AF378073

Rossella Biscotti
The Trial

Mousse

Contents

Introduction

This book marks the closing chapter of a long and evolving
process—a space to gather the voices, materials, and questions
that shaped *The Trial*, a work that explores the legacy of the "April
7th" trial against members of the revolutionary movements Potere
Operaio and Autonomia Operaia. The publication includes the
full transcript of *The Trial*, a six-hour audio work edited from
hundreds of hours of trial recordings, video stills, installation
views, and the documentation of performances dating from 2006
to 2024. It also features newly commissioned texts by Giovanna
Zapperi, Daniel Blanga Gubbay, and Michael Hardt, as well as an
interview with philosopher Antonio (Toni) Negri.

That conversation took place in Toni's Paris apartment
on 2 January 2020, the last time I saw him in person. Over the
years, we had met many times in Venice, Rome, Berlin, and Paris,
exchanging ideas and e-mails regularly—but this was the only
time we sat down to speak about "his" trial and why it mattered
so deeply to me.

The legacy of Autonomia Operaia's ideas, their political
imagination, and the transformative power they represent—
set against the ferocity of a legal system designed to extinguish
them—has kept me engaged for a long time now. I wanted to
reclaim the trial: its substance and space. To edit every spoken
word, to cast concrete onto its architecture.

In 2006, when I first entered the Aula Bunker, the high-
security courthouse at the Foro Italico in Rome, escorted by a
carabiniere, I was immediately struck by the space, and how it
expressed the coercive decadence of its legal structure: the cages
with their thick white bars, the rows of wooden benches bolted
to the floor, the outdated electronic equipment, security cameras,
piles of cables, the green carpet—which was being vacuumed
at that moment—and the broadcast station at the far end of
the public seating area. Opposite, a long table with a few microphones on it stood on an unimpressive platform; at its centre
was the judge's leather chair on rotating wheels. Spelled out in
shiny letters above was LA LEGGE É UGUALE PER TUTTI.[1]
Below the platform, a small chair supported by four metal legs
was positioned in front of a standing microphone. This is where
the defendant sat, alone, facing the judge, with the public arena
at their back and carabinieri at the side.

This structure was housed in a white, wide room, emblematic of rationalist and fascist architecture. It looked like
a film set. We walked around and asked to see the cells beneath
the courtroom—neglected half-ruined spaces, their walls covered
with written messages. A narrow staircase connected them to
the cages above. We climbed up, retracing the steps of countless

1   "All are equal in
the eyes of the law."

defendants, and watched the courtroom slowly come into view. We could imagine it full of people: journalists, family members, friends, lawyers, and prosecutors, all separated from us by the thick white bars.

I remembered this room from TV broadcasts and newspaper photographs, but nothing precise about it. I began to investigate the history of this place, and that of the April 7th trial (1983–84), where more than 70 people were indicted, including professors, activists, philosophers, and artists accused of armed struggle against the power of the state, facing life imprisonment.

Over the years, I requested access to the building several times. In 2009, I shot a 16 mm film inside the empty space. I felt it wasn't enough. I wanted to break the strict choreography imposed by the architecture, to see people move through it—up and down, in and out. I wanted to hear voices and rewrite its narrative. I met with former defendants and began to see the courthouse through their stories. I reconstructed the trial through daily newspaper articles published in *Il Manifesto* and archived trial recordings from Radio Radicale. I began shaping space, information, and politics into a series of artworks, presented in various institutions over the years.

I was the last person to inhabit the high-security courtroom before it was dismantled. Before leaving I collected all the keys I could find. Today, they are often exhibited with the performance set. I unbolted some benches and took them with me. They are now part of *The Trial* and used during the performance as seating for the audience and interpreters.

The making of this project and its continuously shifting forms and translations has involved many people. It has often intersected with current political events. In 2014, the performance at e-flux in New York was paired with a reading group organised with members of Occupy Wall Street. The excerpt of the Turkish translation in this book was commissioned for a group exhibition at Depo Istanbul, a non-profit art space founded by philanthropist and activist Osman Kavala, who was imprisoned by the Turkish government on accusations of orchestrating the Gezi Park protests.

The Trial continues to generate conversations, alliances, and a shared sense of possibility, allowing space for a new political and aesthetic imagination. A network of friendship has grown around this work.

I wish to thank the former April 7th trial defendants, their families and friends, and everybody who has walked alongside me throughout this journey.

Rossella Biscotti

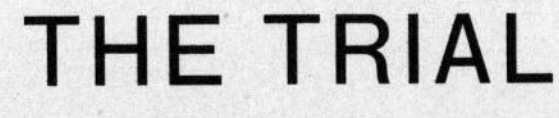

THE TRIAL

THE TRIAL

PRESIDING JUDGE
Severino Santiapichi

JUDGE *A LATERE*
Nino Abbate

PUBLIC PROSECUTOR
Antonio Marini

DEFENDANTS
Cecco Bellosi
Augusto Finzi
Chicco Funaro
Alberto Magnaghi
Silvana Marelli
Antonio Negri
Paolo Pozzi
Franco Tommei
Emilio Vesce
Paolo Virno

***PENTITI* [INFORMANTS]**
Carlo Casirati
Mario Ferrandi
Paolo Morandini
other voices

WITNESSES [FOR THE PROSECUTION]
Severino Galante
other voices

DEFENCE LAWYERS
Tommaso Mancini
Giuliano Spazzali
other voices

PLAINTIFF LAWYER
Fausto Tarsitano

ATTORNEY GENERAL
Oscar Fiumara

Courtroom noises, a continuous murmuring reverberates in the space, sound of microphone inserted in the holder.

JUDGE

Please sit down.

Long pause, room noises, camera flashes.

JUDGE *A LATERE*

First interrogation 10 April 1979, substitute Prosecutor, Pietro Calogero.

JUDGE

[reads quickly, without pausing, and in a mechanical tone]

Question: Have you ever had the opportunity to speak on the telephone with Dr Alessandrini?

Answer: No.

The office points out to the accused that Dr Emilio Alessandrini had declared that he believed he had recognized Negri's voice as the voice of the member of the Brigate Rosse, who was Mrs Moro's telephone interlocutor.

The accused answers: I reiterate that I was not the one who made the telephone call and that I am very surprised that Dr Alessandrini could have expressed such an opinion.

The office provides the accused with his diary of 1978.

The annotation "article to beat numbers" referred to on page thirty in April respectively to articles to be written for publication in *Rosso*. The issue refers to the beats. Paolo surnamed Pozzi, resident in Milan, collaborator as writer for *Rosso*; BC and Alfa ostensibly is the title of an article to be written. As far as BO is concerned I do not recall at this present time which person these initials refer to, it could even be the title of an article to write for *Rosso*. The name Balestrini that often features in my diary refers to that of a dear family friend: Balestrini Giancarlo.

Bologna, Magnaghi, the expression MM Mediterraneo on page nine in January 1978 of my diary refers respectively to Sergio Bologna, my assistant at the University of Padua and profess ... *[unclear]* MM means Mater Marxista which is the title of my series for the publisher Feltrinelli. Magnaghi Alberto ostensibly had to prepare something for this series. Mediterraneo refers to an international conference organized by the Faculty of Architecture of Milan which was then in preparation in the area of the Mediterranean, Your Lordship *[unclear]* asks whether the word area that features in the diary refers to a publishing house and what relation I entertained with it. To the question of whether I was ever interested in Feltrinelli's project and what it consisted of, I reply that in 1958 the Istituto Ricerche Feltrinelli published my first book but in that period I had no relations with Feltrinelli. In '68 I had, together with Massimo Cacciari, relations with Feltrinelli, the publishing house, for the publication of a booklet on Marghera workers' struggles. I don't know what the Feltrinelli project means. I had relations with the publishing house for my works. The continuous contribution began after the death of the publisher.

The accused is asked to clarify whether he wrote or edited, that is to say whether he gave advice about the document titled "Evaluation of the Situation" and in which among other things is written "in this effort it is important to continue to organize the movement in the passage that we have defined from one hundred flowers to one hundred nuclei."

The document is shown to the accused for him to view.

The accused declares: the handwritten correction that I notice in the text is not mine. Nor does the text look like one of mine for stylistic reasons. I am not in the position to indicate who could have transmitted it.

Question: Whether the content of the pamphlet "Potere Operaio per il Comunismo" [Workers' Power for Communism] and the attached erratum is all or in part your work, that is to say whether it is the product of collaborative work in which you have participated.

Answer: This is not a pamphlet of mine and I have not collaborated in its writing. I have never been a member of the Comitati Comunisti Rivoluzionari, which is the designation I read on the first page.

Question: With reference to what you declared in pages eight and nine of the first interrogation, say who the people are who supported the leadership line of the BR [Brigate Rosse] and their initiatives as a moment of unification between the movement and the members of small groups that supported the clandestine and terrorist line.

Answer: I find it difficult, in fact impossible to answer the question. With respect to the claim made by the Paduan public prosecutor that after the dissolution of Potere Operaio there was a split between two lines, I want to underscore that this charge is completely untrue. Potere Operaio did not dissolve over a disagreement between two lines: a more centralizing against a more diffuse one. Potere Operaio was dissolved over the necessity to reconstitute a class factor, starting with its rooting in working class and proletarian autonomy, which the structure, the liturgy and the ideologies of the group no longer allowed. In response to the question from the defence, I clarify that the dissolution of Potere Operaio represents a radical mass option for the reopening of spaces for mass political self-organization, and therefore the opposite of clandestine. *[coughs]*

The office informs the accused that magnetic recordings, the Vesce file, have been acquired by the proceedings; the interventions at the third organizing conference of Potere Operaio, Rome 24–26 September 1971. In relation to your intervention, which evidences that since then the accused defended the view, in the organization, that appropriation on the one hand and militarization on the other were absolutely conjoined terms and that the timing of the conflict and that of organization had to go together.

I am asked for details regarding the handwritten annotation that appears in the leaflet titled "Agreement reached for Giulietta" [an Alfa Romeo car model]. I examine the leaflet Federazione Lavoratori Metalmeccanici, zona Sempione. I recognize the pencilled writing as mine. These are discussion notes used to organize the struggle against Saturday shifts. "Patrol" means picket to prevent scabs from entering the factory. "Camp" and "Rosso" respectively refer to the metropolitan campaign and the magazine. "B Out article" refers to an article also on the issue of Alfa to be written—not necessarily by me—for the magazine *Black Out*.

In response to the question from the defence that *[stumbles over words]* takes note that the telephone box utilized by the member of the Brigate Rosse who telephoned Mrs Moro corresponds to the Rome Termini Station phone number 42 45 29, the accused declares: I most categorically deny that on April 30th I had been in Rome and that I had made the phone call for which I am charged in the warrant.

The defence demands Negri's release for lack of sufficient evidence .... *[unclear]*

Report on your relations with the co-accused of the events in via Fani. Reply: *[coughs]* The lawyer Siniscalchi seizes the opportunity of this question, the questioning *[unclear, reading fast, eating his words]* my question can be found etc., the lawyer Spazzali declares that he cannot agree to *[unclear]* requests to present his defence in relation to the elements of the probing he is responsible for.

Statement arguing that on several occasions Negri formulated the programme for, on the one hand perfecting the quality of military action of the Brigate Rosse, and on the other strengthening the mass actions of Autonomia Organizzata by coordinating both through centralized structures.

Statement arguing that Negri alluded to the structures of Brigate Rosse and Potere Operaio as connected structures and according to which he participated in determining the direction of the Brigate Rosse.

Revelation made by a member of the BR to a person who subsequently informed the judicial authority, and declaration regarding the links between the BR and Potere Operaio.

Statement arguing that militants of Potere Operaio in Padua had weapons and explosives for military training at their disposal.

Statement arguing that Negri taught the technique of making Molotov cocktails.

The accused is shown exhibits number 0, 1, 2, 3, 4, 5, and 6 of the paper *Controinformazione* recovered in his home, and is invited to examine them and report on how and in what role he collaborated with the realization of said issues and whether his articles were published in them. The defence observes that in this case we are confronted with the inversion of the burden of proof. The accused declares that currently he avails himself of the right to silence. The accused is shown some handwritten papers of his Archivio Massironi texts with a series of questions and answers ostensibly drawn from the writing of an interview published in *L'Espresso*, and clarifications are sought with reference to them.

Question: In the study of the architect Massironi, amongst the papers belonging to you at the Feltrinelli Foundation, pamphlets and flyers of the Brigate Rosse were found. The accused is questioned on the content of the notes he handwrote, Archivio Massironi, and concerning the first where the need for a link between the mass movement and vanguard action is indicated. This is the absolutely unavoidable terrain of armed struggle. The second reads *[unclear]* class, Franceschini. The exhibits are shown. The accused is questioned about the content of two handwritten annotations, Archivio Massironi, the first in pencil which, amongst other things, reads: "Dualism of power, insurrection, taking power, emancipation and militarization section." In the second note, written in pen, it can be read: "The possible reopening of the wage front must follow and hit the junctions of power. *[the reading becomes abstract, isolated phrases resoundin the room]* A leap in class struggle. Appropriation as a synthesis of wage and armed struggle. Taking responsibility for power. The party as directly responsible for taking power, and that isn't yet there. Fighting for this without for this reason underestimating the need to also maintain the dualism of today's situation."

The documents are exhibited. Letter copy dated Padua 30 June 1978 from Antonio Negri that reads: "I must apologize to you for ...." *[interrupts himself]*

The accused is shown the thirteen typewritten papers concerning the thesis on crisis and the typewritten cover letter, Archivio Massironi, where amongst other things one finds the definition of neo-revisionist faction groups: Il Manifesto, Lotta Continua, Avanguardia Operaia, and the claim that the USSR reproduces the forms of imperialist exploitation and the global division of the market.

Social democracy is defined as the specific form of the terrorism of multinationals. It is added that the historical compromise of Italian communism is entirely placed within the horizon of democratic socialism; the multinational organization of workers is promoted and workers' construction of support bases is evidenced and it is concluded that armed struggle represents the only fundamental strategic moment and that only armed struggle—whose articulation is linked to the organization of the party in its development, in its consolidation, in its extension—can allow mass struggle to hit the system.

The accused is shown four typewritten pages entitled "Dopo le ferie" [After the holidays], Archivio Massironi, with an addition in pencil that resembles your handwriting and ends with the locution: "to publish after the document of the Siemens Alfa Romeo Pirelli assembly in Milano [unclear] Hamburg comrades."

The accused is questioned on the content of said document where one can also read: "IRA, Viet Cong, Fedayn, Tupamaros, these are the incessantly repeated cries of 300,000 comrades, this is the level of working class struggle in Italy. The political-military shift has turned into an almost obligatory one. [isolated phrases reverberate in the reading] Organizing the occupation of the factory, armed pickets, sabotages, blowing up the office of the scabs' trade union, putting on trial and condemning the functionaries of the bosses.

"Our interests today: the consolidation of revolution, of revolutionary organization and its extension and deepening. Our interest today is the irreversibility of civil war."

Report on your relationship with Nicotri Giuseppe, Ferrari Bravo Luciano, Vesce Emilio, Zagato Lauso, Ferrari Roberto, Piperno Francesco, Scalzone Oreste, Dalmaviva Mario, Pancioni Gianfranco, Marangio Giovanni Battista, Balestrini Giancarlo.

The accused is shown exhibits. "To spread in the jungle, to create impregnable sanctuaries and to provide ourselves with a mobility infinitely superior to that of the adversary. Attacking the enemy on a terrain favourable to us, inviting him to train on our territory, prudently carrying out attempts to create liberated zones and determine an exceptional mobility of organization."

"DC [Christian Democrats], PSI [Italian Socialist Party], PCI [Italian Communist Party], everyone plays his own game to get space within a single anti-worker project. The role of directly attacking the revolutionary left is assigned to the PCI. It is the consultant for this crude provocation aimed at muddying the figure of Walter Alasia and the *Paese Sera* journalist Giorgio Manzini. Communist proletarians will remember everybody; and let all men of power remember the West German iron attorney Bubak; let them remember Tramoni, the peeping Tom of Renault, who has been reached by proletarian justice; let them remember Doctor Pisano, who has recently been exemplarily punished. Communist memory goes back a long way."

USHER

The court.

Pause with some noises in the courtroom, the microphone is moved from one holder to another.

JUDGE

Virno, you are also charged with the counts you were notified of in your indictment. In your case as well, the rule applies of asking whether you intend to respond?

VIRNO

I intend to respond to all charges and all questions. And I'd like to make a general statement before I am questioned.

JUDGE

Go ahead ....

VIRNO

I'd like to state that I have never been involved, in any way, in the activities I am accused of taking part in. The accusation of terrorist activities, in particular, is in many ways an insult to a long period of political militancy. I have never felt anything but contempt for underground action, for political action not conducted in broad daylight. I have shunned such choices; I have fought against them politically. In declaring that I am innocent of the charges brought against me, although I do not know the exact legal difference between the two terms, I would also like to state something more: I feel it's important not only to show my innocence as clearly and convincingly and truly as possible, but also, in the positive sense, to try to show that the things I really was involved in doing—because I've done many things over these last fifteen years from a political and social standpoint—that these things I really did do are not a crime. The legal difference probably escapes me, but from the standpoint of, how shall I put it ... common sense, there is one. It's not just innocence and non-involvement; it's the attempt, though without too much hope, to show that what I really was involved with in an active, tangible sense is not a crime. Because the problem comes back to that: until we arrive at a more unbiased, realistic assessment of a great—and also terrible, but also extraordinary—period of struggle and social transformation like the 1970s, we won't be free. Maybe sooner or later we will be freed from prison, but we won't be truly free until people's assessment of that period of struggle changes. We won't be truly, deeply free until people's assessment of that period of struggle changes.

I think that fifteen years later ... after the period of 1968, many of the people involved—despite their merits—many of the people involved at the time have been overcome by a general feeling of exhaustion, of subjugation, or even a sense of finality and death, a sense of failure and defeat. I think that for the most part there is no reason for this general feeling of subjugation and defeat that seems to have crept into many, too many of the people involved at the time; this new sort of motto that says "obedience is right and rebellion is impossible" which seems to have gained circulation in recent years since the late 1970s, I think ever since 1968, we have focused on a single theme, a single message, a single goal: radical, material, political criticism of the modern barbarity that is salaried work, subjugated work, repetitive, parcelled-out work. And I think that from this standpoint, in terms of this radical *raison d'être*, the movements of 1968 have not failed. The movements of 1968 have achieved their goals. In our society, in an irreversible, though often invisible way, salaried work, subjugated work, is now irreversibly considered, by the younger generation, to come at an excessive cost to society, an unbearable expense, something no longer necessary. In the early 1970s, this basic element, this, shall we say, *substance of what was hoped for* within our political activity, was combined with the tradition of communist revolution. We were revolutionary communists, albeit heretical in our tenets. Later, in the second half of the 1970s, we changed our language. We changed our language, we changed our way of thinking. We deeply criticized the very concept of political revolution. We broke, definitively, with the tradition of the historical labour movement, in the sense that we ceased to be extremist—if there is something that one cannot accuse our movements of in the second half of the 1970s, this "our" naturally including many different things, it's extremism. Because to be extremist you have to be extremist compared to something else, something further to the right, something more moderate. If one is radically different from that something else, in the way one sees things, in the way one acts and thinks, one cannot even be called extremist.

I find that from this point of view 1968 reached its aims and then deflated like a balloon: its protagonists, who are valiant people, have sagged because they have often looked at this movement, this very radical and decisive transformation, with out-of-date perspectives and schemes.

I must say that in this trial, in that cage behind me, I have ... almost all of my co-accused ... I don't know most of them at all—I have met them in prison—very many others I hadn't frequented at all since 1973, the year of the end, of the break of Potere Operaio. The only accused among those that have been imprisoned with whom I have had an assiduous frequentation—which does not mean political association, but assiduous frequentation, yes—is Lucio Castellano. Other co-accused who are not here, with whom in the second ... after 1973, I have had a political relation, which has not in any way been an associative relation, are Libero Maisano .... I have been a friend of and have frequented Lanfranco Pace ... in the second half of the 1970s I have sporadically met Oreste Scalzone. With the others—there may still be one or two ... and Franco Piperno of course—I have only had occasional political relations and in any case not in terms of political association. With respect to all the other co-accused, who are seventy in total, I have either never met them or have had a relation that was interrupted by the end of Potere Operaio. I am sorry about this because—I repeat—they are valiant people, people who I would have liked to meet, with whom I would have liked to debate, discuss ideas and themes throughout the 1970s. I am very sorry about it but it's a fact. It is a cut-and-dry fact.

This is what I wanted to say at the beginning of this interrogation.

Long pause.

JUDGE

Vesce had asked to speak.

VESCE

[from the cage] Yes, Mr President.

JUDGE

Go ahead.

VESCE

Thank you. I wanted to communicate that I suspend my protest, my hunger strike from today. In the last fourteen days I have been able to note that great attention has been paid by the political forces, by public opinion, by the people of the prisons—if I may use this image—who have protested and through their active participation have shown their solidarity with my aim, which was to sensitize public opinion on this huge problem, which is preventive detention, which is infinitely extended. I have received very many testimonies in prison: telegrams, letters in which everybody somehow felt a participant in this initiative. In Verona, eight or nine days ago—I don't know for sure—thirty prisoners even started a hunger strike. Today I suspend mine, bearing these things in mind. But also bearing in mind what the situation is in our country. And so I say and underscore I *suspend* [my hunger strike], because if in the next few months there is no positive development and promises are not maintained, there will be many of us going on hunger strike against preventive detention. And not just against preventive detention but also against all those laws that have been introduced in the last four or five years, which have determined conditions that it would be immoral for us who are experiencing them not to denounce and rebel against them. I am referring to the many cases of prisoners who let themselves die in protest. I am also referring to cases that this court knows already, because they are the cases of accused in trials that will be judged in this very courtroom, and for this reason I say, repeat and underscore again that today I *suspend* my hunger strike in order to restart it unless the barbarism represented by—I repeat—preventive detention is immediately stopped. Thank you.

JUDGE

Negri.

Pause, microphone noises reverberate in the room.

JUDGE

Negri then, *[clears throat]* you manifested your need to proceed year by year in the chronological order of the various facts you are charged with. However, our own need is to gain an overall vision of your personality for the aims such a view serves to the judges of the trial. In the trial proceedings we find references, here and there, and they are actually rather numerous, to your person, and we have a series, or a heap, of your writings. I begin with a note of a personal character found in a diary of 1974 where you say: "I am forty years old, I am an intellectual, the experience of via Jacini is over." This is a personal annotation in one of your diaries, and I link it to another personal note found in *Domination and Sabotage*, wherein you write:

> Nothing reveals the enormous historical positivity of workers' self-valorization more than sabotage, this constant activity of the sniper, the saboteur, the absenteeist, the devious, the criminal that I find myself experiencing. Every time I wear the balaclava I immediately sense the warmth of the workers' and proletarian community. This solitude of mine is creative; my separateness, the only collective reality I know. Nor does the happiness of the outcome escape me. Each act of destruction and sabotage redounds upon me as a sign of the connectivity of class. Nor does the potential risk offend me; quite the opposite, it fills me with as feverish an emotion as the awaiting of a lover. Nor does the pain of the adversary strike me; proletarian justice has the same productive power of self-valorization and the same faculty of logical conviction.

Well, given this, let's say, autobiographical note, or opinion of yours, I also find in the proceedings, including the ones we acquired recently, which I prefer because the rest of them are all well known, I find something that invests this personality of yours more closely. But first I want to read you a passage from the declaration of Ferrandi Mario to colleagues, which the public prosecutor has acquired for the trial. This passage allows us to introduce the other issue, on the relationship between Autonomia and terrorism.

And this is what Ferrandi claims:

> *[reading fast]* The kind of project that was being carried out and to which we referred to at the time, entailed that this experience on the one hand, and on the other the experience of the so-called diffuse struggle of the movement, were consolidated in an organizational form that was different from the extra-parliamentary, public, legal, bureaucratic groups with their mechanisms of elected representation and leadership, and inadequate to confront the realm of illegality, and from that of the Brigate Rosse, that is, close workers' groups, even clandestine, with no public physiognomy and no possibility to expand. These forms of organization had to be put in contact and communicate with the whole universe of social struggles. When they managed to do this on their own, all the better. But in case they did not succeed, then this structure would intervene with initiatives that could fill this gap and close this scissor.

This is not an isolated voice in this trial: it is one of the many ways the accusations against you have taken shape and been attested. So, I have touched on that manner of yours of being an intellectual, and on that way of yours of wearing the balaclava. And then I mentioned these versions, after all, of a different mark, which portray you as the person responsible for the ideation of concrete criminal actions you have been charged with. Let's see if we can introduce an organic debate on all of this. This is my primary requirement.

NEGRI

[clears throat] It seems to me a rather difficult requirement to fulfil. But I will try anyway …. Let's start with the statement by Ferrandi, the "rabbit," I mean, a very intelligent young man as he especially demonstrated in his depiction of the Milanese Autonomia, above all when he speaks of concrete events and of what happened, when he makes history of what happened, and where he manages, perhaps the only one amongst the *pentiti* [informants] to portray Milan as a movement with a thousand heads, forces, and openings. That is to say, it is true that Autonomia aimed to merge an overall political project with the complexity of the phenomena of illegality, where illegality is understood as the rupture of the constituted bourgeois order, of the order of production and the order of the State that protects, aids and allows this order of production, wage redistribution, labour etc. From this standpoint, the debate, or the debates that I entertained and that were entertained with the Brigate Rosse until 1974 ….

JUDGE

You know that Fioroni identifies some relations of yours not only with Curcio and Franceschini, but also with Feltrinelli. Let's see to it that these relations are consolidated so as to clarify a bit what is behind a very delicate issue in the charges against you. Let us start with Feltrinelli.

NEGRI

Ah. I have known Feltrinelli since 1958, when I published my undergraduate thesis with his publishing house.

JUDGE

I am talking about Feltrinelli the person, not the publishing house.

NEGRI

Yes, yes, I met him in person then, and then had some sporadic contacts with him throughout the 1960s. As you probably know, Feltrinelli was very engaged in this political-cultural work of re-foundation and renewal of, let's say, the culture of the left in Italy.

JUDGE

Well, it was not only a matter of culture: as far as I know, Feltrinelli did not die of culture.

NEGRI

He was ....

JUDGE

He did not die of culture.

NEGRI

Eh?

JUDGE

Feltrinelli did not die of culture.

NEGRI

I am talking about the 1960s and I think that Giangiacomo Feltrinelli must undoubtedly be granted some merits. My subsequent relationship with Feltrinelli dates back to 1967–68. I remember it clearly because it was a chance encounter at Madrid airport. We had a long conversation about Cuba: he was leaving for Cuba and I started to comprehend the political lines he was drawing, rather than for himself, essentially within the framework of international intervention, that of Tricon, the Tricontinental: an internationalist political association with its headquarters in Cuba that engaged in initiatives of the anti-capitalist struggle in both underdeveloped and developed countries. So I must say that Feltrinelli was ....

JUDGE

What do you mean by initiatives of the anti-capitalist struggle?

NEGRI

Bah!

JUDGE

If we could leave abstraction behind and try to understand ....

NEGRI

For instance, in underdeveloped countries he directly supported armed struggle as far as I know. As far as I know, Che Guevara emerged from the Tricontinental with his initiative. Obviously it seemed quite absurd to try to transport the ideology, experiences, and forms of armed struggle as they were being practised in underdeveloped, in third world countries ... to move their methods and ideology to our capitalist developed countries.

It seemed particularly absurd to me and my comrades because we came from the experience of *Quaderni Rossi*, on which we worked throughout the 1960s; one that was originally specifically committed to grasping the determinations of revolutionary struggle in highly developed capitalist countries. *[sound of camera flashes]* You can see how far my attitude and analytical perspective was from Feltrinelli's, who

24

defended and represented in the first person such a theory of a generalized shift, transformation and circulation of struggles from the underdeveloped world to the centre, and of a siege of the capitalist centre. The
disagreement on the fundamental lines of Feltrinelli's theory was very
evident, especially when he started personally practising, and I must
say that until I saw ....

JUDGE

So, until then you didn't see the picture ...?

NEGRI

I didn't think he was personally engaged. I thought his was a propagan-
distic activity of aggregation of forces, so to speak, I could not in the
least imagine that he was engaged in ....

JUDGE

You see, here you touch on a very delicate point, in this chance remark of
yours. I don't want to involve other trials in this court but this court has
a bad practice, so to speak, when it comes to acts of terrorism. In other
trials, this court has really insisted on identifying the personality of some
of the defendants. I am interested in starting with Feltrinelli so that I
can come to Curcio and Franceschini. I want to start with Feltrinelli to
come to the Brigate Rosse, your relations, and your personal relations
with the Brigate Rosse. This is the relevant point: I am not interested in
conjectures.

NEGRI

These things are rather different .... Feltrinelli dies in 1972, March, and
I really don't think that, or I cannot locate my first encounter with Curcio
until March 1973. I must add that my meetings with Curcio focused on
very different issues. I had never known Curcio, I had simply engaged
in a journalistic polemic with him in 1969. Curcio published, between
Trento and Milan, a newspaper called *Lavoro Politico*, and there was
this really strong polemic and attack from Curcio as the representative
of a Marxist-Leninist line—and I don't know if I need to explain to the
court the meaning of this rather Chinese theoretical current—against
us of the current of Operaismo. Anyhow, the discussion then centred on
the leitmotivs of the constant polemic, at the ideological and theoretical
level, between currents like that of the Brigate Rosse and Operaismo.
These are absolutely substantial differences in the model of organization, in the relation between economic and political struggle, and the
overall strategy thereof. In 1969 in particular, our different conceptions of economic and political struggle were emerging, because for
a workerist attacking at the level of the wage meant making the revolution, breaking, that is, the economic equilibrium of exploitation. For
the Maoists, attacking the wage meant carrying out an economic and
unionist struggle that was, if anything, educative, and the starting point
from which to make a leap towards the revolution. I am saying this ....

JUDGE

Excuse me, I would like, you see, I have some experience of studying too, when it comes to the Brigate Rosse. We would like to know something specific on these issues. We have understood, as it is abundantly clear from the proceedings of the previous interrogation, what your interpretation of the phenomenon of the Brigate Rosse is. We understood it, and I'll tell you more than that, it can be appreciated, but here I would proceed by specific events.

NEGRI

It is early 1973, the crisis of Potere Operaio has reached a level of deflagration of the group. I started moving to try to understand what the hell was going on around us. I know that Turin comrades, more or less of the brigades, and in fact from their ideological matrix, what these Brigate Rosse were, concretely, was perfectly understood, I personally realized what they wanted to be between 1972 and 1974. But I found out that they worked at Fiat and were actively involved there.

JUDGE

What do you mean "personal"?

NEGRI

Damn. I mean this: I mean that it's not as if I went there as an organization, or he came to talk as an organization. We discuss, we exchange opinions on an object of study if you want to call it that.

JUDGE

The object of study was the revolution? What was the object of study?

NEGRI

Fiat, in this case.

JUDGE

Let's see what Curcio said and what you said on this object of study that is Fiat.

NEGRI

Nothing. The discussion focused especially on given mechanisms of struggle as they were unfolding.

JUDGE

What was Curcio's position and yours on these mechanisms of struggle?

NEGRI

Bah, I must say that not much changed. I mean, it was actually a case of understanding what was happening at Fiat because there was a huge qualitative leap in the struggle there. In other words, no one was in command, because nobody rules the Fiat shop floors. There were real processes of violence within production, of informal organization of this violence. Above all, the first cases of exit from the factory were being seen: workers marching to exit the factory and occupy, making street blockades, imposed whip-rounds on drivers and such things. These phenomena were extreme defences of the strike that became later rather generalized, but given the size of Mirafiori and its working class, they stood out, so to speak, with great power and efficacy. Even as an illustration, because note that in 1973 the intervention of groups at Fiat was practically over. If only you had experienced that period on my side, you would perfectly understand how to read, in 1973, the development of struggles and this clash with the union structure that really anticipated, in its character, class composition and in the forms of violence it adopted, many of the events that would unfold throughout the 1970s. You would have been effectively taken by .... I wrote half a book on this question. It's not as if you could say that I was wasting time.

Shuffling of paper.

JUDGE

So let's say that you discussed this analysis of the events at Fiat. Let's talk about the second meeting. It was in 19 ...?

NEGRI

It's the second half, towards the end of 1973.

JUDGE

In 1973 ....

NEGRI

Curcio talks about the need to overcome the level of protest. For the first time, he speaks to me of striking at the heart of the State, of the leap from the economic to the political level.

JUDGE

Which is ...?

NEGRI

The terms of the debate are these: even at their highest level, the workers' struggles that developed at Fiat and that we have analysed had reached an unproductive stage. They can't obtain anything anymore. Here we can even destroy their factories, but these masters no longer concede anything to us. At this stage, the question emerging from the workers' vanguards is that of the attack on the State, that is, the realization of an open revolutionary project. And here we discussed this and said goodbye and never met again until ....

JUDGE

You never met again because you disagreed, I suppose.

NEGRI

Because our paths were completely different. In that very period, in the second half of 1973, I was working on the constitution of *Autonomy*, which was the exact opposite both as concept and as practice. This is the difference that was established, and we don't meet again until July 1974. At that point, we meet on request of the Brigate Rosse, this time, as an organization ....

JUDGE

A little something had happened then.

NEGRI

Yes, a few little somethings. On request of the Brigate Rosse, this meeting is mainly called because ....

JUDGE

This meeting is not called or promoted because of this fact ....

NEGRI

It's not due to this fact.

JUDGE

It's called because of *Controinformazione* according to you.

TOMMEI

Are you talking about the meeting at Borromeo's house?

JUDGE

Yes.

TOMMEI

I would like to clarify something, Dr Santiapichi. I was asked to organize a meeting in the area of *Controinformazione* precisely because of my detachment ....

JUDGE

Well, let's clear up the issues please, Tommei. It's not as if the court took part in your experience. What do you mean by "area of *Controinformazione*"?

TOMMEI

I mean ... there was this magazine made up of different people. Given that I said I was no longer interested in it because it was no longer possible to mediate the political line I shared in the context of the political line that the magazine wished to pursue, I wanted to leave. Negri did as much the same. The magazine editors said: it's right to clear some issues regarding the magazine, let's have a meeting with some of the exponents of the Brigate Rosse. Obviously the discussion focused on the political problem of the day: the first action of the Brigate Rosse where two people died. Without a doubt, this kind of warning cut the head off the discussion because on top of the potential dissent expressed against a political and theoretical position, there was also a deep dissent over a practice that I found absolutely crazy and absolutely inadequate to a development, even a revolutionary one, of the Italian situation. This was the practice of political homicide.

JUDGE
So do I understand correctly: in this meeting you discussed this action carried out by the Brigate Rosse, and you and Negri criticized it?

TOMMEI
Yes.

JUDGE
And there was divergence on this issue?

TOMMEI
Yes.

JUDGE
[away from the microphone] Can you bring me Fioroni's?

Rustling of paper.

Long pause, room noises, repeated coughing, footsteps that get closer to the microphone, shuffling of papers.

JUDGE
You never talked about the action in Padua? The Padua murder?

TOMMEI
Yes, I told you ....

JUDGE
You see, I am reading Fioroni's declaration, for the sake of memory, straightaway:

> In July 1974, in the country home of Borromeo, Negri supported this last standpoint but as far as I remember he did not formu-late a concrete proposal. For instance, to ignore the Brigate Rosse claiming of responsibility for the murder and, through the

magazine *Potere Operaio* or other papers of the extreme left, to handle the episode as a feud internal to the Padua Fascist Federation.

TOMMEI

Look, from what I remember Negri was extremely worried that the fact that the Brigate Rosse claimed responsibility for this episode would become a moment of general identification. This was ....

JUDGE

Look, Fioroni's version differs from yours also on this issue: the fact that the murder was not assessed, meaning, no negative judgement was passed on the murder. There was a negative evaluation of the claiming of responsibility in so far as Negri would have rather had the murder interpreted as an internal fascist feud.

TOMMEI

I ....

JUDGE

Wait a second ....

[reads] Negri and Curcio purely exchanged their respective assessment of the fact, and then moved on to discussing other issues that were already mentioned in the previous proceedings. Differently from previous meetings, where no substantial divergences were manifest at the level of strategy and tactics, during the Bellagio meeting Negri's and Curcio's points of view on the objectives to pursue were significantly contrasting. The former, that is, Negri, asserted that from then on the target needed to be turned away from the fascists and towards social democracy, and that the clash had to be with social democracy, where the latter is understood as the PCI, which was no longer a communist party, but a party of social democracy. Therefore everything needed to be built outside and against the PCI. On the other hand, Curcio replied that one could not simplistically establish this equivalence of the PCI and social democracy, and that the contradictions internal to the revisionist logic needed to be accrued, and the minimal objective was to recuperate some of the cadres of that party, whilst the maximal objective was to create a vertical break in it.

TOMMEI

As far as I'm concerned, this is Fioroni's madness.

JUDGE

So in this meeting you simply discussed this murder and Negri expressed his criticism. Did you talk about *Controinformazione*?

Yes we did, in the generic terms of this debate, but ....

JUDGE *A LATERE*
This meeting took place in July 1974. As the defendant Negri has stated in this court, the meeting was to discuss *Controinformazione* precisely because of the dissent that had emerged within its editorial board. Well, were there precedents for this discussion? My intuition is that it's not as if you suddenly met in July 1974 to end the discussion. The debate on *Controinformazione* had precedents, with the Brigate Rosse, it was a debate that started a long time before then ... it had precedents that we will later talk about. What I want to know is how this discussion was meant to be contextualized in the general framework. I haven't understood this, and you will repeat it to me ....

NEGRI
The terms of the issue were as follows: basically, after making issue zero of *Controinformazione*, the paper came under a sort of pressure from the Brigate Rosse. Bellavita asked for this meeting with the Brigate Rosse to clarify that they had nothing to do with it, that the Brigate Rosse had nothing to do with it from a financial as well as a political point of view .... The discussion on this issue actually never even began. As soon as we got there, we started talking about the questions surrounding Padua. And we immediately clashed on the claiming of responsibility for the murder carried out by the Brigate Rosse in Padua. We were absolutely opposed to their claiming responsibility for murders. It was not just my problem. It was simply that the movement, that developed from 1968 to 1969, always had an enormous respect for life.

JUDGE
Nonetheless, these people died. The issue was claiming responsibility for their deaths, for their murder.

NEGRI
Do you realize what it means when, for the first time, forces that saw themselves as part of the movement kill and claim responsibility for murders, which amounts to them saying "do this," repeat this, murder is consistent with the movement.

JUDGE
Do you want me to read this passage?

NEGRI
No, I remember it, the passage reports that during the Limonta meeting we discussed fascistization, the direction towards fascism and social democracy.

So, let's try to clarify this issue because it is all but contradicting what I was saying. The problem is very simple and it is this: OK, on the one hand, always in continuity with a sort of tradition in the movement, there was talk of crisis and fascistization of the State. This means that the State becomes fascist to the extent that the proletariat attacks the State. The form of defence that the State assumes to confront the proletarian offensive is fascistization. On the other hand, there was our argument: we always affirmed that Fascism as a historical formation was completely exhausted and that equally and perhaps more repressive State forms for the development of capitalism would take on the vestige of social democratization, a relation that grips even the corporative interests of the working class against the working class. This is the notion of social democratization: a State form that introduced socialism as a moment of division of the working class. Well, the debate on fascistization is one against a horrible, ugly enemy wearing a black shirt, whom you're faced with, immediately: it's the monster you must shoot at. From this standpoint, I say that there is no contradiction because in so far as I say "it's not true that the State is fascist but be careful because the State is infinitely more able and does not need to wear the black shirt again when it wants to do this and that, and manages to divide people," you must intervene intelligently, you must create ruptures on this point if you want to win, if you want to put forward a revolutionary line. Whereas if you see everyone confronting you as a black shirt thug then it's obvious that on the basis of tradition and all of this, you shoot!

Long pause, silence.

JUDGE

Bellosi had asked to speak. I think it was Bellosi, wasn't it? Here Officer, please.

COCHIS

[from the cage] So, Mr President, I'd like to read a document to be included in the proceedings that was presented this morning.

JUDGE

You can read it.

COCHIS

Thank you.

[he reads] A season of initiatives of struggle has begun in the prisons. Here we do not want to judge the limitations and positive aspects of this mobilization. However, we think that among the agenda items, there is one that we don't often talk about, or not often enough, but that is an essential element to understand the situation in the prisons. Differentiation—which is justified as a necessary evil to maintain security—is in fact used to keep hundreds of political and common prisoners in a state of complete isolation: all the way to their *de facto* annihilation in the *death wings* of Turin, Foggia, Ariano Irpino. We have already talked about the inhumane conditions in which prisoners are kept in these places, which are an Italian version of the belly of the beast. But today we have very concrete data that we can bring to your attention. A cellmate of ours, Dragomir Petrovic, has come out after spending almost a year in these black holes. After suffering a stroke, he was left for a month without medical assistance. The news regarding other prisoners is even more worrying: Pierluigi Concutelli, who has a perforating ulcer, has no medical assistance and on the occasion of two violent attacks was left alone, without even the assistance of a nurse. Renato Vallanzasca, who is affected by viral hepatitis, which is turning into hepatic cirrhosis, is forced to live on two mozzarellas per day. No healthcare for Cesare Chiti, who is affected by a serious renal dysfunction, either. Mario Storina's weight is down to 30 kilograms. And these are just the most glaring examples of the attack on the health of the prisoners and of the denial of medical assistance in Foggia. At Ariano Irpino and on the Delle Nuove wing it's the same story: as is testified by the disastrous health condition of Giorgio Semeria. It is probably superfluous to remind you of the complete isolation—twenty-four hours a day—of the scarcity and poor quality of food, of the impossibility of shopping, and of the fact that out-of-cell time is reduced to a minimum. An odious reprisal—all the more inhumane because slow on the uptake—is taking place against the prisoners *[he*

turns page] of the death wings and there is no security measure that can justify these bestial conditions. If the values of liberation are important, so is the value of life: imposing the closure of the death wings means first of all struggling for the right to life, and against a creeping death penalty. As far as we are concerned, we are and will remain close to our brothers imprisoned in the death wings and to their will to struggle against annihilation.

The document is signed by the undersigned, Bellosi, and by Marelli.

Noises in the courtroom, talking and distant coughing.

JUDGE

Finzi, you are aware of what you are accused of because you received the regular notification in the abstract from the remand, and you also know that you have the right not to answer our questions. Do you have anything to say?

FINZI

Well, I just wanted to make some preliminary remarks. I think that this is a trial that touches upon political issues. That's because I and the others have been political militants, we have been active members of political organizations or, let's say, of movements that existed in different periods and had different life spans, different names .... And so from this point of view I believe that this is a political trial. And I also believe that there is an enormous difficulty here because neither I nor, I think, the court expects that the court would want to formulate political judgements. The court is analysing whether there were crimes, whether there is evidence for the formation of an armed band.

Now, I began to work at Petrolchimico [a petrochemical plant in Porto Marghera, near Venice] in 1960, and let's say that I got involved in politics around 1964—as Sbrogiò was saying this morning—through the trade unions and the CGIL and in 1966 I am already a member of the provincial direction of the chemical workers' union in Porto Marghera. Within the union I started to get interested in politics: not just trade union politics but also politics in general, and this is when I got in touch with what would become the Classe Operaia groups, which were the Venetian editorial board of the magazine *Potere Operaio*. So, let's say that the genesis of my political life dates back to this Venetian group of Potere Operaio. It was with this group and within the union that I operated and gave my contribution with respect to factory issues and factory life. There was a very heavy situation and I am going to spare you all the usual talk about how sad and painful factory life is, but I assure you that it is indeed true. Let me be clear: I was in the factory from 1960 to 1978, for about nineteen years. It's not like I just took a walk inside the factory. I spent a big chunk of my life in that factory.

It is around 1968 that I began to hang out with people who believed that it is possible to give continuity to this kind of contribution external to the trade unions and to formulate proposals and demands: that is, to talk about working hours, ranks, shifts, safety, and about how we could build an industrial dispute even without the trade unions.

In fact, if you want I can read them [documents from that period]. In any case, they are also in my written deposition.

JUDGE

[drowns out the voice of the accused] There is no need ....

FINZI

Just a few to give you an idea:

> *[reading fast]* We must give a precise answer to this capitalist plan. Not just with words but also with facts. They call to work, we call to struggle. Within and outside the factory, at the same time: within the factory against the capitalist organization of labour; outside the factory for social reforms, that is, against the social organization determined by the capitalist system. When we struggle in the factory against the restructuring of production and work by the boss, we also struggle against the capitalist restructuring of society and its political organization. During the last few years the class struggle in Italy, and not just in Italy, has put the bosses with their back against the wall. It has hit them hard, it has put their political power into question, it has provoked the crisis of their system and of their relationship with the masses.

This is a flyer by militants of the PCI and PSIUP dated 5 September 1970.

This is to show that the language is a language that has always been—let's say—within the workers' tradition: it has a hard edge, it's even rough if you like, but it needs to make itself understood by people who live in an equally hard and exhausting way, their relationship to work and their own lives. Talking about reducing working time is not talking about something light. It is not like talking about—let's say—a little present that you can get. Unfortunately, these are so-called objectives for which there has been struggle after struggle. Right in August 1970 in Marghera there were barricades, there were roadblocks. In 1968 there had been the occupation of the railway station. And that did not happen because there were extremists. I don't think that this reconstruction of events works. The problem is that these things happen when we reach and cross certain limits, and when as a result people behave in ways that go beyond what is considered normal. But the point is to see what provoked them, how these behaviours developed. This is the issue on which Potere Operaio was born. And together with Potere Operaio there was also the birth of Lotta Continua, with differences [between the two organizations] that, if we try to look at these today, we probably wouldn't be able to grasp. But the two groups were born at the same time. In 1969 there is an assembly in Turin and from this assembly two groups were born: Potere Operaio and Lotta Continua. They are the two groups that, for better or worse, until 1973–74 will take responsibility for the initiatives we are talking about, which have to do with the issue of the so-called factory guerrilla. So we are dealing with the factory guerrilla. But let's be clear on this, I can reassure you that this language is such that if read with the lenses of the 1980s .... *[stops and then starts again]* I mean, how come these people perform guerrilla actions? What happens, do they shoot the bosses? No, it's not as if we shot at the bosses. There may have been insults; there might have been talk of exploitative bosses. However, when speaking about guerrilla activity, we meant that the factory .... Because, if you remember, we were in the middle of the Vietnam War and some of the slogans were "10, 100, 1,000 Vietnams." So our home-made translation of the concept of guerrilla was that we were like the Vietnamese, we needed to liberate ourselves too. Like them, we need to conquer a space that is our own and not let them walk on us, because we need, for instance, to win equality of pension treatment, sick leave, etc., with the employees. Because we must stop dying in the factory, as it is demonstrated that people die in the factory.

So, it is from this point of view that we talked widely about guerrilla activity in the factory. We studied forms of struggle that would enable us to lose less: that's because wage struggles normally involve very high wage losses. So instead we tried to study the cycle of production: and here you have the sabotage of the factory. It was simply a climate in which things became possible and came up. I remember—this is not to waste your time and bring you back to the past—a platform [of demands] such as the 1968 one at Petrolchimico. It wasn't produced by the elaboration of the central trade unions, as we called them at the time. No. In a cinema venue there is an assembly with 300 people, and at some point a worker stands up and says: "But why do we have to strike in that way? Let's strike every second day. It takes 24 hours to stop the plant. After that they don't have enough time to restart it, and so by striking every second day we hit the boss twice." After that there was a lock-down, there were clashes, because Montedison [a factory] decided to call for a lock-down and send everybody home. There you go: this was to say that this whole thing was born like this, all of a sudden. And so throughout the 1970s we see this surfacing of Autonomia, and I talk about Autonomia from the [early] 1970s—please take note: I want to underscore this. That's because these comportments develop regardless of the will and the directives of the groups, which are always trying to catch up with these comportments, they are always trying to put an ideological hat on them. And so they label what's already there with slogans and names.

In those years the discourse of armed struggle itself was applied to comportments such as those at Fiat, in Turin, where there were workers who started to wear the balaclava—Toni Negri has even written a book on this—and, yes, they started to club some of the managers and commit violent acts within the factory. But let's be clear: nobody organized these things. These things were born out of a certain way of conducting social relations. If we now want to shift the blame to some people, let's be aware that we are making a mistake. I think that this would be a terrible mistake. In the descriptions we have provided of factory struggles in those years, yes, we have talked of armed vanguards, we have talked about militarization, but we have talked about these things in terms of processes, of phenomena that were taking place and that we were trying to understand. We were trying to bring [all this] to productive forms—I am using a term that might not be correct—to living forms, to forms that would not be transformed into moments .... I will read these things to you. It's not that I am trying to—let's say—amend today what was said yesterday. We were trying to direct these moments towards a positive development. And if for some this positive development is a negative development, well that's a political evaluation. If we talk about managing to ....

JUDGE

Please let me interrupt you for a minute. Just to make sure that what you say is clear. You say: this kind of language, once it is located in a [specific] time, some would say in a context, is a language that was used by a whole political milieu, not just by the people accused in this trial. This is your assumption.

FINZI

Clear.

JUDGE

I am saying this to sum up your thought. Sometimes we need to sum up the points. Carry on.

FINZI

Well, I think I have developed, or painted a picture of what my path was. Probably I forgot a lot of things and I'm here to answer questions.

JUDGE

Well precisely to answer these questions we adjourn to Tuesday morning to continue your questioning.

Long pause, room noises, repeated coughing, microphone noise on the stand, rustling of papers.

JUDGE

Since *[clears throat]* according to the accused, the starting point for the construction of two levels, which is our particular interest in terms of the charges—we are not interested in a historical reconstruction of the events revolving around Potere Operaio—is the so-called Rome conference, we can start with that.

NEGRI

OK, in order to understand how the Rome conference is located in the history of Potere Operaio, it might be worth briefly recalling some earlier elements concerning the structure and history of Potere Operaio. Certainly one of the characteristics of Potere Operaio was a strong adhesion to workers' struggles. This was a group in which the ideology, this internal bonding element, was largely built directly upon the experience of struggles—also because Potere Operaio had brought together a series of currents and figures with a decade behind them of theoretical research in the field of intervention in struggles. It's very important to consider this structural element of Potere Operaio, this adhesion to struggles, because Potere Operaio was really like a glove that adhered to these struggles.

On the other hand, Potere Operaio was really a mass of differences. It was a mass of differences because it was composed ... the major poles within Potere Operaio were on one side a certain number of Porto Marghera workers—chemical workers, with a certain expertise in their job—on the other side Roman students, students who came from bourgeois families, with a presence at the neighbourhood level ... then there were other university students, a few in Bologna, Florence ... then there were significant layers of recent, new, migrant workers in Turin. 1968 to 1970, part of 1971: these were exciting years to live through. What needs to be made absolutely clear is that when Potere Operaio was founded, it and the other forces clearly represented the majority within the university, within the schools, amongst metropolitan, proletarian youth in general. And they represented an extremely broad part of factory militancy. We're not talking about little groups here, but of groups of militants that represented a *majority*, an overall majority.

JUDGE

But an overall majority where, hmm? In the country?

NEGRI

Look ... if by majority we clearly mean in terms ....

JUDGE

I learned when I was young that there are crowds, and then there are *crowds*. My professors at university taught me to tell the difference between crowds and *crowds*.

NEGRI

But ... I don't know. You probably studied under Fascism, *[laughing]* which was an ugly period for identifying majorities.

JUDGE

Let's move on .... When one talks of majorities, it seems to me that a certain caution is required, given that this involves a discourse of a historical nature. A certain caution is required.

NEGRI

I'm talking about transformative majorities; clearly I'm talking about majorities, of forces that have the capacity to represent the majority of needs, the majority of vital expressions. In this situation, the approach of a consistent student militancy that connected itself immediately to old union cadres tired of what was now the routine of a minority, determined a type of spontaneous action. Look, the first wildcat ....

JUDGE

I'm trying to understand .... You need to help me understand the language. Someone wrote that we speak two different languages. I *[clears throat]* don't speak a different language to yours. I speak as a judge. You say "this vanguard approach determines a spontaneous phenomenon"—that's nitpicking. In my ignorance, it really seems like nitpicking.

NEGRI

It's not nitpicking. I'll give you a very precise example.

JUDGE

Hmm.

NEGRI

The assembly line functions with a certain cadence.

JUDGE

Hmm.

NEGRI

This cadence requires that—you've seen the Chaplin film, right?—a screw is driven in every so many minutes.

JUDGE

Yes sir. Hmm. It's the work tempo.

NEGRI

Work tempos that you're quite familiar with—these are things that we've seen at the cinema—*[laughing]* there's the time and motion man in the background, measuring the work tasks and then setting the piecework pay rates. Now, spontaneity consists of ....

JUDGE

These vanguards intervene in the work tempo at FIAT? Just on that?

NEGRI

Look, there are lots of things; I could give you the history *[laughing]* of interventions since the first wildcats of 1962–63. Wildcat ...

JUDGE

Yes, we know this.

NEGRI

... means precisely an irregular action within the factory. On the other hand, these aren't things that were invented in Italy. There's a book on wildcats from 1951 by Gouldner, on wildcats in the United States and in Britain. So these are all things that come with modernization. The problem of what this is—which also entails the relationship between vanguard and spontaneity—is something that's been studied in detail. When I block something and I don't do it alone, because my workmates and colleagues—rather than chastise me because it's payday, and if we stop we won't get paid today—tell me, "Well done, we're going to do the same thing!," this is the relationship between vanguard and spontaneity. It's a relationship that implies something, a relationship of force with the boss. Because at this point the boss either sends us all home, or else changes things: slows down the pace of production, for example ....

JUDGE

So the first element of this—let's call it intellectual approach, we can call it what we like ...

NEGRI

Well ....

JUDGE

... this student approach—just a minute, I'm trying to understand your line of argument—at FIAT, for example, is an approach where from the outside, students convince people—to give a more trivial example—not to drive in screws on the assembly line.

NEGRI

You know, it's difficult, in front of sixty thousand people, to convince someone to stop driving screws in. If anything, the problem is different. *[the judge talks over Negri, unclear]* The problem is grasping that people have had enough, their need for change. To what end? With the aim obviously of conquering material conditions that allow you to be happier, to participate in a more ....

40

JUDGE

... OK, let's stop for a minute. You spoke about ideology, didn't you? So much talk of ideology .... Now you're telling me that really it was a question almost of hedonism. Trying to make people happier, St Francis of Assisi and all that. Now I don't want to muddle up different situations, but what was the design behind all this?

NEGRI

The design?

JUDGE

What was the ideological perspective? The perspective didn't just fall from the sky. You've written quite a bit on this score.

NEGRI

The ideological perspective was this ....

JUDGE

It wasn't about making work easier in the here and now; it was about pursuing the seizure of power ....

NEGRI

The ideological perspective was to build the party.

JUDGE

There we go!

NEGRI

Essentially that is. The problem of the seizure of power is a problem that we have always put off until after the constitution of the party's mass base, of the organization's mass base. The question was how to make it so that these quantitatively relevant forces achieved, with their consciousness, with their ability to immediately exercise the power they possessed in any case ... that of producing less or more, for instance, that of developing their protest by spreading it to society ... well, to provide, first and foremost, this fundamental consciousness of their power and thus of their ability to organize.

JUDGE

I only wish to know one thing because otherwise here .... I understand what you're explaining ... but seeing as these are things that you have explained before .... Your positions concerning Potere Operaio seem very clear to me. Your argument is clear. What I have questioned ...

NEGRI

[interrupts] It's the creation of the twofold level ....

JUDGE

... is the creation of two levels. If we need to concern ourselves with the history of the extra-parliamentary left in Italy, we can go and find out what other people have written.

NEGRI

Look, Mr President ....

JUDGE

I would really like to hear you talk about more down-to-earth things. I would really like to know if Fioroni's claim that an illegal structure was set up at the Rome conference is true. This is what I would like to know! We've been concerning ourselves with minor matters. Look, I'm not questioning you about Marxism from the inside, from the outside, as you complained at the preliminary hearing. That doesn't interest me, those are your opinions, I respect them. Let me tell you, everyone has ideas they believe in, I have no interest in that. I am interested in knowing if it is true what Fioroni assumes: that at a certain point in Rome, there was a closed meeting where it was decided to create this secret level. This. If your discourse revolves around this ....

NEGRI

I tried to demonstrate to you how *we could not have held* such an attitude. We could not have set up a second level. This is the discourse that I tried to make, because otherwise ....

JUDGE

Well, then, let's move on to this Rome conference and see what positions were held by each of the participants. There is a synthesis of these interventions amongst your papers, have a look. I have read these things conscientiously, I know these things!

Long pause, sounds of shuffled papers, microphone feedback.

JUDGE

There are these interventions in this session that address these specific themes: armed violence, clandestine work, red bases, the militarization of the movement, illegal work, territorial appropriation. It has been said that you intervened in support of the passage from the struggle against fascism to the struggle against the Christian Democrat-Socialist bloc. Do you understand?

MAGNAGHI

Yes.

JUDGE

In a meeting of the executive, where there was talk of armed struggle, talk of militarization, talk of clandestine work, talk of illegal work ....

The judge and Magnaghi interrupt and talk over each other.

MAGNAGHI

Excuse me, Mr ... I have never ... so to respond more broadly ....

JUDGE

I am saying to you, starting from the assumption that there was this meeting of the national executive, in which Scalzone, Piperno, Finzi, Marongio, Negri, Maesano took part, there was talk of these specific themes. Within this context of matters or arguments—armed violence, clandestine work, red bases, militarization, illegal work, territorial appropriation—there was ....

MAGNAGHI

I understand very well.

JUDGE

There was your intervention that stated the need to pass from the struggle against fascism to the struggle against the Christian Democrat-Socialist bloc. Within this context.

MAGNAGHI

Well, then ... I exclude, in the most categorical way, that in these meetings there was talk of clandestine activity of things of that type. I never heard talk of these things in Potere Operaio. I have never heard in the national meetings—in which I participated—of Potere Operaio, discussion of a specific thing. I heard talk in general of a project of the militarization of the movement, which then was understood as the defence of pickets, defence in the streets—this there was. In the movement, 3 July 1969 in Turin, which was a workers' mobilization that lasted from the morning of the strike until the following morning, was called "the insurrection of Turin" by all the newspapers of the left. It was not called the street demonstration of Turin. So the term "insurrectional" had this meaning of passage from a struggle over demands to the struggle in the streets in these terms. So what was said in these meetings ... from what I recall, there was also talk of the problem of militarization. But I believe that Finzi has testified here about a document in which there was a report—just six months after, I believe, that meeting—on the state of these discourses within Potere Operaio, of what was the organizational breakdown of the process of centralization.

JUDGE *A LATERE*

Piperno, when questioned before Instructing Judge Amato on 29 October 1979, here I read the text verbatim: "had claimed the continuity of these affirmations against the regime and for social liberation." What I'm getting at is, we want to understand the terms of these differences.

MAGNAGHI

Excuse me ....

JUDGE *A LATERE*

Otherwise everything is just vague. What was the difference over the armed party, for example, over the foundation of the armed party and what were the terms of the disagreement, so that we can understand ...? You were at the Rome congress?

MAGNAGHI

Certainly, certainly I heard all the interventions.

JUDGE *A LATERE*

The theme of the Rome conference ....

MAGNAGHI

I too wrote in my intervention: insurrection, the militarization of the movement, insurrectionist themes. That was written in my intervention, the theme was under discussion.

JUDGE *A LATERE*

You weren't a fly on the wall, you participated, you spoke, so you knew what was being discussed. Try to make us understand what was discussed; we have the recordings of that conference that we can check if need be; let's not operate at an aleatory level. There are statements ... do you want Piperno's statement read?

MAGNAGHI

Excuse me, if you have the recordings they are all ... in short it was a public conference with two thousand people, with the press, journalists, the police, everyone listening to what was said. From a distance of ten years you want me to summarize things. I will summarize them, the themes were themes tied to these thematics: the political direction of a vast movement of struggle, there were thematics on guerrilla warfare in the factory, taking over the city, PO at that moment addressed this insurrectionist thematic thinking substantially of accentuating intervention in the South, where there were all these struggles in the villages, etc., etc. I repeat: this is very important. If the discourse of this conference had been followed by an organizational process of centralization that led in this direction, it would have meant that it had interpreted the thoughts of others, it would have become a project with wings. But this is not what happened, as this document of '73 testifies, and Rosolina [another meeting] was the unravelling of this project from day one, so the intentions then of each individual .... I cannot be responsible for saying what someone else wanted, what others wanted. Everyone can tell their own story. So in this sense I won't interpret the thoughts of someone else ....

JUDGE *A LATERE*

Mr Magnaghi, I want to ask you a specific question. Was the conclusion of this conference the need to propose to proletarians the constant practice of appropriation as an intermediary measure before arriving at the revolution?

MAGNAGHI

Excuse me, where ... can you give me the source?

JUDGE *A LATERE*

I will read from the [press] conference held by Negri, Piperno and Scalzone.

MAGNAGHI

Well, if Negri, Piperno and Scalzone gave a conference, they wouldn't have lied about their intentions! They would have meant whatever they said. *[public prosecutor's interjection unclear]* I was not at this press conference, but effectively they gave a press conference in which they said those things here, if it is written there.

JUDGE *A LATERE*

We could ask them.

MAGNAGHI

What? Excuse me ....

JUDGE *A LATERE*

But the debate on these thematics was not limited, as you know very well, to the Rome conference ....

MAGNAGHI

Excuse me, I didn't hear ....

JUDGE *A LATERE*

The debate on these thematics was not limited to the Rome conference, that would be much too reductive, it would be insulting reality, wouldn't it? This discourse was a recurrent one, you were a national leader, the secretary, right ...? Part of the executive committee. You can't say "talk to the others": these discussions you heard as well, your experience regarding .... *[continues to speak as his voice fades out]*

Long pause, silence, courtroom noises in the background, footsteps.

VIRNO

Potere Operaio in Rome was born around two major experiences that I'll mention here, without going into details. The experience of the autonomous mass struggles at FATME, the largest factory in central Italy, over the themes of piecework, of equal wages for all against the looming spectre of skills-based pay schemes. These autonomous struggles gave life in late 1968 to early 1969 to a mass rank and file committee, the true leading organism for initiatives within the factory. Potere Operaio in Rome was born from that rank and file committee, from that experience that lasted for months and months. The other pole from which Potere Operaio in Rome was born was the discourse over science and struggles in the science faculties. So within Potere Operaio in Rome, as in Potere Operaio in general, themes such as the Marxism-Leninism of the Chinese, or internationalism or anti-fascism, were all absolutely irrelevant. The central theme was a discourse on an emerging class sector, the assembly line worker, the worker who sustains, invigorates and promotes the class offensive of that time. We hitched ourselves as Potere Operaio not to an ideology, but to this specific experience of this specific class sector—this is Potere Operaio in Rome. In Potere Operaio I was part of the Rome leadership as the person responsible—or as one of the people responsible—for high school students, for Potere Operaio's organizational work in Rome's high schools. For a short time after that—a few months around 1970—I carried out political work at the university. Then I focussed exclusively on the political-social situation in Tiburtina, I was in Potere Operaio's Tiburtina branch. I focussed on intervention at Voxson, another rather significant, medium-sized Roman factory. I focussed on intervention in the small factories and in general on the proletarian fabric of ....

JUDGE

Factories .... What do you mean the Tiburtina branch? We are aware of other maturations, of other paths that passed through these same streets, through these same factories, through these same neighbourhoods. We would like you to be more specific on this point, so that eventual or existing lines of demarcation and variations in behaviour can be clear, at least to the court. I understand ....

VIRNO

Certainly there was a discourse here—if this is the naturally relevant point—a discourse on illegality. It's one thing in a factory to organize the appropriation of a break that hasn't been negotiated beforehand, without informing the section head, without having first negotiated this with the firm's representatives. Making a ten minute break last for twenty minutes in this way means re-appropriating ten minutes of work time—and doing it illegally, certainly doing it illegally. Or else, staying with these forms of struggle—that I imagine from a judicial/penal point of view are more important—and certainly, on the Tiburtina, in a factory called Sciolaris—we pass by it in the prison vans—one of the small factories that we brought out on strike with the type of support and communication of struggles typical of bigger factories. OK, outside Sciolaris we knew that section heads were trying to break the picket with their cars, in order to enter and break the workers' picket. Or the fascists of the section—the fascists taken into consideration only from this point of view—as a small military patrol that clashed with the workers' struggles. Certainly we tried to make the picket firmer, more solid, to impede and discourage the picket being run down by the section heads' cars. Certainly then there was a terrain, as in all great social transformations, when a hiatus—how do you say it?—a space opens between legality and legitimacy. Many things that certainly were not legal in those years were legitimate in terms of the common sense of hundreds of thousands of people. In the movement I have never understood—forgive me if I provide this really minor clarification—one thing .... *[a period follows of mutual interruptions and talking over each other]*

JUDGE

This distinction between legality and legitimacy is somewhat particular to you ....

VIRNO

Yes, in any case it lived in those years and informed the praxis of those years ....

JUDGE

It is not common amongst jurists, to put it mildly.

VIRNO

No naturally, no indeed, however it was common to many people's way of doing things and way of living.

JUDGE

It's not what I want, look ....

VIRNO

It was in order to explain myself, I wasn't seeking legitimation.

JUDGE

I understand that but ... I understood your way of looking at things, see ....

VIRNO

In any case there's no doubt that Potere Operaio in those years, like the whole revolutionary left, was a revolutionary communist organization. So if its programmatic contents, that brought it to blows with so much of the workers' movement, enough … of the historic workers' movement, of the tradition of the workers' movement, it's enough to think of the theme of the radical critique of labour as such. However it's true that the political perspective was that of the classical, traditional communist movement. This was an important encounter between the new social content emerging in the struggles of those years, and this tradition. Perhaps for the first time, this blend succeeded. It was a living blend that lasted a number of years. What did this mean concretely? That Potere Operaio, like the other revolutionary organizations, posed a primary problem: providing an outlet of power for struggles, for the changed relations of force that verified itself then in the factory, in the labour market in general. Consolidating, fixing this shift in the relations of force, posing the problem of political power. Everyone posed the problem of political power in those years. The historic left posed it with the theme of structural reforms, of the end of the centre-left governments, of a new working class protagonism to re-launch economic development. The revolutionary left posed it: the slogan of Lotta Continua, in terms of the problem of power, was "Take Over the City"; the slogan of Potere Operaio, in terms of the problem of political power, was "insurrection," the slogan of the others was "proletarian dictatorship." This ensemble of words meant precisely what was crucial and specific, in terms of the continuity of mass struggles, of the problem of political power. In this sense, for some years we combined, we entwined the new social thrust of 1968 and thereafter with this strong postulate of the communist tradition: that at a certain point, the problem of political power was posed. We said "insurrection," the others said "Take Over the City," others said "proletarian dictatorship." Lavoro Illegale … since Lavoro Illegale was explained by others, I won't elaborate on this.

JUDGE

Just a minute, excuse me for interrupting you. I am taking this opportunity, because you are present, and you have a particular intellectual *[microphone noise]* experience also here in the capital, in order to clarify at least the meanings of a flood of words. For example, you said "insurrection." We have a charge that concerns precisely armed insurrection. But clearly whether these were words or not, blood flowed in any case. I am not saying I am in your debt. I do not owe anyone anything; we will see who is responsible. The word "armed struggle" is present, as it is present in your movement. And it is constantly, I would say obsessively present, in all the journal productions etc. *[unclear]* So I would like you to clarify *[coughing in the hall]* the meaning that you have given to this term "armed struggle."

Like others, I am trying to explain this point as best I can.

I am referring to your experience, particularly here in Rome.

... of my experience. However to be clear I ... I will answer your question straight away, however to be clear ....

See, I am concerned with this in relation *[microphone noise]* to what in the charge sheet is considered almost a qualitative leap, a re-foundation, almost a structuring of an organism—at a famous conference in Rome—with different articulations, but that had as its means—according to the charge—the practice of armed struggle. You touched upon the discourse of "Illegal Work." It can be given whatever label. Be aware that what the court requires is this: to have these points clarified. Therefore you are given, you are allowed to express your point of view, namely the point of view of someone who must defend himself from these charges.

No, I meant that, in revolutionary communist organizations, the problem of violence is a problem that to some extent is judged to be pertinent, important, or in certain phases even central within an experience of changing society. The difference between an armed struggle organization, between a communist organization (which also considers the theme of violence and its organization—including its preventive organization—to be pertinent) and an armed struggle organization, as one would say in the second half of the seventies, is this: that the armed struggle organization is not a public, political organization that seeks to construct mass struggles, that is attentive to the masses' every murmur, to use the old rhetoric. It is an organization that judges the armed struggle as strategic. That is, that judges armed struggle to be content to be carried out immediately. The use of weapons. The armed struggle is, for the terrorist organizations of the second half of the seventies, both an immediate identity of militants, a way of living, as they had theorized, and then immediately the whole political program is this: fighting. A communist political organization like Potere Operaio or Lotta Continua posed the problem, as communists always have done, that social struggles, having reached certain limits in terms of expansiveness, encounter or clash with the State monopoly over violence. Namely, that certain things are prohibited, yet mass struggles, if they are to grow, must try to undermine them all the same. And this is certainly not just principally the problem of central political power. It is the fact that there are empty houses, and that it is certainly a crime to occupy them. It is probably an even more serious crime to defend the occupation of these houses against the police. All the same, it is worth trying to undermine the State monopoly of force in relation to these empty houses that the homeless want to occupy. So the problem is posed for a communist organization in the early seventies, as a long term perspective, in the sense that everything was strenuously commensurate at the mass level.

Naturally I remember from the [court] proceedings that Fioroni says that at the 1971 Rome conference there was a meeting, at which participated some of my co-accused, at which Potere Operaio's Lavoro Illegale was formed. I know that ... I participated in all the conferences of Potere Operaio of which there were four during its existence, up to the last one at Rosolina—to my cost, naturally—there was no such meeting, I don't believe that there was such a meeting. I deny that there was a meeting of this type. Lavoro Illegale: *Illegal Work* is part of the classic literature of the workers' movement: it is the title of a Bertold Brecht poem that sings its praises. It is part of those defensive measures against power that the movement adopted, and that Potere Operaio set out to adopt systematically in the mass struggles. And that seemed to us very miserable, very unpleasant to call "servizio d'ordine" [the body of stewards that defended other participants in a political action]. Upon whom must we impose order? The other comrades of the movement? Those occupying the houses? Workers?—acting in that way sat well with the student movement at the Milan State University, it was all the fashion in San Babila [a Milan neighbourhood dominated in the seventies by neo-fascists]. We preferred to call it Lavoro Illegale. It was bombastic in a different way, but still much better and more significant than pretending to impose order on people. It was the work of the stewards' organization. This is my experience of Potere Operaio, I can only insist on this point and to confirm searching ....

JUDGE *A LATERE*

Excuse me, I understand this whole discussion, but I want to point out some things. In this context of violence of which you speak, of illegality, it happened that Valerio Morucci was made responsible for Potere Operaio's stewards' organizations: is that correct or not? He was a Roman leader, almost a national leader ....

VIRNO

He was responsible for the stewards' organization. For the stewards' organization of Potere Operaio certainly for a period, in Rome, but it's not as if I was saying this because I had, for a period of time, a leading role in Potere Operaio. This is something any one of the five hundred militants of Potere Operaio in Rome would say, any one of them.

JUDGE

Do the plaintiff counsels have any questions? Does the public prosecutor? Then I adjourn until tomorrow for the questioning and we start discussing these issues.

Brief pause, room noises, whispering in the room.

JUDGE

The word to the attorney general.

Microphone noise.

ATTORNEY GENERAL

Mr President, in the document entitled *Proposal for a National Document on the Deadlines of 1972*, volume six chapter one, the defendant states:

> A shift in the masses is occurring from working class struggle towards the armed struggle for power. It is necessary to throw the whole weight of our intelligence and organized power onto the material anticipation of this shift.

In another document, *First Draft of the Thesis on Crisis*, volume six chapter three, the defendant states:

> Armed violence is one of the forms of struggle that becomes crucial in the phase of the coming conflict. Only if this practice can be built the revolutionary organization of the European multinational worker. *[re-reading the previous sentence to correct himself]* Only on this practice can the revolutionary organization of European multinational workers be built. The terrorism of the masters must be met by red terror: the ability to hit all those responsible for the capitalist initiative and their servants, the ability to make the masters pay an ever higher price for every one of their anti-worker initiatives.

The defendant continues:

> From the revolutionary standpoint, there are two sides to armed violence, both of which must be pursued and tenaciously organized: on the one side, as mass violence, as the armed arm of the struggle of the proletariat and the working class that is no longer winning simply because the barycentre of capitalist power is no longer dislocated here; on the other side, as the direct action of the cadres of the organizational vanguard, as the ability to make explicit, in the form of an armed offensive on the institutions of capital, the degree of violence required by this conflict, the ability to free the terrain of all of the obstacles that the capitalist organization of society places against the spontaneous and autonomous raging of the struggle. And finally, as red terror: the ability to identify and strike against the single targets of proletarian struggle, to respond, blow by blow, to the violence of the masters and the State. Whilst in the first instance the building and use of the tools of proletarian violence is strictly, albeit not mechani-

51

cally, linked to the political maturity of the mass vanguards of the movement, and the material and timely unfolding of the conflict, in the second instance, the organization autonomously takes full political and organizational responsibility for every initiative.

Therefore, in the first document there is a shift from class to armed struggle. In the second document there is a reference to armed violence, identified on the one hand as mass violence, as the armed branch of working class struggle, and on the other hand as the direct action of the cadres of the vanguard organization, and finally, as red terror. We ask the defendant what he meant to say when he spoke of red terror.

Long pause, background noises.

JUDGE

Answer this question.

NEGRI

I don't know. Those documents certainly need to be placed in the classical Marxist body of work in which these issues are discussed, agitated around and continuously proposed for their suggestive power. The problem is clearly one of understanding how to locate the issues, and these writings, in my experience and that of my comrades. Undoubtedly this kind of writing is placed in a phase when *[clears throat]* the assessment of the crisis we were entering was particularly intense. It is also true that these writings are generally from the period of '71–72 when, in fact, the issue of insurrection was being developed by Potere Operaio and then subsequently came under criticism. I don't think that, for instance, when we speak of red terror, referring to a reading that goes from Lenin to Togliatti, one can identify, in itself, I mean *[laughs]* ... it's out of the question that in these debates there are, I would say, elements of an apology for violence, this is undoubtedly the case. But I don't think that, in and of themselves, any determinate organizational directions were defined. I don't know if I've sufficiently answered.

ATTORNEY GENERAL

President, as we sometimes hear them say in Parliament, this answer leaves me completely unsatisfied. However, at this point we present the photocopy of the cover of two issues of the paper *Potere Operaio*, number forty-five and forty-six. In issue forty-five we read: "Democracy is the rifle over the workers' shoulder." In issue forty-six we read: "Proletarians, we need to rebel, organize, and take up arms." We request that these photocopies are acquired as part of the proceedings.

NEGRI

I would like to point out that ....

JUDGE

Show me first ....

NEGRI

I would like to note that "democracy is a rifle over the workers' shoulder" is the slogan, a slogan used throughout the struggles of these years .... There are covers of *Lotta Continua* and other papers that report exactly the same slogan. If I'm not mistaken, in this issue there is a photograph of a large piece of graffiti on the walls of the Alfa Romeo factory, which reads "Democracy is a rifle on the workers' shoulder." The problem is completely linked to the defence of democracy, to the ideology of resistance, and the slogan is linked to this kind of ideological and political development. "Proletarians, we need to rebel, organize and take up arms" is exactly as you see it ... above it there is a photo of Lenin speaking in Red Square. They are slogans that traverse the working class movement, are part of a patrimony that one can more or less question, but which belongs to the whole of the working class movement as such.

JUDGE

The lawyer Spazzali had .... *[clears throat, whispering away from the microphone]*

JUDGE

How many more questions do you have?

Long pause, room noises, whispers away from the microphone.

JUDGE

You may speak.

DEFENCE LAWYER

Excuse me, President, I must raise an issue and ask the court to pause for a moment of common reflection on a question that I would like to submit to your attention. During the time spent on the interrogation of the defendants I cannot deny that I have become perplexed and my perplexities have eventually become real concerns. The first concerns an assertion, often reiterated by the court, that must surely correspond to the truth, that is, that the court has engaged in a notable practice, or bad practice as they have named it, in trials of terrorism. The second perplexity I have is that this court, and perhaps this is my main perplexity, has reported and declared, which is also true, that it has perfect knowledge of the general history of these ten years, and in particular it stated that it does not, rightly, intend to re-write this history. But in my view, if this claim is true and right, we still cannot forget two salient aspects of the hearing to which I must draw your attention. The first aspect is that the charge for which we have been remanded and are now being tried for is dense, rich and full of history. It's the history that can be read in the pages of the summons to trial, from the affirmation that "we must follow Gramsci and Togliatti to defend the working class" to that which confines us to "the rubbish dump of history" in the last pages of the order of this court. All this is history, and it is a history well known to everyone, everyone! Because it is epochal and reconstructs an entire complex period and in this reconstruction of an epoch there are, and there float, single islands of charges levelled against us. It is a fact that this reconstructive and historical background never became a real background; instead, it submerged the picture upon which the figures of the crime had to be drawn. The accusation is all background. The notion of organization, its history, later through the emblematic figure of my defendant Negri, who seems a Palamedes with all the fish hooks on which he, wrongly, in my opinion, has been dragging along with all the other defendants. The almost physical representation of this organization *[emphasis on each word]* is what must be said, explained, discussed, this defendant of mine must be granted the time to tell! And then, to conclude, I, more than anyone else, have no desire to see my defendant Negri exempt from any kind of questioning. On the contrary, I think this is absolutely healthy. *[more emphatically]* But first and foremost! Now! Immediately! It's necessary for him to sit on that chair, to speak for however long his defence necessitates. To speak of this organization. To tell all there is to reveal, or communicate, or explain, or claim responsibility for himself. *[quieter tone]* Because I believe that, and here I conclude, such huge accusations ranging from insurrection to a permanent conspiracy to subvert or even belonging to an armed gang, spanning over ten years, and deserving four years of imprisonment, rightly deserve four hours of direct and uninterrupted intervention from my client. So this is my demand: let speak Antonio Negri today, for the time he deems necessary to illustrate his defence.

PUBLIC PROSECUTOR

But, President, it seems evident to me, I don't think this question needs that long to be resolved. I think that the court has accepted Negri's wishes. Ha, the defendant is not simply charged with crimes of association. *[raising his voice]* He's not simply charged with conspiracy to subvert! He's not just accused of belonging to an armed gang! He's not just accused of armed insurrection! The defendant must respond to specific crimes! He has robberies, possession of weapons! He has murders, kidnapping! Well!

DEFENCE LAWYER

Yes, the defendant ....

PUBLIC PROSECUTOR

[constantly interrupting the lawyer and shouting] These are facts he must be called to answer to! These are crimes he must be called to answer to! Not only crimes of conspiracy and association!

DEFENCE LAWYER

Yes, yes, but ....

PUBLIC PROSECUTOR

So it's right that the court, naturally, asks questions on specific facts, because what are these facts after all? They are the crimes as means!

DEFENCE LAWYER

Listen ....

PUBLIC PROSECUTOR

Crimes as means through which we know what end crime is achieved!

DEFENCE LAWYER

Listen ....

PUBLIC PROSECUTOR

And so I believe that it is actually proper to start from specific crimes! Because you always contested this to us: facts, the facts! You claimed that we never charged you with specific facts. Today! We are .... Aside from the fact that we have always charged you with specific crimes and the reading of the interrogation can give ample evidence of this, because it is those who don't wish to listen and don't wish to see that keep saying *[an indistinct murmuring rises from the courtroom]* that throughout the hearing *[shouting]* you were not charged with all the specific elements!

Murmuring continues and the judge suddenly slams the desk.

JUDGE

This is not permitted! It's absolutely not permitted! To anyone.

Long pause, courtroom noises.

Long pause, room noises, confused and sustained voices.

JUDGE
We can start with the witnesses [for the prosecution]. Tommasini.

JUDGE *A LATERE*
For the folder of the witnesses of the chamber .... *[unclear]*

JUDGE
Is this Mrs Tommasini? Wait before you take a seat, Madame. Acknowledging your responsibility under oath, say "I swear." Take a seat, Madame. *[brief pause, microphone noises]* Any questions? I don't think so. Sit down, Madame.

UNKNOWN
Lawyer ....

JUDGE
Where? Ah, there is *[unclear]*, hidden in the middle .... Acknowledging your responsibility under oath, say "I swear."

LEPRI
I swear.

JUDGE
Take a seat. You are Lepri Stefano, Lepri Stefano paper 1,007 ... 1,833.

UNKNOWN
No questions.

UNKNOWN
No questions.

JUDGE
Sit down please. Ask Mrs Toniolo to enter. Yes. Mrs Toniolo, then? What other texts are there here today ...? *[away from the microphone, unclear]* Bailiff.

JUDGE *A LATERE*
Ah, yes, here comes that other witness.

JUDGE
What other witness? That is .... *[unclear]*

56

Long pause, room noises, confused and sustained voices.

JUDGE

Who has questions for Carraro Renato? *[unclear voices from the room]* Carraro Renato, yes. Come, come, why not. Wait before sitting down. Wait, wait! Acknowledging your responsibility under oath, say "I swear." You must swear, you must say "I swear," Madame. *[raising his voice trying to be understood]* You must swear to tell the truth and nothing but the truth, say "I swear"! Eh? Did you hear me now? Then say "I swear," Madame. Come here, come on. Wait before you sit, wait, wait! Say "I swear." *[rustling papers]* Take a seat. *[sound of microphone turned and placed in the stand]*

JUDGE

Your name?

MR BERASSITO

Berassito.

JUDGE

Aware of the resp ... wait before sitting down! Wait before you sit down! Say "I swear." Your name, sit down. What's your name?

CHAIRMAN OF FACE STANDARD [FACTORY]

[replies, unclear]

JUDGE

Sit down. Gio ...? What are you at Face Standard?

CHAIRMAN OF FACE STANDARD

I am the current chairman ....

JUDGE

The current chairman of Face Standard.

CHAIRMAN OF FACE STANDARD

[talking over the judge] ... of Face Standard.

JUDGE

Any questions?

UNKNOWN

No.

JUDGE

Take a seat thank you.

Long break, room noises, coughs, papers rustled.

SCIARETTA

[unclear]

JUDGE

What? Sciaretta, what? Gennaro? Sciaretta Gennaro? Sit down please. [brief pause, papers rustle] Lawyer Gatti, please. Wait a minute. [unclear] Then we suspend everything. [microphone noises] Who is the other witness? Before calling them I just want to know their name. Where is the bailiff? No, but I haven't asked him to bring him here yet. Can you tell me who this witness is? [raising his voice] How many witnesses are there? Who are they?

UNKNOWN

[voice from the room, away from the microphone] Rivierina, Trentin and .... [unclear]

JUDGE

What?

UNKNOWN

[voice from the room, away from the microphone repeats raising his voice] Rivierina, Trentin and .... [unclear]

JUDGE

Trentin. [cough from the room] I'll have him immediately. Now I have him .... [unclear] Come. Come, come. Acknowledging your responsibility under oath, say "I swear."

TRENTIN

I swear.

JUDGE

You are Guido Trentin. You declared that you were a technician at Savelli and controlled the typographical work on that volume of *Autonomia*.

TRENTIN

Yes, yes.

JUDGE

Do you confirm these circumstances?

TRENTIN

Yes, yes, I don't remember ....

JUDGE

[not giving Trentin the chance to finish] Sit down, you can go, thank you.

TRENTIN

Thank you.

Brief pause, room noises, unclear voices.

JUDGE

Zicoli, let him enter. Any question for this witness? Because he is extraneous to this trial, he ended up here ... the miracles of bureaucracy. Acknowledging your responsibility under oath, say "I swear." Sit down please. No, no, no! You can leave actually, I wasn't interested. I didn't summon you, it was the public prosecutor. Another witness, come on!

Long pause, room noises, unclear voices.

JUDGE

Tommei.

Long pause, noises in the hall, coughing, microphone sounds.

JUDGE

Make yourself comfortable. We have some charges before which you claim your complete innocence. *[brief pause]* I would prefer us to proceed, at least as far as my questions are concerned, by addressing each matter in turn. If you would like to make an introductory statement, I have no problem with that, in any way.

TOMMEI

I would like to make a very short introductory statement explaining to the court who I am, beyond what is said in the trial documents. Basically my political life began many years ago. I was active in parties of the Italian traditional left, I distanced myself from them around the middle of the sixties, and I participated in the movement that was formed in '68 in Italian universities and in '69 in the factories. With this movement I did not participate as a militant within any of the organized groups. In this period, we can say, I was active with the movement largely on the cultural front. Namely, together with Fo, Rame and other comrades, I founded La Comune, which was a great cultural experience in those years. In fact, this circle had 25,000 members in Milan. Towards the end of '71, I grew close to the Gruppo Gramsci, a group with some very distinctive characteristics, in the sense that it negated itself as a group from the moment it was founded, and that took as its statute the impulse for workers' self-organization. I moved away from this group as well around the middle of '72, after which all my political activity basically revolved around service structures. My relationship with Negri began in that period, and it was a purely cultural and political relationship, one of open debate. I participated in the journal *Rosso*. I was one of the founders of the second series of *Rosso*, what we can call the *Rosso* of Autonomia, and I participated from the beginning in this political project that was based largely on the self-organization of proletarians, on the self-organization of factory workers, on self-organization in the neighbourhoods. In other words, it always denied any form of organization that could be directed from above, that reproduced a political class. What I would like to clarify emphatically to this court is that for myself, as for many of my co-accused, none of us, starting with myself, have ever thought of or planned to establish an armed group as such. Nor have we ever conceived of a terrorist form of violence, or the practice of homicide. And this holds for my whole experience within Autonomia afterwards. I believe that the

area of *Rosso* in Milan, where it began and carried out its political practice, was absolutely never in the majority—rather, it was an extremely
minor experience. And I do not deny there was a connivance—largely
if not totally—towards subversion in that period, and also a use of violence. A connivance that completely ended from a political point of view
with the end of Autonomia at the Bologna conference of '77, but that
ended in substance after the demonstration at which the police agent
Custrà was killed. Our rupture, from the point of view of practices, of
connivances, of proximities, with a world whose direction we no longer
understood. And this was a total rupture. I am ready now.

JUDGE

Tommei *[clears throat]* ... in the course of the inquiry. Further to what
I said: a discourse that is worth developing further. In the course of the
inquiries, and sometimes within this debate, various perspectives have
been provided of your conduct, in the light of one of your personal documents that you have disputed in the inquiry. It is one of your documents,
a letter to Negri in which you speak of the "little cousins," meaning by
this the Brigate Rosse. You speak of an imminent victory, or of a line that
will prevail within your organization. You know that there is someone—
we will hear from this someone—who holds that you were in charge of
the stewards' organization of Gramsci [the group].

TOMMEI

So far as I know, the stewards' organization of Gramsci ... basically it
was one of the few political groups that by its nature, and because it was
founded later than the others, and dissolved earlier, never had stewards'
structures. And I was never personally responsible for any stewards'
structure, never. I mean, if I had been I would have no problem saying
so, because the stewards' organizations were, let's say, an absolutely
legal thing, from an internal point of view, even if they often moved on
the terrain of illegality.

JUDGE

According to someone else, you were the driving force ....

TOMMEI

I don't understand ....

JUDGE

According to the statement of a witness, you were the driving force of
this organization whose existence you are disputing. And according to
another person, you had entrusted Fioroni with ... *[pause]* according to
Gavazzeni, those famous three million for buying arms in Austria.

TOMMEI

Perhaps it would be worth clarifying this problem of monetary relations
between myself and Gavazzeni.

JUDGE

[interrupting Tommei] Let's clarify it. Let's clarify it, while we wait for that document to arrive.

TOMMEI

Gavazzeni told me that this money was to buy arms in order to liberate Ulrike Meinhof. Which seemed to me ....

JUDGE

In order to liberate?

TOMMEI

In order to liberate Ulrike Meinhof. This was one of Fioroni's many fantasies, as he went around seeking money that he probably then used for his own survival. Using—as was done in that period—and very probably it was easier to get money from some intellectuals or whoever by telling them that it was to buy arms or to break someone out of jail, rather than for buying a Gestetner machine for printing leaflets—so we need to remember the mood of those days, from this point of view. I believe that the problem of so-called armament was then a problem, very much part of the overall debate of the whole left, because it was '73. The problem of armament was not then linked, as it would become years later, to a problem of an armed initiative or terrorist initiative. In that precise historical moment, the problem of armament was linked to the danger of a coup: this was the time of Chile. The problem of a defensive type of armament, against a coup, was completely within a debate that concerned not only the newly born Autonomia on the fringes, but that concerned the whole extra-parliamentary left, and perhaps the parliamentary left as well. Such that this kind of attitude was not so strange then. So that I believe that from this point of view the matter would hardly surprise Gavazzeni. Still, Gavazzeni—and we will see him again, here—knew very well my views concerning the constitution—to put it that way, with a language that didn't exist back then—of a so-called armed group. Namely that I was completely opposed to that type of political conception. However my proximity not only, at this point with "violence" in quotation marks, but also with these .... *[pauses]* As for the problem of a coup, personally I had never agreed, that is personally, I had never thought it necessary to collect arms in anticipation of a coup, because politically I couldn't imagine that a coup was a real danger in Italy, however ... *[pauses]* thousands of people around me thought absolutely differently. Groups who have never been charged with engaging in armed struggle thought in this manner: from Lotta Continua to Avanguardia Operaia.

So I hope that I have explained myself. I really don't have any more to say.

JUDGE

So Fioroni would have approached—you say—Gavazzeni asking him for three million lire ....

TOMMEI

[the two begin to interrupt and talk over each other] In order to buy arms
to be used ....

JUDGE

In order to buy arms ....

TOMMEI

I don't know if in Austria or where ....

JUDGE

They were .... Here, for example: in your personal experience, were there
requests from the BR to you or to one of your comrades for arms or
explosives?

TOMMEI

In my experience, never.

JUDGE

There were never any.

TOMMEI

Nor in my experience have I ever requested explosives or arms from anyone.

JUDGE

You know that there is someone who says—we will hear from this someone—that there was also some dissent over kidnapping people, over
practices of that type that were intended to be undertaken. There are
rumours in the trial ....

TOMMEI

Yes, yes, there are statements in the trial. I refute them absolutely, I have
never contemplated kidnapping anyone.

*Long pause, indecipherable voices away from the microphone, noises in
the hall, distant coughing, rustling of papers.*

JUDGE

[reading] Around November–December '72

—this is from the questioning of Pilenga on 7 June 1980—

I was visited by Fioroni, who I already knew, but in a totally superficial way. He was looking for somewhere to stay and since I lived alone, he asked if I could put him up for around a month and a half. During his stay at my place and afterwards, we discussed politics, and he raised amongst other things the danger of a fascist coup in Italy. I was convinced by his words, also because the political climate of the time lent credence to that hypothesis. One day Fioroni asked me if any people I knew had apartments that could be used as safe places for comrades in the case of danger. He suggested to me that I make my place available for meetings. I agreed. Various meetings were held in my house, meetings I didn't attend as they took place while I was at work. The people who participated in said meetings were the leaders of this organization, which then had no name. After a couple of months, around March–April '73, I joined a small group that was part of said organization. The function of the group to which I belonged was to find safe accommodation for comrades in difficulty. I had always considered that our activity was a defensive function against the danger of an authoritarian turn.

I will continue reading because there is some mention of another minor matter.

In the course of my group's meetings, talk developed of the organization's self-financing. Every so often Negri participated in the meetings, providing a sort of lesson on the political situation and on links with the working class etc. Moreover Negri himself also raised the problem of the organization's self-financing. Negri addressed the problem of self-financing in general terms. Negri said that the working class needed to defend itself from price increases through proletarian expropriation.

So the first point: we desire to know something about these expropriations. Second, since there is talk of appropriations, expropriations, it seems to me that there is a difference in your language between appropriations and expropriations. The nuances are different, and we want to know the difference when you refer to these expropriations and these appropriations.

NEGRI

We are in the second half of '73. As I have already tried to explain, there was this kind of absolutely informal aggregation of old groups, in the attempt to make contact with the factory assemblies. Pilenga's group, what I know of it, was an old group of Soccorso Rosso.

JUDGE

What group was that?

NEGRI

It was an old group of Soccorso Rosso, of Milanese bourgeois who gave, who committed themselves to internationalist assistance, first of all; in the second place to assisting those persons who—within the ambit of the class struggle—needed help.

JUDGE

Needed?

NEGRI

Huh?

JUDGE

Needed?

NEGRI

Help! The fact, it was something ... you need to enter a bit into the climate of the period, the existence of these traditional Soccorso Rosso groups was an absolutely common thing. *[coughing in the hall]* The name Soccorso Rosso has a long history of commitment to this aid work, support. It's what in French they call the work of *soutien*. To give an example, the heyday in Europe of Soccorso Rosso groups in internationalist terms was the period of assistance for Algeria, above all in France where—for example—all those French soldiers who refused the call up so as to avoid going to fight in Algeria ....

JUDGE

[interrupting Negri] Just a minute, we were in '73!

NEGRI

I know, but I'm telling you, it was the moment of expansion of this type of ideology that was consolidated and expanded during '68, '69. We are in '73, that is on the margins of '68, '69, '70, of that period. Pilenga's group was a group that moved within this type of ideology, of behaviours. What absolutely needs to be understood is that there was a stack of these kinds of initiatives, initiatives that simply sprang from what was an ethical behaviour.

JUDGE

What I have asked you is this: have you met this Pilenga, did you hold these meetings, did you participate in these meetings at Pilenga's house and did you participate in the meeting that discussed self-financing? And in this connection I have asked for elucidations on expropriations and appropriations. So we are seeking for you to clarify these points: if there were these meetings, if there was talk of self-financing, what expropriations and appropriations meant in your lexicon, or in that of Autonomia in that period. I think I have understood the difference between the two, but I would not like to make an error. We will see in a little while if these meetings occurred, if there was talk of self-financing, in what sense and what these terms meant.

NEGRI

Well, I knew these people. The relationship with them was not an organizational one in terms of someone telling them what to do or assigning them tasks. Because the point of reference wasn't Negri, it wasn't any of Negri's friends, it was simply this work of coming into contact with the assemblies in order to earn the right to speak, to participate, at this level of organization. All that began to happen only towards the middle of '74—and we will speak of this later—after *Rosso*, the space in via Disciplini, began to become a central reference point. As for this period, as they say, one needed to march towards that objective. There was no kind of organizational relationship. Because this organizational relationship could not be filtered through my function, which was simply—in that phase—one of proposing general political themes. In that moment there was talk of appropriation, it's true that there was talk of appropriation. What appropriating meant in absolutely general terms was this: in that continuous struggle which is the working day, which is the relationship between the labour performed and the labour that is accumulated by the boss, accumulated and transformed by capital, there is the question of appropriating, in an absolutely continuous manner, ever greater amounts of one's own labour, and therefore of one's own liberty. This is in absolutely general terms. In particular terms: in so far as this society seems to be dominated not simply at the level of the factory, but within society as a whole, by rules imposed to expropriate proletarians, what's required is to conquer spaces of liberty, to break these chains of domination. Expropriation: expropriation is an illegal form of mass and individual appropriation. Expropriation, as you know well, is considered acceptable by the classics of communist literature. Is it more criminal to found a bank or to expropriate it? That is a question from Brecht, and it is *[laughs]* classic literature. Is it more criminal to create profit or to distribute it according to just rules? These are discourses that were made within the climate of that time, there is no doubt about that.

JUDGE

The specific question I asked you is this, I am not interested in the classics or otherwise of Marxist literature. We can all find something out about that. Whether or not something is a classic is a judgement that each of us can make on the basis of our own culture or interests. My question is much simpler, we don't need Lenin or anyone else pronouncing from on high, let's avoid that. Did you talk about possible bank robberies, for example?

NEGRI

No.

JUDGE
And did you carry out, for example, bank robberies?

NEGRI
That was ruled out.

JUDGE
Oh! Robberies for example of pay packet deliveries?

NEGRI
That was absolutely ruled out.

JUDGE
Stealing works of art?

NEGRI
That was absolutely ruled out.

JUDGE
You ruled that out. My question concerned this, nothing else. We will hear Pilenga and we will see what she has to say on this point.

Long pause, noises in the courtroom.

JUDGE
Does the plaintiff lawyer have any questions?

PLAINTIFF LAWYER
Mr President, the court order contains a declaration by Gavazzeni, in which he states that the accused and Negri had spoken to Gavazzeni of the necessity for a cadre training school. What I want to ask the accused is this: if there existed a cadre training school, and in what sense.

JUDGE
Please respond.

TOMMEI
[away from the microphone] I think that I answered yesterday on this problem of cadres we were for ....

People talking over each other, unclear.

PLAINTIFF LAWYER

Cadre training school, let's talk about that.

TOMMEI

I don't know, I don't understand ....

JUDGE

Cadre school, we are talking about cadres here.

TOMMEI

I never contemplated establishing a school for cadres with Gavazzeni. Probably, perhaps we were talking about organizing some conferences on some specific topics, but a school for cadres with Gavazzeni, I really don't think so.

Long pause, background noises.

PLAINTIFF LAWYER

May I? So the text from Miglierina—this episode is likewise in the court order—states that after the dissolution of Potere Operaio, contacts were made between ex-members of the Gruppo Gramsci, including Madera, Pozzi, Arrighi, etc., and exponents of Autonomia, amongst whom Miglierina cites Negri, Finzi, Tommei, who openly supported the necessity of mass illegal activity, and mentions in particular, occupations, self-reductions, sabotage, appropriations. What can the accused tell us on this point?

Brief pause.

TOMMEI

I think that this is all true, in the sense of Autonomia in that period, and I agreed on the matter of appropriations, sabotage and occupations.

PLAINTIFF LAWYER

There are no further questions, Mr President.

Brief pause.

JUDGE

Thank you. Please move the microphone.

Brief pause, the sound of footsteps, a microphone inserted in its stand.

BELLOSI

[from the cage] Well then, Mr President, what happened in those days in Rebibbia was, we could say, the blatant demonstration of *[coughs]* the State's binary prison policy. On the one hand, *[coughs]* that of promises—for now—of a vague reformism for categories of prisoners; on the other, the most obtuse repression. And when I say obtuse repression, that's because it really was: that is, in the sense that what happened demonstrated this in the most unequivocal way. What I'd like to do then is to briefly set out the facts. *[clears throat]* The section in which I found myself, Rebibbia's differentiation section, G7, was managed in an arbitrary way. Arbitrary doesn't mean authoritarian, it means simply that the same problem would be addressed one way on one day, and in the exact opposite way the next. Such a management style could only exacerbate tensions. Precisely for that reason we had sought for some time a meeting with the prison director in order to see how to defuse these gratuitous, artificial tensions, which stemmed from the way the section was run. The response was a rising of the level of tension in the final week, leading on the Friday to one of our comrades being placed in an isolation cell charged with having said something that a guard had misinterpreted. At that point we decided to conduct an absolutely peaceful form of struggle, what can be said to be the only peaceful form of protest allowed to prisoners: delaying our return from the recreation walk in the prison yard. This peaceful form of protest was met by a heavy military response: we were forced back to our cells, the director had promised to meet and instead this turned out to be a trap that led us to be placed one by one in isolation. The next day, we were penalized for this absolutely peaceful form of protest with fifteen days of solitary confinement, and some of us—who had simply *beaten* upon the bars, but had not hit any people—received twenty-five days in solitary. This meant that we weren't able to talk to each other, no television, no radio, no nothing, no groceries, in the sense that we couldn't buy anything, not even groceries. The article we were saddled with was number seventy-two of the prison regulations, paragraph twenty, which speaks of the *promotion of revolts or disorders*. Tell me what promotion of revolts or disorders there is in staying in the exercise yard. Examples of this kind, isolation of this type, occurred only at Trani after the revolt, or at Fossambrone after a killing. At Fossambrone and Ascoli people were given thirty days solitary in the branch, after the killings there. *[clears throat]* One last thing, we appealed to prisoners obviously in the other cages to show us their solidarity. This wasn't about political lines, but rather an unjustified, obnoxiously repressive measure, for which we had no problem seeking solidarity from prisoners in the other cages. I must say that we received solidarity from the other prisoners. In order to allow us, one at a time, to spend half an hour a day outside, the separated prisoners of G7 in the other wing of the section gave up their yard time for the next two weeks.

JUDGE

Please.

The sound of a microphone being mounted in a stand.

FUNARO

[from the other cage] In the name of the prisoners in this cage, we want to express our solidarity with every form of peaceful protest that struggles to improve prison conditions, therefore we welcome Cecco Bellosi's request, and associate ourselves with their peaceful struggle for better living conditions in prison.

JUDGE

Negri.

Brief pause.

JUDGE

I have authorized this request, passing it along to the bailiff who is competent to decide. *[brief pause]* Negri.

Long pause, noises in the court, distant coughing, sound of footsteps approaching the microphone, protracted rustling of papers.

JUDGE

Concerning this cadre school. You know that we have—you have heard them publicly here—the testimony from Borromeo. Borromeo has spoken of his experience in La Comune with Fo, of becoming close to Tommei. Of the proposal that Tommei made to him at a non-public level, at a secret, off-the-record level. Call it what you like. And here Borromeo's testimony, returning again to the point of expropriation and appropriation, speaks of surveys and studies that Borromeo had made. Here *[clears throat]* Borromeo agreed to identify accommodation for workers evading arrest, or for people who had had run-ins with the judicial authority. You have heard Borromeo's declaration *[clears throat]*, and we will see if, from your way of seeing, these statements of Borremeo concerning these facts are true or false.

NEGRI

[clears throat] With all probability, I think that a group like that of Borromeo, involved precisely in finding houses, falls exactly within that tradition of which I spoke before, the tradition of Soccorso Rosso assistance. I am absolutely certain, or at least so far as I can remember, that this activity had nothing to do with finding houses, finding hideouts. Because here we have to be very clear: when Borromeo speaks of this kind of work that he says he undertook, we must be very careful not to

superimpose categories, images, stereotypes that are stereotypes of armed struggle, of clandestine struggle.

None of this was really part of the activity of Borromeo, of Pilenga, etc. This is an activity linked in the first place essentially to the tradition of struggle ... *[corrects himself]* to the internationalist tradition. I remember that in Milan, for example, throughout the sixties, I continually encountered for example people seeking refuge from Latin America, Spaniards, people who took refuge in these houses provided by people like Borromeo or Pilenga. These things are absolutely typical of a certain type of Milanese red bourgeoisie. I say this for Milan, and from my personal memory of the fifties, at the end of the fifties, the early sixties, the Algerian *reseau* [networks] were made up of the same people. When they speak precisely about these houses, Borromeo and the others speak of this old tradition that they kept alive. In the second place, above all in the years around '73–74, the coup/counter-coup discourse began, and with it a new accentuation of this history. *[judge clears his throat]* So all this has nothing to with, this searching for houses that undoubtedly took place ... meanwhile I don't think that any houses were obtained, of any kind ....

JUDGE

[interrupting Negri] Look, excuse me Professor Negri, look, here it's not so much, only, a question of finding houses, it's not so much seeing ... *[interrupts himself]* for us these things clearly have an innate penal importance. We have the law and we must apply it, beyond the ideological valences of behaviours. What interests us about Borromeo is his testimony that looking for houses was not looking for houses as the final legacy of French resistance to the Algerian war. It was looking for houses for a compartmentalized organization. In fact I have already alluded to the work that Borromeo undertook for the information-gathering network, for the information-gathering service of this organization. It's not so much house hunting embedded in this work. For Borromeo, this house hunting was part of an information-gathering branch, and then there were other branches. This is the discourse. This is the whole discourse of this organization.

DEFENCE LAWYER

I don't want to interrupt you, perhaps I have misunderstood, but if I remember correctly—I don't have Borromeo's transcript here—this question of research was not perhaps that research of independence from those ....

JUDGE

[interrupting defence lawyer] There was research that he ... on the reactionary structure. And then there was research on a specific subject, we will see this research, we will see it tomorrow. Here *[clears throat]* Borromeo's perspective is that, Borromeo's testimony is not house hunting, I repeat it again, so as to maintain a tradition of internationalism

or whatever you call it, but house hunting for an organization that is structured and compartmentalized.

Brief pause.

JUDGE

You have denied the charge of handling stolen identity cards and driver's licences. Some of these papers were then used to help the material authors of the Argelato incident to flee the country. Scalzone was caught in '75 with one of these driver's licences; there is testimony here from Casirati, Fioroni and Borromeo. What do you know of these matters, of these identity cards and driver's licences?

NEGRI

I have never heard of these identity cards outside the documents of the court remand.

JUDGE

You have also denied charge thirty-one, the theft of a stamp collection valued at one hundred million lire, property of Lorenzo Seguso *[unclear]*, 10 August 1974 in Venice. A theft carried out by Casirati for the purpose of financing, what do you know about this matter?

NEGRI

[speaking over the judge] I know absolutely nothing about this question.

JUDGE

Then there are crimes associated with an attempted robbery at the Marconi Institute in Padua, do you have anything to declare on this point?

NEGRI

I know simply *[laughs]* that it does not exist even in the particulars described.

JUDGE

Does not exist ....

NEGRI

No, it does not exist in the sense that there never was a cash carrier, no one remembers any running after any cash carriers, the cars mentioned by Casirati were never found, etc., etc., but, I have no idea ....

JUDGE

And we come to the attack at Face Standard. And here Borromeo says that you tasked him with looking the place over. You would have participated in the meeting, you would have spoken to Borromeo beforehand, given him this task, and you would have explained to him the reason for the action.

TOMMEI

As for the Face Standard action, I absolutely did not participate in either
its planning or in discussions concerning the action from an organizational point of view. I never gave Borromeo things to do concerning this
action. I did speak a lot about this action. Because everyone spoke about
it in that period. I won't deny it, I found myself rather in agreement with
the methodology, on how it was carried out. Between that and having
had organized relations or planning or reviewing this action afterwards
[interrupts himself] ... before anything else I would like ... perhaps in the
initial part of discourse, I would like to clarify this matter again: in that
period I did not belong to any organization.

JUDGE

You know that Borromeo says that he would have received from you the
task of inspecting these places.

TOMMEI

I never gave Borromeo a task of that nature.

JUDGE

So that would be false testimony by Borromeo.

TOMMEI

So far as I am concerned, yes.

Long pause, courtroom noises.

JUDGE

At this point I can read—if you wish—the statement that you made. If
you want to read it ... because I would like us to avoid then having to ask
if this or that is true.

Indecipherable voices in the background.

JUDGE

If the public prosecutor agrees to let you read this.

PUBLIC PROSECUTOR

No, I want them to read it, so that the jurors can hear what the witness
has said.

UNKNOWN

Put forward your questions.

JUDGE *A LATERE*

I confirm the statement that I made. I was hired at Face around mid '72, practically straight away ....

JUDGE

We will get the juror to read it directly ....

JUROR

[reads quickly, without pausing, and in a mechanical tone] I entered into contact with a group of young people at Face. It was not yet a collective, this group of people was more or less linked to the Gruppo Gramsci of Milan. They carried out a para-union activity: the Gruppo Gramsci was concerned primarily at the beginning with the counter-culture, in that its members had a perspective on personal matters, that started from the deepest personal relationships, bearing in mind not only the political as such, but also what it meant to change relations between people. At a certain point the Gruppo Gramsci dissolved. I believe that Potere Operaio dissolved around the same time, and some people who came from that political experience began to get involved in our collective. The change that these people brought to the collective was a greater incitement to intervention within the factory with leaflets etc. One day around September–October 1974, while making coffee, Giordani told me that there was a further level, without explaining to me precisely what that was. He invited me to an afternoon or evening meeting, and I went. Funaro was there, it was the first time that I saw him, and he spoke of the intention to set fire to Face Standard's premises in Fizzonasco. He didn't explain the details. About a week later we were invited to an expropriation at a supermarket in Quarto Oggiaro. I took part, knowing what it was about, but entered with many other people. Then there was this episode in which we went—I think it was a Saturday—to that place on the Ticino where there was Funaro with another blonde girl that I never saw again, he called her Sandra. It was with the collective—I don't remember now, I think there was Sabatelli, Giordani, I'm not sure if Dell'Acqua was there, Lazzaroni wasn't because he came later, and my husband. Funaro filled up this bottle, threw it against some rocks, and said that this was a Molotov. We watched the Molotov explode, then that was it, and we went home.

Indistinct voices in the court.

UNKNOWN

Not guilty on all counts.

JUDGE

Can we take five minutes?

Long pauses, noises in the court, steps.

FUNARO

It happened that immediately after the fire, which occurred on a Sunday, between Saturday night and Sunday morning, the following Monday there was a very alarmed meeting of comrades from Face at Daniela's house, to try and make sense of what had just happened. There was a lot of concern on the part of some comrades of the collective like Piero Sabatelli, who was the most concerned; Luca Boneghi, who like others was as much concerned whether the action was the work of the Brigate Rosse. It was a very normal evaluation meeting—very normal given the situation, I mean, for the proximity—and was followed by another two meetings, all three held in the same week, as usual.

JUDGE

[interrupting] In which it was clarified, in which it was clarified that the action was not the work of the Brigate Rosse.

FUNARO

[judge talks over Funaro in part, indecipherable fragments] In which it was clarified that the action was not the work of the Brigate Rosse.

JUDGE

[interrupting] You explained to them that it wasn't the Brigate Rosse.

FUNARO

But there was a long and heated discussion on this matter, Mr President. I maintained that ... sustaining means literally giving support, like a rope holds a weight. Maintaining functions also figuratively speaking, like to affirm, to support or defend an argument.

JUDGE

Let's avoid equivocations, generic statements. Here ....

FUNARO

Mr President, I have told you ... *[ironically]* but I cannot say, I cannot say that I have maintained .... I can simply tell you this: that in the discussion, I declared myself to be extremely in favour of what the fire had accomplished, that is clear.

JUDGE

I do not want to know, I do not demand to know, forgive me, sometimes the words .... I would like to know how things went. You are a defendant,

I use the means that the law provides me, including these hearings, in order to know fragments of truth, parts of the truth, the whole truth, unfortunately I don't know everything in total. The lady there says that at a certain point—*she* says before, you say afterwards—you spoke of the Face Standard [incident]. You say the problem was that some people believed that the action was undertaken by the Brigate Rosse, today you tell me that you explained—as she says—that the action wasn't by the Brigate Rosse. Is that it?

FUNARO

Well, not really. I simply said ....

JUDGE

Let's see how it was .... *[coughs]*

FUNARO

I simply said that on the basis of the statement that had been made: a) it seemed to me that the action was legitimate b) that it didn't seem to me to have been a Brigate Rosse action because the style in which the leaflet was written, the distribution of the leaflet, which was widespread and massive, indicated that this was not the work of a clandestine organization, but rather of an organization or a group of comrades relating however to an area in which politically ....

JUDGE

[interrupting Funaro] The lady there says that you—she said you—went to her house. You say without doubt that there was a discussion of this attack upon Face Standard. You say that this discussion occurred not before—as this lady claims—but afterwards, and you tell me that it was not the Brigate Rosse but rather a group of comrades, you say a non-clandestine organization, is this what you are saying?

FUNARO

Broadly speaking.

JUDGE

Broadly speaking.

FUNARO

The situation was more articulated obviously, clearly there was a more articulated discourse. Namely the discourse began with Chile, in substance.

JUDGE

I know that it began with Chile, OK, Funà! I understand these things, I also know how to read between the lines with things you've written, dear God!, that's not what's being said, we know how to read, OK ... what's in this discourse.

FUNARO

I have nothing further to say on this.

JUDGE

OK, if you have nothing further to say, sit down.

Long pause, rustling of papers, coughing in the court.

JUDGE

The other charge that is being disputed is that of having participated in the meeting that decided on the attack at Face Standard. What do you intend to declare on this point? Let's see what you say in your defence. If you have a statement to make, make it ... this attack on Standard.

NEGRI

The attack on Face Standard.

JUDGE

Yes.

NEGRI

Well, perhaps .... It would be useful to try and describe the situation in which this attack on Face Standard occurred.

JUDGE

We could describe the situation, but I would like to know something about this, what you intend to say to this charge, charge number thirty-three. We must make a judgement on this. If you want to set something down, I have no problem with that. If you then want to explain the situation to us, do so, I won't stop you. You need to explain the situation then, go ahead.

NEGRI

Perhaps, it would be worth remembering 1974 and the level of things that I knew and did then. Namely, that I did not concern myself, sadly, with clandestine organizations. I concerned myself with politics, cleanly, talking with people. I did not concern myself with Casirati, I did not concern myself with the theft of stamps. The money that I needed I obtained through my political work. I claim my total non-involvement in this series of grubby stories that have been thrown at me. I would simply recall that 1974 was, for me, a crucial year from the point of view of the organization of Autonomia. That is, of the organization of a political force, organized and with roots in the factories, that was founded and carried forward by men who engaged in politics and desired better things for people, exactly as I did. That at the same time the bosses carried out a state coup in Chile. That, at the same time, in Italy there were strong whisperings of a right wing coup. That all this determined moments of serious imbalance within the factories and within ... society. That the Communist party in this phase was gripped by an extremely profound change in political line. A political line that, in talking of wanting to avoid in Italy a situation like that in Chile, accepted for the first time to play within the traditional system of power. The Historic Compromise was born, in this period, as a political discourse carried forward by the leadership of the PCI. While, on the other hand within the PCI, groups were formed that attempted to arm themselves against a coup ....

JUDGE
[intervenes away from the microphone talking over Negri] Unclear.

NEGRI
That attempted to arm themselves, to organize themselves in an armed manner against a possible coup. This was the situation of those years, of that year in particular. This is the situation in which we discussed politics and we attempted to end that crisis which had followed the dissolution of the groups. 1974 was this for me; this is what I remember of 1974. That was my life in 1974.

JUDGE
So, let's say negative with regard to the position relating to crime number thirty-three. Let's move to crime thirty-six: Argelato. And here the issue becomes a lot more complicated. And it becomes more complicated because we can also approach it on the basis of the statements that someone made in front of the Milan criminal court, of which I was reminding you the last time. Let's hear your thoughts on this matter of Argelato where a person died.

NEGRI
I declare that I have absolutely nothing to do with the whole Argelato affair.

JUDGE
At sheet 914 of the seventh volume there is the statement made by Sandalo about the Argelato episode during the preliminary inquiry. Sandalo declares in the text:

> In addition, with respect to the facts of Argelato, in which the non-commissioned officer of the Carabinieri Lombardini encountered his death, I was told that this action had been decided and carried out by the organization to fund both the magazine *Rosso* and the clandestine structures.

[Statement] One. Ferrandi, Let's start going some way back with Ferrandi:

> *[reads]* For instance: in the attempt to define a model for the development of the organization that would enable it to reproduce itself, a series of practices was introduced, such as the disarmament of night watchmen: another episode for which I am charged (this is in Milan). In your neighbourhood, in your area, near your home, you must study a night watchman—even at the risk of being noticed: this is important. Choose an elderly person, someone who is unlikely to react. Find a street door, a corner, a time when nobody passes by. In short, start thinking like this. We were spreading this kind of plague.
>
> I always talked about this affair, the Argelato affair, with Roberto. I know little or nothing about who participated in it and how it happened. But what I know is that the Emilian Communist Party was attributed a role in the events that led to the Argelato gunfight and to the arrest of those involved in this event. In this sense: in Emilia Romagna there was a network in the organization within which—still according to Roberto: I know nothing first hand—there apparently was a connection to the Communist Party, in the sense that one of the militants of the organization also had a relationship with the Communist Party. It isn't clear. The fact is that through this mole the Communist Party had got to know of a planned provocation or robbery that was going to happen in that area during those days, and it had apparently alerted the police that there was this possible provocation under way. It is likely that at the time the Communist Party already considered these emergent groups—Gatto Selvaggio, etc.—which were present in Bologna—as groups of provocateurs, and so it kept an eye on them. This is how the Argelato gunfire happened. A few hours after the robbery, the people in this group, including those who hadn't directly participated in the Argelato events but were connected with those who did, were arrested one by one, or in any case they found themselves with the police at their door.

Rosso, 15 March–April 1975:

> Shut up or we talk about Argelato. This is what opportunistic cops of all sorts seem to be saying. But we are the ones who want to talk about Argelato because it is our stuff. That's right, it is our stuff: the same as every time youth rebellion, workers' rebellion, marginals' rebellion cannot find a way to organize and explode in a limited and spontaneous way; the same as every time comrades move on a terrain that is still inadequate with respect to the development of the mass movement; the same as every time we cannot find a solution to our own personal situation in this society based on competition and repression;

the same as every time we find ourselves alone with our rage against exploitation and family; the same as every time we read in a newspaper that one of us died at work or from an abortion or was shot by a Carabinieri lieutenant. It is our stuff and we want to talk about it.

These are the charges against you for the Argelato episode. If you have something to say, say it; if you don't have anything to say, don't speak.

NEGRI

If you could please indicate the charges against me.

Whispers.

JUDGE

In Milan there have been other statements by other people on this issue ...

JUDGE *A LATERE*

Mr President ....

JUDGE

Excuse me, Dr Abbate wants to intervene ....

JUDGE *A LATERE*

I just wanted to ask that we read the charges based on what Bonavita says. Please let's read the charges based on what Bonavita says.

NEGRI

Charges ... what does he say? I don't understand ....

JUDGE

What Bonavita says.

NEGRI

Charges ....

JUDGE

What Bonavita says.

NEGRI

Bonavita: I don't know what Bonavita says. Please tell me.

JUDGE *A LATERE*

What happened in the Palmi prison, let's see what Bonavita has to say.

PUBLIC PROSECUTOR

In a passage in Bonavita's statements we read:

From the inside we believed that it was a spontaneous event. Or at least we could only see the spontaneous component without being able to perceive—as people outside could do—that behind it there were small groups that were pushing. I mean, to provide another example, that there were these old leaders who sent kids to do robberies—and I know of the Argelato one—making them believe that they operated in connection with the BR, which was absolutely untrue. In sum, by using the magazine *Rosso* and the political area close to it, Negri and Tommei then used big names for practical purposes, to put their hands on and control the small neighbourhood groups, the proletarian youth circles. These spontaneously tended …. But here they [i.e., the groups] found those big names who militarily directed them, armed them, and then gave them political space in the magazine. Negri and Tommei's function was to elaborate and give political orientation. For the practical production of this strategy they used those big names I have mentioned, and that certainly included Alunni—when he was in Palmi he told me that he was responsible for the circle of Porta Romana, to which belonged the group that shot Custrà—and also others, including perhaps Strano Oreste and Marocco Antonio.

Regarding the connection to the BR in the Argelato robbery, Marocco states in the text and he says it better ….

DEFENCE LAWYER

Mr President ….

PUBLIC PROSECUTOR

Just a moment, a moment please and then you can dispute as much as you like!

DEFENCE LAWYER

It's not that I want to interrupt.

JUDGE

Public prosecutor! Give them to me ….

DEFENCE LAWYER

Mr President, if we read it now ….

PUBLIC PROSECUTOR

No, no, Mr President.

Yes, I met the Ticinese [group] when I was detained in Fossombrone ….

DEFENCE LAWYER
Excuse me Mr President, if we read it now there is no point ....

PUBLIC PROSECUTOR
He was one of those who were going to join me in the escape. He told me of the Argelato episode and said that he had previously met both Negri and Tommei, who had introduced themselves, one as an irregular and the other as a regular member of the BR. They asked him whether they [i.e., the Ticinese group] were prepared to participate in an expropriation, a robbery to finance the press of our organization, the magazine.

Pause.

JUDGE
The passage from Bonavita's statements that interests me is this, and it is specifically about the Argelato robbery. The accusation is that these old leaders sent kids to do robberies. He called them names ....

NEGRI
I am perfectly aware of that.

JUDGE
He talks about painted ....

NEGRI
I have read it. I have read the statements.

JUDGE
Painted old whores.

NEGRI
I wish to make you aware that my opinion of Bonavita is possibly worse than Bonavita's opinion of me. Anyway ....

JUDGE
He said: painted old whores. It's in the text.

JUDGE *A LATERE*
I'd like to know whether he witnessed this scene .... *[whispering]*

Brief pause, footsteps approaching the microphone.

VIRNO
In the Palmi prison out-of-cell time is in the afternoon, from 1 to 3 p.m. ....

JUDGE
And when did this event take place?

If I remember correctly, it was during the early days of January of '79. The proceedings were, so to speak, relatively formal. There were specific charges—let's say, both ideological and specific—against the prisoners from Autonomia who were in that courtyard in Palmi. The charges laid by the public prosecutors (in inverted commas)—including Alfredo Bonavita—in that summary trial were three. And none of them concerned, even in a distant and indirect way, the Argelato affair. The atmosphere was chilling. This is because in the courtyard of a special prison the shifts between charges, judgement, verdict and punishment are very quick. There were three charges. The first regarded the episode that has already been discussed in this court: the split in the [editorial board of] *Controinformazione* magazine.

And what was the charge against you, if I may ask?

The charge was the radical dissension of the [members of the] editorial staff from the emergent Autonomia groups in Milan—as they have testified during the last few days in front of this court—with respect to the elements of the approach of the Brigate Rosse and political line for this magazine. The second charge against these accused prisoners—but I will say more, against the accused prisoner, Toni Negri, who was in a corner of the courtyard (we were all around him)—was the one that was perceived as the most serious and, so to speak, the capital, decisive one. This second charge was that we hadn't been willing to—and this somehow intersects with what Bonavita has declared—in the sense that we had been systematically unwilling, had refused to endorse what in *their* language they called a "*combat line for the spontaneity of the '77 movement.*" For militants with that kind of political formation—Marxist-Leninist, Stalinist—this is a very serious accusation: because it translates into not having adequately *equipped*, which is to say with weapons, spontaneity, the spontaneous movement. Which is in turn translated into an accusation of irresponsibility for having rejected a militaristic horizon, a *combat line*. Their language is more apt to make you understand their thought. There is this strong relation [between language and thought]. And here there was an element of extraordinary violence, of the chips being down, which becomes all the more understandable when we think about the third element of their charges. As the court will remember, December '79 and January '80 was a chilling period in Italy, which in the communiqués of terrorist organizations, in which a man who had been killed was a defeated man, was presented as "Logic of Annihilation." That was when they targeted uniformed policemen because they were policemen. This was in December–January: there was a series of killings in Rome and Milan. And this was the generalization of the armed struggle line. On this issue in Palmi we were a minority—but you still fight your battles even when you are a minority: even when the conditions to express a minority line aren't the most comfortable you still fight your battle—and we expressed all our contempt, as communists, our aversion, our enmity towards something like this. And this retrospectively radicalized all the charges going back ten years. This hallucinating scene lasted two hours. This is a scene that nobody who hasn't been in a special prison can understand and that in any case everybody who was there still remembers. This is not the only instance. This is not the only one: this isn't the first time that in the arguments of the Brigate Rosse we find suggestions that we then find ourselves facing as criminal charges: that is, *irresponsibility*, the same irresponsibility that they expressed as "you refused to take the '77 movement to the armed struggle." It is the same thing.

PUBLIC PROSECUTOR
Excuse me, Mr President. I'd like to know who are these "public prosecutors" in inverted commas, these accusers. Alfredo Bonavita?

VIRNO
Alfredo Bonavita was also there.

PUBLIC PROSECUTOR
And the others?

VIRNO
Then there were some of the historical leaders of the Red Brigades.

PUBLIC PROSECUTOR
All right, say it to the court. Because if we want to be rigorous, the public prosecutor has only introduced one set of minutes ....

VIRNO
Here, there is a problem .... I obviously have no feelings, except hard feelings or feelings of enmity, towards these people, but there is a problem: that these people, who as far as I am concerned could even be the Nazis of Ordine Nuovo, today are in the special prisons under Article 90. And with respect to people who are in special prisons under Article 90 I say nothing.

PUBLIC PROSECUTOR
There goes caution! There goes rigour! So how can the public prosecutor accept the truthfulness of your statements? Only from the statements themselves?

ATTORNEY GENERAL
And then you want the truth! Then they want the truth! Then they want the truth!

PUBLIC PROSECUTOR

Here you invoke rigour, you invoke caution, and then you don't put us is the position to do our job?

VIRNO

This isn't a decisive element.

PUBLIC PROSECUTOR

And this is the situation in which we find ourselves!

JUDGE

This is a statement made by the accused, Mr Virno.

PUBLIC PROSECUTOR

Then do not call for caution and rigour from the public prosecutor.

JUDGE

[low tone, away from the microphone] Oh Good Lord! *[resumes, speaking loudly into the microphone]* Let's move forward, if people must be heard on this issue, then we will hear them. We will hear Bonavita, other people, the people's jury, the presidents of these bodies .... Let's adjourn the hearing to 3.30 this afternoon.

Long pause, noises in the courtroom.

JUDGE

Go ahead, Funaro asked to speak. You're welcome to.

JUDGE

Please bring him a microphone.

FUNARO

A brief announcement, Mr President. On Friday morning, four of our comrades from the Area Omogenea [Homogenous Area] of Rebibbia: Lanfranco Caminiti, Andrea Leoni, Totò Campisi and Paolo Lapponi, who were given extremely harsh prison sentences during the trial of the Unità Combattenti Comuniste [Communist Combat Units], have started a hunger strike. We express our full solidarity with these comrades. We ask everyone who is in favour of bringing the emergency to a close, today, everyone who wants to see the end of an absurd and useless state of war, everyone who appreciates the moral and political value of the choice of political dissociation; we ask them all to join us in this protest. Thank you.

JUDGE

Negri then.

Long pause, noises in the courtroom, random voices away from the microphone, coughs.

JUDGE

Your position as an MP, or future member of parliament, having not been ratified by the election office yet, unless the court examines the other issue, if the court itself must establish it according to Article 68 of the constitution, or whether it is Parliament or not, at the moment, your position is, let's say, an unofficial one. Therefore, we obviously need to carry on our own interrogation.

NEGRI

In this case, I would like to exercise the right to silence. For reasons that seem clear to me. I would therefore be extremely grateful to the court if they accepted my request.

JUDGE

It is your right. This is your right.

NEGRI

Thank you.

JUDGE

Let's proceed with the interrogation of the next defendant: Pozzi.

PUBLIC PROSECUTOR

Mr President, the public prosecutor acknowledges the defendant's exercise of his right to not answer questions from the public prosecutor, the plaintiffs and the defence lawyer. Consistent with the usual custom, at the end of every interrogation of a defendant, the public prosecutor must put forward requests for the preliminary inquiry. He must, first of all, ask to hear from, either as a witness or as a defendant in a connected trial, Marocco Antonio, to have him come to report on the following circumstances before the court: that in the Palmi prison there was a unitary structure named Comitato Unitario di Campo [Unitary Field Committee], to which Curcio, Franceschini, as well as Vesce and Negri, belonged. That one of the issues dealt with by this committee was how to manage the current trials against the militants of the Brigate Rosse and Autonomia. That Curcio and Franceschini insisted on the thesis of the guerrilla trial, whilst Negri defended the thesis of a self-defensive trial that would simultaneously be an attack on institutions, proposing the use of the debate with a twofold objective: on the one hand, as a tool for stating one's own innocence, and on the other hand, with the unwitting support of the press, radio and television, as a moment of restatement of the validity of the revolutionary positions of Autonomia. That, always on this issue, there was a furious row between Franceschini and Negri, during which Negri is supposed to have said to Franceschini: "You'll end up like Baader, if you fail to manage the spaces the system is offering you." *[whispers in the courtroom]* To which Franceschini replied: "With this pretext of managing spaces, you will end up looking wicked." I request to hear Savasta Antonio, who will be able to report, as head of that branch of the Brigate Rosse, on his contacts in Veneto with exponents from the Autonomia of that region. He can also report what Valerio Morucci proposed to the Brigate Rosse, during a meeting of the leadership of the Roman branch.

Voices of protest are raised in the courtroom, the judge requests order, the public prosecutor is interrupted by voices and screams in the courtroom.

JUDGE

[hitting the desk with the gavel] Silence.

VESCE

[away from the microphone, few words can be heard] This isn't a courtroom .... This is an insult to justice, Mr Public Prosecutor, what you are saying now ....

JUDGE

OK.

PUBLIC PROSECUTOR

Defendant Vesce, I am acting in conformity with all previous hearings. I am only introducing to the court testimonies *[raising his voice to cover Vesce's]* that have reported on those events. Whether those events occurred or not will be clarified to the court later.

VESCE

[shouting from the cage, away from the microphone] You are insulting justice with Marocco's statement, because in Palmi Calabro, you know, I fought against terrorism and put my life in danger, do you get this? Because you locked us up all together, after the Brigate Rosse had threatened us. *[constant noises of camera flashes]* And today I find myself in this courtroom, accused of having been part of a field committee that had to decide on the killing of people. Do you understand what I'm saying? This is an insult to justice!

PUBLIC PROSECUTOR

Exactly ....

JUDGE

Vesce .... Please with that video camera, move away from it for a minute!

PUBLIC PROSECUTOR

[with rising agitation, raising his voice, then shouting to cover Vesce's response] Vesce here we have statements that we must take into account, we cannot not take them into account! We want to know when these people will come before the criminal court, whether they will confirm them or not! *[Vesce continues to shout from the cage, inaudible because of the public prosecutor's voice]* We cannot keep these declarations in the drawer! We have the duty to tell the court and you too ...

JUDGE

[overlaps and speaks to a third party] Miss, note that the defendants have left.

PUBLIC PROSECUTOR

... there are people who say these things. We have the duty to say these things. We cannot keep them hidden from you, the court, but especially from you, who have the right to defend yourselves from these statements. *[shouts resound in the courtroom]* This is the only spirit that animates the public prosecutor, to put before you, who have always demanded to know, "what the charges are, and their sources." And the public prosecutor rightly indicates them. And he also identifies all the events which you need to defend yourselves on.

Empty tape.

Microphone noises.

JUDGE

This court notes:

> *[reads]* three fundamental issues need to be taken into account. First: the close interdependence of the positions of all the defendants both in terms of the hypotheses of the accusations relative to their crimes of association, and in terms of the projection through individual behaviours of the single common aim assumed in the contestations. This is of particular relevance when it comes to the defendant Antonio Negri who ascribes a determining role to the formulation of the charges. Second: today's statement of the defendant Antonio Negri that he wished to exercise the right to silence for the rest of the hearing, whilst awaiting the results of the elections and potential concession of the authorization to move forward. Third: the imminence of the publication of the results from the official election offices. Linking these elements and, above all, due to the binding need to proceed in a single treatment of the cause, comes the need to postpone the debate until after the election results have become known and the procedure for the authorization thereof been granted. For these reasons, I postpone this hearing to the 26 September 1983, 9.30 a.m. Hearing suspended.

Long silence.

Noises, voices.

USHER

The court.

Brief pause, sound of gate opening.

JUDGE

[clears throat] The court has produced an arrest warrant for the defendant Negri and this morning we have acquired the results of preliminary investigations: the so-called suitcases of minutes of the researches of the defendant himself.

PUBLIC PROSECUTOR

President, I can only ask that we proceed in Negri's absence, whilst waiting for the minutes.

JUDGE

The court, upon request of the public prosecutor, orders to proceed in the absence of defendant Negri. Come Vesce.

VESCE

Mr President, today we cannot evade our obligation to express a point of view on the events of the last few months.

JUDGE

Excuse me, wait a minute, it's better if you come here so we can all hear you.

Long pause, microphone noises, room noises, voices, coughing.

VESCE

I was saying, well, that we cannot evade the obligation, and do not shy away from it, to express our point of view on what's happened in the past three months. In jail, we have become aware, being careful observers of what happens outside, of the attention that public opinion is paying to these events, and we realize the significance of this attention. Today, what is probably asked of us is an assessment of what's happened, one that would probably satisfy the feelings of vengeance and aggression that we have seen ... that we were able to read in the newspapers' chronicles of these days. No. We are calm and resilient in our continued and tenacious defence of our political identities and our individual histories. We have followed the parliamentary debate and naturally and simultaneously, whilst following the debate, we had to register those forms of irreducibility ... the irreducibility of some positions that for years we have been fighting in prison, is not only a legacy or culture of prisoners, we could see that this culture of irreducibility also exists in parliament, this inability to look forward, to free oneself of the burden, of the conditions and feelings of revenge. Everyone who warmly supported Negri first but then allowed for his re-arrest to be voted for, that extremely strange alignment that took shape in parliament ....

JUDGE
[interrupts Vesce and closes his microphone] I am not accustomed to .... Let me speak, I am not accustomed to silencing a defendant, but let us keep outside of this trial and away from our presence all comments on the political powers, or comments on what has happened elsewhere. Let us please deal with this trial.

DEFENCE LAWYER
[away from the microphone] Could I intervene, on this question of the request for house arrest?

JUDGE
We will discuss it as soon as the public prosecutor has seen it. Defendant Pozzi, please.

Long pause, voices, microphone noises.

JUDGE
Pozzi, you have recurring charges against you, most recently in the remand to court. The first question is obviously aimed at whether you refer to these statements or not.

POZZI
Yes, I refer to these statements and naturally I intend, if you allow me, before starting this interrogation, to clarify what my position is at the moment, after years, also considering, Mr President, that it is very difficult to answer during a hearing, because you never, in my opinion, know what you are being charged with. Mainly, my first preoccupation, now as throughout the course of my interrogation, is that of not allowing for charges to fall on other people. If that was to happen, and it is always possible, especially if we think of the climate to which I was subjected in the first and second interrogation, Mr President, clearly one could not even dream of naming a person who had collaborated on *Rosso* in any

way. However, if you allow me, I would like to start with a brief overview of my political history.

It isn't easy to give a picture of one's life, and is even harder, I believe, in front of a criminal court. A man's personal convictions and ideals are not separate from his social life, and are almost always the same as the values of his generation. Belonging to a given generation means being influenced by its values and sharing in some or all of its mistakes. Even today, my second thoughts are heavily influenced by the state of captivity in which I have been living for almost four years now. I have been a subversive; there is no question about that. I started out in 1966, I was 16. I have been a revolutionary. Nowadays that word may prompt a smile, but back then, in '68 and in the seventies, it was no laughing matter. Every generation has a shared vision. For our parents it was the Resistance, at least for many of them. For us it was Che Guevara, the legendary Giap, the revolutions in the Third World, the demonstrations in the streets. But our vision was richer than our parents'; it was an imaginary of revolt at all levels. We wanted a total revolution, different from the traditional communist kind. A social revolution that would change all relationships between people, not just the ones involved in production. Women were asking us their own questions, saying there could be no communist revolution without women's liberation, that nothing had a point unless the relationship between us and them changed. Children were asking to be loved whilst being allowed to live free of love's oppression. We hoped and tried to live out this uncertain, improbable revolution. My generation has been a subversive one. I don't hide it: I made my own contribution, perhaps not a small one, to that subversion of society. Where? In the field where I worked best, the field of culture, and more specifically, the sector of alternative media, or "antagonistic" communication as it was called back then. Over the course of the seventies, I also worked as a militant in the movement and in fully-fledged political groups. I was active in Lotta Continua. I was an organized autonomist in the political experience of *Rosso*, as well as an autonomist in other informal movements, or what used to be called a "loose autonomist" [It: *autonomo sciolto*]. The police were always aware of these activities of mine. I was investigated on multiple occasions by the judiciary, and the antiterrorism squad of Lombardy had me under daily surveillance for almost two years, as you can see from the records. My activities were thus anything but clandestine. I was a subversive, and all these papers were subversive. I was inside the subversive culture of the seventies, but I was always opposed to political assassination. I took part in illegal demonstrations with thousands of people, but like thousands of people, I never killed anybody. Trying at all costs to construct a political continuity between Molotov cocktails and assassinations, talking indiscriminately about all violence having a common root, about the corrupting influence of bad teachers, is something I find wrongheaded and egregious. My generation has been defeated. Part of it, the part that is still free, is either living in exile, and unfortunately from there has contributed nothing to the political debate, or else has remained in Italy, mostly giving up politics. Some, unfortunately quite a few, have tried to offload the burden of their defeat, sending hundreds of people to jail. A third group, my own, ended up in prison. And in prison we have even risked our lives sometimes to defend life. Like others at Palmi, in Fossombrone too, when the Brigate Rosse held a referendum on whether to kill Judge D'Urso and later, Patrizio Peci's brother, a few of us said no, and repeatedly emphasized that we were opposed to death under all circumstances. Choices such as these, of culture and of life, led to the creation of the Aree Omogenee. I am a founder of the Area Omogenea at Rebibbia and am proud of that. I would like to say one last thing: in Italy violence is often ascribed to the culture of Autonomia or that of the extra parliamentary left. But the culture of subversion in Italy and the world was something more, and much broader.

From the US universities, to the French and German 1968, to the workers and proletarian struggles of the 1970s, to the most varied forms of artistic expression: film, music, theatre, people who were absolutely extraneous to Autonomia and yet as subversive if not more. And to conclude, I would say that there is a great figure haunting the collective imagination of my generation, the collective unconscious of us thirty year olds. It is Colonel Aureliano Buendía, that character from the novel *One Hundred Years of Solitude* who promoted thirty-two insurrections, and lost each one of them. He ended up a defeated man, shut up in a house, crafting little golden fish. I would hope—we would hope—that this Court will not force us to craft little golden fish shut up in a cell, for our entire life, and will give us another chance at life on earth.

JUDGE

Let's adjourn in ten minutes, then I will ask you some questions.

Long break, noises, coughs away from the microphone, camera flashes.

JUDGE

So, Pozzi. *[brief pause]* This court deals not with solitudes. This court deals with concrete events that are integrated, in the hypothesis of the prosecution, with elements of crime. You know that in the assumptions of the investigating judge it is neither simply a matter of your collaboration with the paper *Rosso*, nor of what you wrote on that paper, but rather, beyond the writings, it is a matter of the material comportments you had. You, as I've just told you, are alleged to have taken part, according to this person, in the "subjective secretariat" of *Rosso*. You know, from the debate, here, in the interrogations of other people, that moments of contestation, in one form or another, coagulate around this definition of subjective secretariat. Let us try to clarify this point: that of your belonging to the subjective secretariat and, prior to that, the presence, existence, or whatever you wish to call it, of this subjective secretariat in and of itself.

POZZI

The subjective secretariat is a mere invention, of Barbone and some Milanese public prosecutor. This must be said straightaway. There never was a subjective secretariat that had any form of command within the area of *Rosso*. The area of *Rosso* as such, and also the area of Autonomia Operaia in Milan, was extremely varied and complex, composed of completely different subjects. I wanted to speak about this another time but I'll do it now. There are historical phenomena that you must really take into account. For instance: half of this area of Autonomia was made up of women. Women did not obey men. In a feminist discourse it was impossible to rule women through a subjective secretariat. Commanding was impossible! It was impossible because the modulation of the movement was such that it was impossible ... a structure such as the one Barbone has in mind, of a subjective secretariat, is the strategic leadership of the Brigate Rosse.

JUDGE

Is it necessary to command women?

POZZI

Rosso, no ... given that the area ... I gave you a small example ....

JUDGE

I didn't understand. No, excuse me, can you let me speak?

POZZI

It's absurd, even from the point of view of .... I mean ....

JUDGE

I don't understand, do women have to be ruled?

POZZI

Yes, they have to. If the subjective secretariat had command over anything, it would have had to command half the area of Autonomia made up of women! I am telling you that this is historically absurd because it was impossible to command anything in Milan, including women. It was impossible to rule in Milan. There were different centres of political energies. I don't know how else to define them. They were: the secretariat of the workers political collectives, who met in via Sebastiano del Piombo 11. And Barbone forgot this because it is not convenient to him to remember, here is the dualism of the centres, and he only thinks about the subjective secretariat. There was the coordination of school students, the coordination of the neighbourhood collectives, there was the editorial group of *Rosso*. It was structurally impossible to manage to ....

JUDGE
[interrupting Pozzi] What centre of energy was this editorial group of *Rosso*?

POZZI
Well, I could define it as a political and cultural ambit, also because I cannot find ... then it is up to you to decide whether it is an armed band or a subversive association.

JUDGE
Barbone speaks of subjective secretariat in a different way; you know this better than me. You say that this is an invention of his.

POZZI
It's an invention.

JUDGE
OK, we will hear Barbone.

POZZI
I wanted to say something else: *Rosso* and the area of Autonomia as a whole, as a philosophical dynamic—because it is the only way to name this new way of doing politics—never had centres of unified command as an internal structure.

JUDGE
To sum up what you've said, Pozzi. You said that *Rosso* did not have a subjective secretariat; you claim that it did not place into being comportments that can be subsumed under what we call criminal doings, that is, comportments that could ....

POZZI
It depends; it depends on how you interpret it .... That is to say: I took part in illegal protests that were not authorized by the police. That was normal at the time. So I am not saying ....

JUDGE
It was normal for you.

POZZI

It was normal for a set of people, and there were many of them, because otherwise it would be impossible to understand this enormous phenomenon in Italy that displayed such comportments. Mr President, I said that I am speaking of then and now. I cannot deny that at the time it was not such an incredible thing to have three or four guys organize in twenty, thirty or forty to go to a supermarket and do some so-called *proletarian shopping*, it wasn't something one needed a subjective secretariat to decide, Mr President. It was a normal comportment. I realize that it is criminal, as was gate-crashing into concerts, Mr President. *Rosso* did not organize the gate-crashing into concerts of the great rock and pop artists. They came to Italy, demanded five thousand lire for the ticket, the concert is enjoyed and the ticket not paid. I didn't tell anyone to do this. There were hundreds of people who did it. I contributed, as I said, perhaps not in a modest way, to this subversive culture in this country. I am asking whether it is possible that, before sentencing the seventies, this court might care to recognize that there wasn't only *Rosso* in Italy. Perhaps it knows that. There are a considerable number of cultural productions, from '68 until now, that made a full apology for violence and subversion. From Godard's films, *La Chinoise, Loin du Vietnam,* Bellocchio's film *La Cina è vicina* and so on and so forth. I saw my first Molotov in an Attilio Bertolucci film, if I'm not wrong, entitled *Prima della rivoluzione*.

JUDGE

And then did you use these Molotov bottles?

POZZI

But ... Mr President, everyone used them because it was a question ....

JUDGE

No, but did you use them?

POZZI

It was a question of self-defence.

JUDGE

But no, I asked you a question ....

POZZI

I answer yes.

JUDGE

You say yes.

POZZI

A question of self-defence because they practically shot on you. In Milan there was a death every three or four months. At this point it was an automatic mechanism of defence. After this, I am not saying that it was fine. But it is a social phenomenon that must be comprehended as such, and as such must be understood—hence the discourse of *disassociation* at Rebibbia.

JUDGE *A LATERE*

President, on this statement I wanted to ask for a clarification. *[clears throat]* Let me read from the text, because I wrote down what you said:

> *[reads]* There was militarist pulsation within the area of *Rosso*, this is clear ....

POZZI

[interrupts] And the area of Autonomia, in its broadest sense.

JUDGE *A LATERE*

And the area of Autonomia ... I am asking, given that we judge defendants with a name and surname who took part in that editorial group of said area, which of the current defendants were part of the editorial of *Rosso* at the time, and which of our defendants participated in meetings where the militarist question was debated within Rosso.

POZZI

You want names from me? Well, I've said it from the start that I do not name people. So this is quite impossible.

JUDGE *A LATERE*

We judge defendants who have names and surnames.

POZZI

Who was in the editorial of *Rosso* out of these ones here in the cage? Toni is no longer here, he was in the editorial of *Rosso*. Tommei, for some periods, when he wasn't in prison, has been in the editorial of *Rosso*. Funaro never was in the editorial of *Rosso*, obviously he came by because the editorial meetings were open and held in via Disciplini. Of the others in the cage absolutely nobody has nothing to do with *Rosso*, the paper, as far as I know.

ATTORNEY GENERAL

I will carry on, can you give me the ....

JUDGE

The word to the attorney general.

Microphone noise.

ATTORNEY GENERAL

Mr President, "Struttura di Rosso—Brigate Comuniste" [Structure of *Rosso*—Communist Brigades]:

[reads] The structure of *Rosso* was the following. There were four organisms: the paper's editorial board, the local secretariat, the workers' secretariat and the prisons commission. These four organisms formed a so-called subjective secretariat from which arose a small executive.

Barbone provides a detailed description of all these bodies and, on the subjective secretariat, he claims:

[reads] These four organs plus the logistical one were politically and operatively directed by the subjective secretariat, so called because it was made up of leaders who were self-designated with no representative criteria. Among them were Negri, Tommei, Funaro, Mancini, Pozzi, Mainardi, Pancino, Fabrizio Ventura, Laura Motta and Alunni. From this subjective secretariat emerged a smaller executive, which was not a more important organism as such, but rather a select committee with the aim of planning single initiatives and confronting any need of the organization in the sense of its day-to-day running, including the financial side. Part of it were, in a sort of rota, Pancino, Alunni, Tommei, Mancini. Having the faculty of selecting people for different activities, they also had the power to give a stamp or another to the general politico-organizational decisions of the secretariat. This organizational structure stays stable until the formal constitution of the Brigate Comuniste, which can be dated to the assault on the Bergamo prison of 1977, the exact temporal collocation that now escapes me. After the formal constitution of the Brigate Comuniste, there were changes in this framework, which I will punctually identify for you. I would also like to add that what I described is the structure of *Rosso* in Milan. This Milanese structure was certainly also responsible for the geographical areas of the province of Varese and Bologna. I knew of the existence of another *Rosso* structure in the Veneto-Padua region, whose contacts with the Milanese one were, to my knowledge, sporadic. I can therefore say nothing of the activities of people unknown to me.

In the hearing before the Milan criminal court, Barbone added:

Therefore, at least in theory, everyone participated in the organization and had to share the armed actions and their inherent dangers. The only exception was made for Toni Negri who, because of, say, his well-known personality, or his role as utmost theoretician inside the organization, excluded himself from the composition of the operative nuclei without this preventing him from participating in moments of decision, organization and structuring of the operative nuclei themselves, precisely as executive of the organization. And this was the only exception, that of Toni Negri, where a militant of *Rosso* did not participate, or did not put himself forward, or was not deemed available, for the armed activities of the organization.

All these statements have been confirmed by those of Pasini-Gatti, Ricciardi, Ferrandi and Marocco. I would like to know what the defendant has to say on these points.

Long pause, rustling of paper.

ATTORNEY GENERAL

[without microphone] During the course of the release of the arrest warrants. *[microphone turned on]* Pardon ....

JUDGE

Sorry for interrupting.

ATTORNEY GENERAL

Sorry.

JUDGE

Here, unless I tell you not to respond, answer directly.

ATTORNEY GENERAL

In the course of the written declarations, I heard that the Brigate Rosse, in the prison of Fossombrone, asked you and ...

POZZI

[overlapping] Not me.

ATTORNEY GENERAL

... asked your other comrades to vote on the killing of Judge D'Urso. Can you tell me how and why, in your view, it happened? I mean, how come the Brigate Rosse asked you and the others to even take part in this decision?

POZZI

Well, as usual we haven't understood one another. I didn't say that the Brigate Rosse only asked me what ....

JUDGE

You said that they held a referendum.

POZZI

They held a referendum in the prison of Fossombrone as they held one in all the prisons of Italy as you know well because it was the Brigate Rosse who told you these things. Back then it was common practice for the Brigate Rosse to ask what the people in prison thought about the vicissitudes, the actions they partook in. In Fossombrone, there was a sort of referendum. I, with a few others, who are now all part of the Area Omogenea, said no. I said that it didn't make sense; that I was against murder at all times and under all circumstances. At this point I can only let you imagine the atmosphere: it was terrible. Because someone who spoke like that, for them, was an enemy, a traitor. We went on like this for a year. I took my walks with four other people in the concrete box of the prison, which is a sort of rectangle, like a shoe box, 30 x 15 m of reinforced concrete, with really high walls. Nobody spoke to me anymore. No one spoke to me because I was an enemy of the people. I talked to very few friends, four or five, with whom I finally managed to leave the special prisons and come to Rome to found, with others, the Area Omogenea of Rebibbia.

JUDGE

Anything else ...? Public prosecutor?

PUBLIC PROSECUTOR

President, I only have one question because obviously confronted with this position of the defendants I can only wait for the arrival of the *pentiti* and for them to report what they said in the preliminary investigation, so that we can finally have this confrontation. I only wanted to read one page from the remand to court, and link back to what the defendant has already stated during the interrogation. In this passage of the remand to court, I read:

> The organization was able to supply the participants of the demonstrations with firearms, not only with hundreds of Molotovs; and with its militants it piloted the marches along the agreed route, identifying the objectives to strike against according to a predetermined political line.

This is what Barbone said, then we will see the confrontation:

> [he resumes his reading] The motive of the demonstrations— claimed Morandini—was always secondary because it was about finding any pretext, or creating it, to take to the streets with weapons. There are precise directives imparted by the top of *Rosso* and other armed organizations. The weapons, though centralized by *Rosso*, were entrusted to the responsibility of each collective, to the people who were linked to *Rosso* and participated in the coordinating meetings, Morandini continues. The modes of execution of the marches, adds Pasini-Gatti, including

the internal distribution of weapons, were planned in detail at the table of the leaders of *Rosso*, amongst whom was Pozzi, who practically led the marches.

Having read this passage, or reminded you of this passage, Pozzi, I wanted to know how many demonstrations you took part in and what role you had in them, having admitted that it was customary at the time to make and throw Molotovs. Or to use Molotov bottles to determined ends.

Let's talk about weapons, Mr President, because I wanted to see, given that the preliminary investigation speaks of weapons, which is why *Rosso* was charged with the organization of an armed band, not only for being a paper, but also because of the organization that revolved around *Rosso*, well, I wanted to know whether beyond the Molotov bottles that were commonly used in that period, weapons were also used during marches. Who made these weapons available to the protesters? You know that we have an infinite collection of testimonies where weapons are used and centralized by *Rosso*. Didn't you ever see these weapons?

PUBLIC PROSECUTOR

One second, prosecutor, I am doing the contesting, don't intervene here ....

POZZI

Well, there's no question that there were people, groups of people, who went around armed at demonstrations. I'm not one to deny this. As for me, I had very little to do with these groups, I had nothing to do with them, I knew some of them but in no way were they centralized. Second point: this idea that the area of Autonomia in Milan coincided with *Rosso* must be completely debunked. Because it's not true. There is another remand in court, of Dr Piaciotti, that explains the other half of Milan. Or the other three quarters of Milan, of the area of Autonomia, which are Senza Tregua, Prima Linea and so on and so forth. Therefore every time one talks about the square in Milan, one needs to realize that it's useless to still talk about this single centre that unified all the demonstrations. It's absolutely false. There were lots of diverse political and neighbourhood groups.

PUBLIC PROSECUTOR

Here we are talking about arms centralized in the paper *Rosso*.

POZZI

It's not true!

PUBLIC PROSECUTOR

I wanted to know from you as the head of the editorial board, as the leader of *Rosso*, have you ever sensed this arms depot that was in *Rosso*?

POZZI

That I was the leader of *Rosso* is Barbone's statement. It's not as if only because Barbone says so I am the leader of *Rosso*, good God! Who is this person, God Almighty? Anything he says, he's right? Moreover, it seems to me that in Milan there were some little problems on how the murder of Tobagi went, weren't there?

PUBLIC PROSECUTOR

Look, it's Morandini, not Barbone, who speaks of arms depots.

POZZI

Leave Morandini aside, I never saw Morandini so I can't even tell what kind of person he is.

PUBLIC PROSECUTOR

Anyway, leader or not, these weapons, were they there or not? Did you ever sense that ....

POZZI

I ....

PUBLIC PROSECUTOR

About this arms depot?

POZZI

All I read on the official documents is that they found the weapons on the 28 March. I don't know. Ask Barbone about this .... Don't ask me! It's not true .... I didn't have weapons! What do I have to tell you? I can't tell you something I don't know ....

JUDGE

OK, thank you. Does the defence lawyer have any questions for the defendant?

JUDGE

None. Please sit down. You can go. Erm. Strano, Tommei ....

PUBLIC PROSECUTOR

Tommei, let's listen to Tommei.

JUDGE

Then let's have Tommei ....

JUDGE

Some say *[clears throat]* about your activity, that in that demonstration in Milan, no? You are said to have been a protagonist of the disorders. You were at the head of this march, according to some rumours in the trial.

102

TOMMEI

It's true.

JUDGE

What does it mean, and what happened? What did you do? If you could be more specific on this issue.

TOMMEI

I'd like to clarify for a moment.

JUDGE

Clarify ....

TOMMEI

No, no, I would like to clarify the context of the situation. *[coughs]* So, as far as I'm concerned, given that we keep talking about these armed demonstrations and the like, I would like to clarify the general situation. First of all, as far as I know in Milan there were no more than three armed demonstrations, as far as I know. One where I am charged, in a trial in Milan too, with breaking into Confapi [a small businesses association] and participation in it. The second, this one you are charging me with now, concerns this armed protest at Assolombarda [an Italian Entrepreneurial Association]. And a third one, the one where Custrà got killed. Well, on 11 March, irrespective of what the rumours from the *pentiti* are .... *[interrupts and starts again]* On 11 March almost all the comrades of the area of *Rosso*, as of the whole of the Autonomia of Milan and other Italian cities, came to Rome for the national demonstration that is also in the official documents here. *[coughs]* Basically I find myself in the situation, which I chose, to go to the square for this march to see what could happen, also because the environment and political situation at the time in the area of Autonomia—which was not that of *Rosso*—because the area of Autonomia in Milan as I tried to explain yesterday was very varied and large, and even the area of *Rosso* was not a party-like area where command could find any expression. *[coughs]* I found myself in this demonstration and in this demonstration I managed to mediate a situation that in my opinion could become desperate. That is, in via Mulino delle Armi I found myself having to mediate a situation where a part of the participants at the march thought they had to engage in an assault of the Prefecture, something that in my view could have ended up in a full-on bloodbath. I personally opposed this initiative for two reasons: first, by saying that it was a mad idea at the level of the consequences it might have caused. Second, on the basis, and this is probably a secondary issue, that we were against an attack on the State, and thus opposed to this where the Prefecture was a symbol. At this point I said: "Let's go and protest by Assolombarda, let's go and demonstrate there." This decision of mine was accepted by the majority of other people who convinced those who wanted to attack the Prefecture too. Then, by Assolombarda, people, some people, among whom, what a coincidence, all of the *pentiti,* took out the weapons they kept in their pockets and shot at the windows of Assolombarda.

JUDGE A LATERE

President, a specification.

JUDGE

Yes, yes, please.

JUDGE A LATERE

But, did you enter the premises of Assolombarda?

TOMMEI

What?

JUDGE A LATERE

Did you enter the premises of Assolombarda?

TOMMEI

There was no breaking into the premises of Assolombarda. Absolutely none.

[SOMEONE AWAY FROM THE MICROPHONE]

In '76?

UNKNOWN

'76.

UNKNOWN

'76.

Long pause, room noises, background voices, papers shuffled, coughs.

JUDGE

Ferrandi, please sit down.

Pause, ambient noise.

JUDGE

So, in what we may call a historical excursus—I mean: historical with reference to your own history—we have Assolombarda [a 1977 demonstration against the Lombard Industrial Association], then we have the Confapi episode, and finally the Custrà episode.

FERRANDI

[in agreement] Hmm.

JUDGE

You have described this Custrà episode in front of the Milan Criminal Court.

FERRANDI

Well, what happens there is that *[clears throat]* ... there are some incidents. We must reconstruct the episode—otherwise we do not understand. *[sniffles]*

JUDGE

Reconstruct it as you prefer.

FERRANDI

There are incidents. This man who is a police agent dies. Pictures are taken and some people from Porta Romana are identified in these pictures. Well, there is a first batch of pictures where these boys from Cattaneo [a Milanese high school] who were connected to Barbone and who had shot are photographed. They were recognized at school, so in the following days they were arrested. In addition, a rumour had started to spread in Milan that the collectives in Porta Romana had become .... *[interrupts himself and restarts]* I mean, we were attributed the responsibility for anything that happened in Milan. That's because we had become famous as a result of some unfortunate displays, such as when I took out a rifle at Assolombarda, etc. *[sniffles]* So when the events of via De Amicis take place—in which, yes, some of us were personally involved, but together with many other groups—immediately the rumour that started to circulate in Milan ... aside from the risk of identifying the two, that is Svampa and Pasini-Gatti, who had been fully photographed, the collectives from Porta Romana ... we were completely wrong-footed by this episode. And here there is something that I have been meaning to say for a long time. In short, armed struggle ... there are aspects that in my opinion have never been understood by my ex-comrades, who still don't understand them. In short, armed struggle has its own internal dynamics, which must be respected. Once you trigger it, then it becomes something that works on its own, you cannot pilot it. You are no longer able to use political devices to bring it back to different patterns. This episode—the episode in via De Amicis—is typical of this approach: we didn't bring weapons to do ... to kill people. We brought them for specific purposes, to defend ourselves or for break-ins, for certain actions. But what happens? In this case it happens that a plan was circulated, which was to go in front of San Vittore [a prison in Milan] to cause trouble with the police, who then would have certainly charged into us. Then from San Vittore we were supposed to retreat to Porta Genova, where we would have raided the offices of Democrazia Cristiana or things like that. The plan went wrong because ....

JUDGE

But ... its function was to ... it had been organized to go to San Vittore ....

FERRANDI

Yes.

JUDGE

To provoke clashes with the police ....

FERRANDI

Well, it's not that we wanted to provoke clashes with the police, but we took it for granted that as soon as we arrived at San Vittore the police would have charged into us: we took it for granted ....

JUDGE

And what were you supposed to do when this happened?

FERRANDI

Retreat to Porta Genova, which is the neighbourhood adjacent to San Vittore.

JUDGE

[questioning Ferrandi] And what were the weapons for?

FERRANDI

We systematically carried weapons, basically to defend ourselves. In my own case, in those days I was armed for another reason ....

JUDGE

[interrupting Ferrandi] But what were you supposed to do at San Vittore?

FERRANDI

Nothing. This was the issue: the day before there had been the killing of this girl in Rome. So we called for a march of the whole revolutionary left. But at the same time in the days before the march there had been a small blitz, one of the first ones against Autonomia, *[sniffles]* and there had been several arrests. So it was a matter of somehow asserting our own discourse against repression by separating from the main march of the revolutionary left and doing our own march to San Vittore. It had been planned that afterwards, "if there is an incident as soon as we arrive at San Vittore they [the police] will certainly charge us" ... because the route had been agreed to by the extra parliamentary left groups with the police and there was absolutely no authorization for this kind of deviation. So at that point there were going to be incidents and we would have retreated to Porta Genova, where there were supposed to be people who said "let's do the offices of Democrazia Cristiana." There were even those who thought that we could have robbed a small armoury. They said: let's make this kind of statement. But what happens? That the march arrives in front of San Vittore and there is this kind of confrontation, but there is no charge. We do not feel like provoking the police. The same for the police: probably because there were just a few of them and they had not expected this to happen. We stand opposed to each other for some minutes. There is tension, a lot of tension. And then what happens? There is an unexpected situation. The march restarts in order to go and join the gathering in Piazza Duomo, from where it had started, and a line of police cars with their sirens blaring arrives—probably late for meeting us at San Vittore. They probably didn't even know that they were going to come across this march, which had been improvised then and there, and so nobody could make any prediction. This line of police cars with their sirens blaring arrives from via De Amicis right when the march, after leaving San Vittore, is crossing a side street. By now we were—I am not sure—about five hundred metres from San Vittore. The line of police cars with the sirens blaring arrives, all of a sudden, and what happens is that those who are in that particular spot see the line of police cars coming with their sirens on, and this triggers the normal reaction: that is, we make a barricade, we try to protect the march from this line of police cars that were coming with their sirens blaring. In fact, the line of police cars ... the usual clashes begin: absolutely normal clashes, the traditional clashes that took place in the streets in those days ... we stop the tram, we move some cars, we try to build some barricades, the police start shooting tear-gas canisters, we start launching Molotov cocktails. At this point some people—OK, including some of our people, and others who were there—start shooting on their own initiative. But there is no premeditation and even those who start shooting do it on their own initiative, without us from Porta Romana ever having decided, including at that very moment, to open fire on the police. This happens: there are people who open fire because the level of circulation of weapons had by then reached such a level that nobody could control it any longer. For instance, these high school students from Cattaneo were students, they were sixteen- or seventeen-year-old boys ... none of us had given them weapons. They wore their own weapons. One of them had stolen the weapons from his father, who had been a partisan, and had brought with him a P-38. Another one had a Beretta pistol: I don't know who had given it to him. And so they start shooting. *[sniffles]*

And we have this mess. Incidentally, some of us didn't even realize what had happened at that moment. There was a lot of confusion: smoke from the teargas canisters ... shootings ... the police agent falls and we don't know about it ... the march restarts, regroups and arrives in Piazza Duomo, where there was the rest of the gathering for the march. In the evening we switch on the radio: "police agent dead." Damn. At that point starts, starts .... *[interrupts himself and restarts speaking]* In addition there is also this spectacular event: the different phases of the shooting have been photographed, we have color photographs even, *[nervously laughs]* which start coming out in the newspapers. In the pictures there are people from Porta Romana. *Zap!* The rumour spread that it was the people from Porta Romana. There is the problem that this dead agent is a weight on the entire Autonomia and—at least on this occasion—these Autonomia groups offload the responsibility on the shoulders of the Porta Romana collective.

JUDGE

Did Funaro know that there was this death in Milan?

MORANDINI

Yes, gosh ....

JUDGE

Did you talk about this Custrà?

MORANDINI

Yes, he said you are the usual bandits of Romana Vittoria.

JUDGE

You are?

MORANDINI

The usual bandits, adventurists of Romana Vittoria.

JUDGE

So, Funaro criticized you.

MORANDINI

Certainly. Even though he once had said—I remember this very well because he said it to me—"Communism is also five minutes of power in a bank with your pistol drawn." It was Funaro himself who said this to me: "This is what communism means."

JUDGE

Funaro said to you "Communism is five minutes" ...?

MORANDINI

"Is also five minutes, armed, in a bank." This is to say ... he was very much in agreement with what we were doing. The fact that I have never seen him armed ....

JUDGE

That's it. I'd like to find out something about the period in which you were in *Rosso*. Did you ever participate in robberies?

MORANDINI

Do you mean bank robberies?

JUDGE

Bank or other types of robberies ....

MORANDINI

I participated in expropriations. The so-called expropriations, which are ....

JUDGE

Robberies, for instance bank robberies?

MORANDINI

No, no, never.

JUDGE

Never. Thefts?

MORANDINI

Yes, if expropriations count. They are also types of theft. They serve to continue the political project ....

JUDGE

[interrupting Morandini] Have you ever discussed the organization's weapons with Funaro?

MORANDINI

No, I don't think so.

JUDGE

You don't think so. When you arrive in Rome and meet Funaro, what do you talk about? Did you know each other?

MORANDINI

We certainly did.

JUDGE

And what did you talk about with Funaro? Funaro was undoubtedly an intellectual. He must have given lectures, taught courses, etc. You must have got your ideological training from someone. You said to me, "the first time I heard of *Domination and Sabotage*" [title of a Negri book] and so on, was with that little Face Standard flyer. Did he give theoretical classes?

FERRANDI

I honestly cannot recall it. If you mean ... in short, I am terrified—that's it—by the idea of putting forward the theory of the so-called *evil teachers*. Because although I think that the leadership of *Rosso* has grave and precise historical responsibilities—at least as grave and precise as those of the people who, like me, subsequently materially carried out something even more absurd—I mean—the discourse of the armed struggle .... *[interrupts himself and restarts]* What I am trying to say is that from my point of view when we talk about this leadership we are talking about political responsibilities. I mean, I don't feel like presenting myself as someone who has been manipulated by someone else. The choice of the armed struggle was my own choice. I wish to make this much clear. That is, that's all ....

JUDGE

That wasn't the meaning of my question ... the jurors of this criminal court have instructed me to ask you some ... what's your juridical position?

FERRANDI

I am charged with a homicide in Milan in the trial against Prima Linea: The homicide of a heroin pusher.

JUDGE

The homicide?

FERRANDI

Of a heroin pusher.

Long pause, courtroom noise, paper shuffling, background noise.

JUDGE

In relation to this Assolombarda demonstration of 12 March 1977, for this is what we are talking about, during preliminary inquiry you declared in front of the public prosecutor:

> *[reads]* By now I was also involved in the militarized groups at the demonstrations: in particular, the groups that were always in the first few lines at every demonstration. The first noteworthy demonstration that I recall was the one that culminated with

110

a shooting in front of and against Assolombarda. I recall that although I participated, on that day I was behind and not among the armed people. That's because—all of this is in inverted commas—I hadn't been formally recruited—still in inverted commas—among those in the first lines. In any case, I could still distinctly see Tommei who was giving precise instructions to the demonstrators: not just about the route to be followed and the formation to be kept, but right in front of Assolombarda, where precisely as a result of his instructions, the shooting against the offices started.

MORANDINI

You have all my minutes with you ... isn't that so?

JUDGE

So? Haven't you said these things to the public prosecutor Spataro?

MORANDINI

Yes, except that there is an inaccuracy that I have detected when I reread the minutes, which I have in fact corrected. Because, probably, when minutes are prepared ....

JUDGE

[interrupting Morandini and questioning him] Can you describe this demonstration at Assolombarda to us? Can you tell us: what did you do?

MORANDINI

Yes, I have some memories of the moment of—let's say—the clashes. But I can't recall where ... how ....

JUDGE

[starts raising the tone of his voice, interrupting Morandini and questioning him] Did you participate in them? Let's start from the beginning. At what time did you go to the march? Can you recall this? Who did you go with and where did you go ....

MORANDINI

I don't have exact memories of that day. I just remember the biggest events, such as the shooting.

JUDGE

Let's look at things.

MORANDINI

I can't remember ....

JUDGE

Did you go to this Assolombarda march armed?

MORANDINI

No.

JUDGE

No, you weren't armed, not even petrol bombs?

MORANDINI

Nothing.

JUDGE

You didn't have anything on you.

MORANDINI

I had ....

JUDGE

Did you go with others?

MORANDINI

In fact, I recall that I had a dislocated shoulder, so ....

JUDGE

You had a dislocated shoulder, you joined this demonstration. Were you on duty as a steward at this demonstration, or were you not?

MORANDINI

No, I was not involved.

JUDGE

Had there been a meeting of the Romana collective for this march or hadn't there?

MORANDINI

I cannot recall anything like that.

JUDGE

You cannot recall. Did you go to this march on your own?

MORANDINI

Yes, I mean, on my own ... to get to the march? I think so.

JUDGE

You think so. Where were you within the march?

MORANDINI

Me? In practice, I was close to the usual group in front, close to the Romana Vittoria group.

JUDGE

Close?

MORANDINI

To the Romana Vittoria collective.

JUDGE

Close to whom?

MORANDINI

Close to the Rabbit.

JUDGE

Close to the Rabbit, close to Barbone?

MORANDINI

Barbone, Pasini-Gatti, others … those I knew better.

JUDGE

Was Tommei close to this group?

MORANDINI

Hmm … Tommei was there … at some point I saw him …. I wouldn't be able to say where he was during the march. But he must have no doubt been somewhere around there, because I remember seeing him when the shooting took place.

JUDGE

Well then, let's see how this march unravels. Let's see what gets done at this march.

MORANDINI

So, the demonstrators march along via Larga and when we get to the corner where Assolombarda is located—I didn't even know that that's where Assolombarda is—a group of people leaves the march and they throw a few petrol bombs, others shoot with pistols at the building's bulletproof glass windows.

JUDGE

Do they shoot from within the march?

MORANDINI

Yes.

JUDGE

That's some of the people from your Porta Romana group, isn't that so?

MORANDINI

Yes ... I don't know about this.

JUDGE

You don't know. Didn't you see anyone shooting? Someone with a face ....

MORANDINI

I saw people shooting from a distance. They were masked, as usual, so I wouldn't even be able to recall the people I knew. These are very confused situations. That's also because—as I was saying to you, as I wanted to say before—these marches weren't regimented, they were quite disordered, not like those ....

JUDGE

This march to Assolombarda: was there a deviation or was Assolombarda along the route?

MORANDINI

I don't know about that. In the sense that I was following the march, but I don't know ....

JUDGE

Did the whole march move to Assolombarda?

MORANDINI

Yes, the whole march.

JUDGE

And then what did you do? Did you surge backwards?

MORANDINI

Yes, we surged backwards. Most people hadn't even ....

JUDGE

Most people?

MORANDINI

Hadn't even left the main march, obviously most people hadn't even stopped in front of Assolombarda.

JUDGE

So only part of the march stopped.

MORANDINI

Yes, those ....

JUDGE

Would one be correct in thinking that only those at the head stopped?

MORANDINI

This ... I cannot recall whether it was the head of the whole march or the head of a section of the march ... that is, whether there was another [march]. I can't quite recall this. Also because there wasn't only ....

JUDGE

So, was Tommei in the group that stopped in front of Assolombarda?

MORANDINI

I saw Tommei in front of Assolombarda, right when ....

JUDGE

What was Tommei doing? Was he disguised?

MORANDINI

No, he wasn't: that's why I remember him well.

JUDGE

What was Tommei doing?

MORANDINI

No, he didn't have his face covered with a handkerchief. Nothing: he was very agitated.

JUDGE

What do you mean by agitated?

MORANDINI

I mean that he had his back to Assolombarda, he was outside the march, he was yelling. I don't know what he was saying, I didn't hear.

JUDGE

Yelling? What do you mean?

MORANDINI

Let's say that he looked like someone who was behaving as if he was giving ... he was telling people to do something but people weren't doing it at all ....

JUDGE

People?

MORANDINI

Something like ... I didn't hear his words but his attitude was as if he was trying to stop these people who were leaving the march to go and shoot at Assolombarda.

JUDGE

So, was he trying to prevent these people from shooting?

MORANDINI

Yes. I don't know, something ....

JUDGE

Yes or no?

MORANDINI

Yes, I didn't hear his words, but ....

JUDGE

So, you thought that Tommei was agitated because he was trying to stop these people who were shooting?

MORANDINI

Yes.

JUDGE

Is that so?

MORANDINI

My hypothesis is that he didn't know that people were supposed to shoot and because he had ... I remember that Tommei erm ....

PUBLIC PROSECUTOR

You have declared different things from ....

JUDGE

No, please be patient ....

All of a sudden they raise their voices and speak at the same time. Incomprehensible voices from the courtroom.

PUBLIC PROSECUTOR

No, Mr President ....

JUDGE

No, be patient. Please be patient. Morandini: don't answer ....

MORANDINI

I can explain ....

JUDGE

[shouting and interrupting Morandini in a peremptory tone] Morandini!

Long pause: excited and incomprehensible voices far away from the microphone.

JUDGE

[reading fast and in a mechanical tone] There is a point. I have in mind the cages of the Milan trial against Autonomia, from which you and your comrades have managed to remove yourselves. You say you feel no responsibility for the likes of Barbone and Morandini. Maybe … I am holding a bench warrant: robbery and illegal possession of weapons. It contains the names of many of us. At number seven there is Barbone Marco, born in Bari on 19 September 1958. It refers to the expropriation of the supermarket in via Moretti, in Quarto Oggiaro, which took place—still according to the bench warrant—on 19 October 1974. When we organized that expropriation Marco Barbone had only turned 16 the month before. You have compared those expropriations to the assaults on the bakers' shops in Manzoni. For you that expropriation had been a milestone in the construction of a mythical new workers' movement. The chapter in the *Betrothed* with the assault on Grucce's baker's shop starts like this: "What was happening in Milan under Renzo's curious and disbelieving eyes had precise causes: that 1628 had been the year of famine and plague." In 1974 you published *Worker's Party Against Work* and in a prose that is perhaps more elusive than Manzoni's you say that the problem is finding the mediation needed for determining that workers' power is stable on the offensive terrain. Here I have another bench warrant, still with Barbone, dated December 1974: possession of explosives and setting fire to the headmaster's car. I have seen again Chicco Funaro on television: he was next to you in the cage at your trial. Although he still has a lively demeanour, he looks older, his hair is grizzled. And yet it felt like yesterday when with Barbone and the others we had organized the small team that set reactionary professors' cars on fire. And it feels like yesterday the memory of his home behind Santa Maria delle Grazie. Another bench warrant: this time it's damages, devastation, illegal possession of weapons and the aggravating circumstance of having been more than ten [people gathered]. There is still Marco Barbone. Among the others Franco Tommei makes an appearance. Destruction of the offices of the Confapi in via Mozart, Milan. Franco, in your old cage, is the one who has changed the least: sardonic smile, something about him reminds you of a satyr. I see from the warrant that he was born in 1936: he is approaching 50. I remember him under

the Confapi offices when they were burning like a torch, in front of the Autonomia march that was waiting for us. People were shouting "Confapi is burning," and he was rhythmically clapping his hands and marking the beat, with his eyes that were smiling in that unique way of his: they switch on. You know him better than I do. The prosecutor attributes to him the aggravating circumstance of having directed the march and the irruption into the offices of Confapi. When we broke in there were a dozen clerks. I remember their appalled faces when we drew our weapons. About ten pistols altogether. We had collected them at the Liceo Berchet [a Milanese high school]. It was Barbone himself who kept them: they came from the robbery at the armoury in viale Monza. But you can't remember these details: and yet for us these details were how we were unravelling the red thread of the armed organization as we prepared for the development of the struggles.

Short pause.

JUDGE

Then it says:

We get to the terrible spring of 1977. Horror and horrors. The likes of Barbone and Morandini were kicked out of the movement after the death of Custrà and we have nothing to do with it ... maybe. But I have in mind that small room full of smoke in via Disciplini with you, Pozzi and the others barricaded inside to discuss the articles for *Rosso* and to choose the pictures to put in it: always beautiful, extremely suggestive pictures. There is an issue of March–April 1977, a few weeks before the facts of via De Amicis, in which on the first page there is a picture with a group of masked protesters who brandish pistols. For sure, you might not have known who they were: they were Barbone, Morandini, Luca Colombo and Pasini-Gatti from the Porta Romana collective. The picture had been taken at the March 18 march that ended with furious shooting against the glass windows of the Associazione Industriali Lombardi. Among the internal titles of that issue of *Rosso* there was a banner headline that I can still remember. It simply said: Thank You Comrades.

Long pause, indistinct ambient noises, distant coughing.

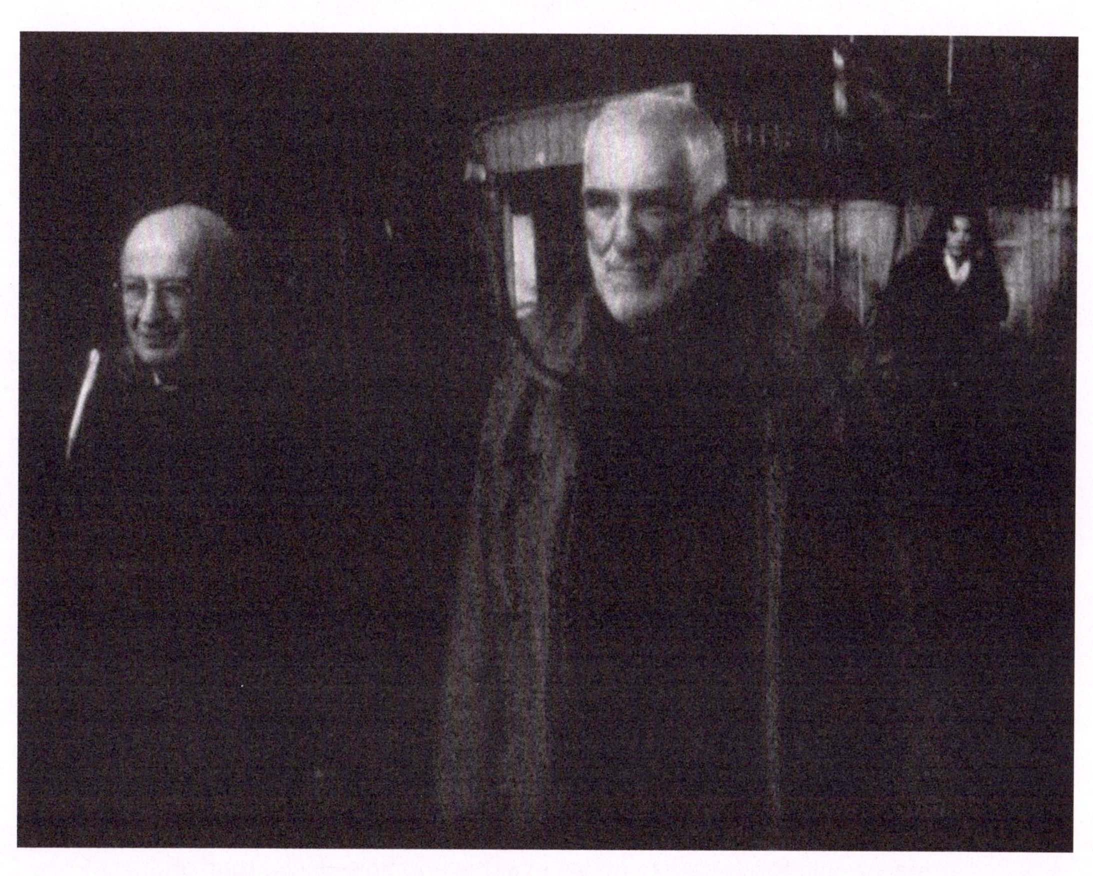

JUDGE

Was it this one?

FUNARO

[speaks away from the microphone to the judge, unclear]

JUDGE

This one, Funaro? This one?

FUNARO

[speaks away from the microphone replying to the judge, slowly approaching the microphone] ... Specific crimes of Ferrandi against whom we have no specific charges, something we have never done before ....

JUDGE

[interrupting] Come here Funaro; speak to him directly about it. Come here. We have no problem with it.

Long pause, noises in the room, footsteps, voices and fragments of speech that cannot be attributed with certainty.

JUDGE

Tell the clerk who needs to add it to the proceedings. Please sit down. What did you want to say?

FUNARO

I simply wanted to say that mine was a slightly polemical joke on the judge *a latere* Abbate, please forgive me councillor Abbate but the problem is a different one. There is clearly a problem here, that of a contention that is, let's say, more political than criminal, and often reflected in taking sides in newspapers, through articles of this kind, etc. I would like to say, to make a simple and brief declaration on this, which is not even a statement, but the expounding of my thoughts and I believe I can also speak on behalf of Paolo, Paolo Pozzi and Franco Tommei. There is no doubt that some political paths, ample, tormented, long and difficult ones must be placed today in their right historical, political and, I would personally add, moral perspective. This is a problem we have felt strongly at various moments of our lives; some of us—I believe—have deeply felt it even during the unfolding of certain events, but this doesn't mean much and is certainly not a matter for judgement, nor can it ever become so. I wanted to say that, starting from this kind of political, cultural, human experience, many of us have gone through extremely complex trajectories, where critical and

120

self-critical choices were made. There is one thing separating me and Mario Ferrandi here, at this point in time, which is not, or is not solely and entirely, the critique of an overall political, cultural and human trajectory. It is the outcome of this trajectory that divides me from Mario Ferrandi, and I must add that I am very sorry about this. This division is represented by the need of a law, of a system of laws that covers and ratifies a human attitude that I do not share and cannot share in, neither because of political ethics, or merely because of political ethics, nor for cultural ethics, or not merely because of cultural ethics, but rather, substantially, because of human ethics. Critical and self-critical trajectories start from historical and political needs and cannot overcome the level of personal crisis. Seeing Mario here, sat down to reconstruct events that are not even that distant from the reconstructions we have provided, and knowing that he has taken advantage of this law, that he *[interruption and then repetition of the point]* has, has come to … he, so intelligent, I have no problem recognizing it: Mario is terribly intelligent and terribly nice. We've all seen it, we laughed too when he told stories that—no matter whether true or false—nonetheless involved us in a cultural fabric that was common to us all. I reassure you, Mr President, I don't want my statement to be …. I only want to take a load off my chest. I reassure you that seeing Mario Ferrandi here taking advantage of the law of *pentiti* and knowing that Mario Ferrandi has named comrades etc., this causes me a truly great pain. Well, this is all I wanted to add.

FERRANDI

Can I say something?

FUNARO

I only wanted to add this: the essential. I have nothing to add.

FERRANDI

What causes me a great pain is seeing you go through a court holocaust for the sake of defending a political experience that is not reducible to the debate on the historical errors to be confronted *inter nos* without confronting reality, the reality even that of these laws you refer to, which I felt no horror in taking advantage of, because amongst other things, they do not necessarily include the need to name, if you feel moral scruples about this. But I simply saw them …. I mean, it was a different dimension: to me, they seemed something extremely acceptable and which anyone could have availed himself of.

FUNARO

[partial overlap] Mario, excuse me ….

FERRANDI

The fact of doing it would have made this kind of moral label fall—which I know too well even on my skin—this label that is stuck on you as soon as you decide to talk. I think that as soon as one accepts the reality for what it is .... *[interruption]* The reality is on the one hand the total defeat of these trajectories of ours, and the irrationality at their basis, and on the other hand the right of the State—who won this war—to demand a price in exchange for the chance for you to think of a life again. To me, this seems acceptable from a moral point of view.

FUNARO

I don't want to and perhaps I cannot respond to all you have said Mario. Because I told you that I have, amongst other things, a curious form of respect for personal choices. Although, frankly, the personal choice you made, and this is the last time I say it, I don't agree with now, I didn't agree with in the past, and I will never agree with. Here quite frankly no one can accuse me of trials of demonization. I am going through an experience that I wouldn't have thought I'd go through ... that could have been a risk inherent to a certain way of conceiving the relationship with the State, politics or culture, but please let's not mix these issues, which are an object of discussion but that ... Mario .... *[reciprocal interruption and overlap]*

FERRANDI

These aren't charges of demonization, the problem is that ...

FUNARO

Here's the problem.

FERRANDI

[unclear] ... You have been in jail for five years probably for stupid things, because you dig your heels in over the fact that they cannot be admitted to whilst maybe people who've caused disasters have been out for a while, and I am sorry about this at a human level. Can you see that? Because I think that your obstinacy and that of your comrades in denying the evidence does not make any sense ....

FUNARO

Mario, I never denied any evidence that was evidence of political responsibility, as I never ... if it was ....

FERRANDI

That ugly reality of the trial ....

Voices away from the microphone.

PUBLIC PROSECUTOR

[far from the microphone] [laughs] I wanted to introduce it myself, this ideal confrontation, with Negri, but luckily Funaro came along ....

FUNARO

Excuse me Dr Marini, but from this standpoint I can do nothing but leave. How is it? *[the public prosecutor imposes his voice speaking away from the microphone, unclear]* Dr Marini, can I tell you something outside the trial?

PUBLIC PROSECUTOR

[increasingly agitated, voices overlap] You are saying the same things that Negri would have said sitting in your place. That Negri, who doesn't even have the courage *[raising the tone of the voice even further]* to confront Ferrandi here.

DEFENCE LAWYER

[raising his voice] This is not true at all, it's not true at all *[punching the desk]* and there are other proceedings of the trial that demonstrate that he does not say the same things! He doesn't say the same things!

UNKNOWN

[female voice] But he isn't Negri .... *[unclear]*

FUNARO

Dr Marini, Dr Marini excuse me ... excuse me Dr Marini ... Dr Marini you are someone—I say this outside the trial—you could be someone capable of carrying out this job with extreme .... *[increasingly agitated]* Dr Marini this is not permissible. You can't tell me that I'm here to represent Negri, Dr Marini, because on this I am forced to leave. My name is Alberto Funaro, known as Chicco, forty-one years old, spent well or not; Toni Negri was one of my best friends for ten or twelve years. *[raising his voice]* This in no way authorizes you to say that I am here to represent Toni Negri! Dr Marini .... This can't go on! *[moderating his voice]* Excuse me Dr Santiapichi, I beg you to postpone all further debate to another time. I am literally indignant.

PUBLIC PROSECUTOR

Ah, I was ... *[unclear]* not to represent.

JUDGE

Come and sit down Funaro ... come on.

Footsteps.

FUNARO

Ciao.

FERRANDI

Ciao.

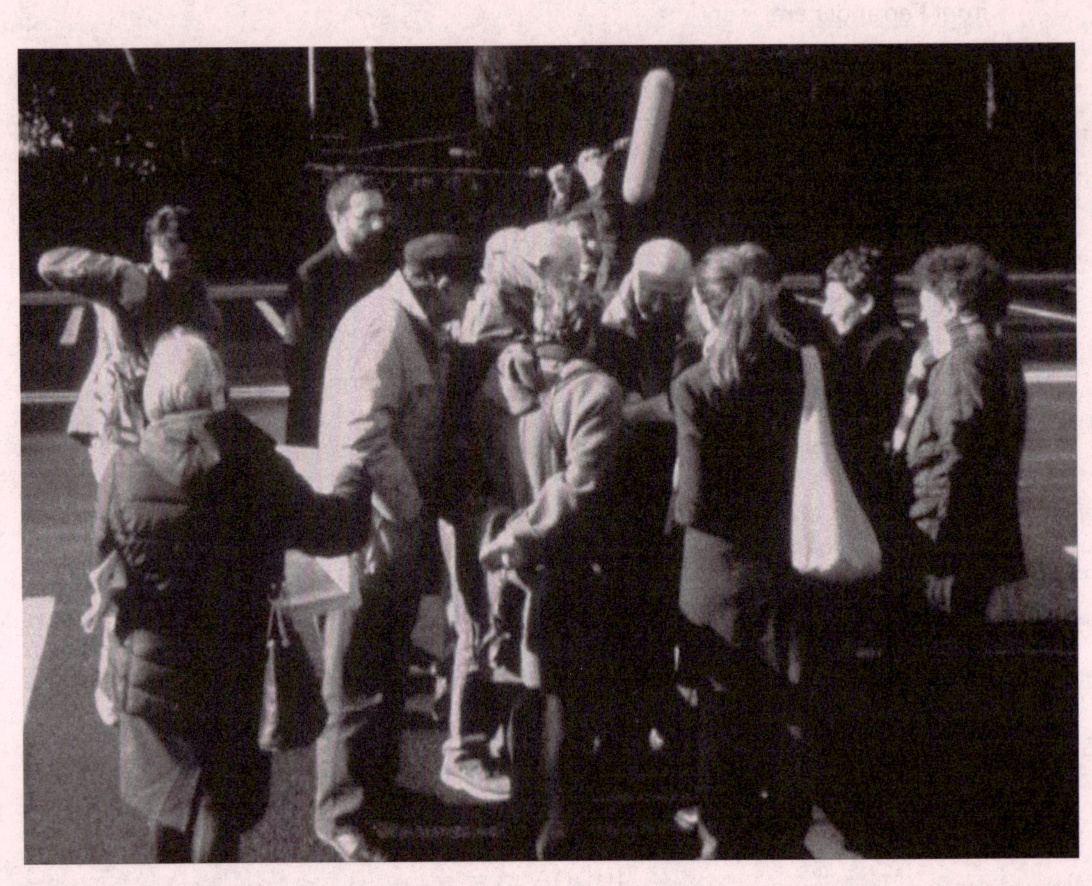

JUDGE

Take a seat, Funaro.

Sigh.

JUDGE

Adjourned for ten minutes.

Noises in the courtroom, rustling of paper.

Long pause, ambient noise, talking, someone laughs, coughing, microphone noise.

JUDGE

Please sit down. *[noise of the microphone being inserted into the holder]*

GALANTE

Thank you.

JUDGE

You have made some statements and in some of these statements you referred to Negri, the accused. You also talked about Ferrari Bravo and Bianchini. Would you mind being more specific?

GALANTE

[laughs] If you wouldn't mind specifying the question: I testified ....

JUDGE

Do you know Negri?

GALANTE

Yes, we used to work in the same faculty, so I know him.

JUDGE

What did you teach then?

GALANTE

Me? History of political parties.

JUDGE

History of political parties. And you know Ferrari Bravo?

GALANTE

For the same reason as above: that is, we used to teach and work in the same faculty.

JUDGE

That's it. In the preliminary inquiry you declared:

> *[reads]* It is widely believed in the Faculty that Negri is the head of Autonomia Operaia Organizzata, whose most belligerent groups are in the faculties of Political Science and Education. They adopt violent and intimidating methods of struggle *[clears his throat and restarts reading]* ... most belligerent groups are in the faculties of Political Science and Education. They adopt violent and intimidating methods of struggle with the aim of destabilizing universal institutions *[corrects himself]* university institutions. It is also widely believed that other adherents to Autonomia include Ferrari Bravo—Negri's disciple—Del Re and Serafini. As far as Bianchini is concerned, his conduct appears ambiguous and there are contrasting opinions regarding his belonging to the aforementioned organization. *[footsteps]* Some time ago I learned from my colleague Giorgio Roverato that in the late 1960s, maybe in '69, Negri taught the technique for making Molotov cocktails in the Fusinato student residence. The other morning, commenting on the recent arrests of academics from our Faculty, Professor Sabino Acquaviva said in front of me, Roverato and the secretary, Marina, that he believed that Negri was one of the organizers of autonomist guerrilla warfare.

JUDGE

Can you clarify these things?

GALANTE

Sure. Regarding the first part, that is the relationship that the people you have mentioned had with the leadership of Autonomia Organizzata in Padua—for that's what I can talk about—not only was this widely believed within the Faculty, but there were also the following types of connections. In the office of Ferrari Bravo—for instance—and of Dr Alisa Del Re, which I think was the same office, there were the following types of activities that took place in front of the academics I have just mentioned: the leaders of the Agitation Committee, which was the local structure of Autonomia Organizzata, wrote the texts of flyers and *tatzebaos* [posters] which were then put up inside and on the walls of the Faculty building, in the Faculty hall and sometimes even outside the Faculty building. Sometimes when I was passing by the corridors I had to put up with having to watch the preparation of this material .... I saw them writing .... I don't know exactly what they were writing, but when they put up those flyers I could read them. There were also similar links in terms of political themes. I mean, I could see this at the beginning, when assemblies were called to which everybody could participate and so I could also participate. The demands of the autonomists, of the (in inverted commas) students of the Agitation Committee were also supported by the academics who endorsed the same politics, the same political attitude: both normal politics and politics that on the contrary were oriented towards demands that, as far as I know, were outside the existing laws. I am thinking, for instance, about the self-managed seminars, about the minimum "political" mark and so on.

JUDGE

That's it. What can you tell me about the self-managed seminars?

GALANTE

Well, I have brought a small dossier with documents by Autonomia, including flyers. I'd like to read one if I may. It says:

> [clears throat and reads] The proposal of self-managed, funded seminars, with a guaranteed mark, has moved forward in those faculties where this has been allowed by the power relations between proletarians and academic control. It has also set in motion moments of political confrontation favourable to the mass structure in other situations. The seminars have been used by the proletarians [clears throat] as a first moment of organization towards the imposition of their overall needs, as moments of struggle that allow them to confront on the one hand the capitalist structure of the university, and on the other hand to impose their command on the city, housing, transport and so on.

I have a bit of a habit of thinking as a historian and so I follow the documents …. If you take the time to follow the documents that I have here with me and also other documents, you then see highlighted some of the things that I and others physically experienced within the Faculty: that is to say that the self-managed seminars were an instrument used by Autonomia to self-organize within the Faculty. Secondly, the self-managed seminars aimed at recruiting new adepts to the organization, providing generalized and militant political training—as they used to say—for the cadres of the organization, and they were also a covert instrument for attracting to the organization a broader militant mass that would then impose what they called the de-structuring and destabilization of the Faculty as a centre of command of academic power. They were also sites from which further activities could be directed towards other faculties such as Education and the Humanities—this was claimed in a series of flyers—and towards the city. For that's where they formed the nuclei that—as it happened on 15 November 1977— would then operate using Molotov cocktails in the city suburbs, or in the suburb of Portello on another occasion. That is: there was a centre from which what I consider terrorist, or in any case violent activities were organized and radiated outwards.

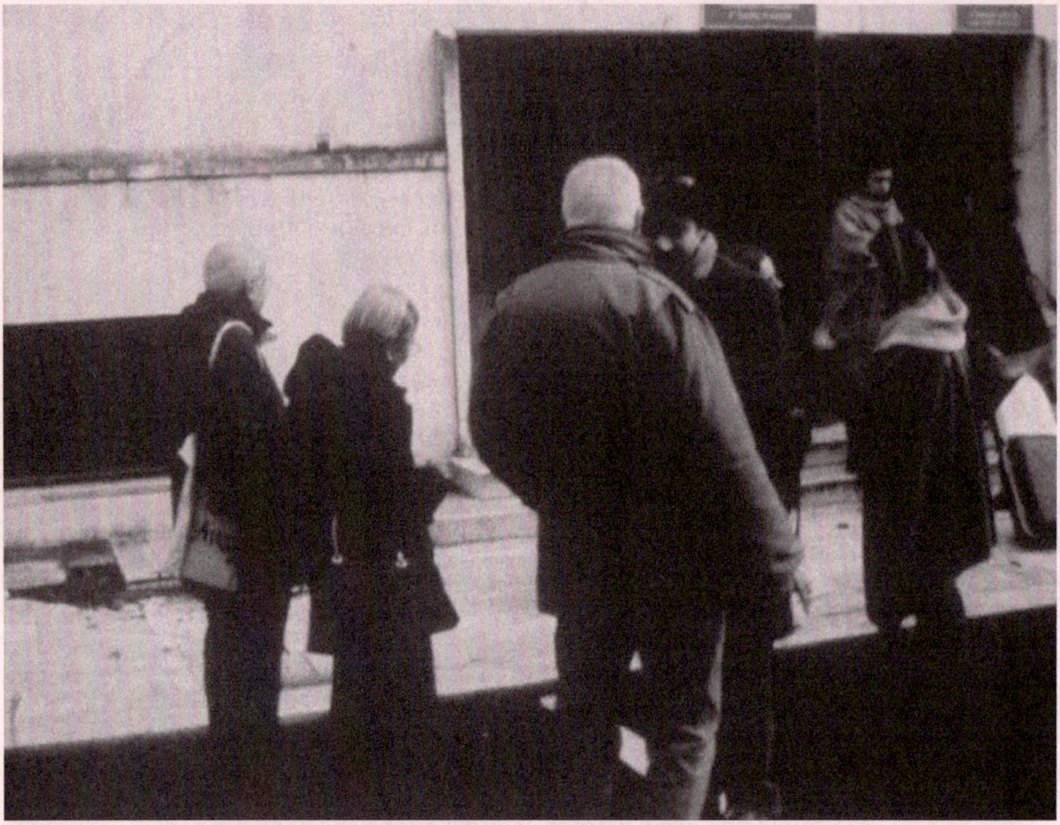

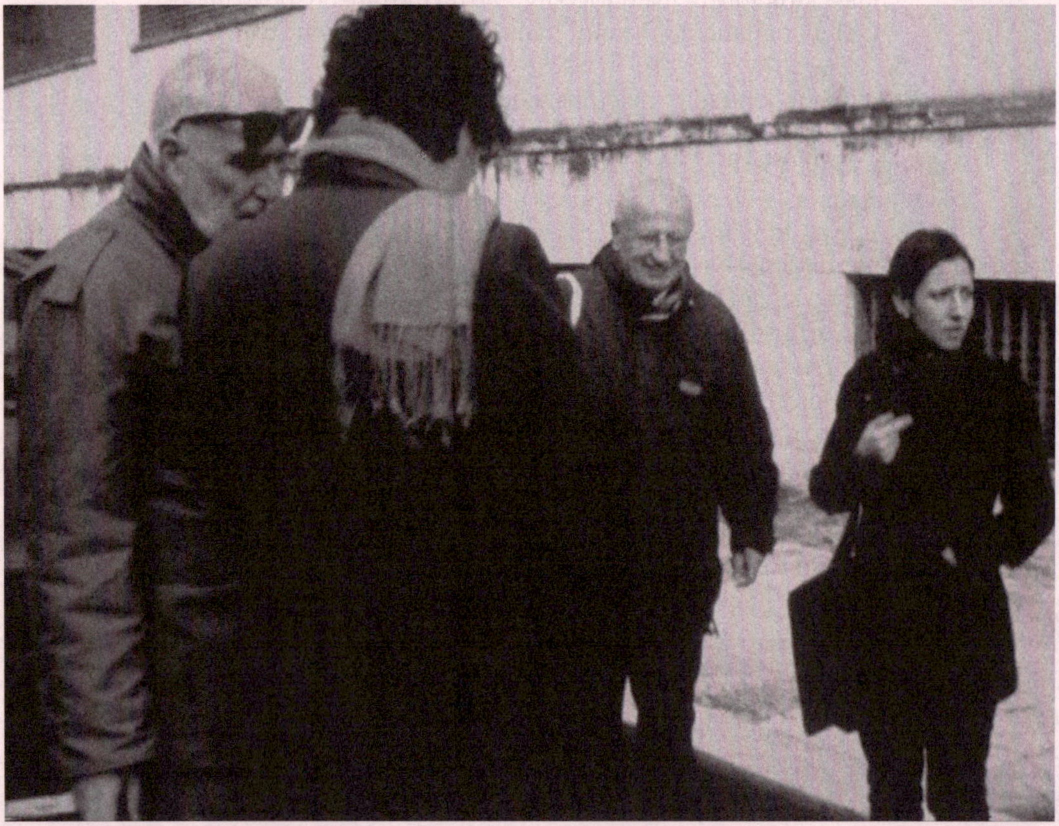

JUDGE

Please give me folder number one. Do you understand? Please don't remove these folders from my table. Here.

Long pause, noise in the courtroom, coughing near the microphone, paper shuffling, background noise.

JUDGE

[reading fast with mechanical intonation] During the 30 January 1979 search in the house of Magnaghi a paper was seized, "The Collaborator and Training," on which are written the names of Pietro de Giudici, Giambattista Marongiu and Oreste Scalzone. It is to be excluded that it refers to issues related to professional didactic activities, all the more so because the list includes people with the most diverse qualifications. In truth, a screen was created within the Faculty of Architecture in Milan to provide a cultural and scientific cover behind which individuals such as Scalzone, Magnaghi, Marongiu, who operated undisturbed and with the financial support of the State, could propagandize subversion and organize their adepts.

Here there is a reference: Lombino, seven, seventh file, sheet number 1,784; Barbone, seven, fifth file, sheet number 1,006:

Some photocopies of the flyer concerning the homicide of Walter Tobagi were produced with a photocopying machine of the Faculty of Architecture in Milan.

See also: regional National Accounts note etc.:

[continues reading] The motivation for the choice of Prof. Marongiu by the Faculty Council is incomprehensible.

And so on.

MAGNAGHI

Not a single *pentito* in Italy has associated me, even by hearsay, with any participation in subversive activities. And that's even though the interrogations of many of these *pentiti* reveal that they have been widely asked about me: especially the *pentiti* of the Milan area, where I have lived permanently for the last ten years. Nothing. Nobody has anything to say. The only witness whose testimony in a note refers to an issue that has something to do with me—that is to say, the famous question of the Faculty of Architecture—is a certain Lombino, act number seven, file seven, sheet number 1,784, which supports the phrase on which I commented before: "In truth, a screen was created within the Faculty of Architecture behind which" individuals like me "operated undisturbed." And then there is: "Lombino notes ...." I have checked what Lombino says. In his testimony Lombino says: "The Faculty of Architecture ...." *[he stops]* I must premise that I don't know this Lombino. I understand that he said that his brother was enrolled as a student. I think I read this in his testimony, but I am not sure.

> The Faculty of Architecture had become a place for discussions, for various groups

—here I think he is talking of 1975–76, but the dates are all mixed up—

> whose shared matrix was clearly their belonging to the area of Autonomia. There were various assembly structures from the factories in the Milan area, such Marelli, Falck, Carlo Erba, Telettra, Unidel, whose point of reference was the now dissolved Cocori line. I must say that the Faculty of Architecture had undoubtedly become the designated place for these meetings because of the help of people who had historically belonged to Potere Operaio—Scalzone, Magnaghi, Perelio Augusto, his wife, Stevan, and others—who were academics within the Faculty.

Then there is an illegible word.

> They wanted to turn the Faculty into a laboratory for meetings with large masses of the proletariat.

If it were so I wouldn't be in the least ashamed of this.

> In particular, this was a coherent line put forward by Magnaghi in his teaching on Territorial Planning. I add ....

—this is still Lombino who is talking—

> that I am not aware of any real link between the people I have mentioned and armed organizations. In fact, neither Magnaghi nor the other people I have mentioned ever participated in the assemblies—these assemblies that involved the various facto-ries—nor did they participate in the open meetings on these themes that took place every fifteen or thirty days.

Now, I want to briefly comment on this because I think that it is import-ant. It is well known that since 1968 the Faculty of Architecture, like very many other Italian universities, had been the designated place for public meetings of the most diverse political organizations. It is also well known that the managing structure of the Faculty where I worked for twelve years always guaranteed the availability of some lecture rooms to all the student organizations, which could therefore use the building for their political assemblies and public, non-public or private meetings, etc. This is something that was practiced in almost all universities at least until 1977—here we are in fact talking about 1975–76. So, together with the majority of the lecturers I always promoted the political availability of the university. Therefore, in order to take place, the workers' assemblies that Lombino talks about didn't need any particular intervention by ex-members of Potere Operaio, as someone *makes* Lombino say here. And they make him say that Perelli Augusto had been a member of Potere Operaio when in fact he had been a member of CSIULP. He had never been a member of Potere Operaio. The same with his wife, Sandra Bonfiglioli, who had also never been a member of Potere Operaio. Cesare Stevan is a member of the Socialist collective of the university ....

JUDGE

[talking at the same time as Magnaghi: some of the words are incomprehensible] It's not that someone makes him say. He says. Please go on.

MAGNAGHI

He says ... if he is wrong ... but what a coincidence, Mr Judge: in these statements by the *pentiti* everybody becomes a member of Potere Operaio or Autonomia. One wonders how. Let it pass, excuse me ....

JUDGE

Let it pass, ignore these considerations ... these are hypotheses that relate to specific instances of crimes. That's when people say this kind of thing.

MAGNAGHI

He says, he says, Lombino says ... but how come this Lombino who knows nothing about this whole thing says that they were all ex-members of Potere Operaio. And he hints that there is a link between being an ex-member of Potere Operaio and the political availability of lecture rooms for factory assemblies. Which is complete nonsense because the whole Faculty Council hosted for three days even the homeless people of via Tibaldi, complete with the forced removal by the police and the criminal charges laid against all the lecturers. Imagine that. The reasoning that in those years ex-members of Potere Operaio were needed to guarantee the political space for workers' and students' assemblies doesn't hold up. But what is most clear is that when Lombino is prompted by the investigating judge to find an activity connecting me with the armed groups, he contradicts the reasons for which the testimony is referred to in the note. That's where the judge says: "There was a group .... There was Magnaghi who pretended to work as a lecturer but in fact organized subversive stuff." At this point they ask Lombino: "And what did he organize?" Lombino says: "Nothing, I don't know, he didn't organize anything." On the other hand, the purpose of this testimony .... I'll report something interesting, even though Lombino's testimony would be enough to defend myself. On 19 June 1981 in the newspaper *Repubblica*, this Lombino says, among other things: "The artful message of some magistrates who left me in solitary confinement for over a year has led me to give evidence on my militancy. This has become an information pool used to strengthen circumstantial evidence against others, including manipulating the written minutes. This is the reason why I retracted all my interrogations some time ago." This is what I have found written in the 19 June 1981 edition of *Repubblica*. *[pause]* Oh, that's it! After this statement in which it is said that I acted undisturbed using State money they insert a note. I am still talking about the text of the remand because that's the one in which I am charged. So:

> *[he reads]* Some photocopies of the flyer regarding the homicide of Walter Tobagi were produced with a photocopying machine of the Faculty of Architecture in Milan.

Full stop.

JUDGE
[unclear, far away from the microphone] "Were?"

MAGNAGHI
Were produced with a photocopying machine ... some photocopies of the flyer ... were produced with a photocopying machine of the Faculty of Architecture.

I have read this and have asked myself what the insertion of this phrase could mean: placed there, after the statement that I acted undisturbed. I was already in prison. Let's not even talk about this episode ... this terrible episode. But what does the insertion of this suggestive phrase mean? That in the Faculty of Architecture we supported the printing of terrorist flyers? Does anybody know that in the Faculty of Architecture there is free access to the photocopying machines for students? Or maybe Dr Amato wants to promote a reform of the university that eliminates students' access to photocopying machines and, while we are at it, to the university itself?

Long break, noise in the courtroom, voices, a latch clicks and a metallic door is opened, footsteps, shuffling of papers.

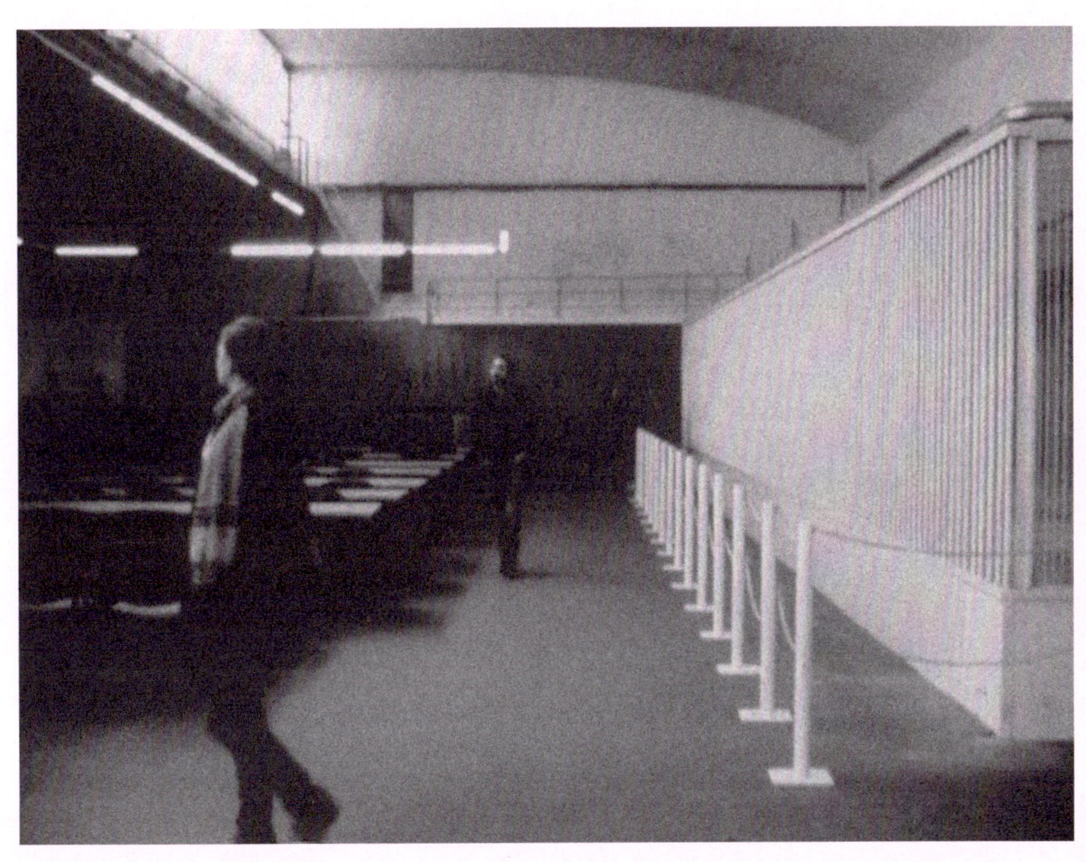

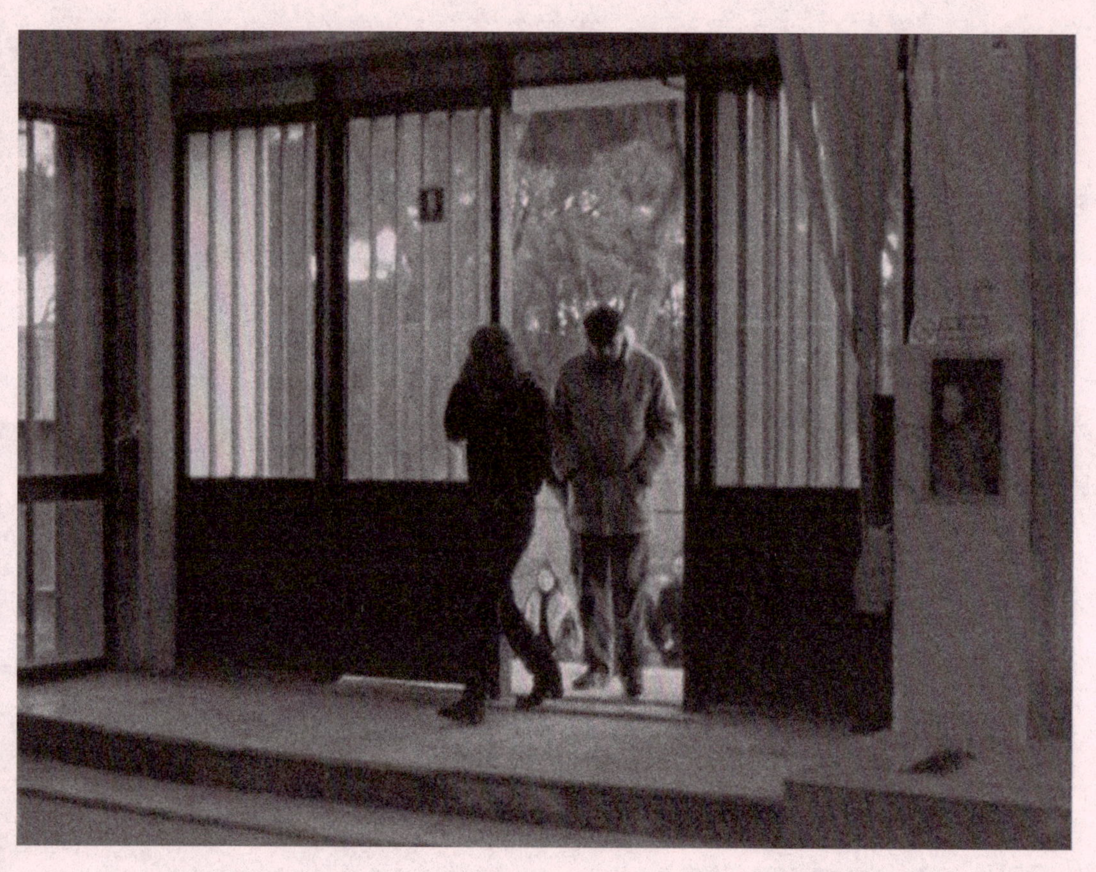

JUDGE

Did you sign the statement presented to the public prosecutor's office by twenty professors from Padua?

GALANTE

Yes, they called us the gang of twenty.

JUDGE

Well, if you could please report to the court the content and the consequences of that statement.

GALANTE

If I remember the statement correctly—for even in this case several years have passed—it was about a series of intimidations and violent acts that had happened in the Faculty. I must also say that I signed other statements and so I may be mixing up things. Anyhow, it denounced ... *[clears throat]* this climate that existed within the Faculty. There were these fairly large groups of autonomist students who came together with completely normal students. On some occasions they came together, four or five of them, and they demanded that they be examined—in a manner of speaking—at the same time by the examination committee, and then they demanded to impose the mark twenty-seven [27 out of 30] or similarly high marks. In the face of this situation repeating itself, a Faculty Council was convened that voted—twenty against thirteen—for the suspension of didactic activities until 30 September. A majority, as I have said, of twenty. The names of these twenty were publicized—I don't know through which channels—and were passed on to students who put them up outside the Faculty and made them public. And so the professors became the targets of threats on a *tatzebao* that was put up in the Faculty hall and were given the nickname—possibly with reference to other gangs—gang of twenty. At the same time, movement assemblies were also organized *[clears throat]*, as I was saying, within the Faculty. That's because the Faculty of Political Science was considered a political space that shouldn't in any way be taken away from the organization of Autonomia: because without that base—which, as they used to say, was a red base—it would have been more difficult for them to organize future actions in the university and in the city. As far as I can recall, this was the climate and this was what the statement referred to, but ....

JUDGE

Thank you. Public prosecutor, please continue.

PUBLIC PROSECUTOR

Nothing. With reference to our interrogations, I was alluding to the interrogation that was answered ... in front of the Investigating Judge Francesco Amato, and I was referring to what the witness was saying about the so-called Agitation Committees. *[coughing in the courtroom]*

Then there is another circumstance about which I'd like to call the witness to say things:

> *[he reads]* On many occasions I had the opportunity to note that there were activists from the Agitation Committee in the university office shared by Ferrari Bravo and Alisa Del Re. The programme of the Agitation Committee was the programme of Autonomia Organizzata, and it unfolded along the following lines: self-managed seminar, political mark, the funding by the University of the activities of the Committee and the provision of equipment and materials for the Committee, such as megaphones, use of telephones, rooms.

This is the question that interests me:

> The methods adopted for the pursuit of such objectives were the use of violence, threats and intimidation towards academic staff and anyone who would oppose their objectives. There were no contestations regarding the seminar, or more precisely regarding the disciplines related to the seminar led by Negri or Ferrari Bravo. Violent acts and threats were on the contrary directed towards the academics responsible for the disciplines of modern history, languages, in particular English, economic disciplines and some of the law disciplines. I add that recently, after the publication of an article by Nicola Scajola in the magazine *Espresso*, I have received telephone threats and my name has also been written on some walls in Padua, on its own and together with other witnesses, with attached intimidating expressions. My name has also appeared on some flyers and has been circulated in a similar way by Radio Sherwood.

With reference to the city: a little while ago you said a phrase, "And then they moved towards the city because there is where they organized the groups and there is also where the clashes took place." In addition to being a University Professor, I understand that you are also a citizen of Padua .... Do you live in Padua?

Short pause, courtroom noise.

GALANTE

Yes, yes, I am a city councillor in Padua.

PUBLIC PROSECUTOR

Can you then please describe, still in the ambit of the discourse about Autonomia Operaia Organizzata, what was the climate that was experienced in Padua in those days?

Short pause, noise in the courtroom.

GALANTE

Well, talking about climate is always an issue ....

PUBLIC PROSECUTOR

[interrupting Galante] The climate with reference to the methods adopted, the objectives and the episodes of violence, the threats, intimidation, etc.

GALANTE

Well, in fact this is ... *[voices of people protesting]* anyhow, anyhow, I'll provide examples .... *[voices overlapping and reciprocal interruptions]*

DEFENCE LAWYER

[speaking far away from the microphone] It is an extremely generic question ....

PUBLIC PROSECUTOR

[raising his voice and overlapping with defence lawyer] There are one hundred attacks! We have the list of episodes! In fact, five hundred, not just one hundred!

DEFENCE LAWYER

You must ask ... you must talk about the individual attacks ....

PUBLIC PROSECUTOR

I ask questions that result from the official records. I don't make up anything.

DEFENCE LAWYER

But the climate! What does the climate mean? The question is too ....

Long pause, ambient noise, voices, microphone noise.

VIRNO

The day before the expulsion of Lama [then General Secretary of the CGIL, the biggest Italian trade union] from the University of Rome, there was an assembly in the Home Room of the Faculty of Arts. This assembly in the Home Room discussed what was to be done the following day, when Lama was scheduled to arrive. I personally expressed the opinion that we should have asked for an exchange of views with Lama himself—that is, that we should have asked for the opportunity to speak immediately after Lama—and that any preliminary opposition to the arrival and presence of Lama at the University would have been a political mistake. That was the kind of position that carried the day within the movement and the following day we were ready to ask for an exchange of views with Lama. But the stewards of the Communist Party came with a militaristic attitude and with the intention of moving the occupying students out of the university and of deleting the struggle writings on the university walls, which I'd say is a way of proceeding typical of the regimes of real existing socialism. They started using fire extinguishers against the protests that came from the movement that was occupying the University and so there were clashes.

Short pause, noise in the courtroom.

JUDGE

[reading quickly, without pauses, with a mechanical intonation]
We are not terrorists, we just want to state a few things, a point of view, some real events, some facts that we have personally experienced on our skins in recent times at the University. Some facts and not just words. At Liviano a climate of general terror has been created for over a month. Nobody can organize meetings or seminars in the Faculty. The students' office is practically walled up. Those who don't comply with the policies imposed by the deliberation of CdF

—Faculty Council, I think—

are put on file and denounced to the police. The police are constantly present inside and outside the Faculty, etc., etc.

Shall we read it all? Let's read it all ....

[continues reading] In the Faculty of Psychology all the rooms of the students' office have been closed. Meetings and assemblies have been prohibited. On Monday, fifteen hours out of sixteen, during a seminar that took place at the entrance of the Faculty, Pettere and his henchmen call for the intervention of the anti-riot police. The search begins: several comrades are beaten up by the police inside the Faculty and two hundred students are identified. On Tuesday, during the Faculty's general assembly

that took place at Pappafava, the eviction of the students by the police was only avoided because of the mediation of an academic. On Thursday 18th at 10 a.m., an assembly in the Morgagni lecture room at the Policlinico, which had been regularly requested to discuss the present situation, was *de facto* prohibited through the denial of permission to use the room. The police and the carabinieri stand as guarantors of democratic order. In the Faculty of Political Science the Faculty Council denies its solidarity with Fausto Schiavetto, an adjunct in the Faculty who has been denounced by Kalogero

—with a K—

for interrupting the Faculty Council. The report is a frame up: the Faculty Council's minutes testify that there has been no interruption. The Faculty Council is more inclined to set up a control committee on the exams in order to second Kalogero's enquiry into the self-managed seminars as nests of subversion. It is certainly not the movement that is trying to exacerbate this situation: proletarians and students who for many months have worked in broad daylight on a political project regarding, in the first place, the permanence of proletarians at the University. We don't take any responsibility. We absolutely refuse the logic of frontal confrontation imposed by the enemy, and on its own ground. We are not so stupid. For our part, we say: first, that we take no political responsibility for a situation that the organs of control of the University want to exacerbate and that can have extremely heavy repercussions; second, that we can no longer tolerate the criminalization of our struggles, the closure of political spaces, the attempt to question the legitimacy of self-managed seminars, the attempt to bring the University back to normality; third, that all the spaces must be reopened and that we must be able to take our exams, which are within a week, without interference; fourth, we are launching a campaign, in the city and in the whole territory, for the re-appropriation of political spaces for the entire movement. In conclusion: we say that all of this is the result of the indications given by the University assembly that took place on Thursday 18th in the Faculty of Political Science, with eight hundred students in attendance who represent all the faculties, and that it will be put into practice, with all its articulations, starting from today. We declare that the agitation is extended to all the faculties, all the high school students, all the neighbourhoods, and to the counter-information initiatives in the villages and the factories. It is appropriate to say that if there won't be fair and positive resolutions we will all take our respective roads. University struggle inter-committees, general assembly.

Long pause, ambient noise, microphone noise.

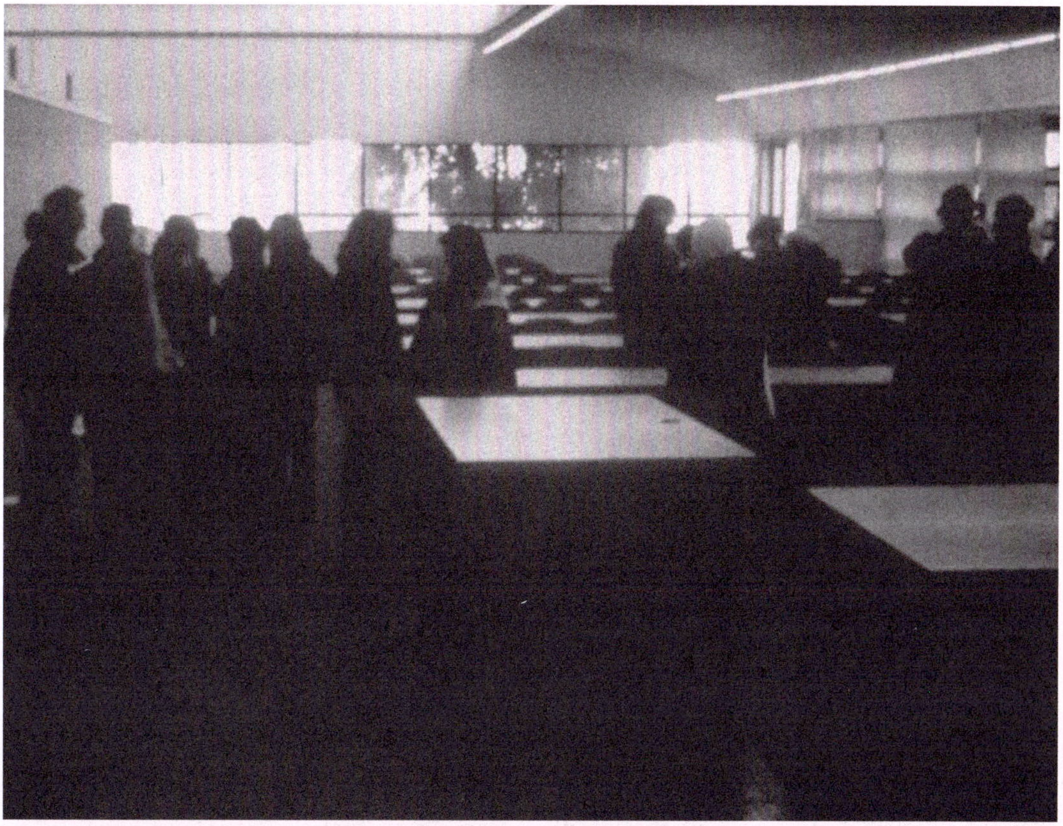

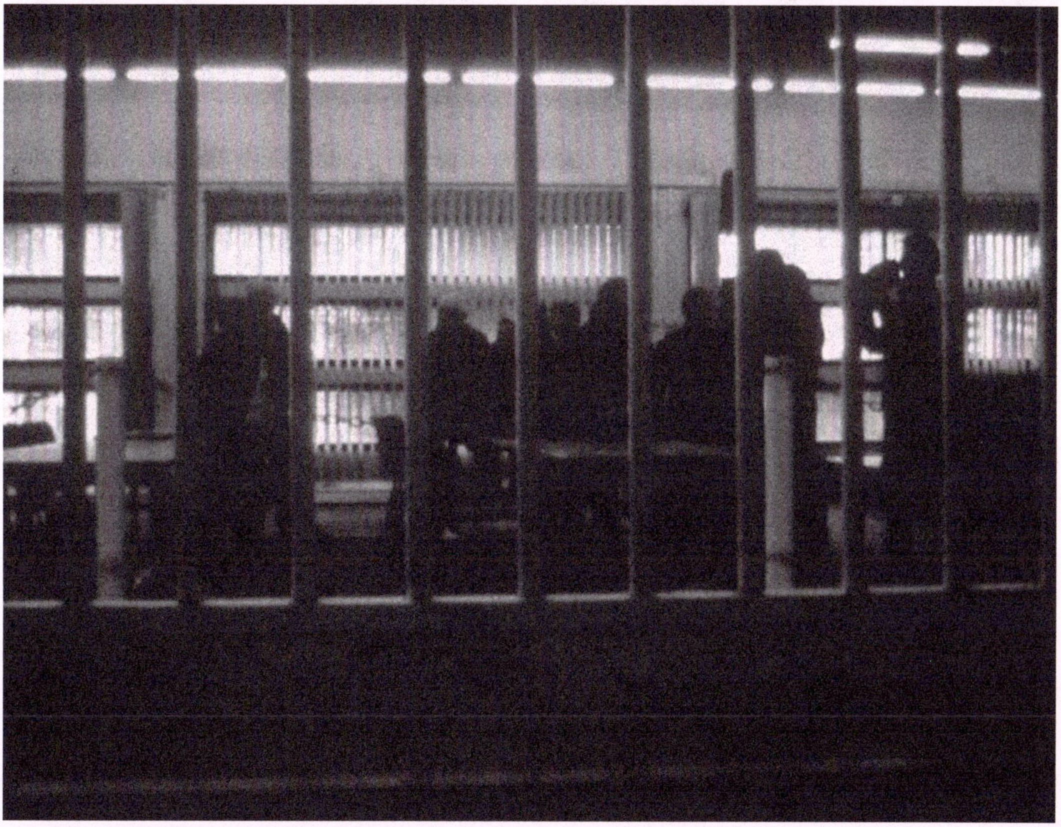

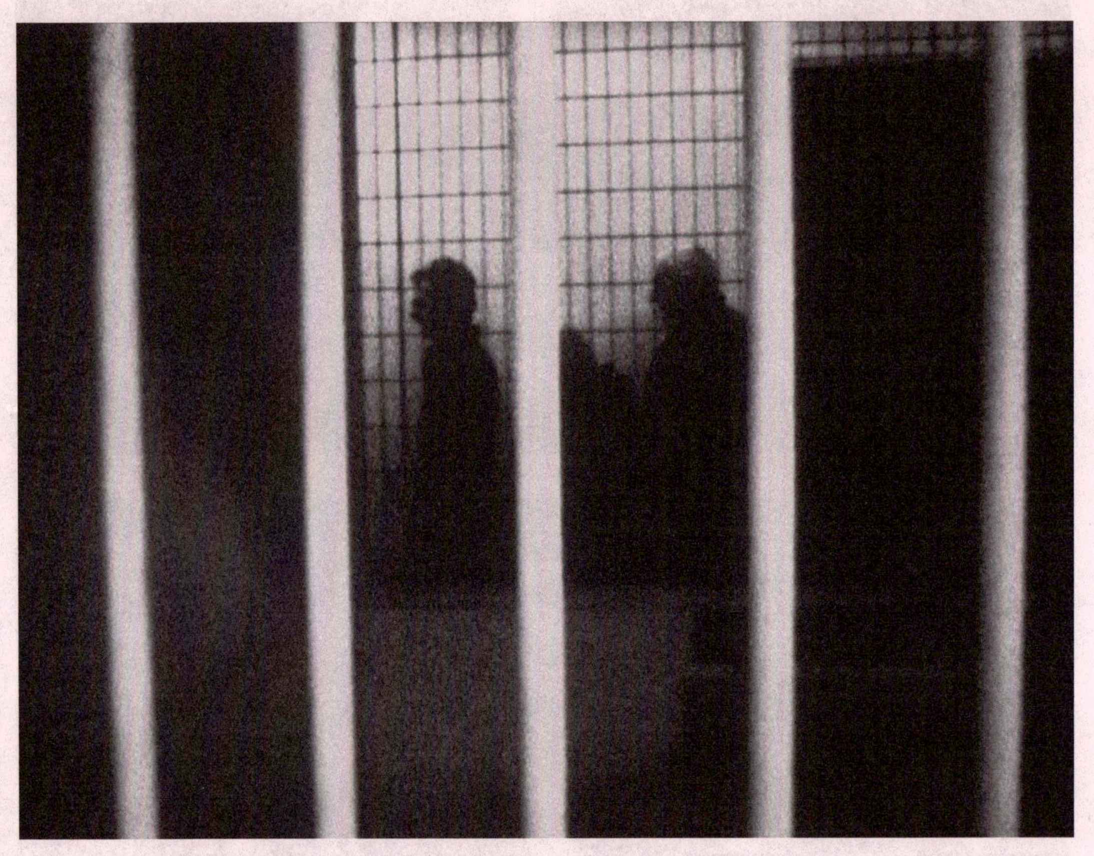

Long pause, courtroom noises, background noise, footsteps.

JUDGE

You are Marocco *[microphone noise]* Antonio I think.

MAROCCO

What?

JUDGE

Your name is Antonio, I think.

MAROCCO

Yes.

JUDGE

You are charged in a connected trial, so you are questioned here according to the formula of the code concerning the free questioning of defendants in a connected trial. Are you going to answer our questions?

MAROCCO

Of course.

Long pause, microphone noises, coughs from afar, papers turned.

JUDGE

You see, *[clears throat]* I wouldn't have told you, but some say that some of these people, irrespective of their alleged responsibilities, which is something this court will establish, worked towards the objective of ending terrorism, whereas you led a struggle against *dissociation*; and they see, from what it seems, in this document, in these declarations of yours before the court, they see a sort of thinking backwards: that is to say, Marocco doesn't come here to tell the truth, Marocco comes here to carry on his battle against people who dissociated themselves from armed struggle. This is the affirmation against you which was made this morning by the defendants.

PUBLIC PROSECUTOR

Can I propose to have Marocco's letter read out?

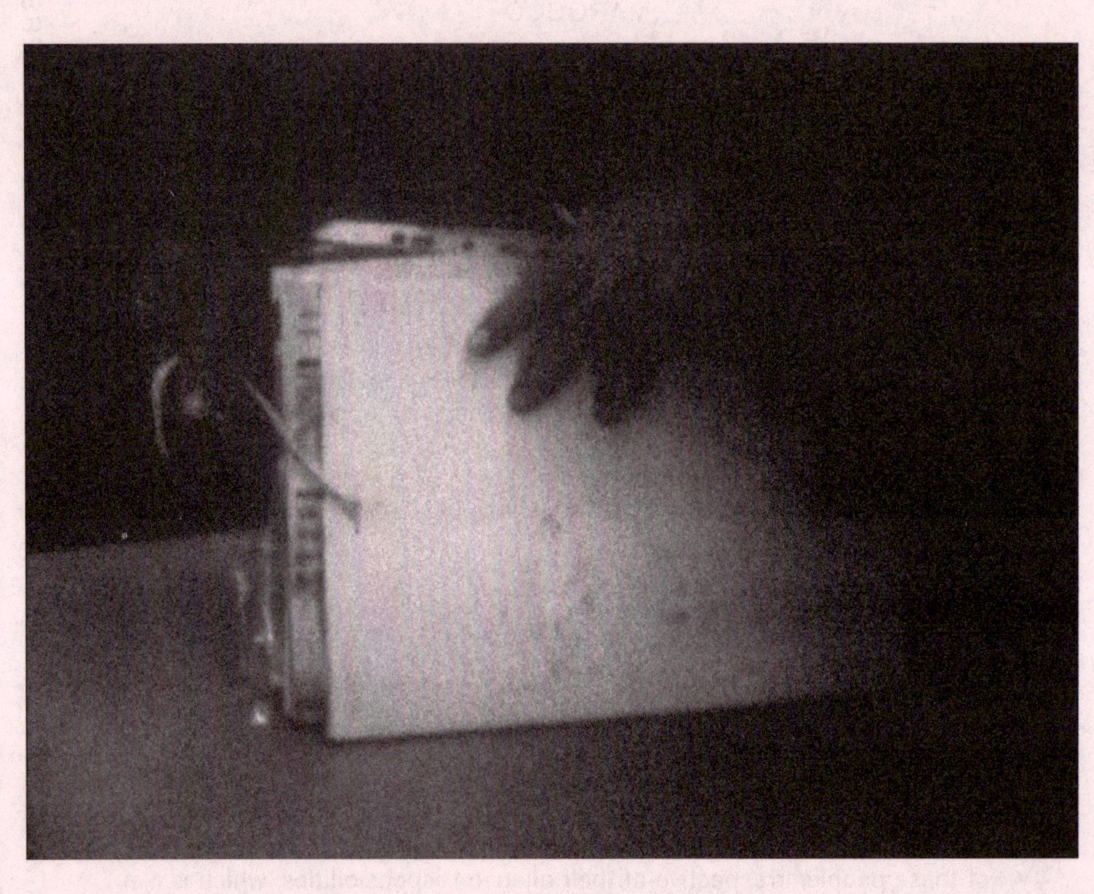

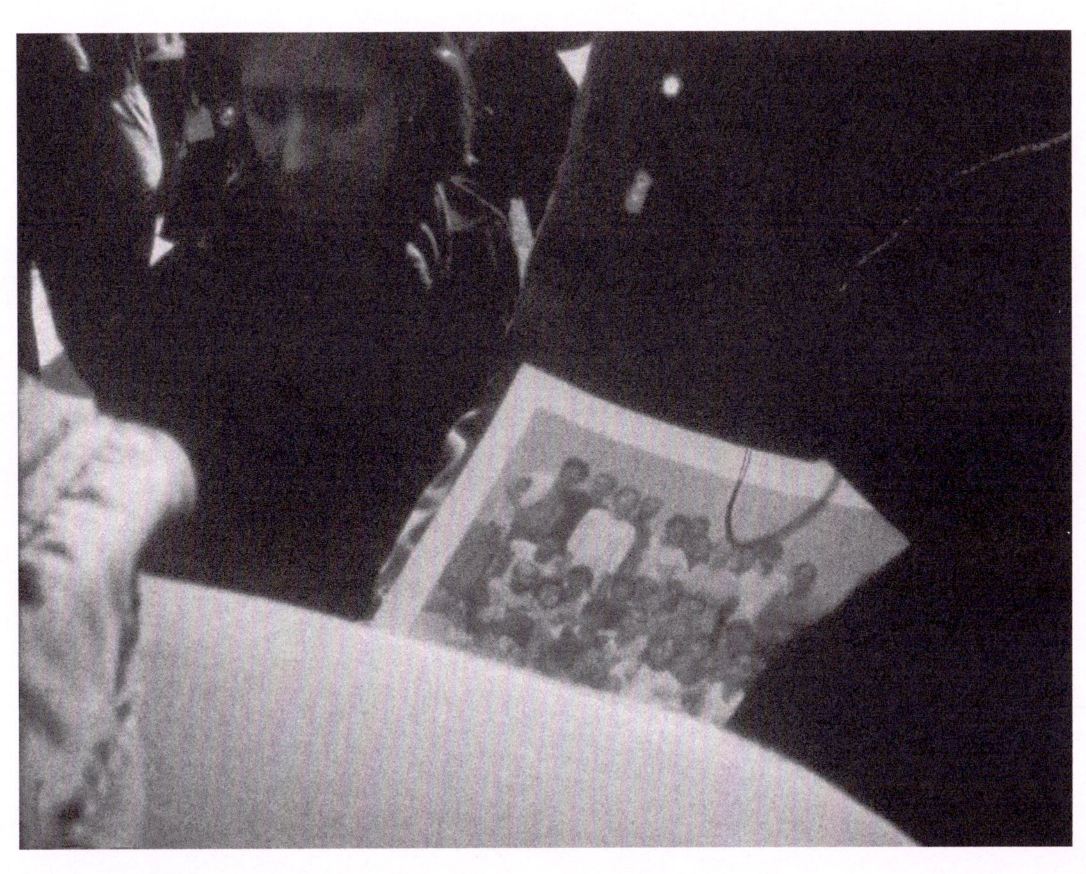

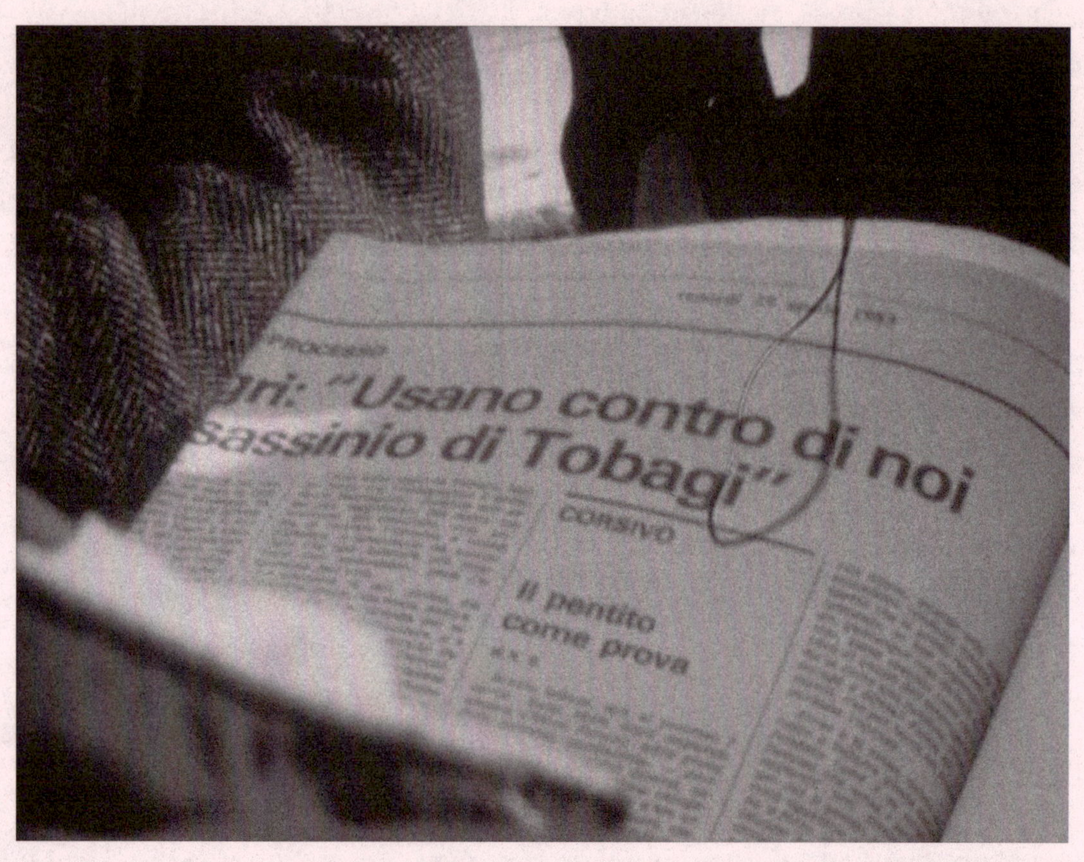
Processo
ori: "Usano contro di noi
sassinio di Tobagi"
CORSIVO
Il pentito
come prova

Long pause, microphone noises, background noise, voices away from the microphone.

JUDGE

Please ....

UNKNOWN

So what happened?

JUDGE

If the defendants want to leave, make sure they go if they so wish. Look. Carry on.

All the defendants leave the courtroom in protest.

Brief pause, diffuse voices.

JUDGE

Bailiff, wait a minute.

Long pause, room noise, opening door, diffuse voices, coughs.

UNKNOWN

Come in.

JUDGE

You, Casirati, are here heard as a defendant in a connected trial. Do you wish to answer our questions?

CASIRATI

Yes.

JUDGE

Casirati, we should start from a bit of a distance, before I ask you if you wish to confirm your questionings or not ...

CASIRATI

Yes ....

JUDGE

... I would like to know when you met Fioroni and how you met him.

CASIRATI

[throughout the questioning he replies with an arrogant and defiant tone] Ask Fioroni, or read the proceedings again.

PUBLIC PROSECUTOR

President, I'm tired *[microphone noises]* and would like to remind Casirati, especially on these last questions asked by the plaintiff counsel and the answers he gave, that he must finally acknowledge his task here before you, because it's true that he is not obliged to take an oath, but I think he is still required to tell the truth. And this is not a commitment you only make before the law, Casirati, but before your conscience. Why am I telling you this? Because there are two fundamental issues and surely we cannot just be referred back to the records of the proceedings, because the records, as you very well know, do not display univocal statements and consistent declarations from the beginning. *[raising his voice]* Why can't you refer back to the proceedings? Because you never said such things. Call on your conscience and finally say all you must say. *[screams]* Really tell the whole truth because it seems that this truth can never emerge in this trial and there have been no less than three hearings. Call on your conscience, because you can't say I refer to the records, because you never said those things on record. Or what you said was very different then.

CASIRATI

I've already told you.

PUBLIC PROSECUTOR

Told whom? You haven't already said it. Then repeat it if you've already said it.

JUDGE

People. *[unclear]*

PUBLIC PROSECUTOR

[interrupting Casirati] Casirati, tell the truth, for .... *[raising his voice]* I beg you, tell the truth!

JUDGE

In other words, the public prosecutor also put before you a question of conscience. The public prosecutor has contested some contradictions and incongruences in your various statements.

Short pause, room noises, coughs.

148

DEFENCE LAWYER

President, *[clears throat]* I'd like to know from Casirati whether it's true that from France he wrote a letter to the investigating judge Caselli, where he charged himself with the murder of the lawyer Croce.

CASIRATI

It's in the records.

DEFENCE LAWYER

I know whether it's in the records. I would like to know whether you confirm that you wrote this letter.

CASIRATI

Yes, I wrote it for a very simple reason: so that I would receive an arrest warrant in France to be able to stay in France and ask for political asylum, and then be able to escape from France.

DEFENCE LAWYER

Do you know Cesare Bianchi?

CASIRATI

Cesare Bianchi?

DEFENCE LAWYER

Yes. Isn't he ....

CASIRATI

I think it was me.

DEFENCE LAWYER

What do you mean it was you? *[laughing]* If you could explain this to the court ....

CASIRATI

You explain it to the court; you know it better than I do.

DEFENCE LAWYER

[laughing] Bah ... you know ... Cesare Bianchi was not me.

CASIRATI

If you know, you explain it to the court, no?

DEFENCE LAWYER

Well, if it's true that you were detained in Bergamo prison in 1980, under the false name of Cesare Bianchi .... Casirati, is this true?

CASIRATI

But you are saying it ....

DEFENCE LAWYER

No, I am asking it, it's not a statement.

CASIRATI

How is it not?

DEFENCE LAWYER

No, I wanted to know whether it's true that you were detained in Bergamo prison under the false name of Cesare Bianchi.

CASIRATI

Well, ask the head of prison, eh?

DEFENCE LAWYER

But you said that you were Cesare Bianchi, excuse me.

CASIRATI

Eh ....

DEFENCE LAWYER

Well, then I ask you something I cannot ask the head of prison, is it true that in March 1980 ....

CASIRATI

[interrupting lawyer] I can't see the absurdity of this question. To cover up what, how and why, since we had been in a state of emergency for some time, and then they hid me under a false name, as they hid all the others?

DEFENCE LAWYER

All the others who?

CASIRATI

All the other *pentiti*. Under false names. If it's useful to you as the defence, I don't know. And I wish to confirm everything and answer you no more.

DEFENCE LAWYER

One more question for Casirati. Casirati said that he refuses to engage in cross-examinations. I would like to know from Casirati whether this refusal applies to Fioroni's hypotheses too.

JUDGE

Is the question understood?

CASIRATI

Yes, I perfectly understand it.

JUDGE

What does it mean? What is your answer? If Fioroni were here would you be available to engage in cross-examinations with Fioroni?

CASIRATI

I would have nothing against it but I'd find it useless.

JUDGE

Well, take a seat.

Long pause, room noises, coughs, diffuse voices.

MARELLI

[reads] Why doesn't Fioroni come? Few seem to show a real interest in publicly asking the reasons behind the decision of Carlo Fioroni—the first *pentito* in Italy—seemingly taken a long time ago, to not appear before the trial. That is, to ask whether his repentance was sincere or not. Fioroni's conscience, in inverted commas, became the issue, a conscience that unfolded throughout the years with the only linear aim to protract the havoc done back then against everything and everyone for his own personal gain, subsequently deceiving everything and everyone through that accusation and now jeering from his safe beaches both truth and morality. It is not the intimacy of Fioroni's conscience that needed to be questioned, but the truth of his statements, and this is what we have always cried for in our desperate isolation. Nonetheless, now the public trial has been going on for many months and, to anyone who has been following it, the real reason why Fioroni does not come to the Foro Italico is crystal clear. Even the public prosecutor of the 7th of April trial, though regarding the exceptional laws of the state of emergency as unexceptionable, has expressed a moral discomfort. His lawyer, the ineffable Gentili, abandoned him, and the press, with some praiseworthy exceptions, tends to silence it all, renewing, with Montanelli, the ethical stance of blocking one's nose with political style. Fioroni then is the salary of fear. No, sirs, it's all simpler and graver: Fioroni is a pure and simple national bamboozler.

Signed by all the defendants of the 7th of April.

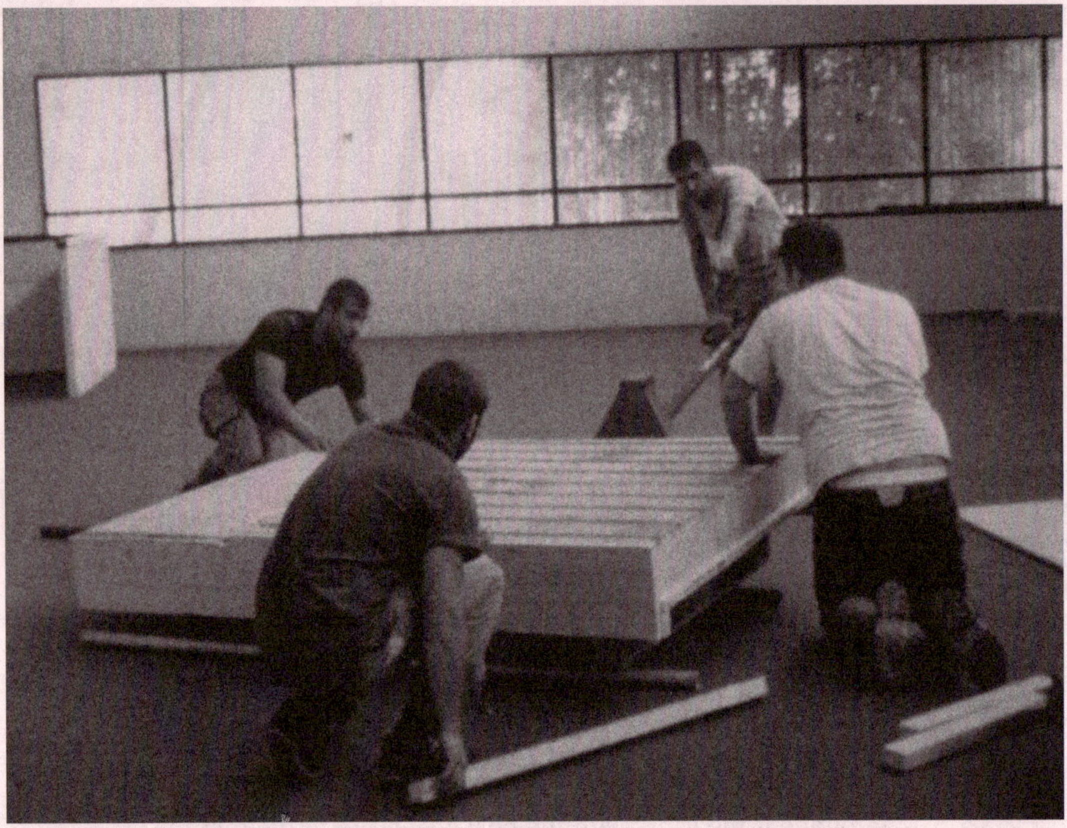

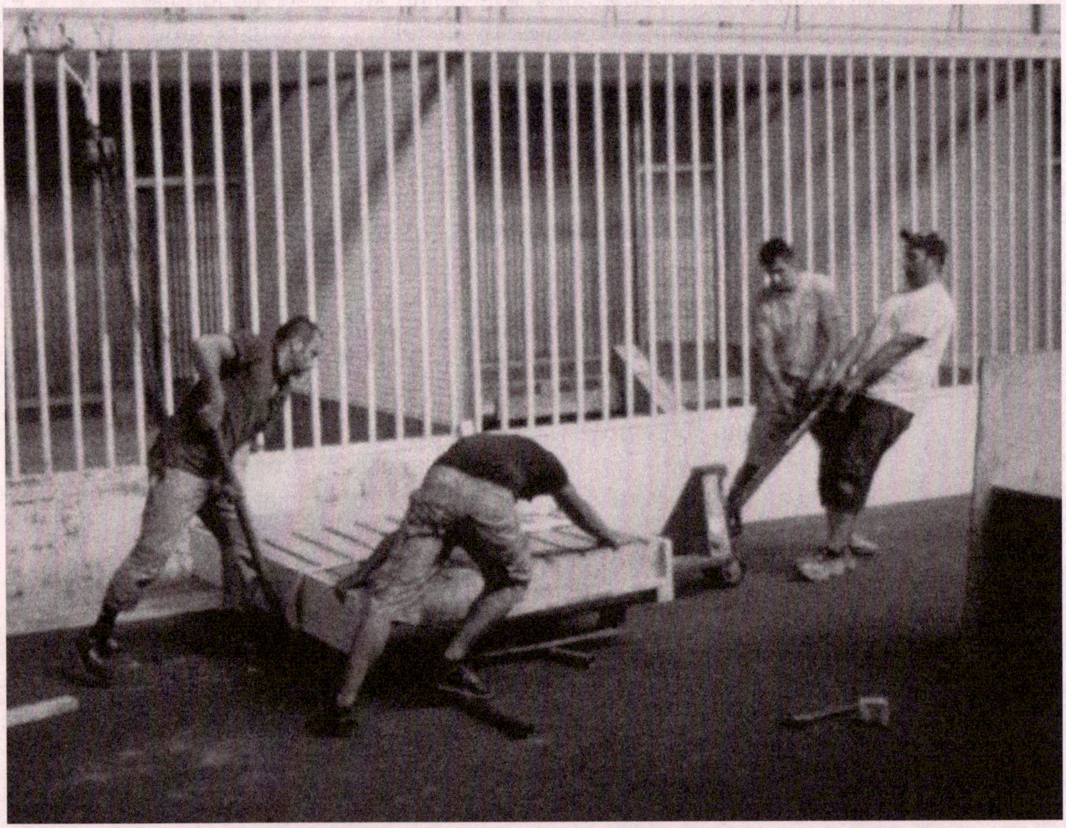

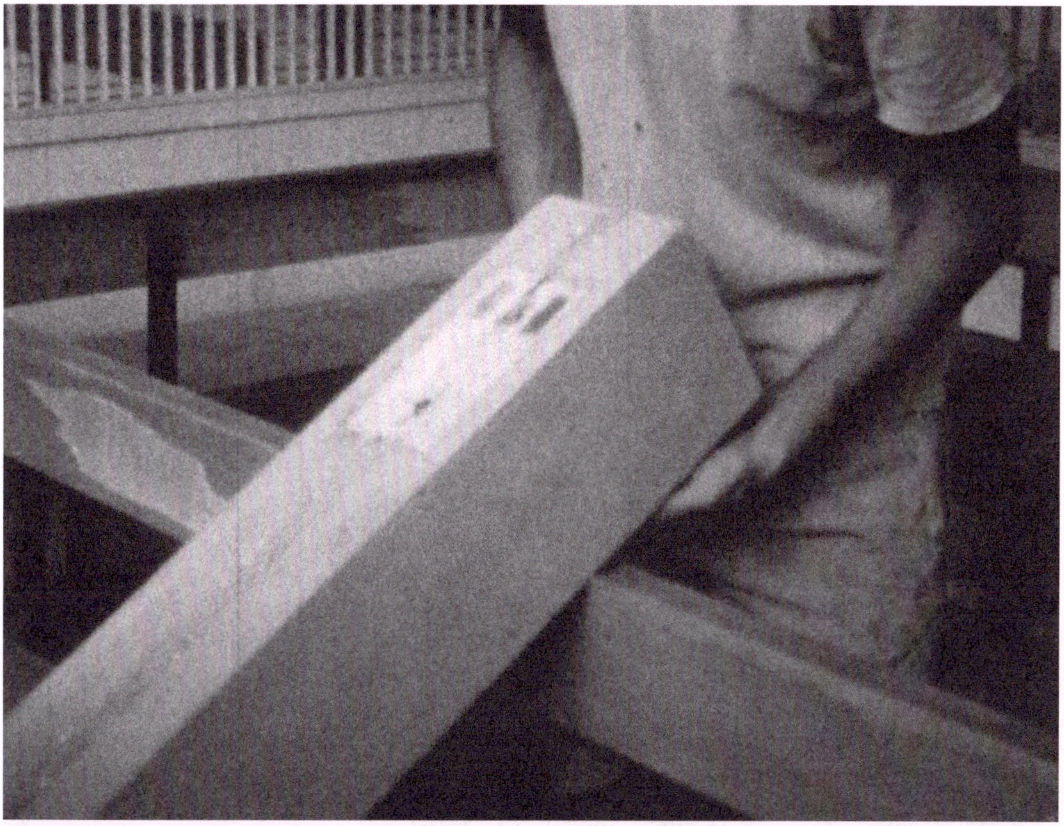

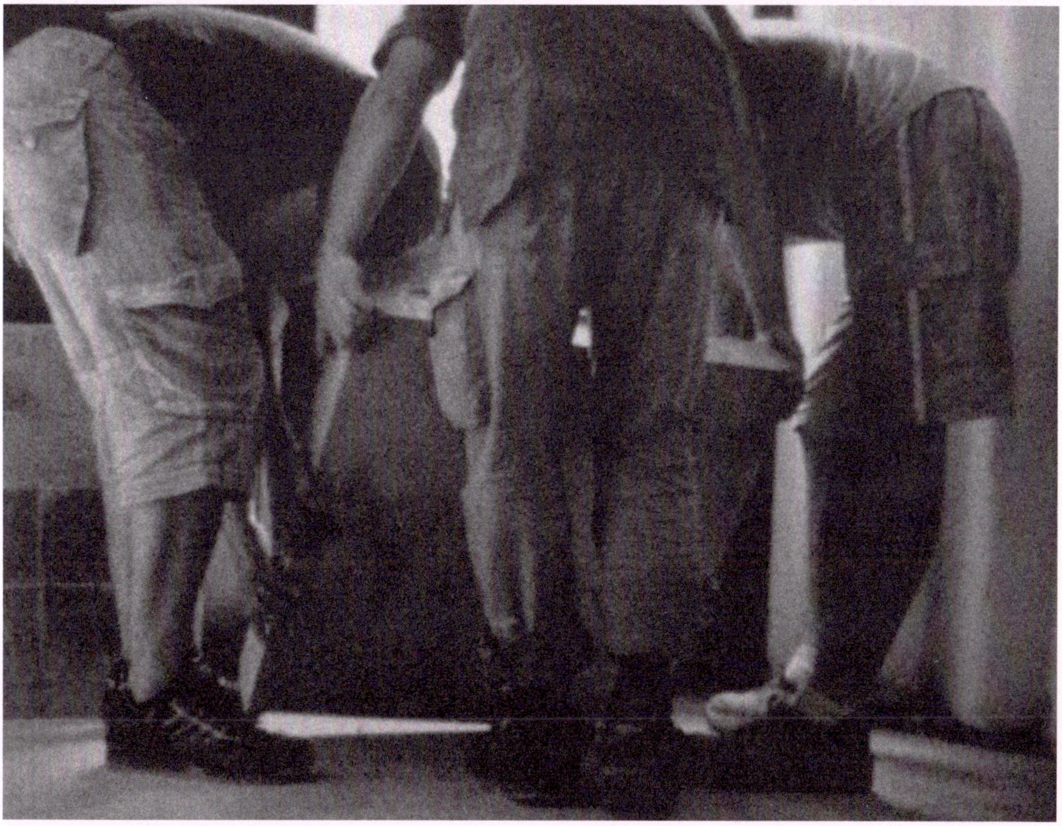

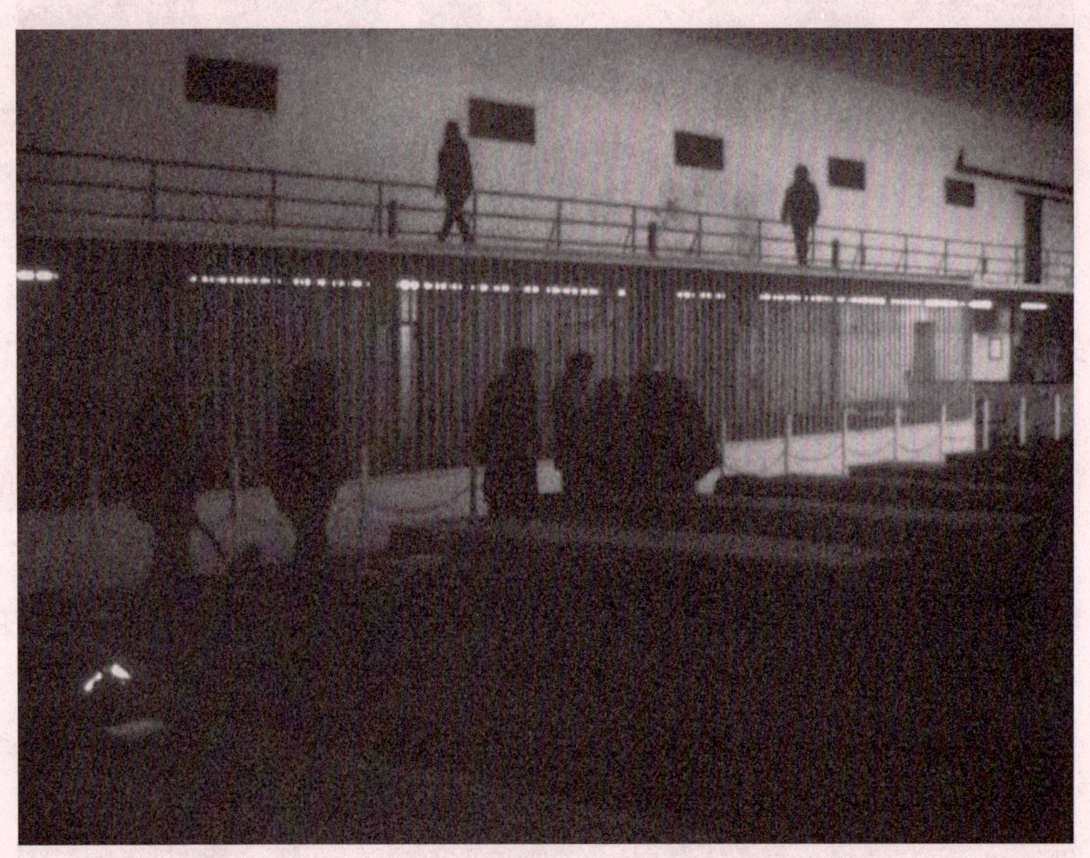

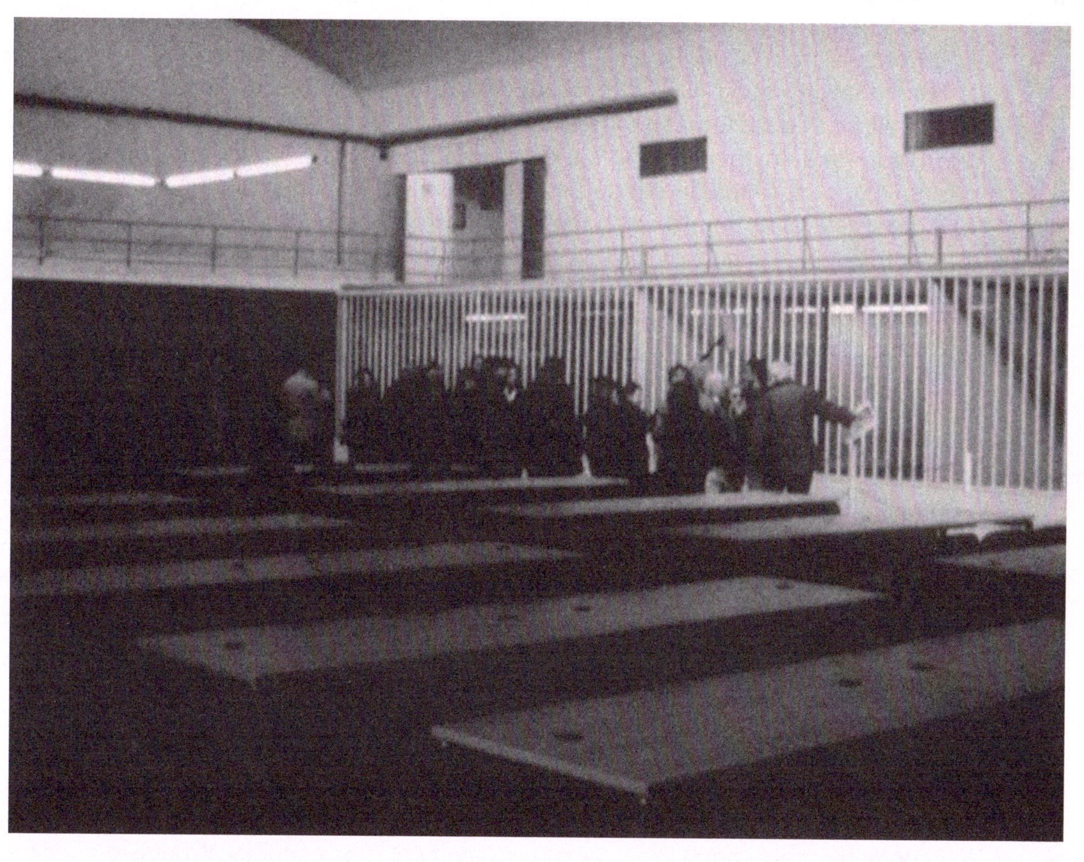

Long pause, room noises, background voices, microphone noise.

DEFENCE LAWYER

President. It's clear that as the defending counsel of a series of defendants in this proceeding, I oppose the reading of all the records of the proceedings .... The reading of which necessitates the consent of the defending counsel of the defendant. I would simply like to say a few words on this issue. One to the popular jury: for several days we have been talking about a reading of these records of the proceedings. First of all, what does it mean to read these proceedings? Because it's possible to read anything during a trial. What it means is very different from the concept of reading in common knowledge. It means giving procedural relevance to a record, that in and of itself would have none due to the lack of a pretext for this relevance. In other words, we ask for or do not oppose the reading of the records of Fioroni because there is no pretext for the relevance for these records that could be a confirmation of these from said witness. Then we will see, and at this point, sirs, if you must evaluate the possibility of a reading irrespective of the content of Fioroni's declarations, but in relation to Fioroni's position in the whole of the hearing, well, sirs, then you must go a little deeper with respect to the declarations presented to you by the head of police yesterday. Because Fioroni's credibility changes a great deal depending on whether he ran away on his own, whether he was helped, whether he escaped legitimately or not, whether he was given a false or a real passport. You were told that Fioroni left with a false passport and that this falls under the general directives imparted by the prime minister for the protection of *pentiti*. But sirs, here we must hear from the prime minister of the time, the home secretary of the time. What general directives were imparted so as to lead to committing a crime? Is there a provision in our court system that legitimates the administrative authorities to release false documents to cover up *pentiti*? Where is this written, gentlemen of this court? Who gives this faculty to these people? What provision gives them this permission to create false documents? I therefore ask, gentlemen of this court, that ... first of all, I oppose the reading not only of Fioroni's but of any other testimony and I oppose the reading of Carlo Fioroni's in particular.

Long pause, noises in the courtroom, coughs.

PUBLIC PROSECUTOR

Mr President, I certainly did not express my moral discomfort, dear Spazzali, as to the alleged validity of the accusations Fioroni put forward. After all, the whole of my comportment in the hearings of this courtroom was aimed at verifying the validity of these accusations also through the questioning of the defendants. Ha, because let us not forget that if there is a relevant voice in this trial that has demonstrated the validity of a large part, if not of all, the accusations or accusatory statements and testimonies, call them as you wish, of Fioroni, well, this voice came from the defendants themselves.

Long pause, room noises, rustle of paper.

PUBLIC PROSECUTOR

[with a tone of annoyance and assertion] We jump, President, we jump over many issues. *[brief pause]* Even *Rosso* publishes the national coordination on 5 June 1976. It publishes a document entitled "Autonomia Operaia Against the Elections. Let's Create Counterpower, Organization Against Elections." *[screaming]* Elections are a fact of democracy, they do not want elections! *[screaming louder, the echo resounding in the courtroom, now rallying]* And yet Negri accepted the election to Parliament that the beautiful rules of democracy offered him, that same democracy that allowed him to escape to avoid this trial and evade your justice. The elections. *[brief pause]* Well, anyhow, aside from ... long-winded locutions. There is a verb, here, that is "to steal." There is a verb that is "to shoot." Eh! Here to kill the cockroaches infesting our ... but what's here though? Who are now the cockroaches? They are no longer the fascists, but all those who ... the social democrats! Amongst whom must be included the communists. *[short pause, breaths and starts calmly]* The paper, Mr President, as I was telling you, publishes the full text of this document, entitled *[mockingly]* "The General Tendency," always by that Negri. But we cannot read this document, suffice it to say, well, let me just draw your attention to the passages that underline the crucial relevance of these papers, the radio and the organizational process of Autonomia, because we are talking about Radio Sherwood. *[screaming again]* And then, Mr President, the litmus test! The litmus test! Because Mr President we have a document in our records, seized from Ferrari Bravo! Actually, the diary of Ferrari Bravo, where, handwritten, we find expressions such as: "Re-vo-lu-tio-na-ry council," "organizational building of Soviet style autonomy," "leaping from the network of collectives to moments of centralization," "organization as a tool of expansion," "centralization is a leap from one hundred flowers blooming to one hundred nuclei," "centralizing and stabilizing the moments

157

of counter-power that power tries to break down," "the importance of the national paper, the radio, etc., propaganda, armed propaganda." Eh? These are the declarations of Ferrari Bravo. So then, when Pozzato comes to tell us that he heard rumours about a revolutionary council, what has he come to say? *[raising his voice, his words echoing across the room]* A lie? Or the truth? *[brief pause]* And what is the most important deadline promoted and organized by the autonomist organisms tasked with this national coordination throughout 1976? It is the national conference, as is written, of Autonomia Operaia Organizzata, which took place in Rome in 19–21 of March. As can be drawn from the respective diaries, Mr President, of Negri and Ferrari Bravo, we can see it in their own diaries! The diaries! The diaries seized! In the proceedings! In the announcement of the paper *Rosso* issue seven of 13 March 1976, we read: "Today violence is the slogan of the masses and the vanguards. Workers' violence in class struggle now borders on the violence of class war." A concept that is exemplified on the last page of the publication through a series of photographs showing moments of a recent guerrilla act of organized autonomy in Milan city centre, characterized by the use of firearms! Roadblocks! Arson! Devastation! This, you must remember this, popular jury, when we will speak of armed insurrection against the powers of the state. The pro-movement! You must remember this! *[screaming louder]* You must emit your memory because this will be the historical memory of the judiciary! We have infinity of reports with mentions of roadblocks, arson, devastation, shootings and fire! *[brief pause, then with solemn intonation]* I want to weigh my words, Mr President, because this is a historic moment, this decision on a crime of promoting the armed insurrection against the powers of the State. *[papers rustling, then he resumes raising his voice, which echoes in the courtroom]* Having said this, Mr President, you must let me conclude by saying that this has not been a trial of ideas. This has been a trial of facts! *[calmly]* Let us ... it's obvious that I'm emotional and raise my voice before such facts. *[screaming]* These facts! These are facts we have debated in this trial, President! Not opinions! Not ideas! *[mockingly]* Here we debated murders, robberies, theft, weapons, weapons, weapons and weapons! Read this charge again. I leave it to you Mr President: it's full of armament! This charge that you cannot even imagine .... The armament we have amongst the charges. But this is what you have to take into account. *[hitting the desk]* What set-up? What framing of the trial? *[resumes a normal tone]* Mr President, I've finished. I've ended my efforts. I don't ask you for an exemplary sentence. No. I ask you for a sentence of truth and justice. Thank you Mr President.

Long pause, room noises, footsteps, silence.

1977 represents a break with the previous tradition. It is the most radical rupture which—to a point—we are still living. What happened? That a movement of struggle, which was anything but marginal, exploded. It has been said many times that it was the peons of the *bidonvilles* of the peripheral neighbourhoods who revolted against the economic crisis. Not at all. As we were interpreting and living 1977, it became clear to us that this was a social subject that was anything but marginal: that, on the contrary, was rich with learning, rich with knowledge, rich with productive capacity; a subject that was probably central in terms of productivity, or that would become central, that was borne out of the [capitalist] restructuring processes. It was the new productive subject that emerged from the [capitalist] restructuring processes. It was a rich subject that knew many things; that knew how to become self-entrepreneurial. A powerful subject, a subject that was anything but marginal. To make the example of the University of Rome, they often were the precarious intellectual workers, they were the workers who even if they were working, attended classes at university to accumulate sociality, information, knowledge. What happened? We thought—just to make a key example—that it wasn't true that the restructuring of production, and therefore unemployment as well as the work mobility that it produces, was in itself a bad thing: it could be that this mobility, this precarious work, contained a strong element of workers' self-determination, of working-time flexibility, of choice with respect to life's times: given the richness that time represents. And this was a real scandal with respect to the themes of those days: with respect to the dogmas of the movement and the trade unions, who said that the main issue was the defence of the job no matter what and resistance to [capitalist] restructuring. We said: in restructuring, in mobility, there can be a different relation with self-determined work, in which the times of the working day are articulated around one's needs and exigencies. All of this to mention a fundamental theme of our reflections around this new attitude towards work: according to which in our view work was no longer seen as some kind of settled destiny which dictates that one starts working at twenty and stays in the same place until it is time to retire. The factory was no longer a life sentence: it was an episode in one's biography. *[coughing in the courtroom]* It was a circumscribed episode with respect to which the response was to escape, to try to move to more fulfilling jobs, to richer productive activities. We interpreted nomadism from job to job, precarious work, mobility as a potentially rich element about which we had to start pondering. This is the first great theme. And for the movement of those days that was a scandal. It was an element of rupture and discontinuity. We said: yes, informal work comes with poverty and exploitation. But we also said: informal work isn't necessarily that archaeological thing in which one works without machines, at very low technological levels. Maybe modern informal work begins to be the work of widespread electronics. Maybe informal work is an extraordinary opportunity to disentangle ourselves from the factory regime. And this is another great element that perhaps today sounds either obscure, or not very significant, or even banal, because many of these elements have subsequently been taken up even by popular newspapers. In those days it was a complete scandal within the movement. These were themes that were absolutely path breaking and scandalous themes. The other great theme was the discourse about the State: if in the first half of the 1970s the new social developments were linked to the classical Communist theme of seizing power—as I was saying before—what we questioned, with respect to what was concretely happening within the movement of 1977, was the very concept of seizing power, of political revolution. I don't know if I am managing to give you an idea of the scandal—with respect to a particular kind of environment, a particular kind of world, which was a world that was experiencing turmoil and struggles—represented by saying seizing power is a poor, miserable thing, let's abandon it. The idea of political revolution itself, the substitution of one kind of State management with another, of institutions with institutions, is a miserable idea that has no relation with the new social movements: critique of the concept of political revolution, critique of the concept of seizing power. We said: at best, with respect to power, for these new social movements there will be the problem of defending themselves from power, of growing by experimenting new forms of life and by keeping power at arm's length. In the debate of those days these were contradictory elements with respect to the commonplaces that circulated in the movement of 1977. But they were elements that were linked to the new experience that we were making.

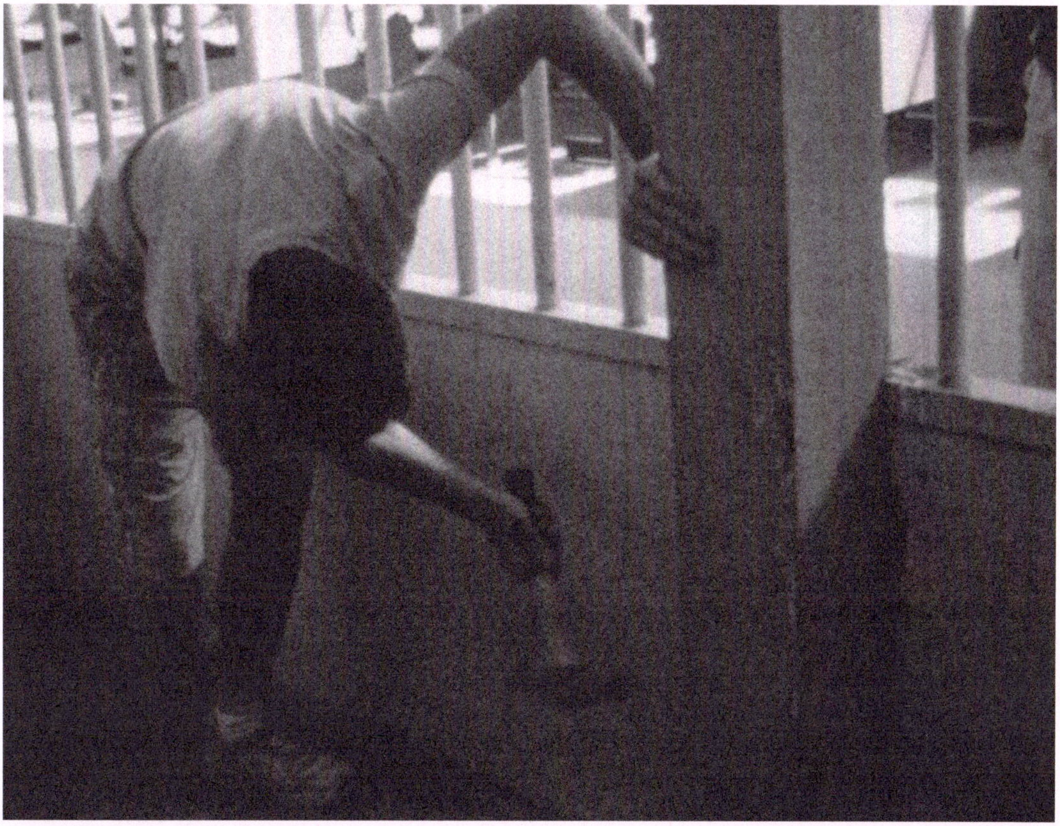

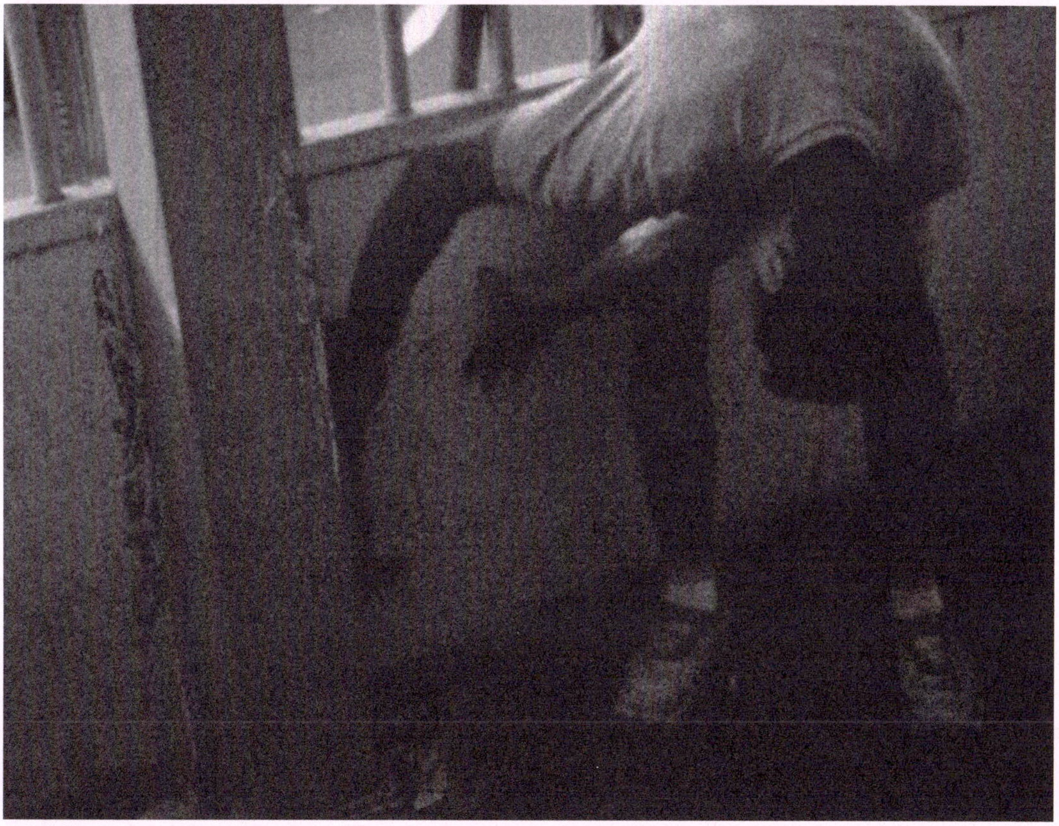

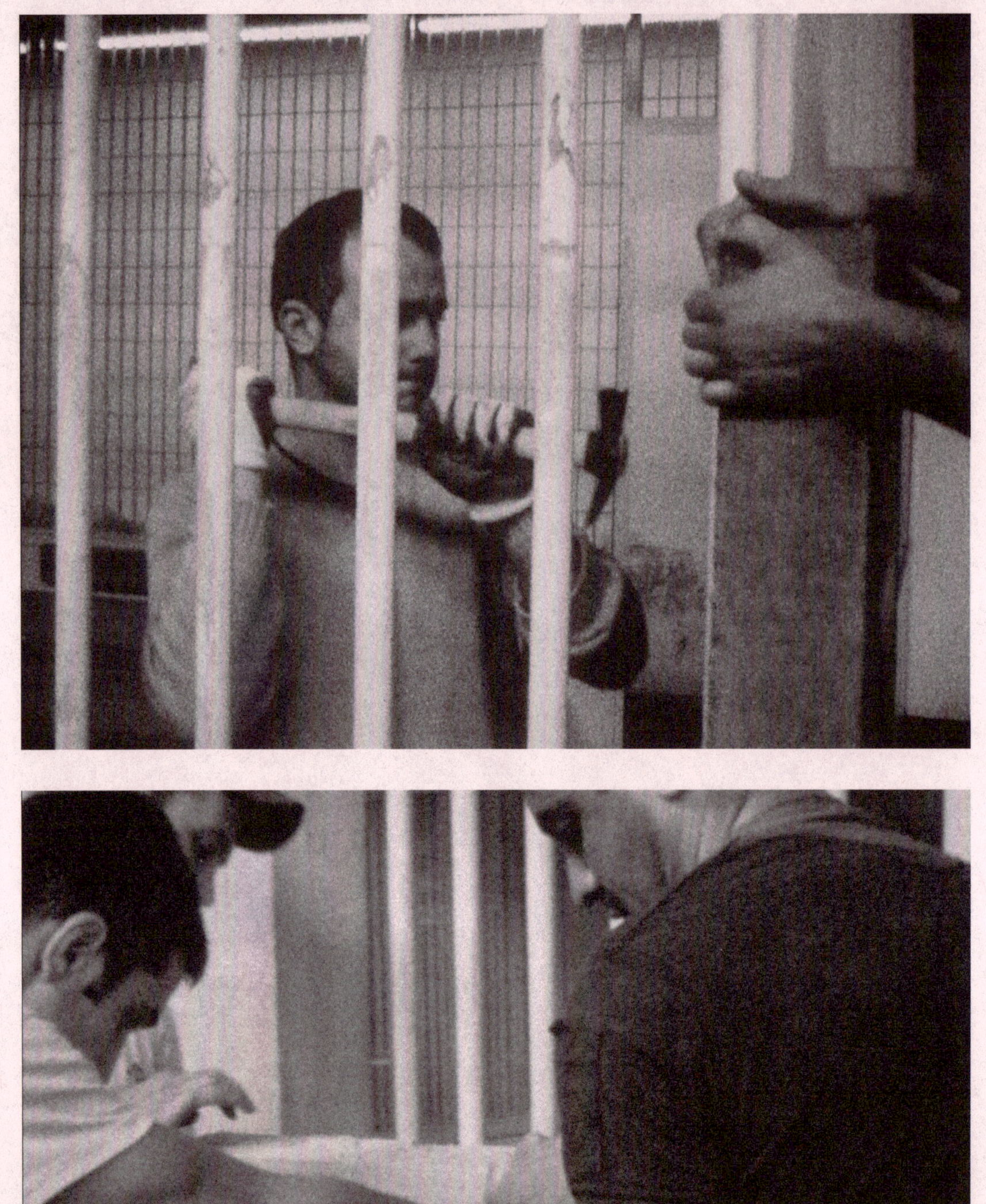

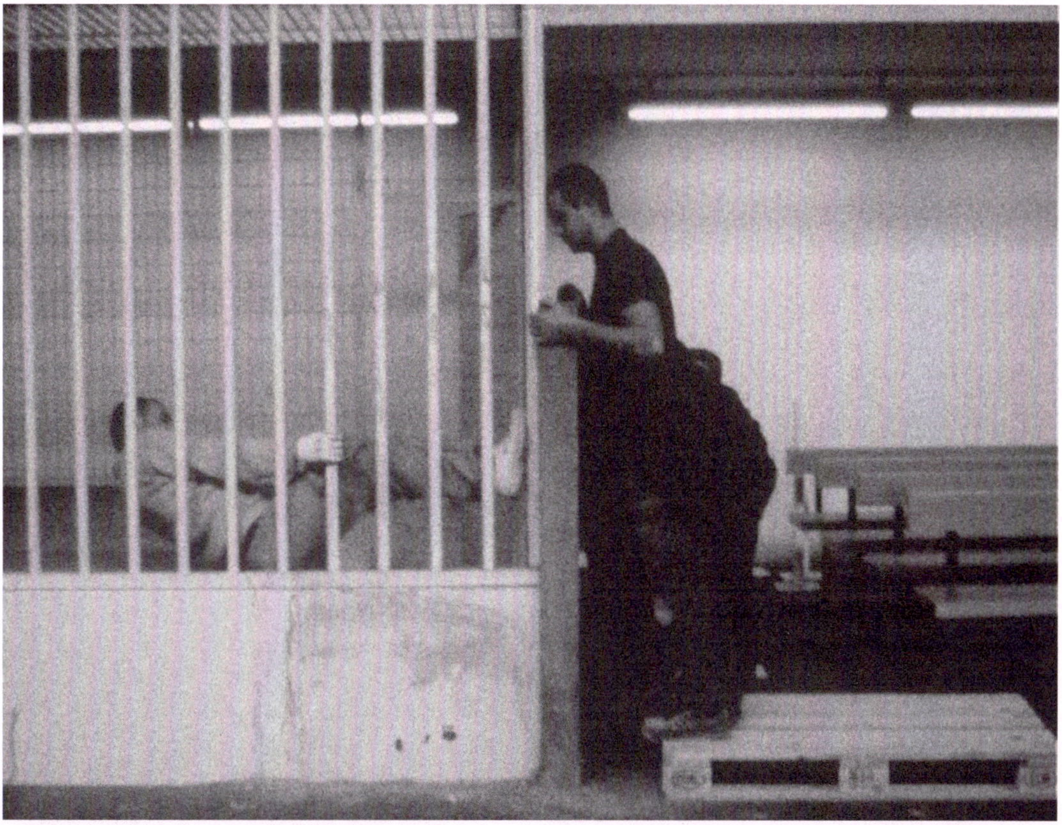

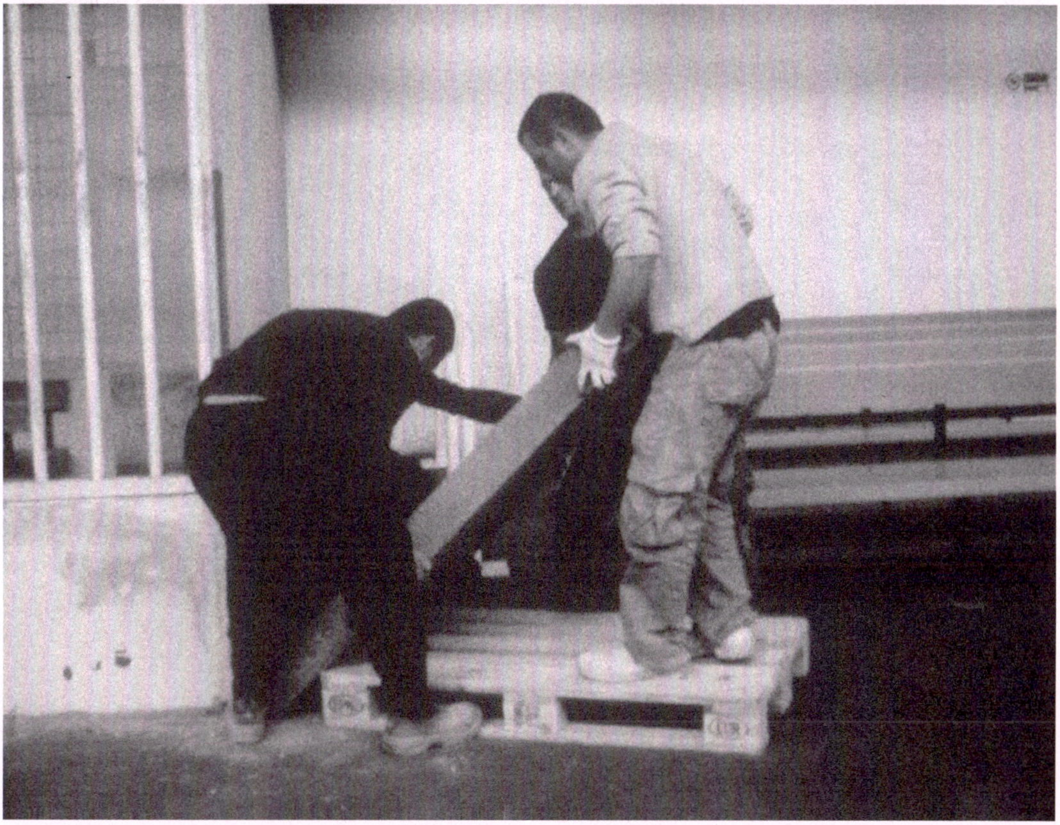

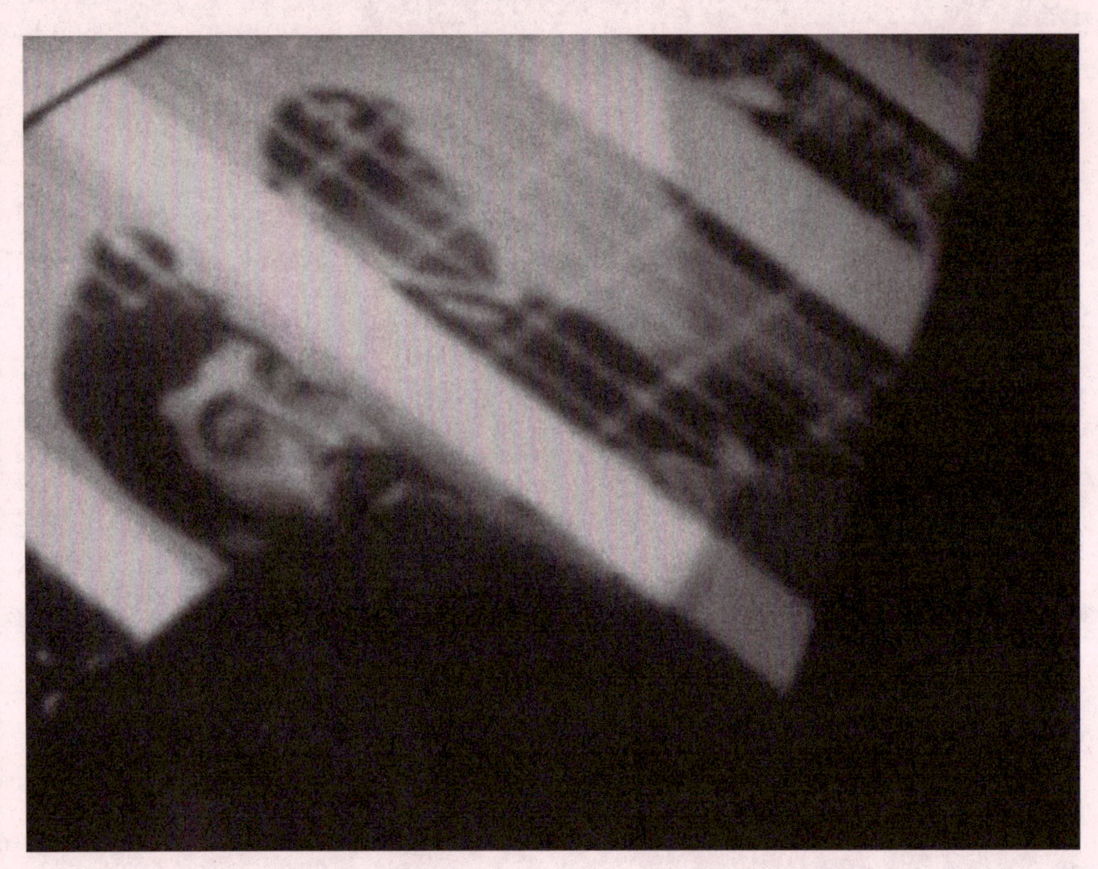

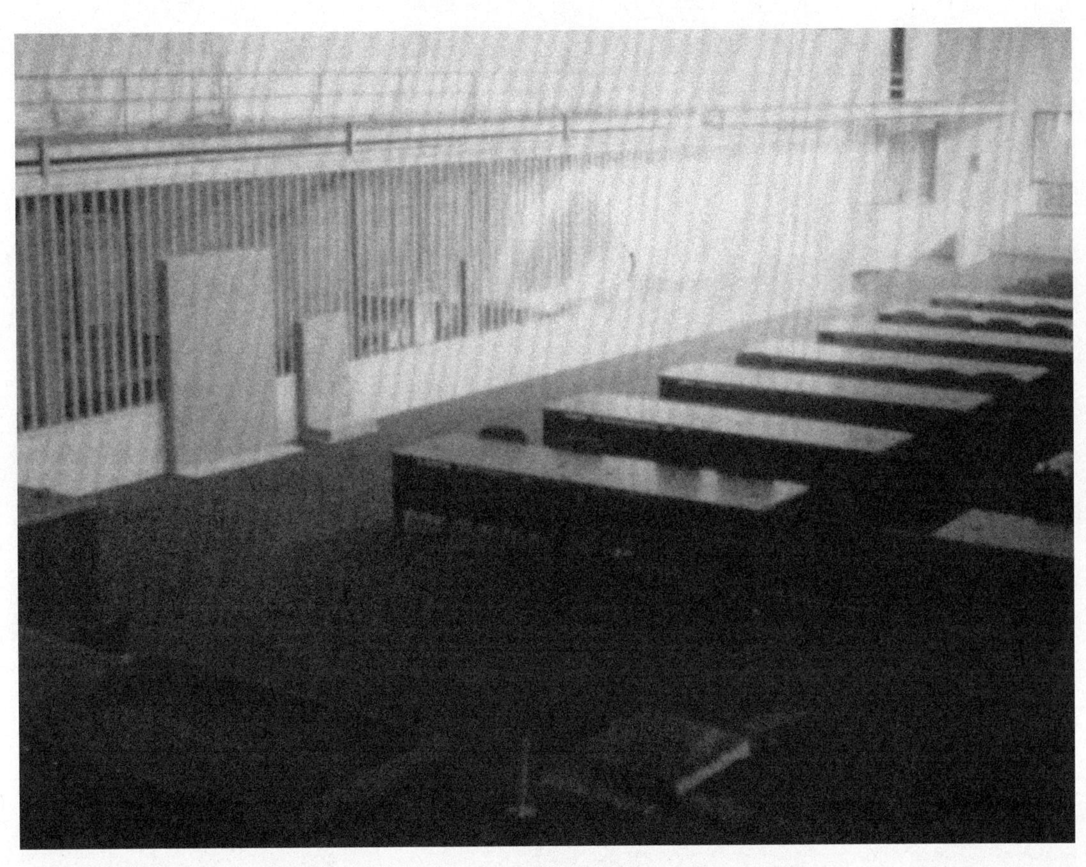

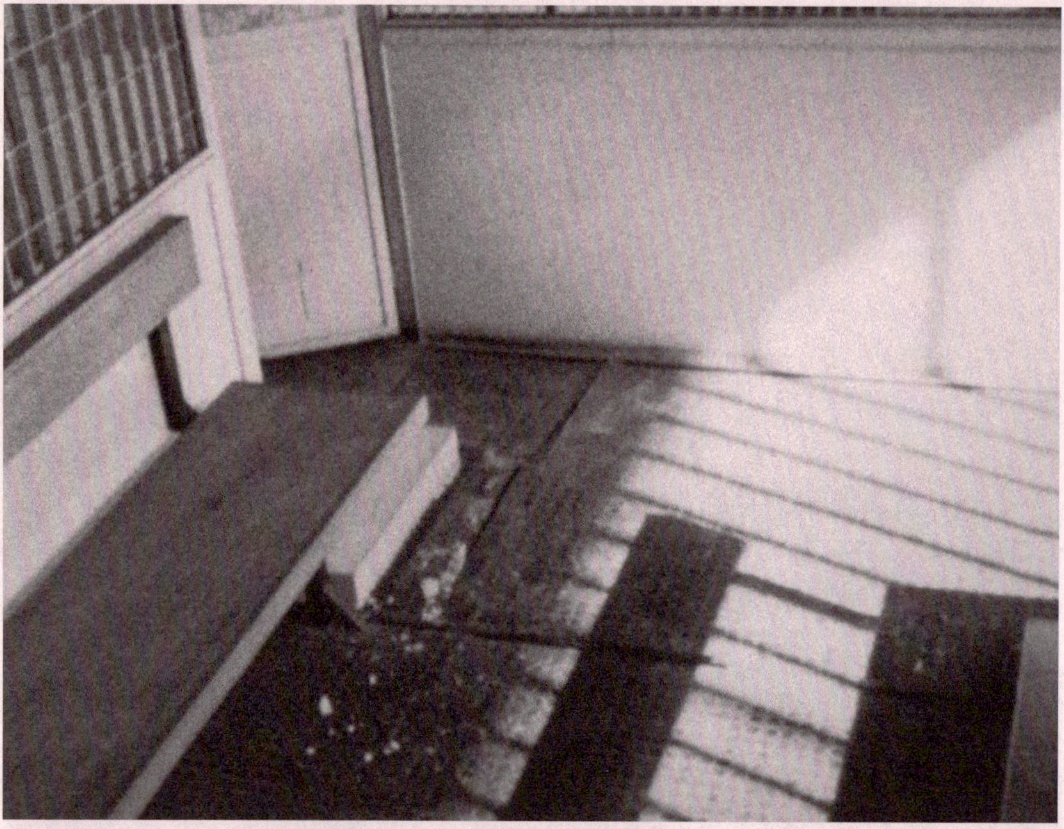

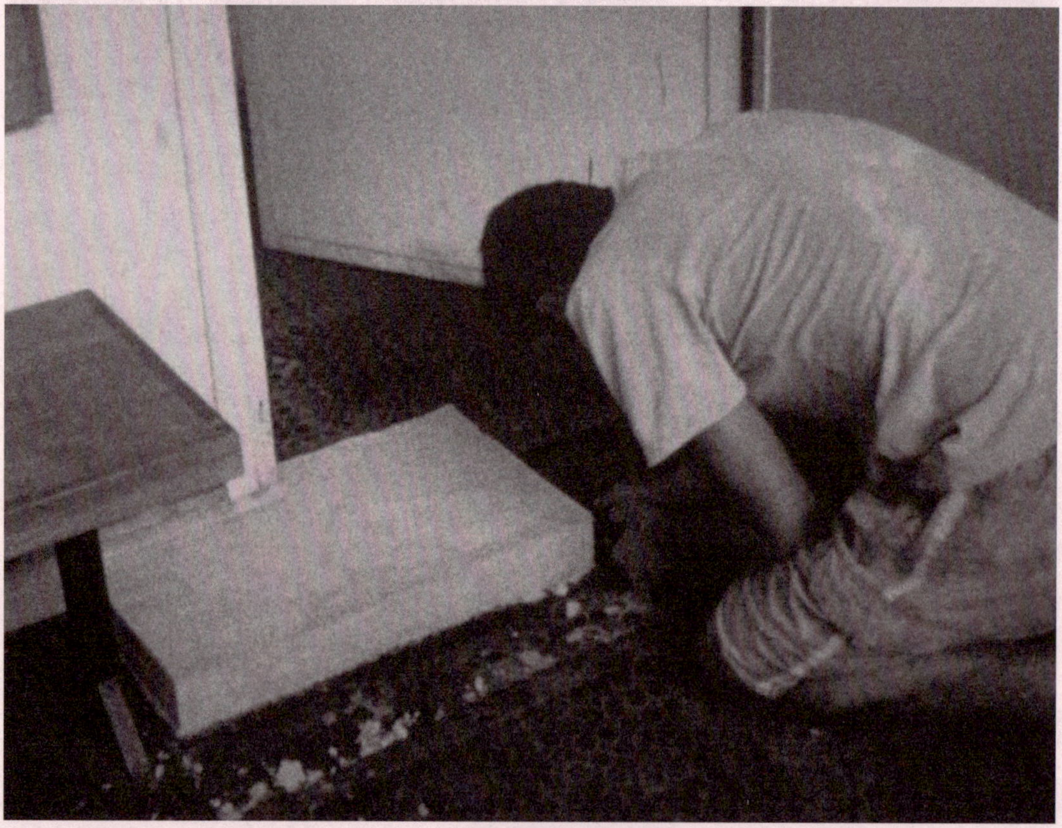

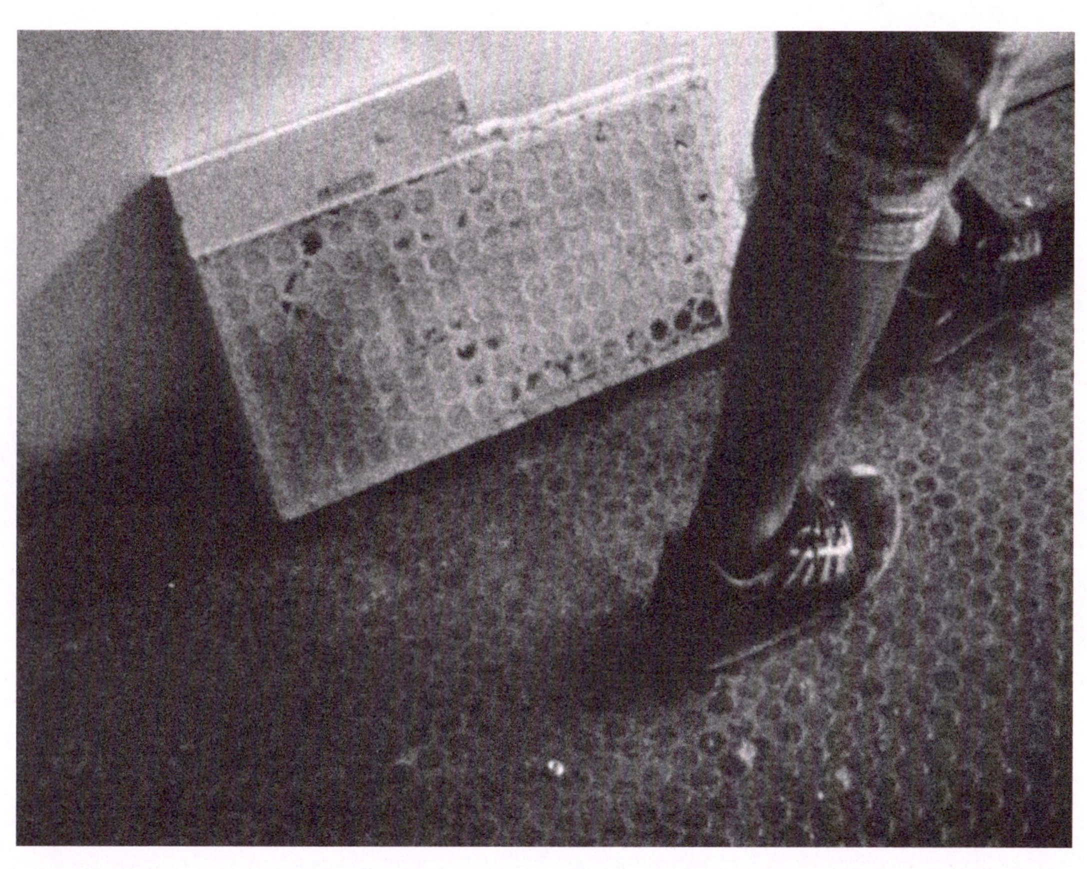

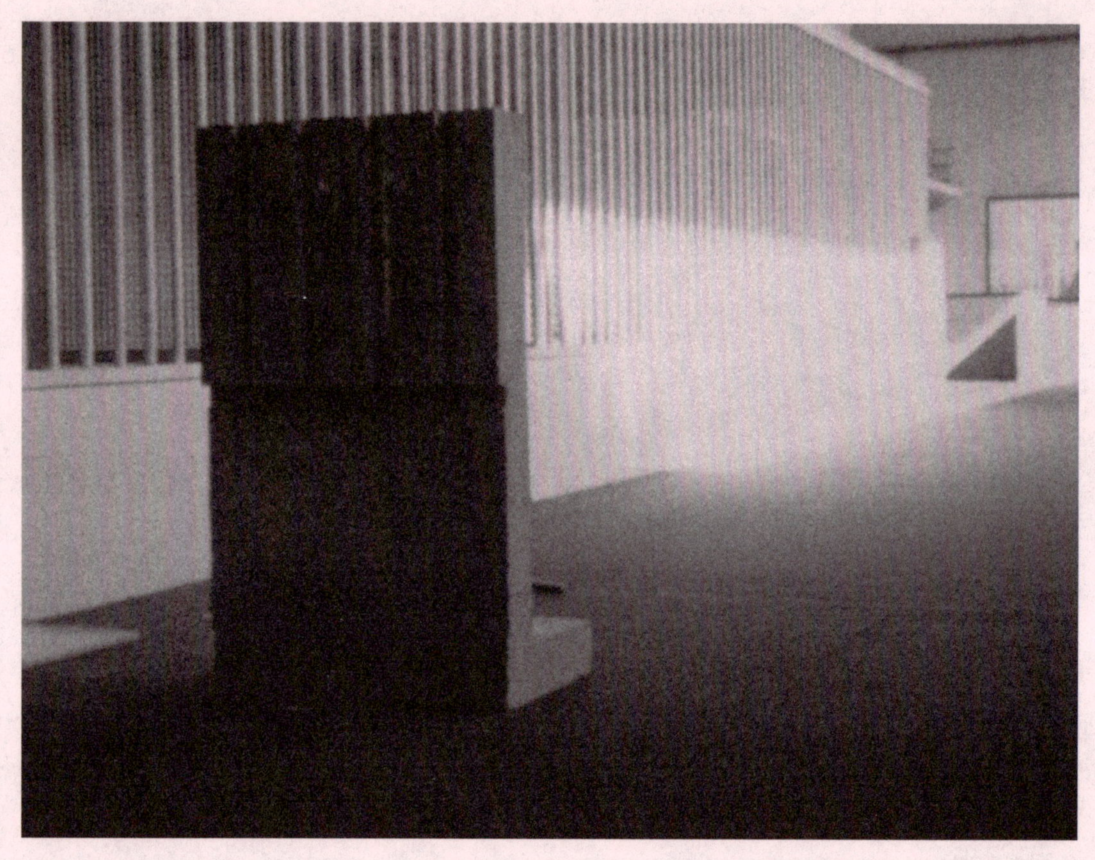

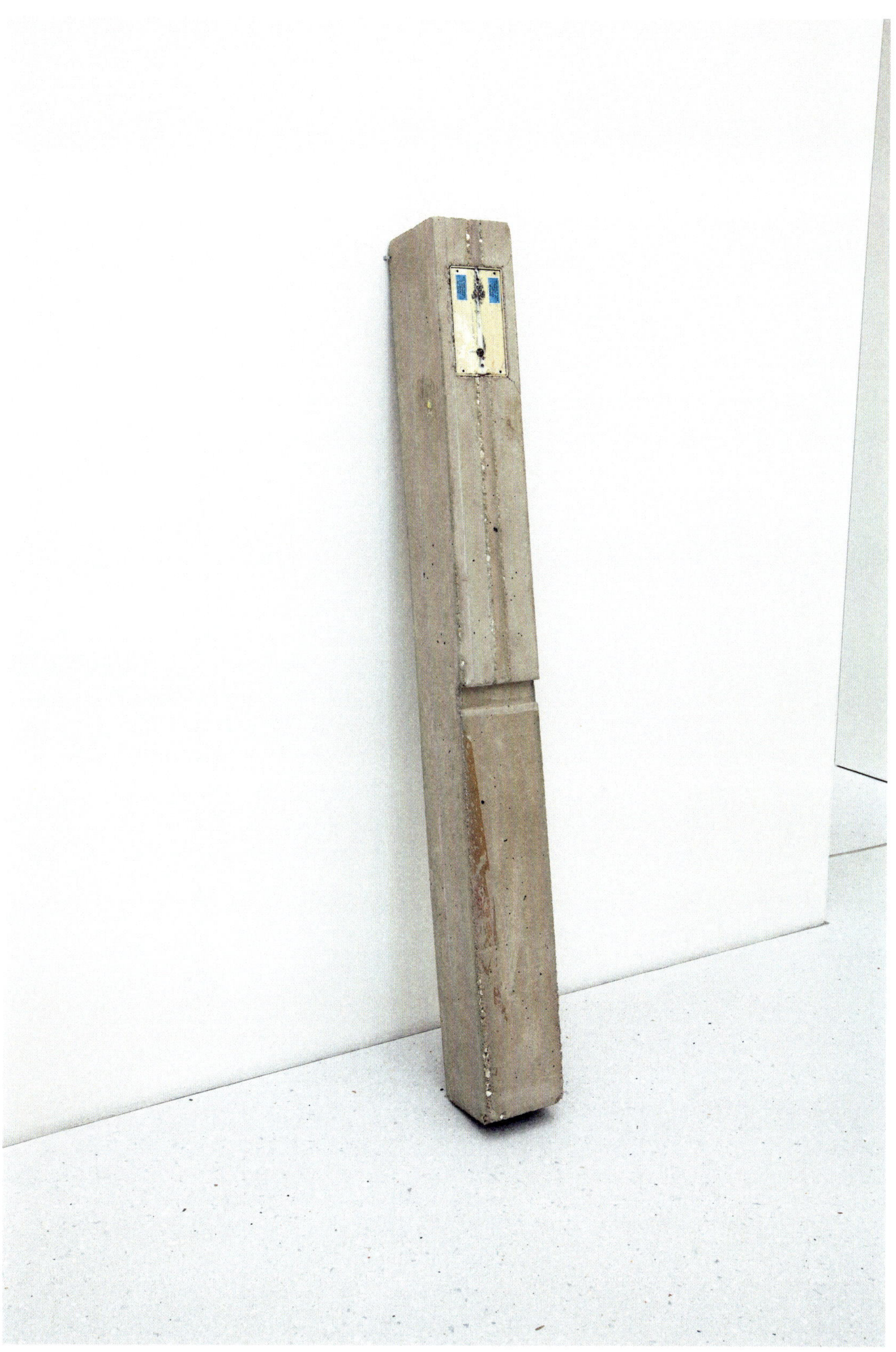

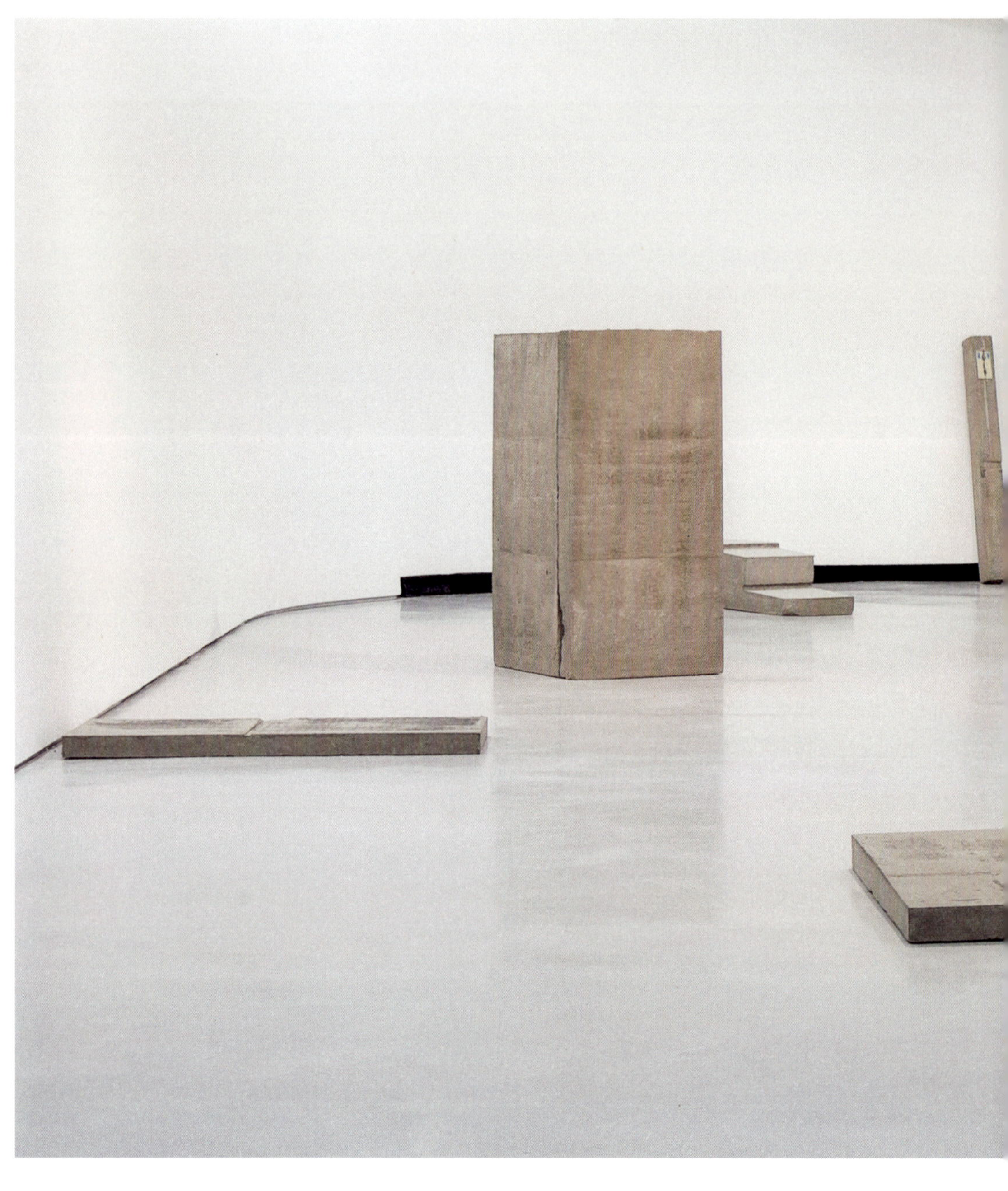

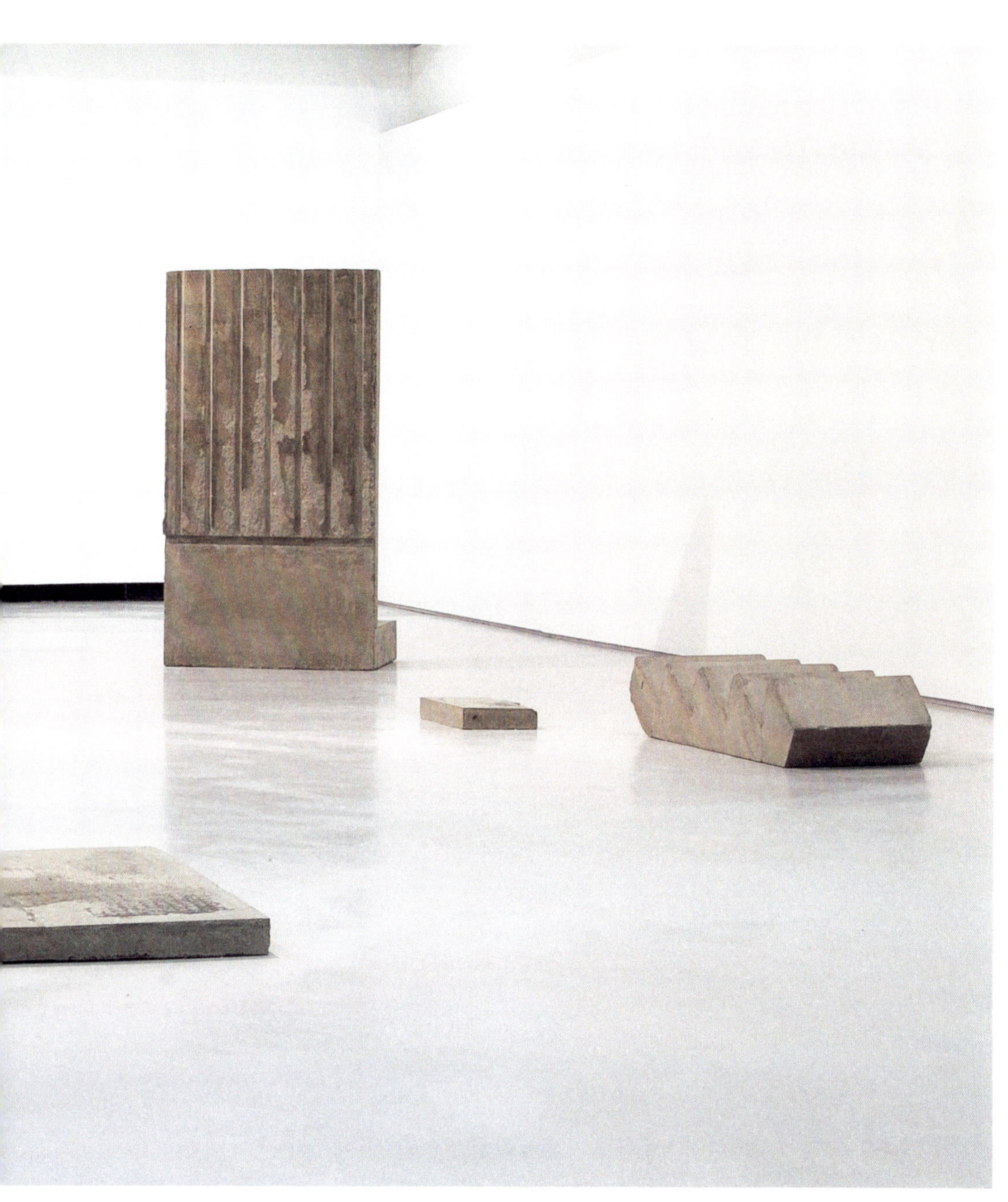

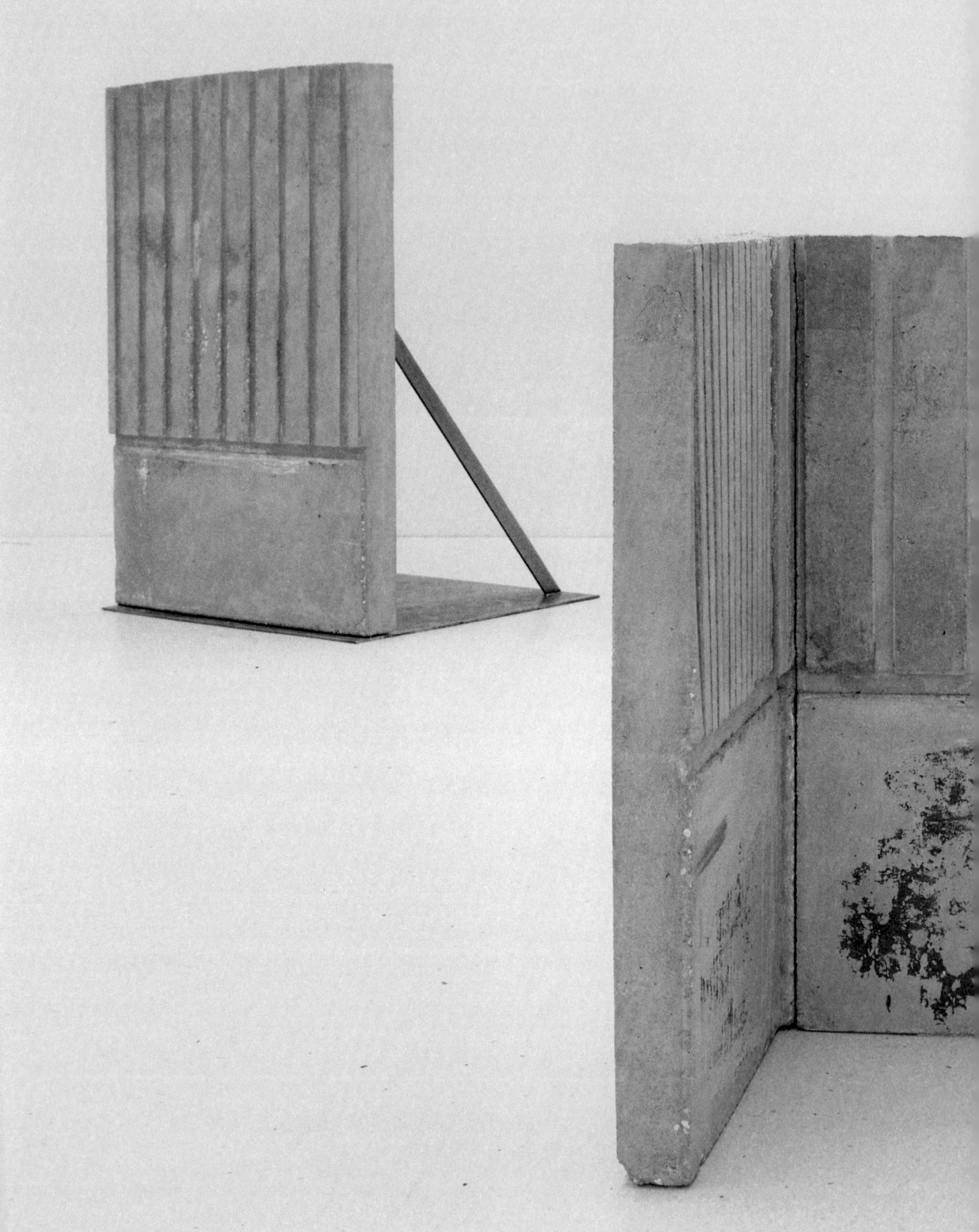

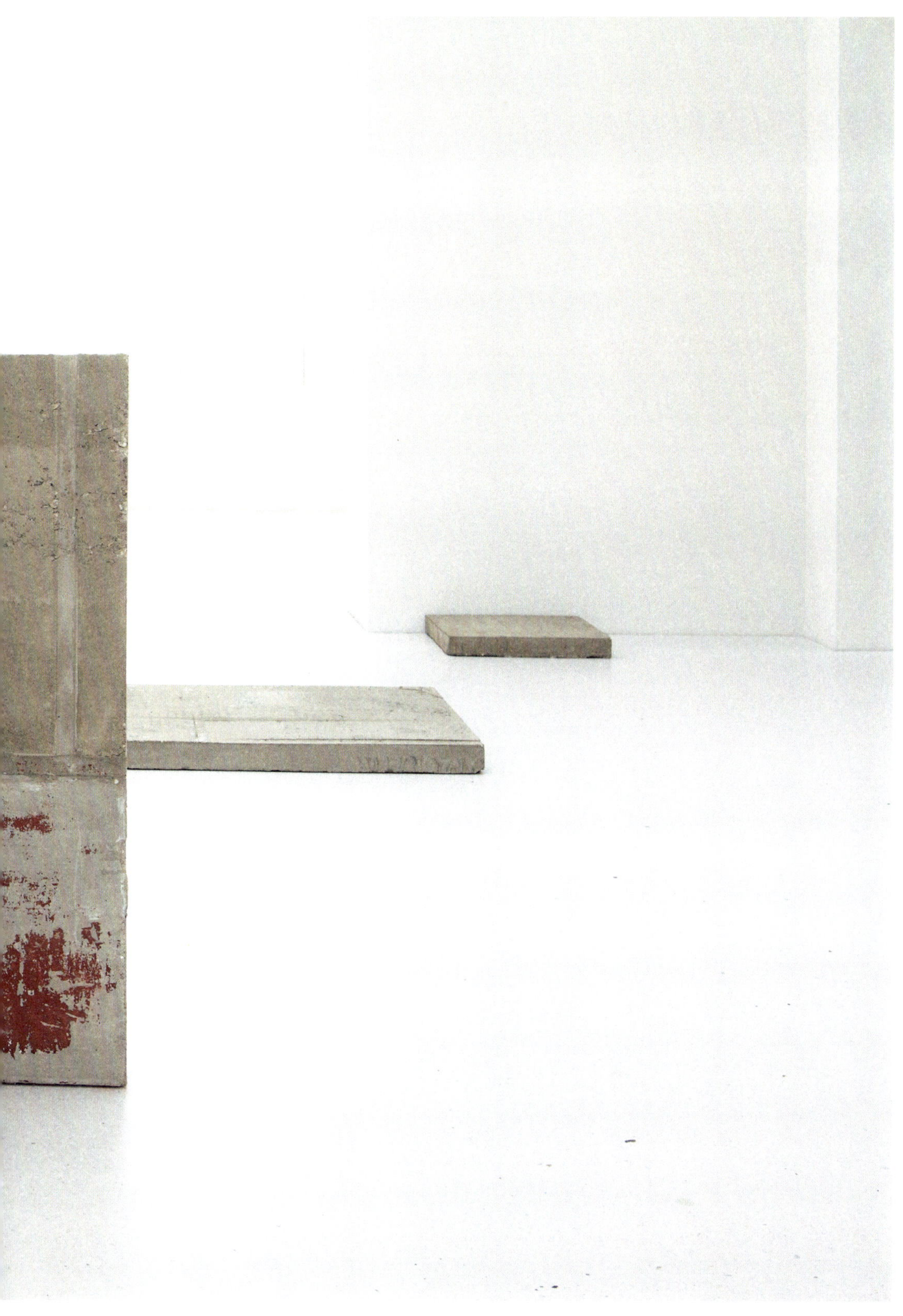

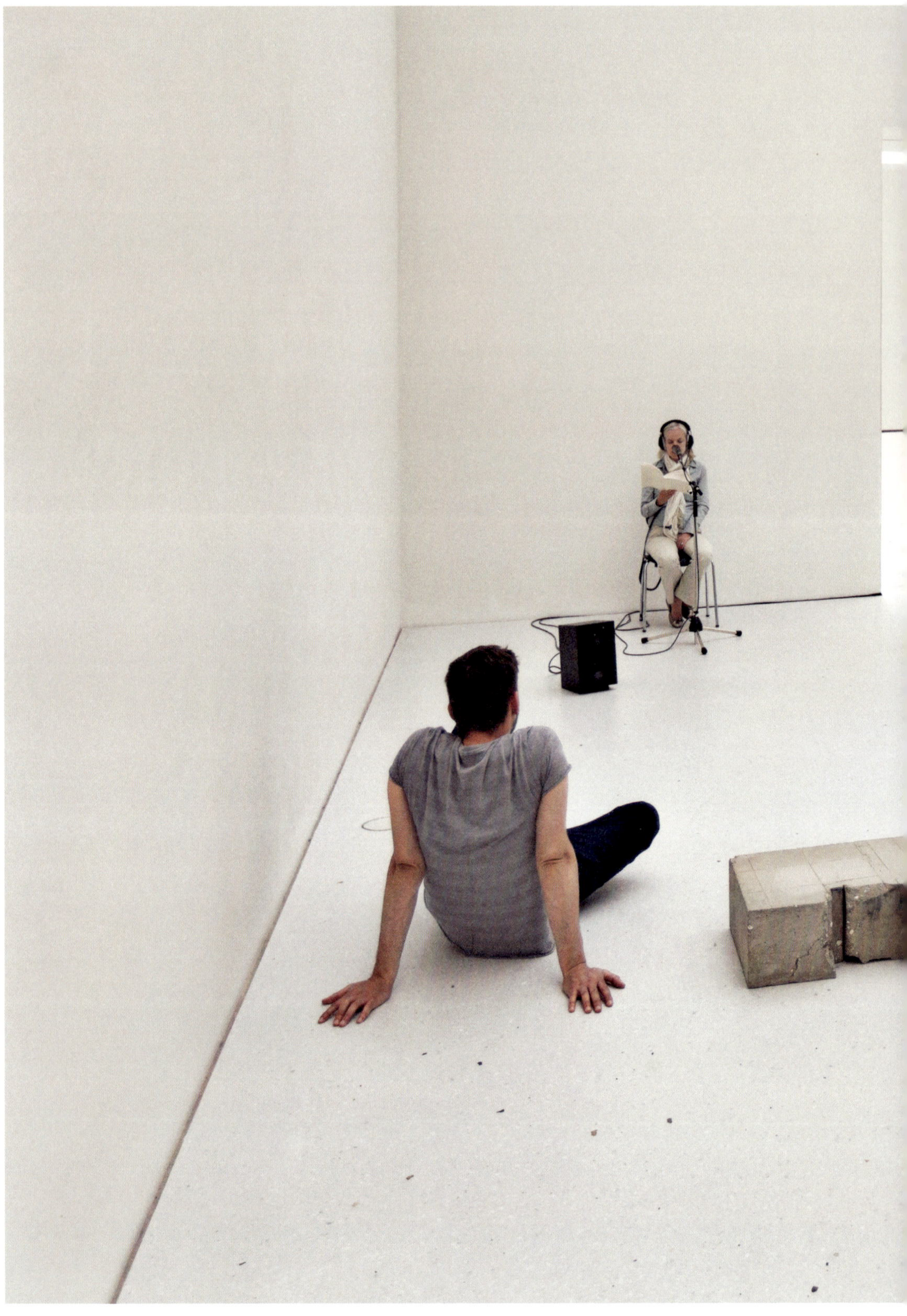

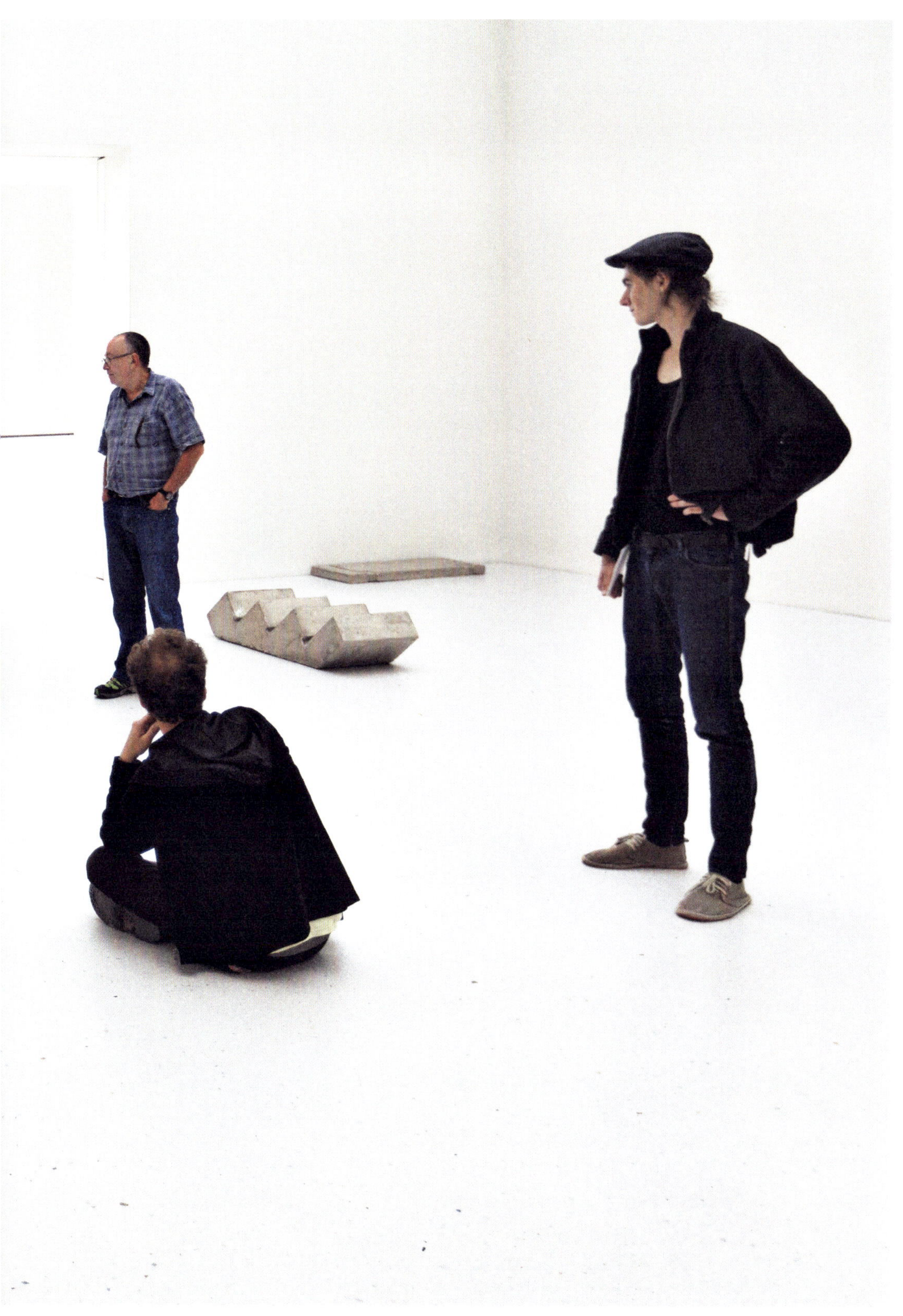

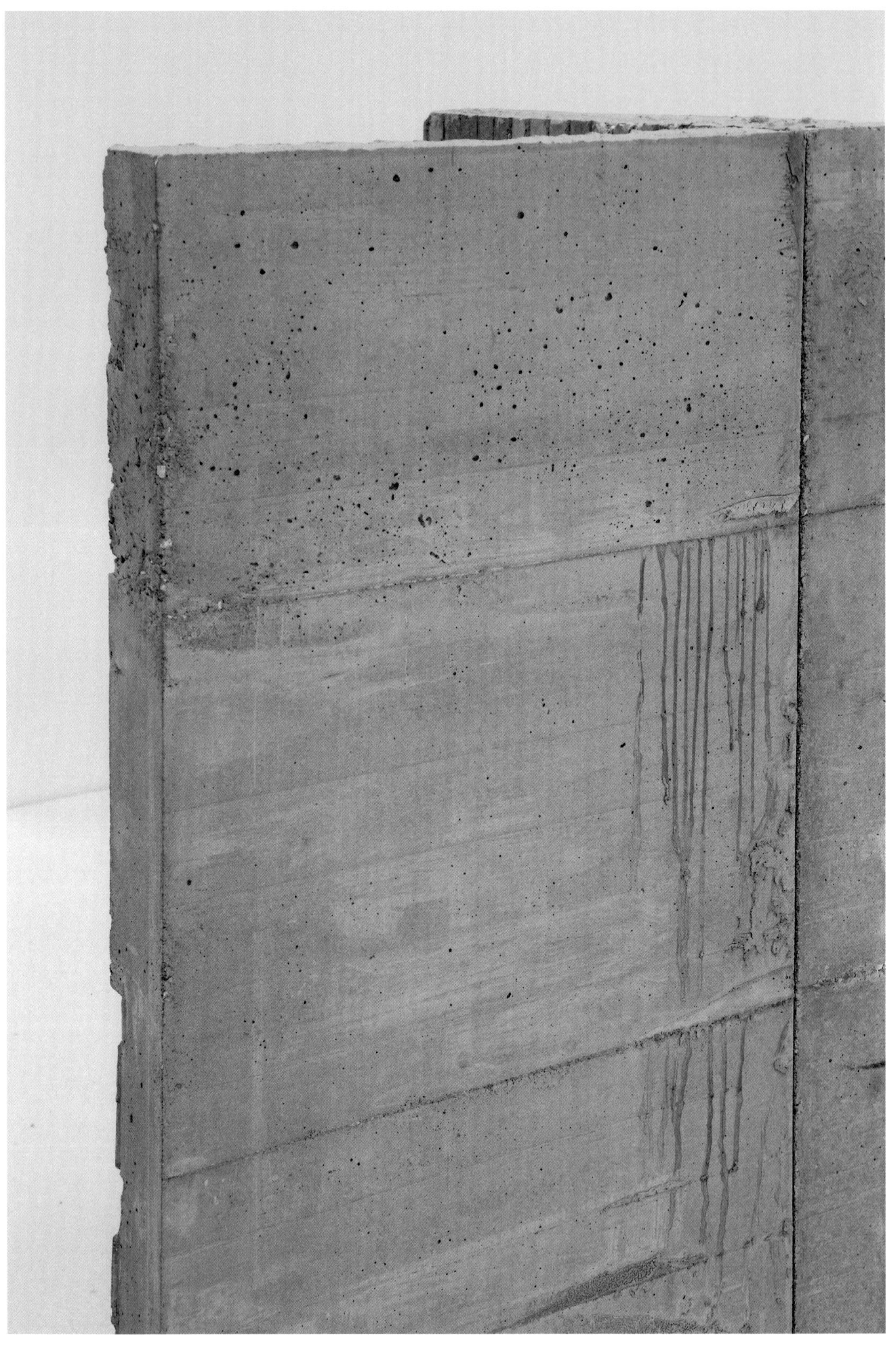

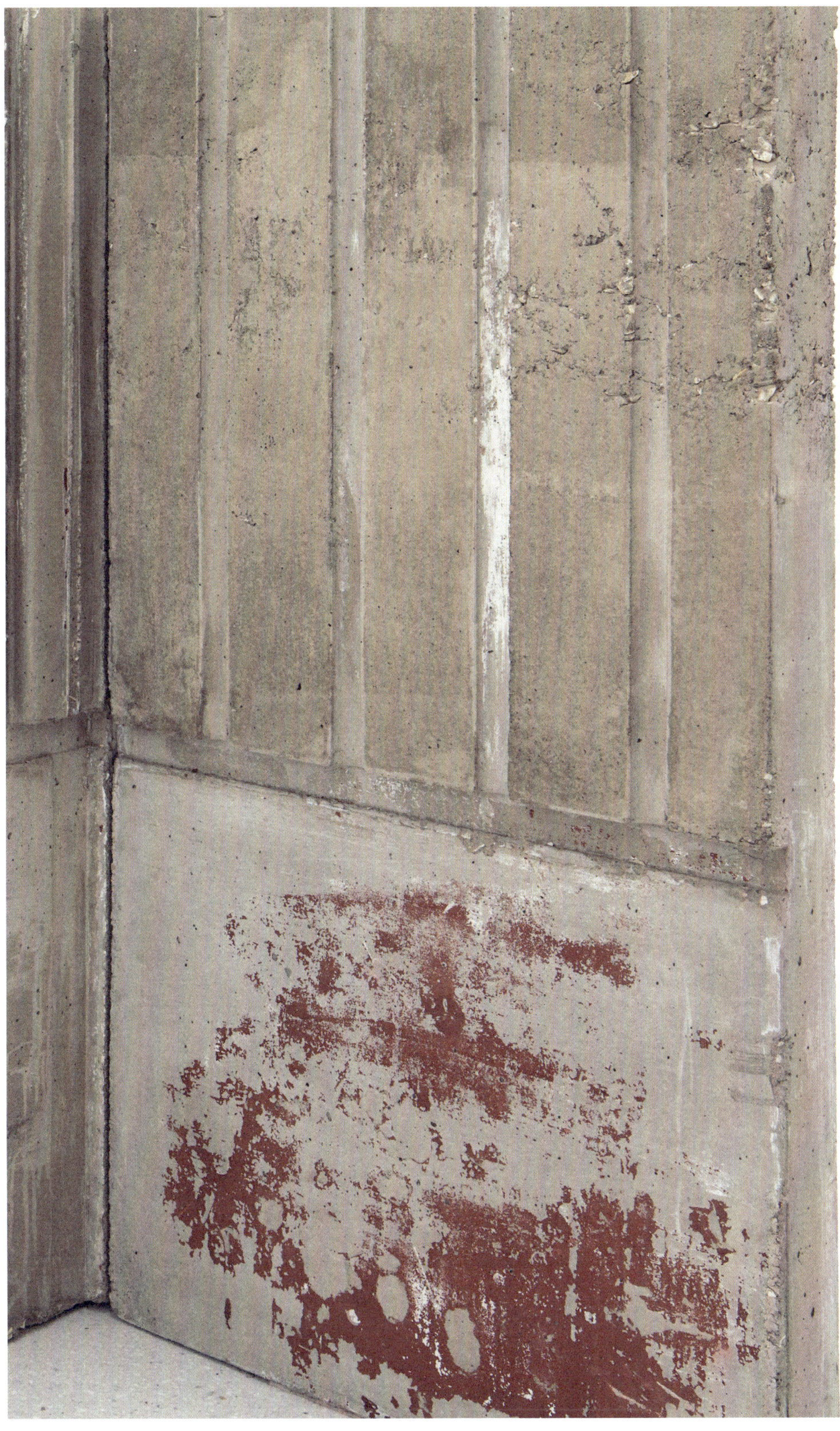

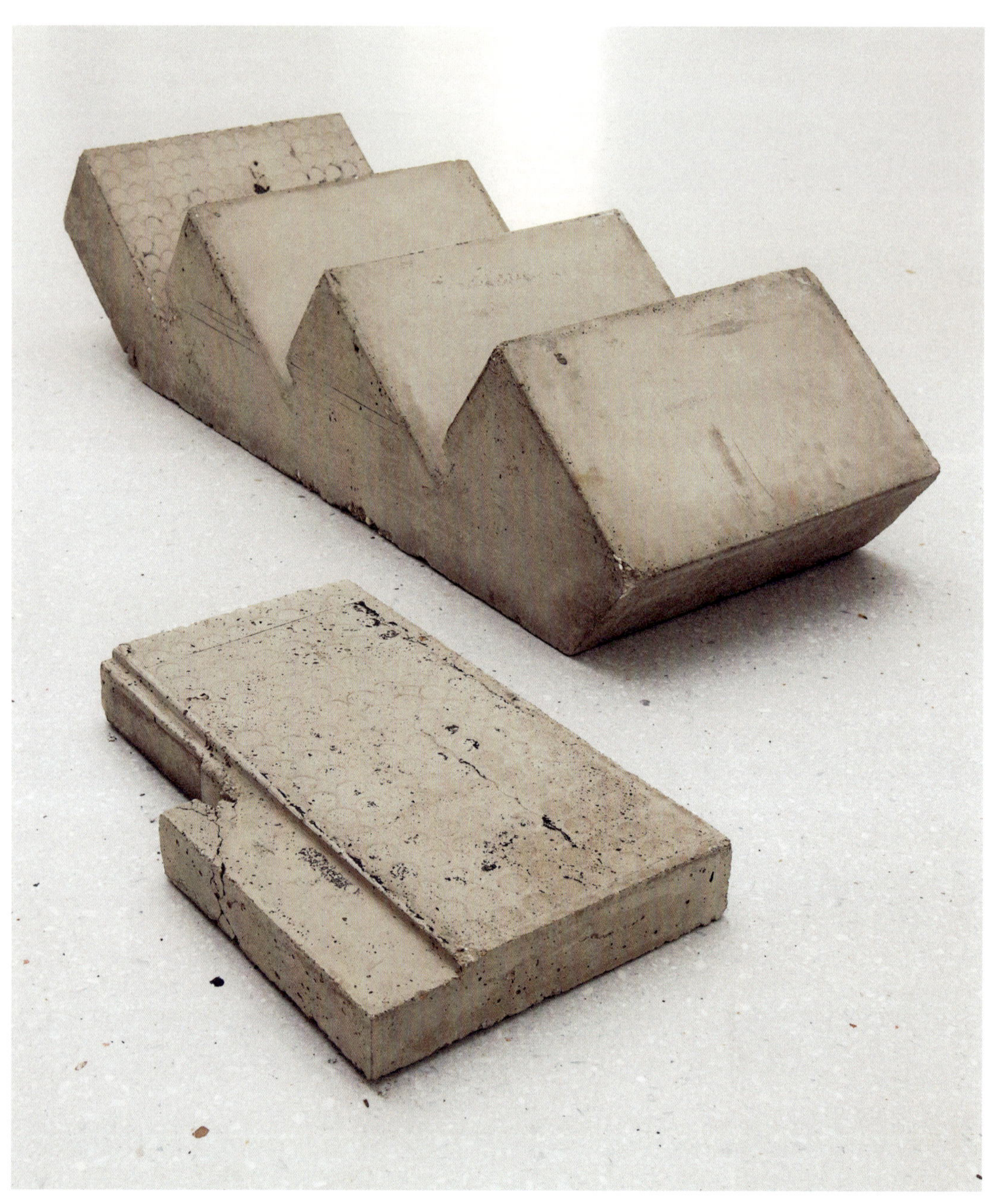

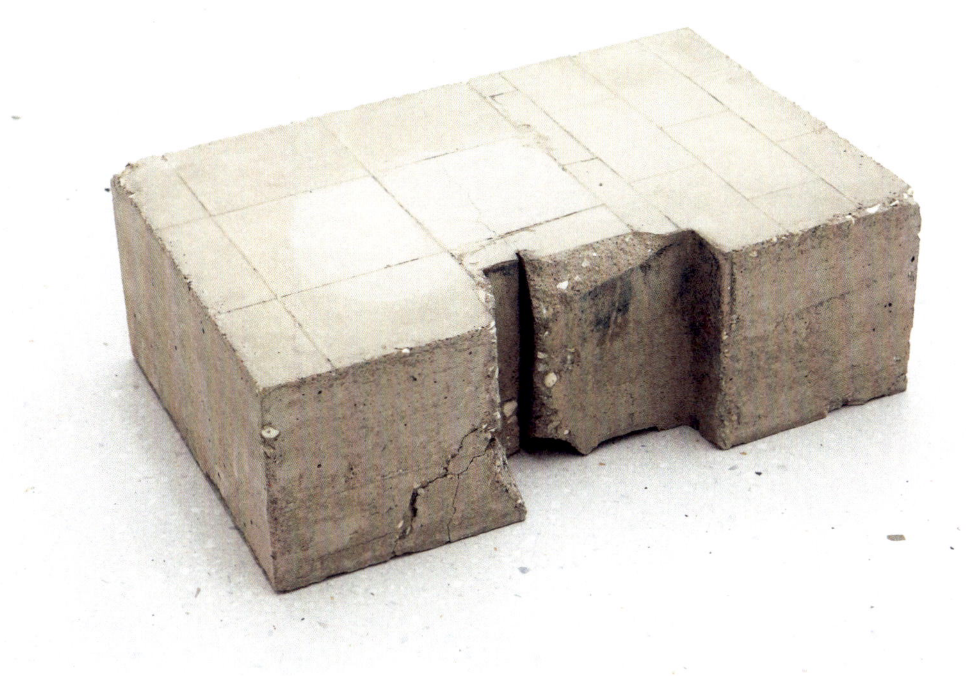

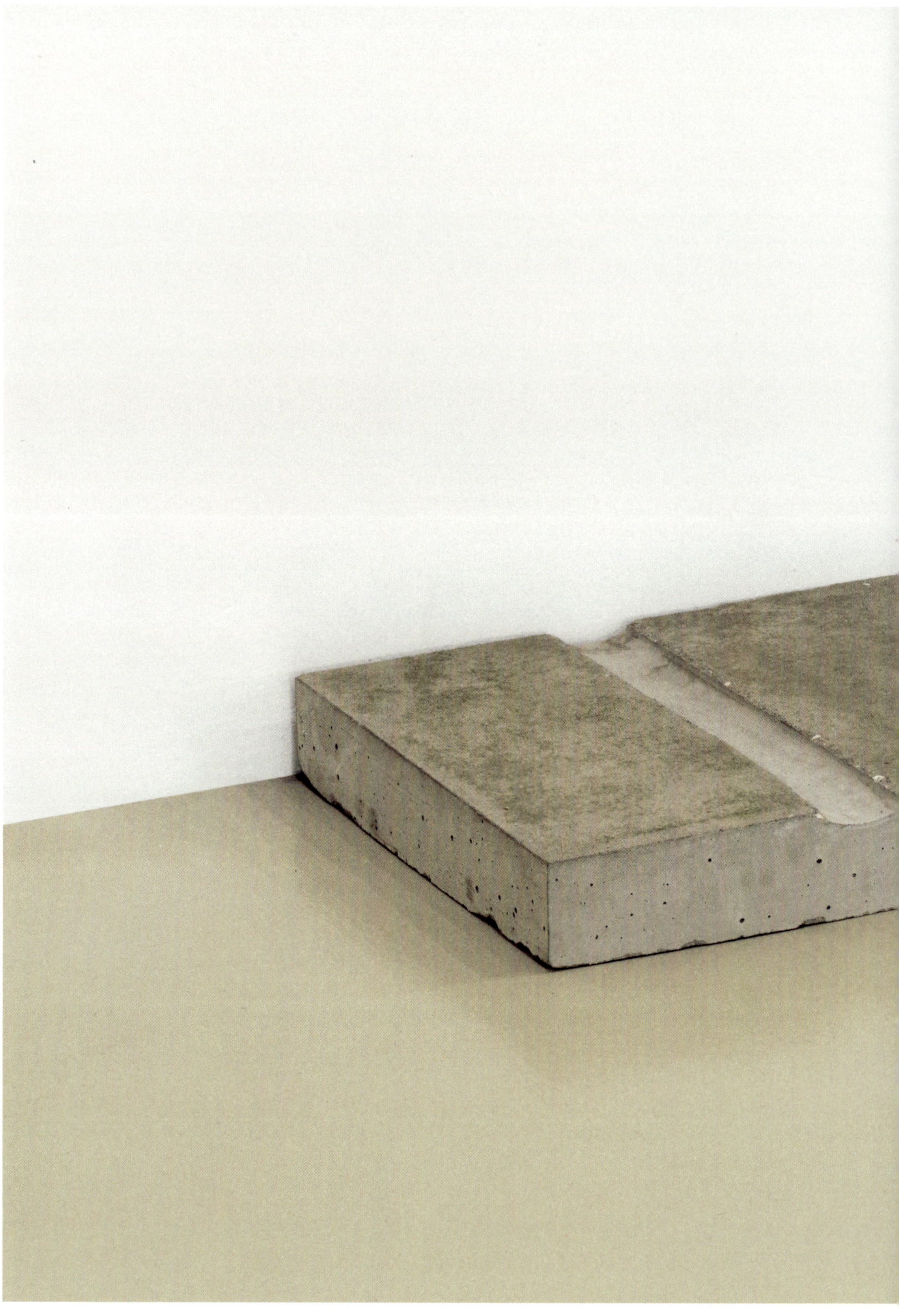

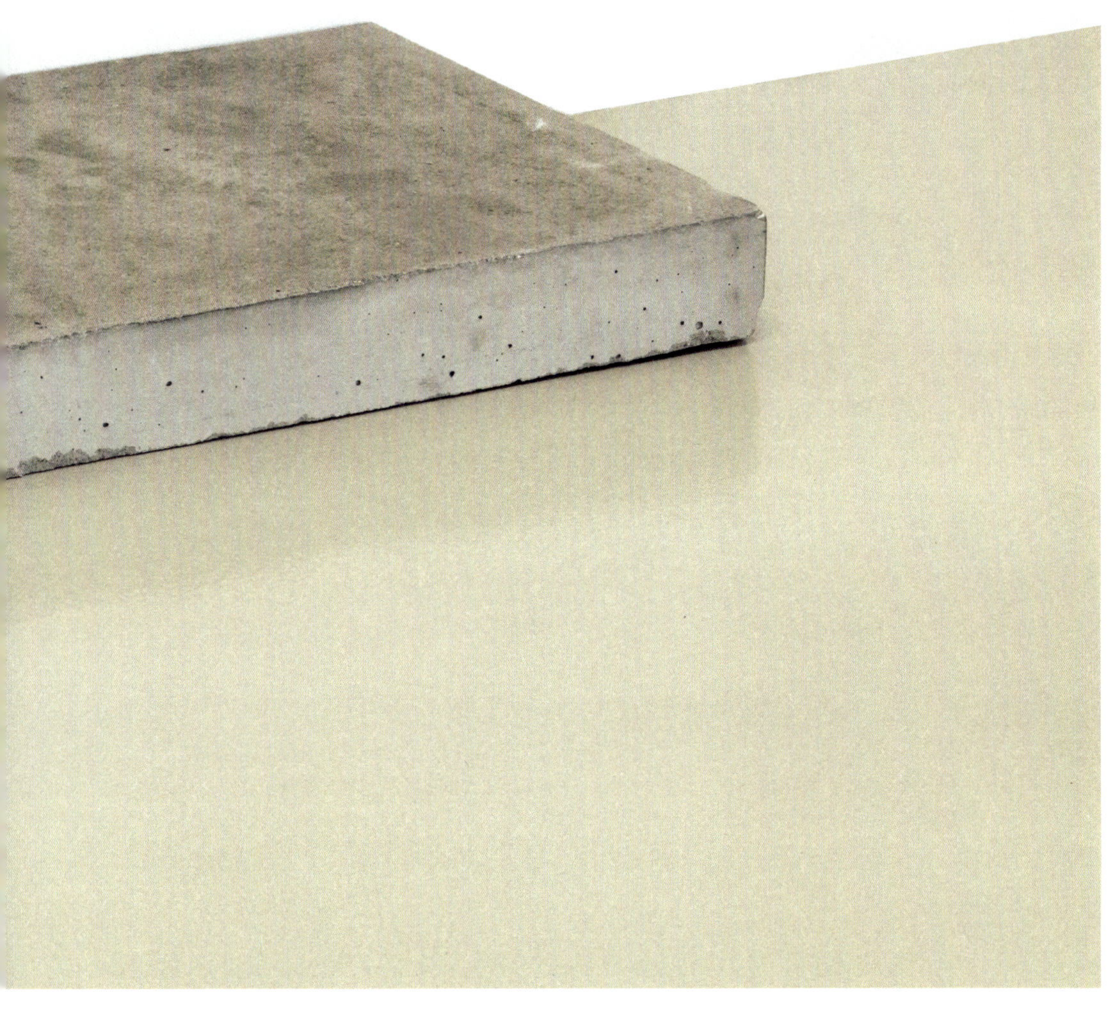

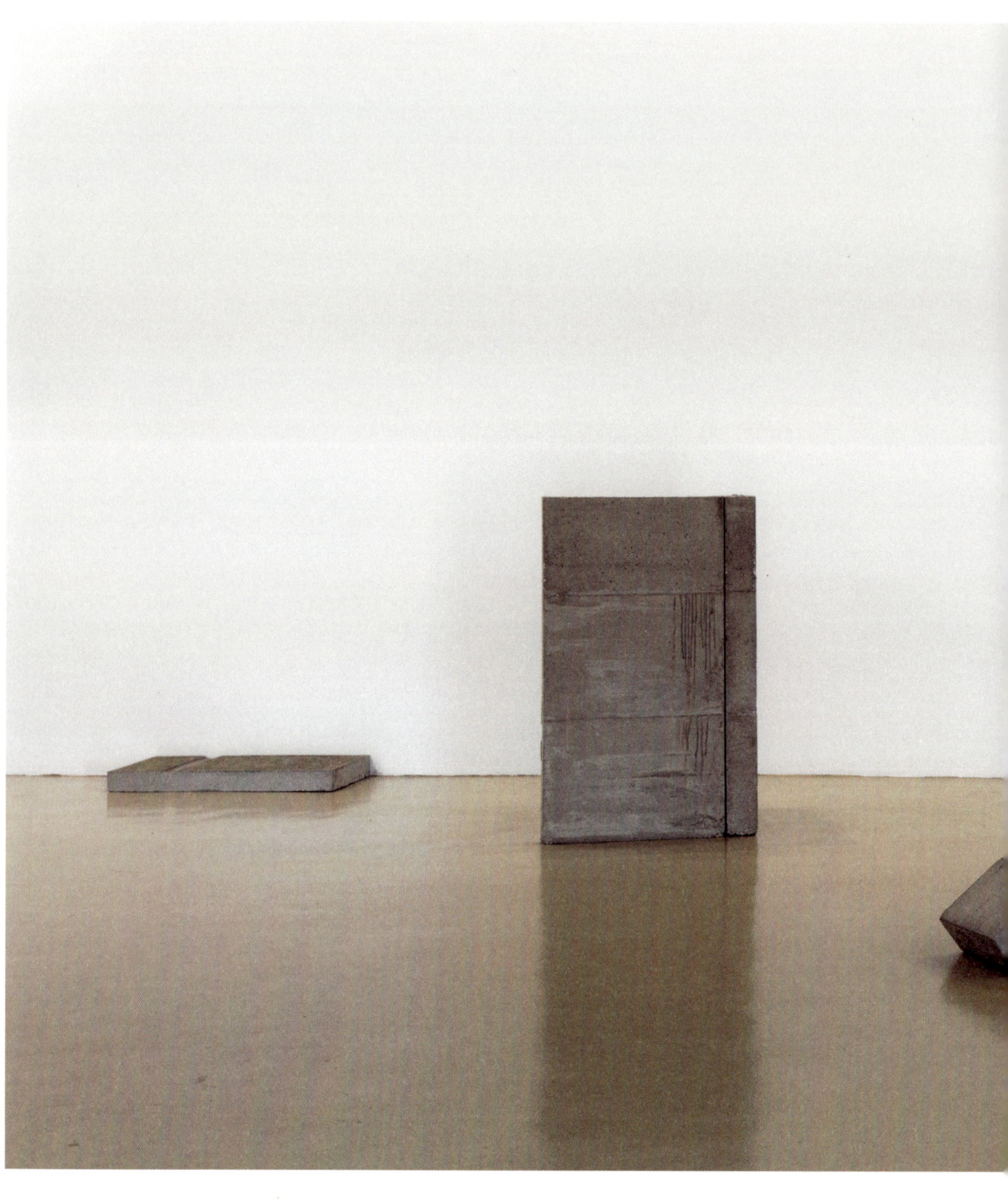

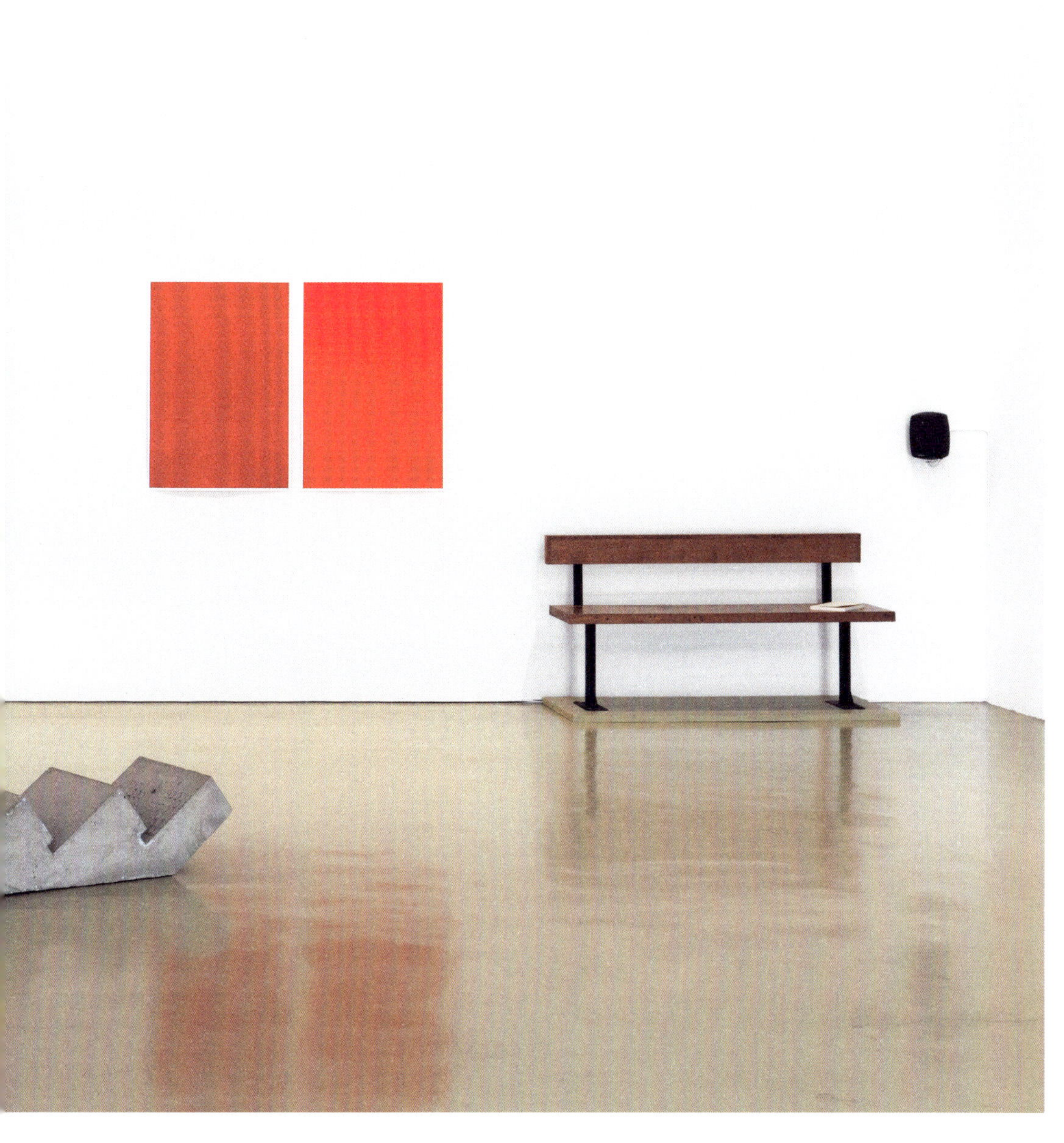

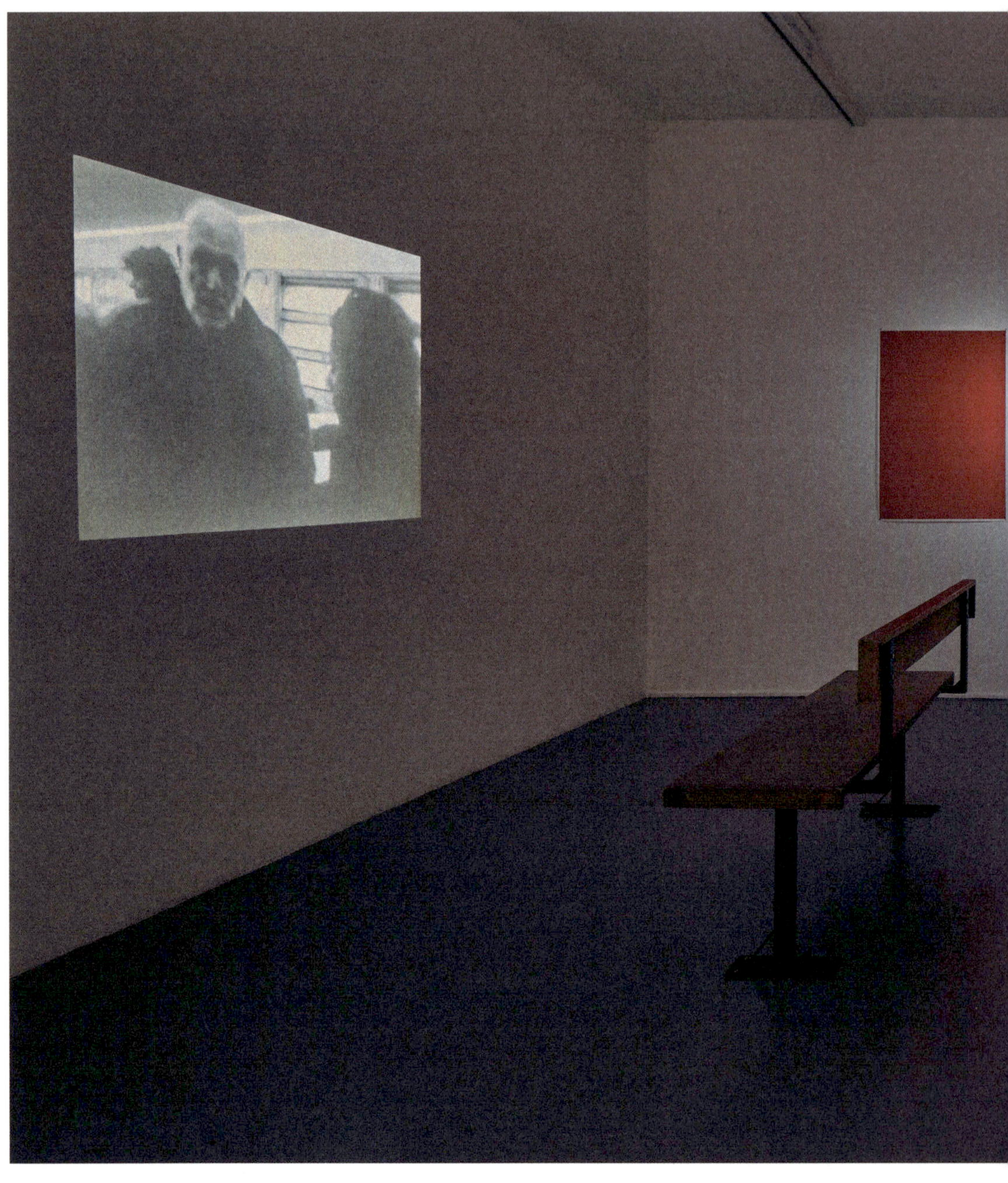

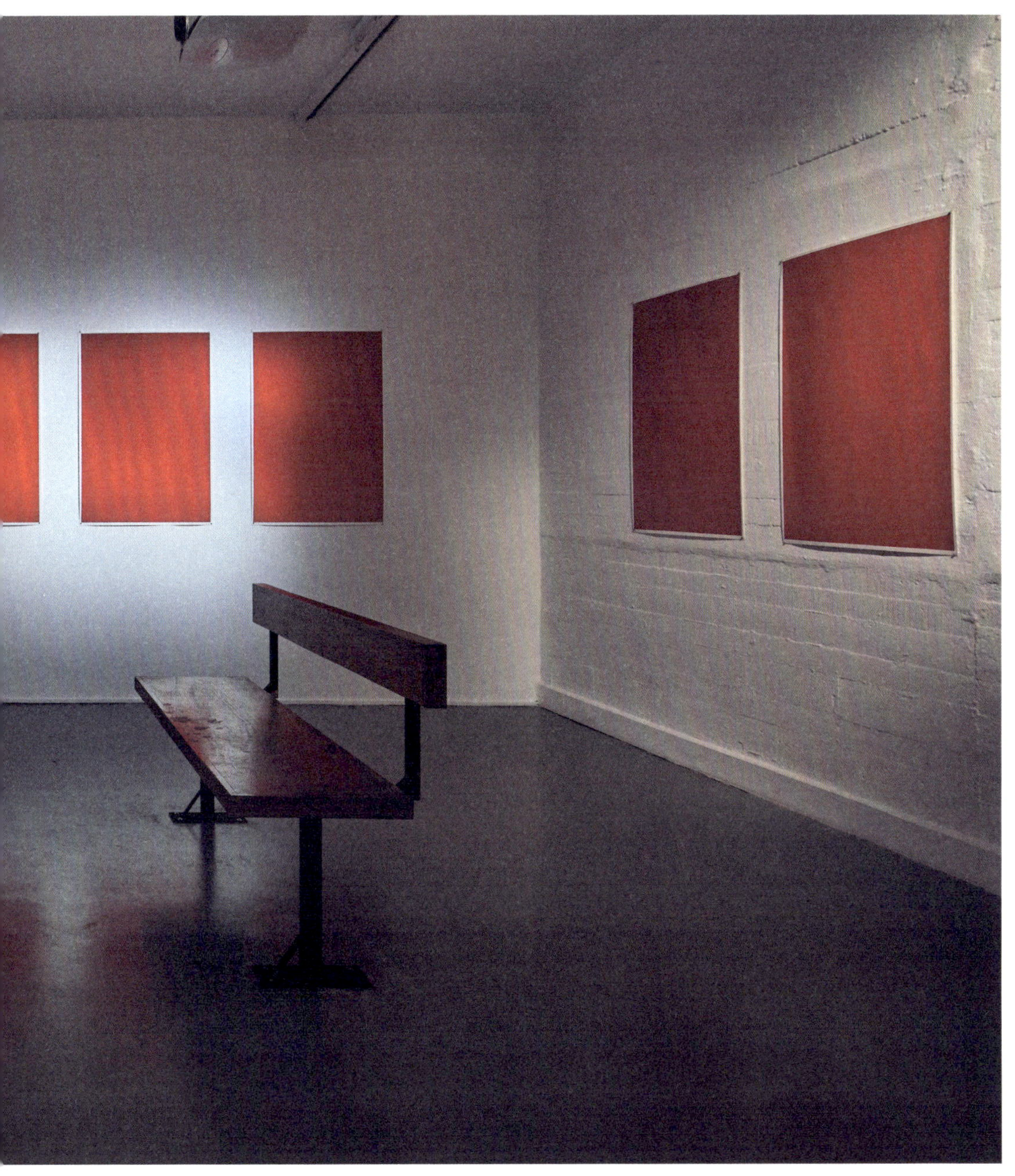

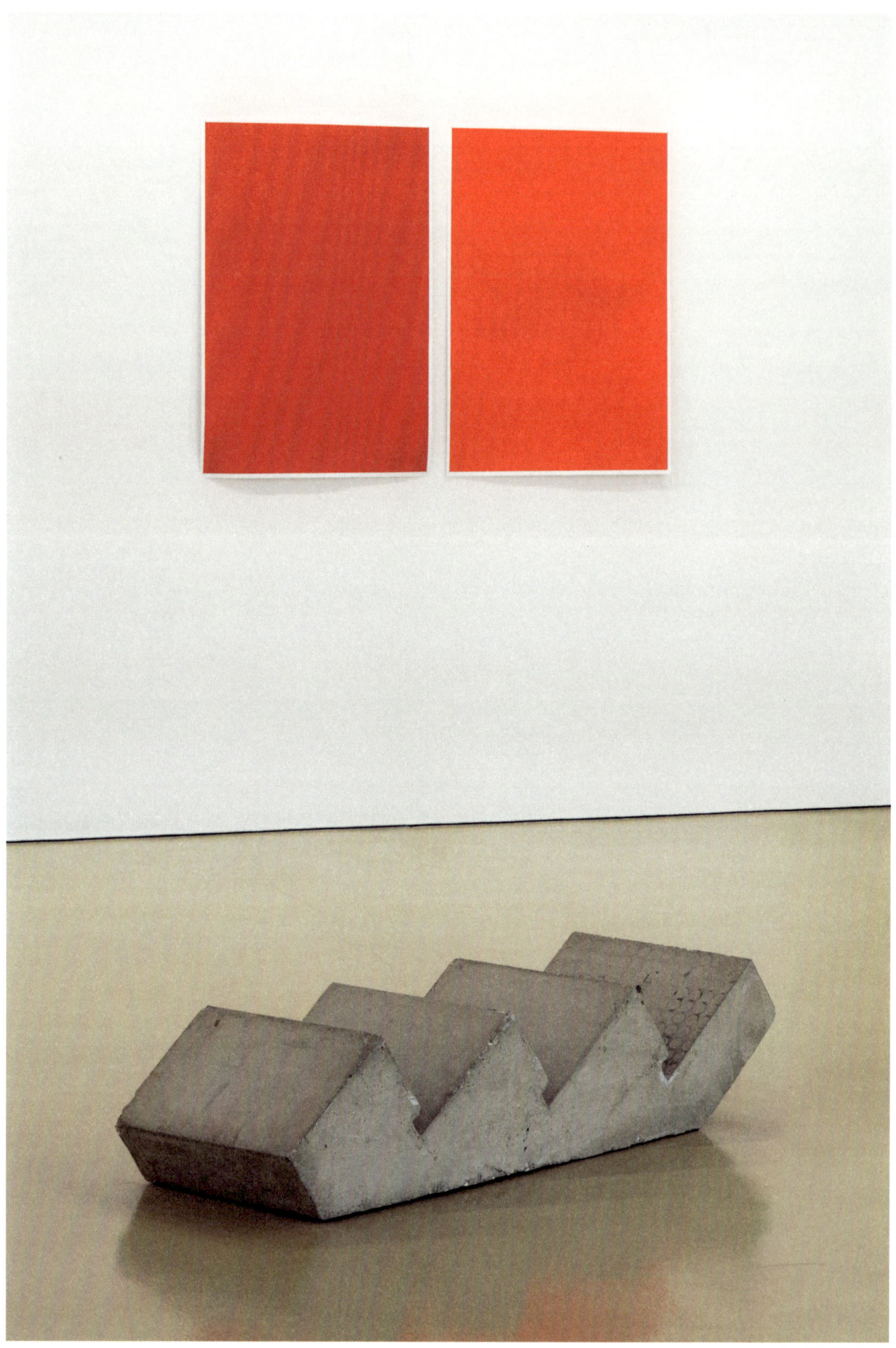

In the Bunker of History: Places, Voices and Materials in Rossella Biscotti's *The Trial*

Giovanna Zapperi

This innovation [of 1968] entailed the discovery of the realm of autonomy, the breakdown of the party system, the liquidation of socialism, a proposition of communist issues, a practical critique of waged labour. All of this was the substance of the imagination in power and it was developed in the space of a decade.[1]

In a recent interview discussing his political and intellectual trajectory, Antonio Negri describes the time spanning from his arrest on 7 April 1979 to the subsequent trial as a period of existential and political reckoning. During his time spent in prison, Negri had to reckon with the political defeat of the Autonomia Operaia [Workers' Autonomy], and the ensuing need do reorganize the political struggle in a radically changing landscape.[2] The so-called April 7th trial, which took place between 1983 and 1984, was one of the key events following Italy's "long 1968," a revolutionary season that lasted for over a decade, before giving way to the transition towards a new configuration shaped by the rise of neoliberalism, the accompanying demise of industrial labour, and the shifts in the composition of the working class, which Negri and Michael Hardt would later rethink via the concept of the multitude.[3] But perhaps, most importantly for Italy's recent history, the arrests of Negri, Paolo Virno, Luciano Ferrari Bravo, Chicco Funaro, and hundreds of other activists on charges of terrorist activity and insurrection against the state marked the end and subsequent criminalisation of the revolutionary forces that had defined the entire decade in transformative ways.

The history of the trial against members of the Autonomia Operaia is inseparable from its now established persecutory nature, summarised as the "Calogero theory," which was named

1 Antonio Negri, "La sconfitta del '77," in Nanni Balestrini, Primo Moroni, eds., *L'orda d'oro 1968–1977*, (Milan: Feltrinelli, 1988/2019), p. 632.

2 Antonio Negri, *Travail vivant contre capital* (Paris: Les éditions sociales, 2018), p. 67.

3 See Michael Hardt and Antonio Negri, *Multitude. War and Democracy in the Age of Empire* (New York: Penguin, 2004).

after the state prosecutor who initiated the investigations leading to the arrests. According to this doctrine, former members
of Potere Operaio [Workers' Power]—an organisation that ceased
operation in 1973, when it merged into the Autonomia Operaia—
were accused of having planned and directed the kidnapping
and ultimate assassination of the Christian-Democratic leader
Aldo Moro by the Brigate Rosse [Red Brigades]. This assumption
was a deliberate attempt to collapse the Autonomia Operaia and
Brigate Rosse, whose purposes, modes of action, and strategies
in fact diverged dramatically. This trial represents a dark page
in the country's recent history; there still has not been a full
accounting of the proceedings and their impact, despite the
major acquittals that would follow years of preventive detention.
There have been numerous attempts to open up a more honest
discussion on the historical circumstances of the long 1968
and its consequences for large sectors of the Italian left, but up
until now, these attempts have largely been dismissed. Equally
important issues—the possibility of political amnesty, the
carceral regime, the repressive measures and the brutality of the
state repression against significant components of the political
movements of the time—still remain unaddressed. Within this
historical configuration, the space in which the trial took place,
the infamous Aula Bunker—a courtroom annexed to Rome's
tribunal, used to host high-security trials in the 1980s—has come
to epitomise the entanglement between judiciary power and state
of exception characterising Italy's own "war on terror." The latter
has been identified—somehow vaguely and yet unmistakably—
with the whole radical left, which in public discourse is often
associated with terrorism and armed struggle. Thus, the memory
of the Aula Bunker brings to mind the repression and the emergency laws which state apparatuses typically use to address what
they perceive as threats to their institutions.

Rossella Biscotti's multimedia installation *Il processo*
(*The Trial*) is based on an inquiry into the history of the April 7th
trial in an attempt to understand the significance of this episode
in Italy's recent past. However, in her work, the events are reac-
tivated in a ghostly manner; rather than provide a documentary
reconstruction of the proceedings, the work speaks to their current erasure and illegibility in the country's mainstream debates.
Whereas Biscotti's piece can be considered within the paradigm
of "artist as historian"—a term coined by art historian and
curator Mark Godfrey—the formal strategies she deploys show
significant differences than those typically characterised as such,
which tend to be based on the use of found images, archival
research and documentary practice.[4] Over the years, Biscotti
has devoted much of her attention to the histories of political
movements, through the exploration of selected sites, formats

4   See Mark
Godfrey, "The Artist
as Historian," *October*,
n. 120, Spring 2007,
pp. 140–72.

and events that emphasise the role of collective action in twentieth century Italy. Her process-based practice always involves a specific interest in places and materials, while at the same time building on the dialogues, friendships and communities that are generated during the research process (and often stem from the artist's own political commitment.) When she first approached the history of the April 7th trial, instead of providing a detailed account of its well-documented circumstances, Biscotti decided to foreground the spatial dimensions and embodied experience of the Aula Bunker. Her research departs from the material apparatus of the courtroom, which she rearranges into a stage-like environment, inhabited by a series of material or discursive traces that have been mobilised in the present.

Inside the Legal Machine

Starting from an inquiry into the architectural structure of the Aula Bunker, Biscotti has undertaken an archaeological journey into the repressed memory of the April 7th trial. She first presented the installation at MAXXI museum in Rome in 2010, then later at dOCUMENTA (13) in Kassel in 2012. Afterwards, it was reassembled in other venues in a variety of configurations, combining sculpture, performance, video and sound in unexpected ways. In its original iteration, conceived for Rome's MAXXI, *The Trial* took the form of an audio installation comprising an eight-hour excerpt[5] from the trial's audio recordings, edited and selected by the artist.[6] Producing a coherent segment from the hundreds of hours of audio documentation necessitated some drastic choices and the construction of a narrative that does not necessarily follow the trial's development, but chooses instead to trace the chronology of events, as told by the defendants. Biscotti's cuts prioritise multivocality and the trial's significance with respect to a collective history. By avoiding the singling out of individual participants, the artist underlines how different defendants often answered the same questions and addressed similar issues, even though each of them was actually facing different accusations. The legal machine was predicated on the need to isolate the defendants from one another, a fact that contributed to the disguising of the political dimension of the trial itself. Listening to these recordings is a deeply captivating experience, as it enables one to dwell upon the political experiences and the theoretical framework developed within the Autonomia Operaia, while at the same time drawing attention to the ways in which the trial was very much focused on indicting ideas overs facts. As Negri would recall years later, one of the fundamental aims of the April 7th trial

5   The duration coincided with the museum's opening time and was an indirect reference to the Fordist notion of the working day as composed of eight-hour allotments for work, sleep and leisure time. For the work's following iterations, the audio was reduced to six hours.

6   The trial's hearings were broadcasted live by Radio Radicale and are still available online on the radio's website: www.radio radicale.it.

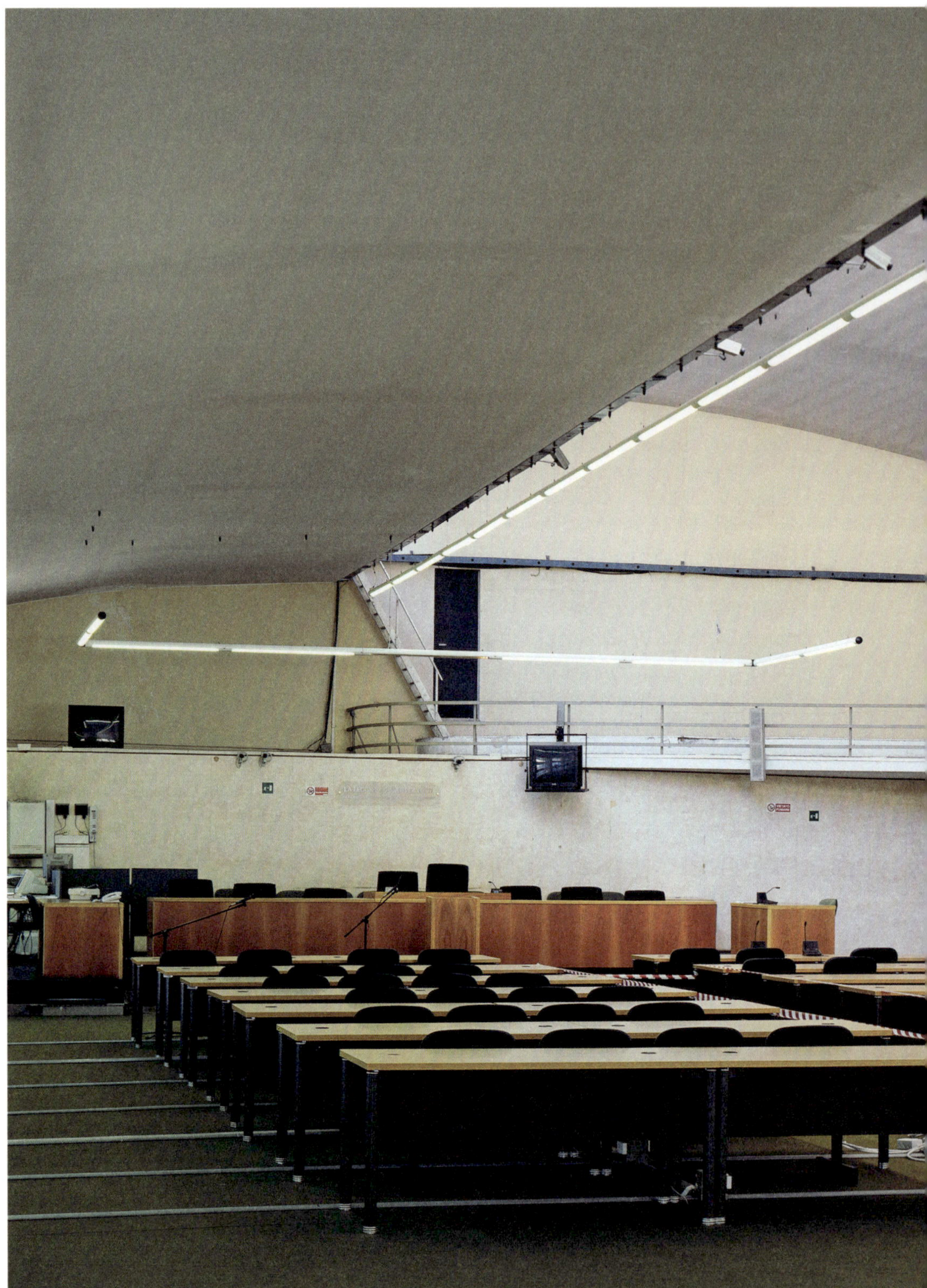

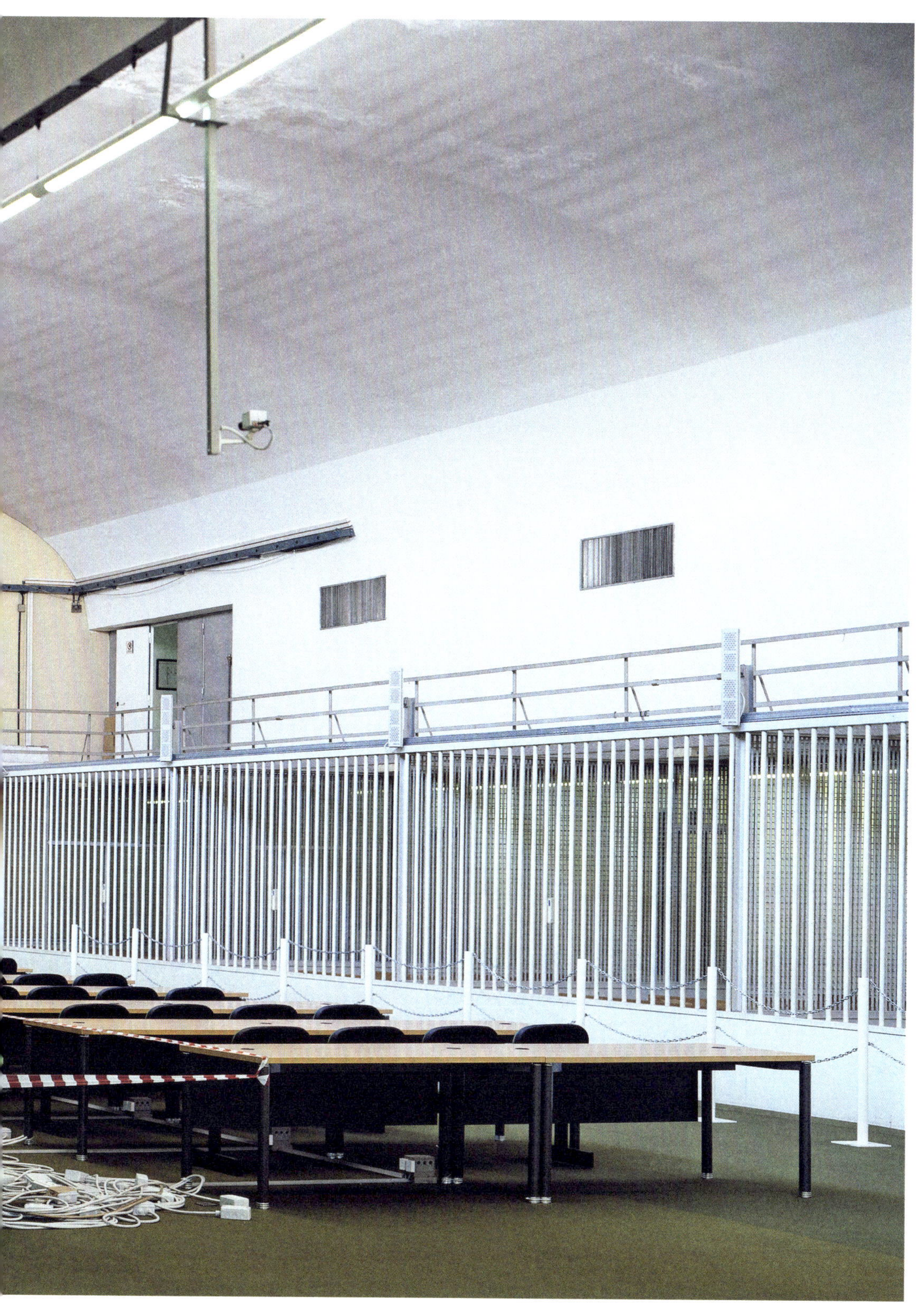

7   Toni Negri, "Via 8 febbraio? No! Via 7 aprile!" (2009), republished in: *Euronomade*, 7 April 2020, www.euronomade.info/?p=13247 (last accessed on 29 May 2020). Most of the teachers gathered around the Istituto di Scienze Politiche at the University of Padova were arrested on 7 April 1979.

was to dismantle the ability of groups of intellectuals to directly connect to the working class struggles in a time of radical re-organisation of the country's production.[7]

Tape recorded in the courtroom decades earlier, in the MAXXI, the voices of prisoners and prosecutors, witnesses and *pentiti* [collaborators] accompanied the visitors' path across the spectacular stairways of Zaha Hadid's architecture into the exhibition space. Here, a collection of eight reinforced concrete minimalist-like sculptures was spatially arranged in a way that suggested a theatrical setting, like an empty stage inhabited by architectural traces. The sculptures are based on casts taken from the elements of the Aula Bunker, which were added when the space was converted into a courtroom in the late 1970s: the cages where the defendants were held in custody; the benches bolted on the floor where they sat during inter-rogation; one of the cages' microphone; the linoleum floor; the stairs leading from the underground cells to the holding cells; and the stairs used as the public entrance. Biscotti based their position in the space on a loose mapping of the courtroom's architectural components.

When Biscotti started to work on this project, the Aula Bunker was slated for renovation that would remove any traces of the building's former judicial function. In this sense, the casts represent a paradoxical salvage operation against the impending dismantling of the room's history. The bunker's original architecture was conceived by Rationalist architect Luigi Moretti in 1934, and completed in 1936. It was designed to host the *Casa della scherma* (House of Fencing), as part of the Foro Italico complex, the monumental athletic centre located on the Tiber's left bank in the northern district of Rome. The complex's architecture is one of the best known examples of Rationalist aesthetics from the 1930s, and has come to epit-omise the Fascist regime's modernising ambitions. Biscotti first embarked on the research that led to *The Trial* around 2006, when she was developing a photographic project on the legacy of Fascist architecture in Italy and its subsequent transforma-tions. In this moment of transition, the empty building was still under the administration of Italy's Department of Justice, before it was handed back to the Italian Olympic Committee (CONI) to be transformed into a museum for sports.[8] The artist, who was already in touch with former members of the Autonomia Operaia, became immediately interested in excavat-ing the changing usage of this building, and, more specifically, its connection to the radical left in Italy. As she approached the Aula Bunker's history, she was guided by the accounts of some of the April 7th trial's defendants, which enabled Biscotti to view the spaces through the lens of their lived experience.

8   The project was eventually abandoned, and, as I write these lines, the fate of the building is still un-decided.

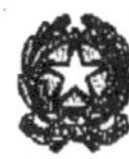

TRIBUNALE ORDINARIO DI ROMA

PRESIDENZA

Autor.-AL/fp

N. di Prot. _113 99_

Roma , li **11 OTT. 2006**

Risposta a nota del ____________________ N. __________ Alleg. N. __________

OGGETTO: Richiesta autorizzazione ad effettuare una visita all'interno della sala della scherma (ex aula bunker della 1° Corte di Assise), sita in via dei Gladiatori (Foro Italico).
- **Kevin Van Braak**, nato a Varnsveld (Olanda) il 22.12.1975, passaporto nr. NL4602057;
- **Biscotti Rossella**, nata a Molfetta (BA) il 11.12.1978, C. I. nr. AJ8991147.

"American Academy in Rome"
Via Angelo Masina, 5
c.a. Dana Prescott
(fax. 06/5810788)

R O M A

Al Comandante Nucleo Tribunali CC.

Al Dirigente della Polizia di Stato

S E D E

Si autorizza, per il giorno **16 ottobre 2006 dalle ore 10.00 alle ore 12.30**, l'accesso all'interno della Sala della scherma "Moretti" (ex aula bunker della 1^ Corte di Assise di Roma), dei due Artisti in oggetto, per effettuare una visita allo stabile per motivi di lavoro riguardante l'architettura razionalista.

Gli stessi saranno accompagnati da personale dell'Arma dei Carabinieri impiegato per la vigilanza dello stabile.

Il Presidente Vicario del Tribunale Ordinario
(Alberto Bucci)

C/forte/visita sala scherma ex aula bunker Gladiatori/

9   T. J. Demos, "A Form of 'Total Revolution.' The Art of Rossella Biscotti," in Bartolomeo Pietromarchi, ed., *Rossella Biscotti: Ten Works*, exhib. cat. (Rome: MAXXI, 2010), p. 13.

The Trial juxtaposes the disembodied sound of the tape-recorded voices, which conjure the protagonists' bodily presence, with the brutalist materiality of the sculptures. The contradiction between these two elements is merely superficial, as, material or immaterial, both can be understood as a set of remains that—by virtue of the indexical nature of casts and recordings—makes reference to the spatial configurations and human interactions that took place during the trial. These elements are reanimated, albeit displaced within the museum, in the form of traces that require interpretation. As it has been observed, the association of voice and sculpture produces a certain opacity in terms of the work's meaning. The concrete sculptures' link to the Aula Bunker remains obscure, resisting an easy correspondence.[9] Biscotti is indeed more interested in mapping the legal apparatus in its performative and material aspects, rather than in reconstructing the trial's circumstances as such. *The Trial*'s performative dimension becomes even more crucial if one considers the work's subsequent presentations. Two years later, the original recordings were interpreted by professional translators at dOCUMENTA (13) in Kassel, rendering the historical testimony accessible to an international audience while also reactivating it via live performance and presence. Whereas the dOCUMENTA presentation comprised both sculptures and performance, further iterations of *The Trial* exclusively focused on the performance, with the translated text being simultaneously typewritten by performers.

The installation therefore suggests the idea of a space inhabited by voices and objects, positioned halfway between sculpture and architecture—an aspect that recalls the artist's early training in stage design. Perhaps even more importantly, this theatrical dimension can be traced back to one of the most distinctive legacies of Italian modernism—Arte Povera—in its exploration of materials within the object-environment relation. As Biscotti explains in a conversation with Cesare Pietroiusti, she is interested in engaging with the material specificity of the places at the centre of her work, which leads her to turn to materials that carry the traces of the place by retaining information about the socio-political environment.[10] This is particularly true if one looks at the constellation of the artist's works that deal with disciplinary institutions, such as the courtroom or the prison. The reinforced concrete in *The Trial* echoes the lead used in *The Prison of Santo Stefano* (2011), or the compost collected with inmates of the Giudecca women's prison in Venice as part of *I dreamt that you changed into a cat... gatto... ha ha ha* (2013); the chosen materials convey both the site and the production process, which is a constitutive part of the work, inasmuch as it always involves a collective enterprise and the building of a community. In the case of *The Trial*, the use of reinforced concrete is

10   Rossella Biscotti in conversation with Cesare Pietroiusti, in: Letizia Ragaglia, ed., *Rossella Biscotti*, exhib. cat. (Bolzano: Museion, 2015), p. 97.

194   Giovanna Zapperi

directly inspired by Hadid's use of the same material for the monumental spaces of the MAXXI. The association between the space of the trial (the Aula Bunker) and the space of the museum suggests a meditation on the entanglement between forms and materials in the conception of buildings intended to represent the nation-state and its various institutions. With its "feeling of cheap and repressive architecture,"[11] as curator Carolyn Christov-Bakargiev put it, reinforced concrete specifically conjures disciplinary institutions, such as the tribunal. The material was nearly omnipresent in post-war Italy, in contrast with the Fascist regime's predilection for marble (a shift echoed in the transformation of the Aula Bunker).

11   Carolyn Christov-Bakargiev, "On Art and Dreaming: The Singular and the Collective, from Cement to Compost. An Interview with Rossella Biscotti," in *The Side Room: Rossella Biscotti*, exhib. cat. (Vienna: The Secession, 2013), p. 84.

Translating History into the Present

Interestingly, the MAXXI museum—inaugurated in 2009 as Italy's first national museum for contemporary art and architecture—is located just opposite the Aula Bunker, on the other side of the Tiber. This play with proximity is key to Biscotti's project, as *The Trial* relocates the traces of the April 7th trial from Foro Italico into the space of the museum. For the exhibition's opening, the artist organised an informal gathering in the spaces of the Aula Bunker, convening some of the people involved in the project: former defendants and their families, lawyers and other friends. The visit aimed at reactivating the legacy of Autonomia Operaia, via collective but intimate encounters, thus reconfiguring the space's meaning via a temporal gap. Whereas the art museum was inhabited by the ghostly remains of the trial, the Aula Bunker suddenly, albeit temporarily, became alive again. The informal gathering, in which some of the protagonists of the April 7th trial were able to visit the empty rooms almost three decades after the events, was conceived as a collective performance, a quasi-cathartic moment offering the possibility of a shared memory across generations.

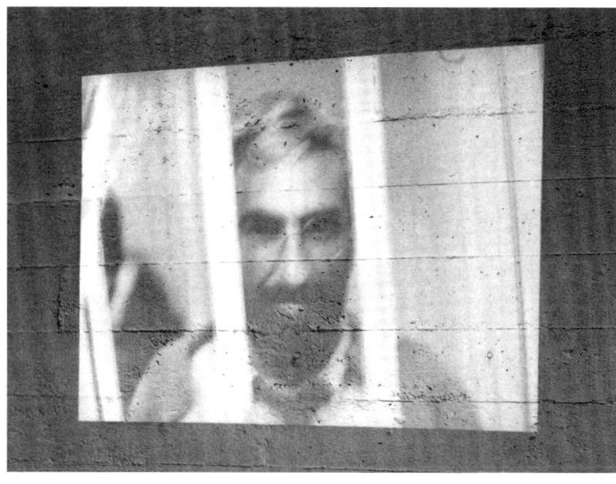
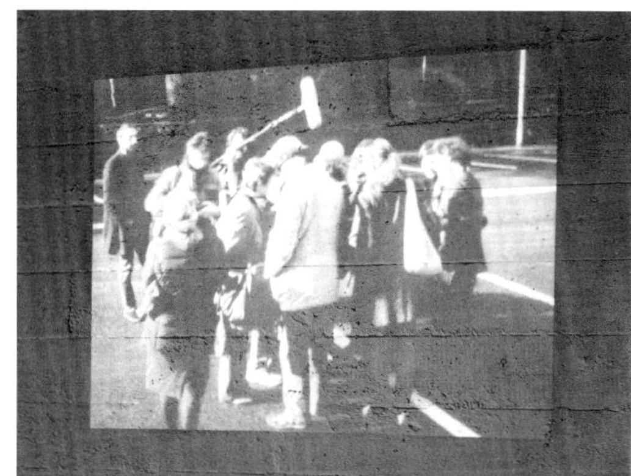

12   Rossella Biscotti
in conversation with
Cesare Pietroiusti,
p. 105.

13   Rossella Biscotti's
email to the author,
30 May 2020.

14   Annette Kuhn,
*Family Secrets.
Acts of Memory and
Imagination* (London:
Verso, 2002), p. 6.

15   The film was first
shown at e-flux in
New York in 2014, and
later that same year
at WIELS in Brussels.
The very first perfor-
mance in connection
with this work was
presented in 2011
at the Rijksakademie
in Amsterdam as part
of the artist's open
studio.

This performative reunion was captured in a Super-8 film that Biscotti edited together with footage filmed during the production of the concrete casts, which were made in the same space. While discussing a similar usage of Super-8 for her project *The Prison of Santo Stefano*, the artist admits that her films are sometimes mistaken for archival materials.[12] This film also embraces an ambivalence: at first sight, the use of black-and-white, the absence of sound and a clear narrative, the grainy quality of the images and the Super-8 itself all suggest family films in the pre-digital age of the 1960s and 1970s, the years at the centre of the trial's hearings. We become aware of the footage's contemporaneity only when we watch how the sculptures were produced. The camera walks us through the semi-abandoned spaces of the Aula Bunker, where former defendants, friends and relatives join the artist in engaging in an informal and rather joyful commemoration. As the artist herself explains in relation to her use of an 8 mm camera, "the footage is a sort of diary of small events in which the act of filming is not separated from the active participation in the life recorded in the making."[13] The fact that the footage suggests the intimacy of a private diary is particularly meaningful in a work in which memories, subjects and temporalities intertwine. Film scholar and cultural critic Annette Kuhn has described family albums as sites in which the personal and the collective come together; as memory texts, they "constantly call to mind the collective nature of the activity of remembering."[14] The memorial quality of the Super-8 film, with its reference to intimacy and community, links to the collective act of commemoration taking place in the Aula Bunker in a way that underlines the work's political meaning. This has to be understood not as a means of revealing the ultimate truth about the April 7th trial, but as the work's ability to produce knowledge, through the exploration of the connections between public historical events, personal memories and collective formations.

The film component of *The Trial* has been shown from 2013 on as a crucial feature of the work's subsequent iterations, as the whole installation shifted its focus onto the performative dimension that was developed for dOCUMENTA (13) (via live translation and the bodily co-presence of translator-performers and the audience).[15] This new configuration emphasises the question of translation, not just from one language to another, but from a specific space, format or epoch to another. Each restaging of the performance was in fact reconfigured according to the local context. Most importantly, it was conducted in the different languages spoken in each venue (English, Flemish, Dutch, etc). A translation is always, at the same time, an interpretation and an adaptation that implies a shift in time and place.

It's an operation that involves language, form and time: Biscotti collects architectural fragments in order to translate them into sculptures and transforms the tape recorded speeches into live performance. Translation therefore does not merely refer to the problem of accessibility, but rather it becomes a means through which the historical event is actualised as part of an experience that involves time, space and the body.

The diverse features composing *The Trial*—performance, film, sound and sculpture—are strongly connected to one another as they reflect upon the problem of translating historical processes into a contemporary perspective. It is no coincidence that, eschewing a linear or descriptive account of the April 7th trial, Biscotti chooses instead to concentrate on the ties connecting an array of fragments: the architectural space and its coercive function as a structural component of the repressive state apparatus; the tape recorded voices as a return of the repressed, lingering over the tangible traces of the trial; the performance (be it the gathering in the Aula Bunker or the live-translations during dOCUMENTA (13)) as a re-enactment that looks at the historical event from the perspective of both live and life experience.

From Industrial Labour to the Information Society

While reflecting upon to the topicality of Biscotti's work, it is hard not to think about the historical circumstances in which her research took place: namely the 2008 crisis, followed by the austerity measures that marked the ensuing decade. On a more local level, the moment also corresponds with the impending fall of Silvio Berlusconi and his right-wing neoliberal government, in which legal procedures have played a crucial role. The economic crisis corresponds to a reorganisation of the capitalist economy, whose foundations can be traced back to the moment of transition that was at the centre of Autonomia Operaia's analysis. These included the acknowledgement of a crucial transformation in the working-class composition, in line with capitalism's radical restructuring, which involved large- and medium-sized companies' response to the workers' struggles that had challenged their operations over the past decades. As the defendants explain in a document written collectively during the trial, the mid-1970s had seen the emergence of a new political subjectivity that refused the work ethics of traditional workers' organisations.[16] This new subject was instead primarily interested in the building of autonomous spaces and the fight for universal income as a means to reclaim life's time (*tempo di vita*) and a liberation from the constraints of the factory, while searching for a new community.

16　"Do You Remember Revolution? A Proposal for an Interpretation of the Italian Movement of the 1970s," document signed by Lucio Castellano, Arrigo Cavallina, Giustino Cortiana, Mario Dalmaviva, Luciano Ferrari Bravo, Chicco Funaro, Antonio Negri, Paolo Pozzi, Franco Tommei, Emilio Vesce and Paolo Virno, published in the newspaper *Il Manifesto*, 20 February 1983 and 22 February 1983 (English translation by Ed Emery online: libcom.org/library/ do-you-remember-revolution, last accessed 1 June 2020).

Biscotti chooses to conclude her edited montage with an excerpt from the trial's proceedings that points precisely to this new political subject. In the excerpt, Paolo Virno describes the transformations affecting the working class by the end of the 1970s:

> It has been said many times that these were the peons of bidonvilles or of the peripheral neighborhoods who revolted against the economic crisis. Not at all. As we were interpreting and living 1977, it became clear to us that this was a social subject that was anything but marginal: that on the contrary was rich with learning, rich with knowledge, rich with productive capacity [...]. It was the new productive subject that emerged from the [capitalist] restructuring process.

Virno also underlines the role played by the emerging information technologies, by stating that despite its exploitative nature, the new informal economy also represented an opportunity to "disentangle ourselves from the factory regime." As Virno and others would later develop, the emergence of this new subjectivity was at the centre of the post-Fordist restructuring of the work force. In this changing configuration, new forms of exploitation took advantage of the workers' ability to react to the technological innovations, their familiarity with the web of communication and information, their ability to negotiate among the different possibilities offered by the job market, and so on.[17] Interestingly, the counter-revolutionary turn marked by the defeat of the Autonomia Operaia and the transition towards post-Fordism also provides the context of the rise of Berlusconi, private TV and the information industry being one of the driving sectors of 1980s Italian economy.

It seems therefore no coincidence that, in the audio recordings she edited, Biscotti decided to emphasise this particular passage, which refers to one of the fundamental issues at stake during the trial: namely the ways in which Autonomia

17 See Branden W. Joseph, "Interview with Paolo Virno," *Grey Room*, n. 21, Fall 2005, pp. 29–30. See also Paolo Virno, "Do You Remember Counter-Revolution?" (1994), in *L'orda d'oro 1968–1977*, pp. 639–57.

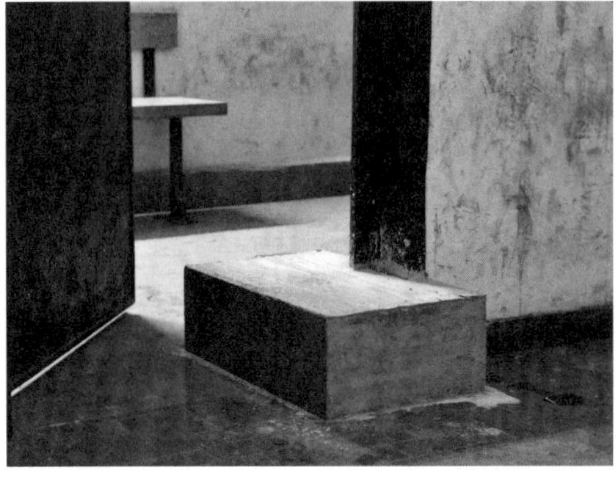

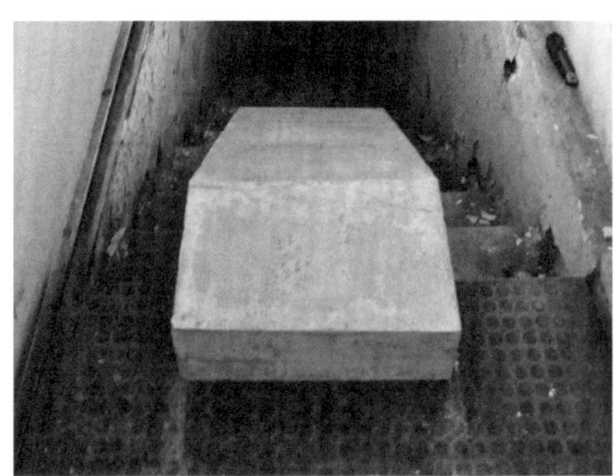

     Giovanna Zapperi

Operaia had interpreted capitalism's ongoing transformation
from a revolutionary perspective. And yet this meditation on the
transformations in the forms of labour within Western societies
brings to mind the attendant shifts that occurred within the
artistic field at the turn of the 1970s. The demise of industrial
labour in the context of the emergence of the post-Fordist economy, with its emphasis on technology, information and informal
labour, significantly affected artistic practices as well. *The Trial*
suggests this moment in the field of the visual arts by juxtaposing the use of reinforced concrete, with its inevitable reference
to Minimalist sculpture and the art of the late 1960s, with audio
recordings that were originally broadcast on radio.

Minimalist and post-Minimalist artists, such as Carl
Andre and Robert Morris, redefined their activity in terms of
labour, thus siding with the working class, while mobilising
materials and procedures that made explicit reference to factory
work.[18] This reference thus implicitly indicates not only a time
of industrial production, but also the moment in which industrial
labour was in the process of being replaced by a new technological environment. At exactly the same moment, an array of other
artistic practices engaged more explicitly with the information
society by turning to video, performance, and other "demateri-
alised" practices. *The Trial*'s resistance to transparency and the
seeming gap between the form and the meaning it conveys can
therefore be addressed within the artistic strategies it mobilises.
In juxtaposing concrete-abstract sculptures with the sensorial
dimension provided by the tape-recorded voices, Biscotti makes
reference to this moment of transition affecting art practices
as well as society at large. In particular, the way in which her
installation oscillates between sculpture, technology and live
performance underlines a certain instability of form by introducing bodily presence within both the sculptural environment and
the historical narrative per se. Idioms that make explicit reference to an epoch of artistic reckoning with some of the issues
raised during the proceedings are introduced as a constitutive

18   See Julia Bryan-
Wilson, *Art Workers.
Radical Practice in
the Vietnam War Era*
(Berkeley and Los
Angeles: University
of California Press,
2009).

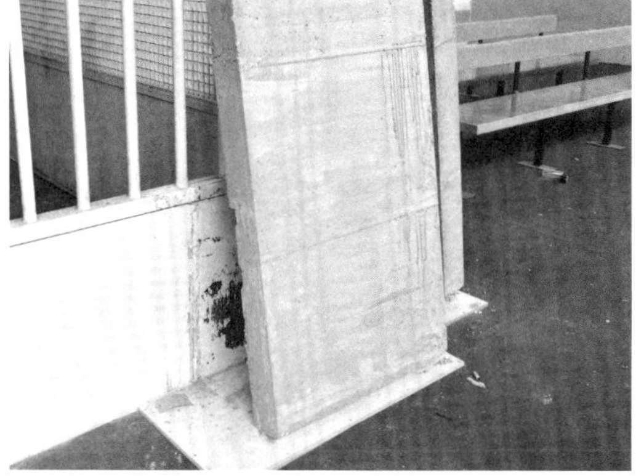

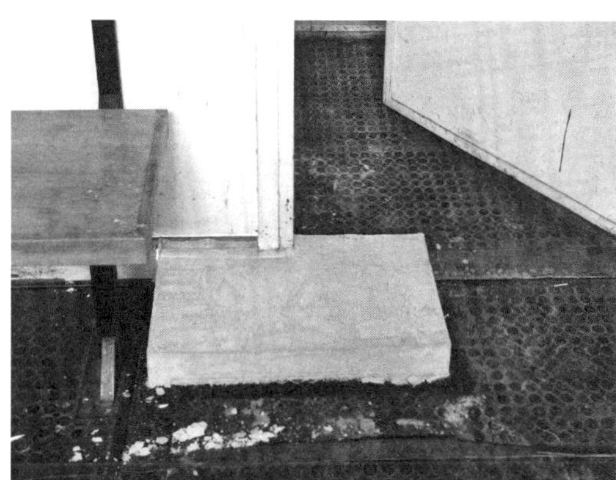

component of a work that deals with that historical moment. In this sense, *The Trial* incorporates a reflection on its own formal vocabulary and procedures within the broader inquiry into the practices, discourses, and theories that were at the centre of the April 7th trial.

In looking at a critical moment of transition that involved both the history of the revolutionary left and the transformation of workers' subjectivity, Biscotti brings us back to the issues at stake during the case against the Autonomia Operaia, whose long-lasting consequences are still visible today. Using a performative mapping of its legal setting, the artist actively reclaims the legacy of Autonomia Operaia for her own practice, therefore stressing its significance for today's critical theory, art and activism.

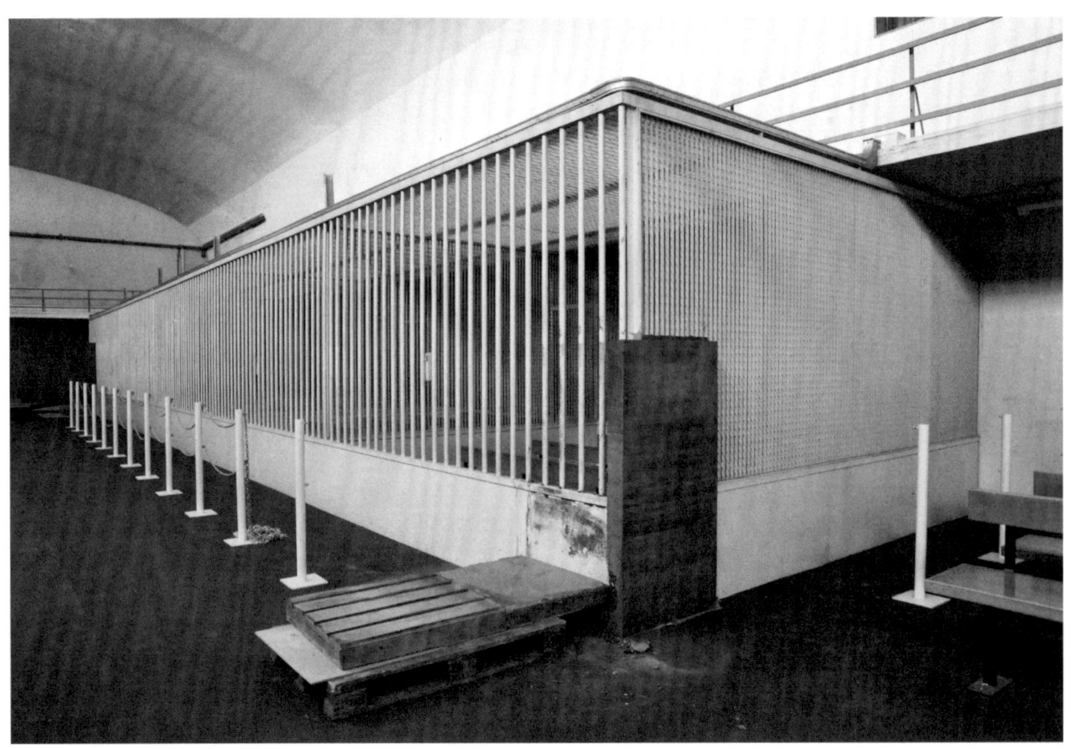

The Interpreter: Translation, Action and Politics

Daniel Blanga Gubbay

On 7 June 2014, I participated in Rossella Biscotti's *The Trial*, at WIELS, Brussels. I was the interpreter of Paolo Virno. I interpreted him in the sense the word takes on in simultaneous translation. Starting in 2010 and adapting to different contexts, *The Trial* developed as a performance based on the April 7th trial (1983–1984)—proceedings against members of the left-wing revolutionary Autonomia Operaia [Workers Autonomy] and other activists close to the movement. A six-hour long version of the recordings of this trial was played in headphones worn by a series of interpreters, who were called upon to offer their simultaneous translation in the local tongue. Years have passed, but this text began at that moment.

1

The interpreter is immersed in an act of isolation and listening: a voice resounds in the headphones, enters the ears, vibrates in the eardrum. The interpreter's gaze is often suspended, vacant, not wishing to be distracted, in a mark of loyalty to that single thread of a voice whose every word must be captured. The whole body of the interpreter is held in a state of total listening, yet their mouth disobeys and starts translating. The interpreters speak but do not hear themselves; they cannot pay attention to the sound of their own voice, because they must remain devoted to the voice they are listening to; because no sooner have their lips opened to pronounce the translation than new words reach the headphones, demanding equal attention. The voice presses on, forcing them to continue. The speech does not halt. So, the simultaneous interpreters are structurally late: they chase content and when they think one phrase is within reach, they realise that another phrase has already formed and erupted from the previous one.

At the same time, another sensation of lateness pressures the interpreter on—something similar to what Jacques Derrida called *différance*,[1] deferral, or the constitutive delay between the sensible and the intelligible. The interpreters start translating with no knowledge of how a phrase is going to end. From the outset, they chase meaning, which in turn might affect their word choice. And whilst running, they try to keep an eye on the horizon, on the ultimate meaning of the phrase. Simultaneous translation carries the interpreter along a fast-paced pursuit, across digressions and turns of phrases—something akin to a car chase in the narrow alleys of a historic city centre. Hesitations grant breathing room, but are also opportunities to revise the meaning of a phrase. The interpreters tail, chase and translate before knowing what is around the corner; they catch a glimpse of the end of a phrase and hit their stride in a vain attempt to grab hold of its body.

In her 1993 essay "The Politics of Translation,"[2] Gayatri Chakravorty Spivak speaks of translation as a form of body-to-body contact. One of the first translators of Derrida into English, Spivak describes her work on the texts of the Bengali poet Sadhak Rāmprasād Sen, concluding that if translation is the most intimate act of reading, the act is erotic rather than ethical: an act of negotiation in the presence of two bodies and subjectivities.

Rossella Biscotti's *The Trial* thus opens with an act that seems to condense—or rather, to translate in a single image (the image of the simultaneous translation)—the different stages of an investigation: from the listening in to tapped phones, to the tailing, to the violent clash of an interrogation.

In doing so, rather than approaching a reconstruction, *The Trial* suggests the possibility of a trial of the April 7th trial itself, and of its investigative and judiciary methods—which remain one of the most controversial juridical legacies of the Years of Lead.[3]

2

The voice moves forward through the headphones, enters the ear, vibrates in the eardrums. The body of the interpreter is filled up with words that are not their own, but that they are obliged to utter. Words are part of an inverse process: they do not originate from the body, but instead enter it, as if swallowed—and from there, they affect it from within, pressing forward to the rhythm of given commands. This language is more than a sap that nourishes and guides the movements of the mouth; it is a substance capable of gradually altering its autonomy. In the translation process, the interpreter and the original voice hold a special relationship: the interpreter is obliged to utter phrases

1   Jacques Derrida, "Cogito et histoire de la folie," *Revue de métaphysique et de morale*, 68/4 (Oct.–Dec. 1963), pp. 460–494; "Cogito and the History of Madness," in *Writing and Difference*, trans. Alan Bass (London: Routledge, 1978), pp. 36–76.

2   Gayatri Chakravorty Spivak, "The Politics of Translation," in *Outside in the Teaching Machine* (London: Routledge, 1993).

3   It is a term commonly used by Italian media and historians to describe the period between the late 1960s and the 1980s, marked by widespread social unrest and episodes of political violence.

in the first person. The interpreters never say, "*Virno* thinks that"; but they say, "*I* think that." And by saying this, they find themselves having to think it. Their palate is stained, they got their hands dirty. Even if they wanted to take them back, they have already spoken those words.

In *The Sacrament of Language: An Archaeology of the Oath*, Giorgio Agamben describes this irreversible power of language, starting with performative verbs: "the performative is a linguistic enunciation that does not describe a state of affairs, but immediately produces a fact, actualises its meaning. *I swear* is, in this sense, the perfect paradigm of a 'speech act.'"[4]

So, what is *this fact* produced in the body of the interpreter over the course of simultaneous translation?

It seems to be two-fold. On the one hand, the interpreters try to be invisible, to be at the service of the speech that animates their body. At the same time, they have no safeguards from the intimacy of what they are saying: they not only are a vehicle for content, they also raise their voice when it has to be raised, sometimes smile when a smile is called for. The interpreters are forcedly transported inside the subjectivity of the voice they interpret, in a desire for identification. Similar to the relationship a medium has with the hosted spirit, here is the double thread animating the interpreter at work: an attempt at anonymity, in the mere service of speech, and the obligation to constantly flirt with the possibility of getting inside a new biography—that of the voice being translated.

This specific dichotomy between obedience and metamorphosis—a dichotomy so foundational to simultaneous translation—seems to magically echo the different points of the political discourse spoken within the Aula Bunker of the Foro Italico during the April 7th trial.

On the one hand, in the filigree of the words of the defence, there seems to lie an idea of political struggle as a kind of service, thus as obedience. In contrast with the nascent society of a progressive re-affirmation of the *I*, political struggle negates the subject and is described as a movement in which individuality is at the service of a cause, dedicated to something other than itself. On the other hand, the trial ends with Paolo Virno's speech on the aftermath of 1977, on a rising interest in job mobility as a possibility of metamorphosis:

> It could be that this mobility, this precarious labour, contained a strong element of the workers' self-determination, of flexibility with the work day [...]. In our view, work was no longer some kind of settled destiny that dictates that one starts working at twenty years old and stays in the same workplace until it is time to retire. The factory

4   Giorgio Agamben, *Il Sacramento de Linguaggio: Archeologia del Giuramento*, par. 23, 2008; *The Sacrament of Language: An Archaeology of the Oath (Homo Sacer II, 3)* trans. Adam Kotsko (Cambridge: Polity Press, 2010), p. 342.

PRESIDING JUDGE
Severino Santiapichi

JUDGE *A LATERE*
Nino Abbate

PUBLIC PROSECUTOR
Antonio Marini

DEFENDANTS
Cecco Bellosi
Augusto Finzi
Chicco Funaro
Alberto Magnaghi
Silvana Marelli
Toni Negri
Paolo Pozzi
Franco Tommei
Emilio Vesce
Paolo Virno

INFORMANTS
Carlo Casirati
Mario Ferrandi
Paolo Morandini
other voices

WITNESSES
[FOR THE PROSECUTION]
Severino Galante
other voices

DEFENCE LAWYERS
Tommaso Mancini
Giuliano Spazzali
other voices

PLAINTIFF LAWYER
Fausto Tarsitano

ATTORNEY GENERAL
Oscar Fiumara

12:00
JUDGE hurriedly reads
transcripts of Negri's
10 April 1979 interrogation
(FR) VALERIA ROVEDA

12:13
VIRNO opening statement
(FR) DANIEL BLANGA-GUBBAY

12:21
VESCE [*from the defendants'
cage*] declares end of his
14-day hunger strike
(NL) CLAUDIA BONAMINI

12:24
JUDGE defines Negri's
character [*extract from
Domination and Sabotage,
1977, and his confiscated
personal agenda read into
the court records*]
(FR) ANDREA CAVAZZINI

12:29
NEGRI on witness stand
(FR) JEAN-FRANÇOIS GAVA

12:46
TOMMEI testifies on
Controinformazione magazine
(FR) ALESSANDRA COPPOLA

12:53
PLAINTIFF LAWYER cross-
examines NEGRI on the state's
social democratization
(FR) ANDREA CAVAZZINI

12:58
BELLOSI [*from the cage*]
reports on the physical and
living conditions of detainees
(NL) CLAUDIA BONAMINI

13:01
FINZI testifies on the use
of guerrilla tactics in the
factory struggle
(FR) SERGE VANDIEPENBEECK

13:15
JUDGE questions NEGRI on Wild
Cats strikes and vanguardism
(NL) SONJA LAVAERT

13:26
JUDGE questions MAGNAGHI on
the audio recordings of Potere
Operaio's public assemblies
(NL) SARAH VANTORRE

13:34
VIRNO qualifies Potere
Operaio's terminology
(FR) DANIEL BLANGA-GUBBAY

13:48
ATTORNEY GENERAL presses
NEGRI on 'red terror'
[*extract from* 33 Lessons on
Lenin, *1977, read into the
court records*]
(NL) SONJA LAVAERT

13:57
DEFENCE LAWYER on the
'ash heap of history'
(FR) GIOVANNI MELOGLI

14:01
PUBLIC PROSECUTOR aggressively
redirects the court through
shouting
(FR) GIOVANNI MELOGLI

14:03
WITNESSES time-lapse
(NL) SARAH VANTORRE

14:10
TOMMEI testifies on his
politics and relationship
with Negri
(FR) ALESSANDRA COPPOLA

14:24
NEGRI clarifies the difference
between 'appropriation' and
'expropriation'
(FR) JEAN-FRANÇOIS GAVA

14:35
PLAINTIFF LAWYER questions
TOMMEI
(FR) ALESSANDRA COPPOLA

14:37
BELLOSI [*from the cage*]
on repressive measures at
Rebibbia prison
(NL) CLAUDIA BONAMINI

14:43
FUNARO [*from the cage*] affirms
Bellosi's call for solidarity
(NL) CLAUDIA BONAMINI

14:45
JUDGE questions NEGRI and
TOMMEI on the Red Aid network
(FR) AMANDINE MÉLAN

14:55
JUROR reads testimony
of a Face Standard employee
(FR) LEONARDO SFORZA

14:58
FUNARO testifies on Face
Standard's factory arson
(FR) SIMONA DENICOLAI

15:02
NEGRI testifies on 1974
and Autonomia
(FR) ANNE HERLA

15:07
JUDGE presses NEGRI on the
Argelato affair [*extract from
Rosso* *magazine of 15 March –
April 1975 read into the court
records*]
(FR) LEONARDO SFORZA

15:12
PUBLIC PROSECUTOR reads
statements from Red Brigades
informants
(FR) LEONARDO SFORZA

15:16
VIRNO on Red Brigades threats
against Autonomia prisoners
held at Palmi high-security
prison
(FR) DANIEL BLANGA-GUBBAY

15:23
FUNARO [*from the cage*] states
solidarity with prisoners
on hunger strike
(NL) CLAUDIA BONAMINI

15:25
NEGRI exercises his right
to remain silent
(FR) LEONARDO SFORZA

15:26
PUBLIC PROSECUTOR calls
informants
(FR) LEONARDO SFORZA

15:30
VESCE [*from the cage*] decries
Autonomia's anti-terrorist
positions
(NL) CLAUDIA BONAMINI

15:31
JUDGE suspends the hearing
after the defendants leave
in protest
(FR) LEONARDO SFORZA

15:39
JUDGE reads Negri's arrest
warrant
(FR) LEONARDO SFORZA

15:40
VESCE [*from the cage*] draws
a parallel between Parliament
and the terrorism network
(NL) CLAUDIA BONAMINI

15:44
POZZI opening statement on
Autonomia's culture
(FR) ANNA RAIMONDO

15:53
JUDGE questions POZZI on *Rosso*
magazine's editorial position
(FR) ALLAN WEI

16:10
TOMMEI testifies about the
1976 demonstrations in Milan
(FR) ALESSANDRA COPPOLA

16:18
FERRANDI testifies on
the 1977 demonstration
and published photographs
picturing a gunfight between
student protesters and
the police
(FR) DUCCIO VIANI

16:26
JUDGE questions MORANDINI
on charges that the defendants
are 'corrupting the youth'
(FR) DUCCIO VIANI

16:37
JUDGE reads Ferrandi's
statement to the defendants
(NL) LORENZO BENEDETTI

16:42
FUNARO confronts FERRANDI
on the ethics and use of
informants
(FR) DUCCIO VIANI

16:53
GALANTE testifies on Autonomia
in the University of Padua
(FR) ELENA SARACENO

17:01
JUDGE questions MAGNAGHI
on the appropriation of
facilities at the University
of Milan for political use
(FR) STEFAN POLLAK

17:09
PUBLIC PROSECUTOR questions
GALANTE on student terrorism
at the University of Padua
(FR) ELENA SARACENO

17:15
VIRNO testifies on the 1977
student opposition to the
trade union police in the
University of Rome
(FR) DANIEL BLANGA-GUBBAY

17:16
JUDGE reads student flyer
stating that self-managed
seminars are not acts of
terrorism
(FR) GAIA CARABILLO

17:21
CASIRATI refuses to answer
JUDGE and DEFENCE LAWYERS
(FR) IRIS MARANO

17:35
MARELLI [*from the cage*] reads
a statement signed by all the
defendants that condemns the
use of informants
(NL) CLAUDIA BONAMINI

17:38
DEFENCE LAWYER objects
to the reading of all the
proceedings' records
(FR) GIOVANNI MELOGLI

17:42
PUBLIC PROSECUTOR pontificates
in his closing statement
(FR) ANNA RISPOLI

17:57
VIRNO on the 1977 emergence
of cognitive labour and its
precarity
(FR) DANIEL BLANGA-GUBBAY

5   Paolo Virno,
in the April 7 trial
recording. www.
radioradicale.it/
processi/457/
processo-7-aprile.

was no longer a life sentence: it was an episode in
one's biography.[5]

During the trial, Virno anticipated a demand: to think in depth
about the idea of flexibility, which was set to become the key
to exploitation in later decades.

By placing the act of simultaneous interpretation at
the centre of the performance—and its essence caught between
obedience to speech and the shifting of identity—*Il Processo
(The Trial)* emerges as a prism through which to reflect the
nuances and complexities of the political discourse surrounding the April 7th trial.

3

However, despite translation being wedged between attempts
at anonymity and risks of identification, it would be impossible
to regard the real biography of the interpreter as insignificant.
In "Politics of Translation," Spivak reminds that there is no
neutrality in the work of translation, even though it is a form
of submission to the rhetorical framework of the text. On the
contrary—and from Spivak's essential feminist, Marxist and
postcolonial perspective—it is always filtered through a weight
of experience, where gender, class, origin and the interpreter's
biography converge.

It is not coincidental that Rossella Biscotti chooses not
to work with professional interpreters, but calls on people who,
in one way or another, have some link to political thought. The
translation might be imperfect, but it opens the wider question
of what it means, after all, to translate, as well as the possibility
that every translation is the superposition of three different
forms of translation.

The Trial has been presented in multiple linguistic contexts. Iterations have been performed in New York, Brussels,
and Moscow, as well as in Marrakech, as a parallel event to the
biennial, and in Kassel, Germany, as part of dOCUMENTA (13).
The original recordings have undergone simultaneous translations into German, Arabic, English, French, Dutch and Russian.
The first form of translation—translation on a linguistic level—
is certainly the most evident.

In Bologna, in 2011, a version of *The Trial* was shown
with a translation from Italian to Italian. This version helps put
focus on the presence of a second level of translation, that is not
only linguistic, but also, one might say, temporal. If in the performance, translation is simultaneous, it is not so in the sense
usually given to the term: that is, as the simultaneous occurrence

of the speech's production and its translation. The voices of defendants Franco Tommei, Carlo Casirati or Antonio Negri, of the judge, the prosecutor or Virno entering the headphones are from 1983–1984, and translating them means not only shifting from one language to another, but from one time to another. It means using now a word that would not have been used thirty years ago, pursuing language through its organic life. So, while translating *The Trial*, interpreters are simultaneously in 1984 and in 2014, in the Aula Bunker and in the performance, in the past with the original voices and in the present with the translation. They are also in the future of the transcription that will be made and remain as a posthumous document of the exhibition. Translation then becomes a place that holds different times together—a single space allowing them to coexist.

Finally, in working with non-professional interpreters—selected for their resonance with Italian political history or present-day activism—Rossella Biscotti suggests a third form of translation. The history of the April 7th trial does not resurface in a vacuum. It always appears at a given time and through interpreters whose present circumstances influence the act of translation. Ngũgĩ wa Thiong'o has defined translation as "the common language of languages,"[6] suggesting in this image the idea that languages communicate with one another through the language of translation, their lingua franca and meeting place. Similarly, *The Trial* opens a meeting space for distant political moments. Its power lies in the fact that it neither reconstructs history nor relegates it to the past, but lets its voices resonate in the contemporary political space. Following linguistic and temporal translation, the third form is political, opening yet another space for encounter.

6 "Kenya's Ngũgĩ wa Thiong'o on the Politics of Translation," publishing perspectives.com, 2017.

4

Work on *The Trial* began in 2010, on the eve of a transnational season of social protests in 2011 across the world, from the الربيع العربي/Arab Spring, to the Indignados movement in Spain, to Occupy Wall Street in New York. In 2013, together with Yates McKee, editor of *Tidal: Occupy Theory, Occupy Strategy*, Biscotti created a reading group to relate Autonomist writings and Marxist theories to the new Occupy movement.

The dissemination of these ideas was also at the core of the very April 7th trial. It is known that, faced with judicial violence, many defendants decided to use the court proceedings not only to defend Autonomia Operaia from accusations of armed struggle and cooperation with the Red Brigades, but also to spread a political idea that was being silenced at the time, allowing it to resonate within the concrete walls of the Aula Bunker, and from there, via broadcasts by Radio Radicale, to the rest of Italy. The trial was not the end of a political moment, but a political moment in itself. By placing these recordings at the centre of the performance, *The Trial* re-enacts this political strategy, turning the performance into an opportunity to disseminate content. The interpreters translate and repeat the phrase they hear in the headphones out loud, and in so doing they make the content audible to others, who might not have had access to it. Through this mechanism of listening and repeating, the structure of *The Trial* seems to anticipate by several months the political strategy of "the human microphone," which, while used in different countries, gained a level of media recognition thanks to its use at Zuccotti Park. Developed to circumvent the ban on amplifiers during the occupations, this technique was adopted to transmit speeches to large audiences. It consists of asking the people in the proximity of the orators to repeat, shouting in unison, what is said, thus amplifying the first voice and allowing for ideas and information to reach a wider public.

This kind of transmission not only disseminates information and content: it also passes on the strategy of transmission itself. In this gesture, what is amplified is not only the speech, but the form of making it audible, and politics as an indomitable form of life capable of bypassing attempts at its repression.

Finally, through the process of linguistic translation at the heart of the performance, political discourse widens the possibilities of its transmission as well. At each iteration of *The Trial*—and therefore with each translation—the words from the proceedings travel from language to language, mouth to mouth, changing and becoming stronger. To quote Cecilia Vicuña, language becomes migrant.[7] Each act of translation is a transmission to another language—and from there, it opens up new possibilities for further transmission. It is again Spivak, in "The Politics of Translation," who reminds us that translation is a crucial tool in the pursuit of a wider feminist agenda, it enables access for women working across languages and reclaims translation as both an act of transnational solidarity and a political gesture in its own right.

Thus, *The Trial* is not only inscribed in a politics of translation, but in a translation of politics: a strategy to make audible something that is not, to amplify its chances of transmission.

Rossella Biscotti's installation dissembles the Aula; she disseminates in space the concrete sculptures, casts of the Aula Bunker's courtroom architecture, prior to its demolition. The room is suddenly open and allows for the discourse it once contained to start propagating again, for the sound waves of a multitude of voices to echo, crash, at times become immersed in, and be translated into the different details of the present.

7   Cecilia Vicuña, "Language Is Migrant," www.poetryfoundation.org, 2016.

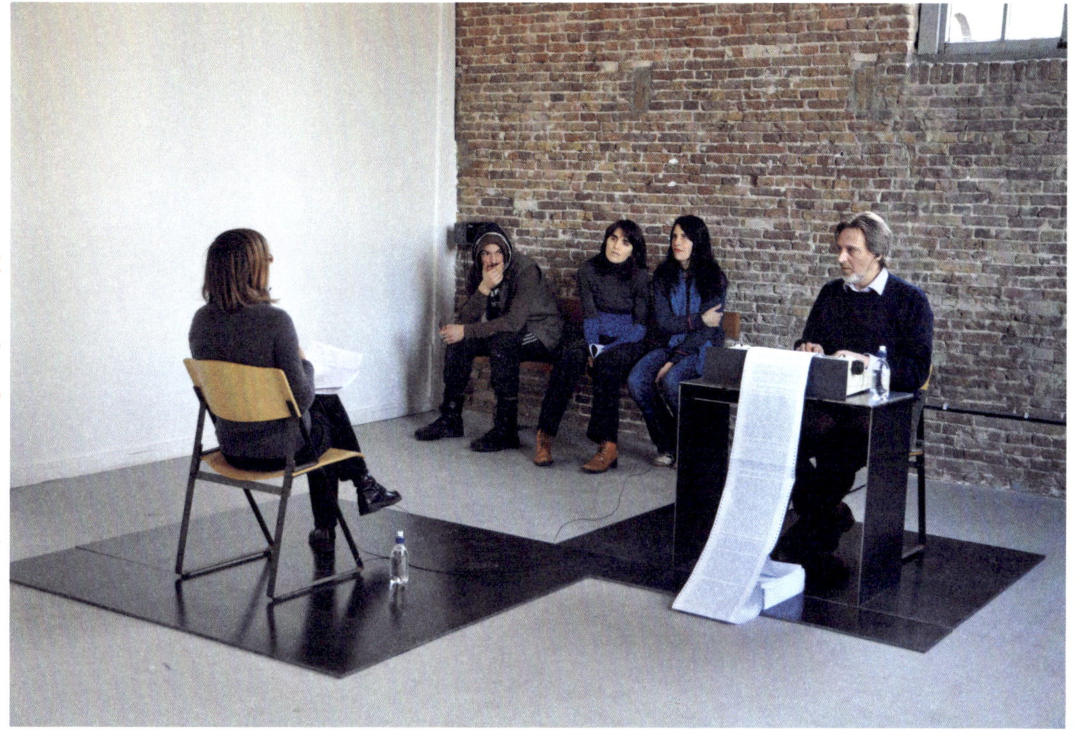

Durational performance with one simultaneous translator (Italian to English) and typist

209

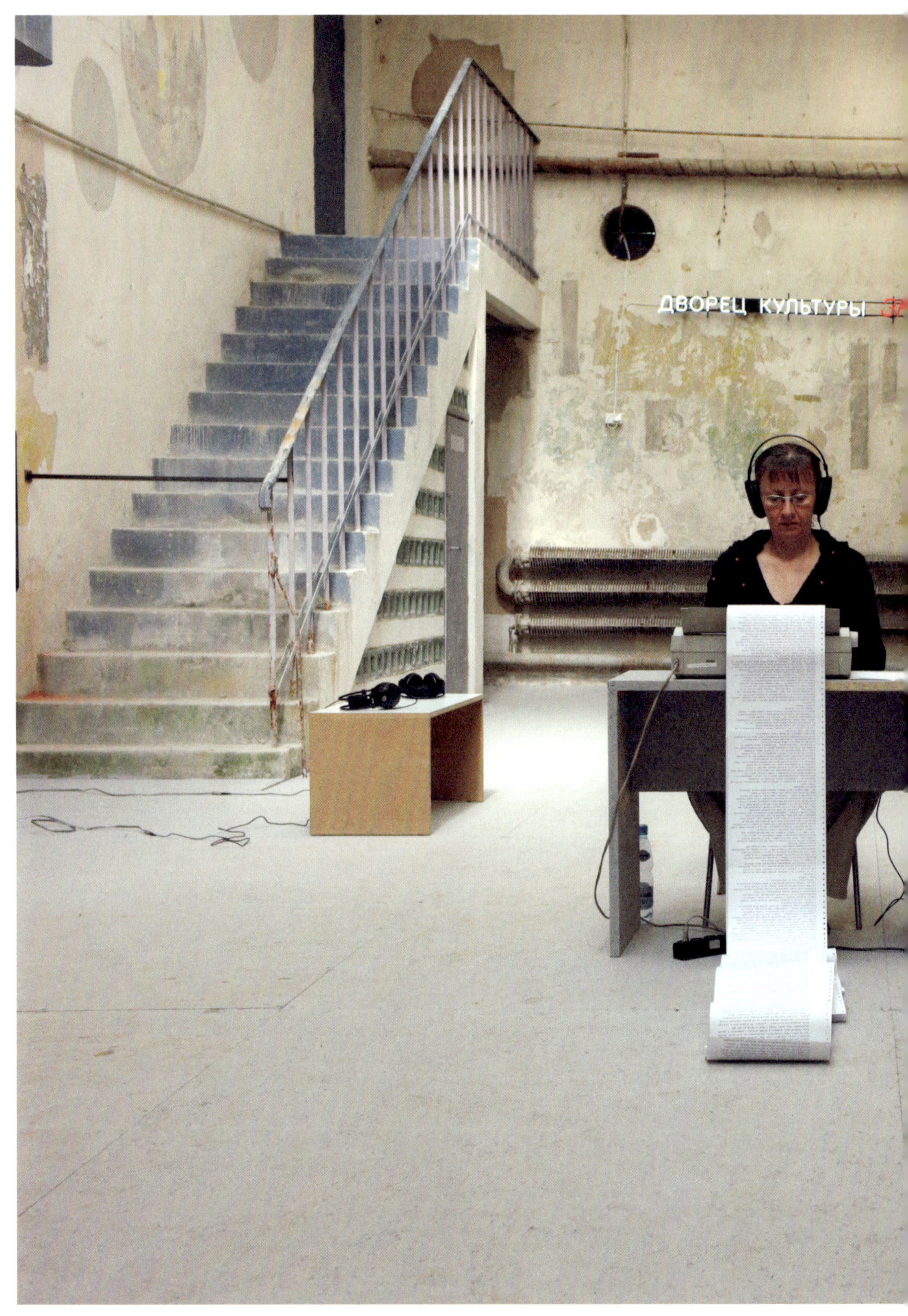

European Culture Congress, Wrocław, Poland, 8–11 September 2011
Durational performance with one simultaneous translator (Italian to Polish) and typist

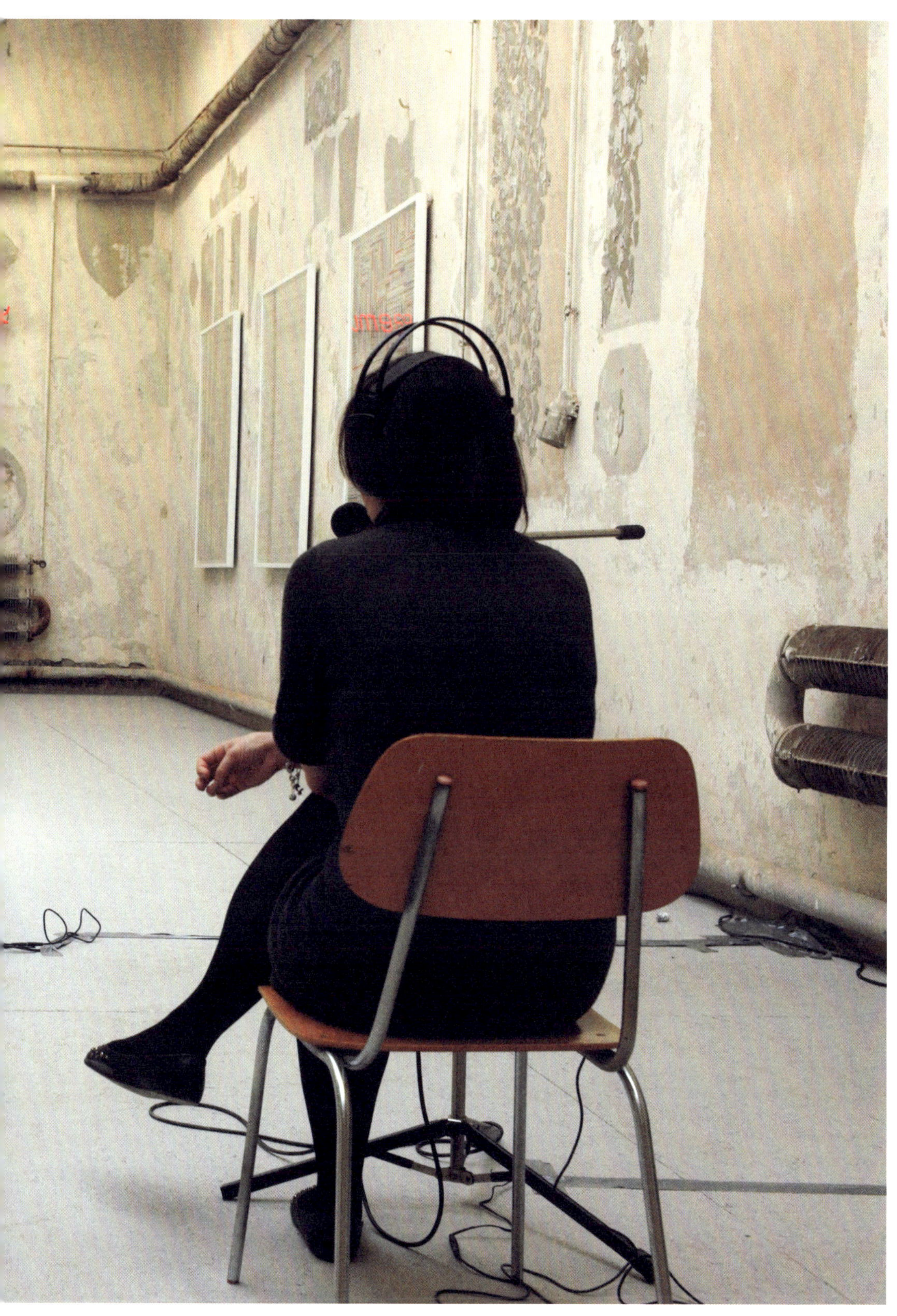

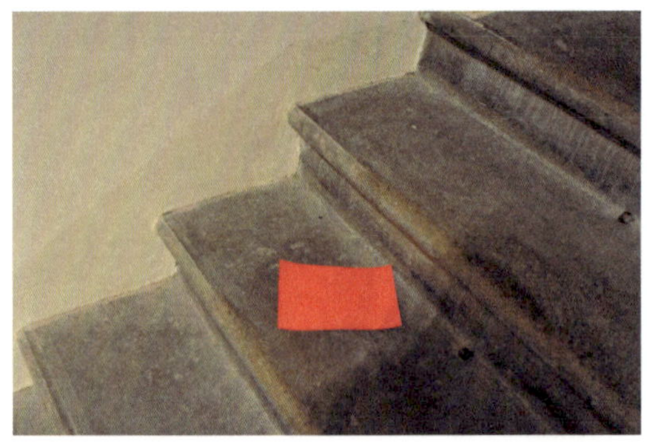
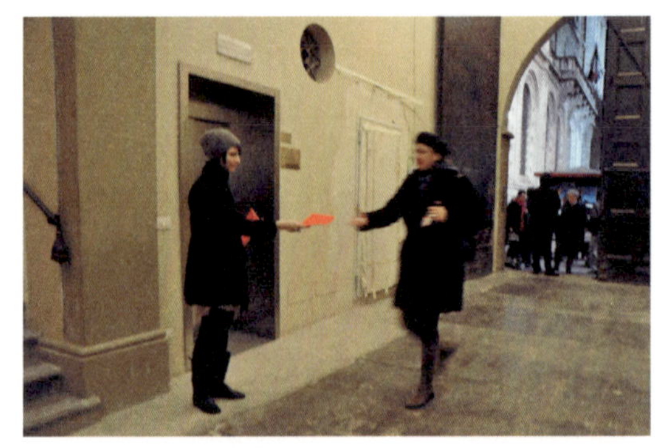
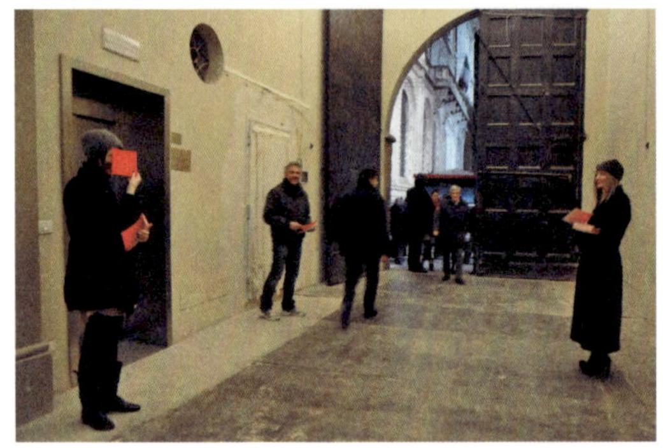
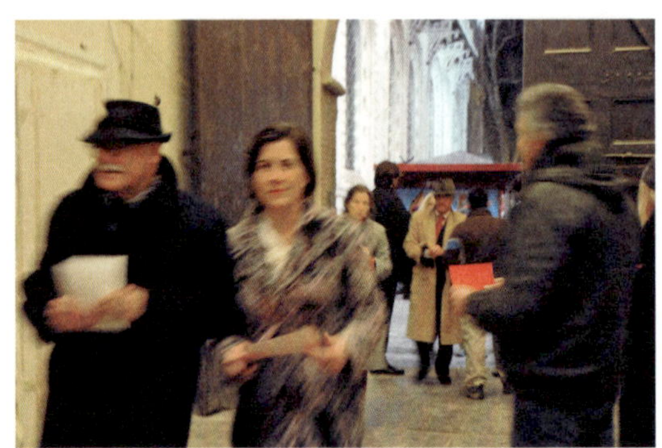
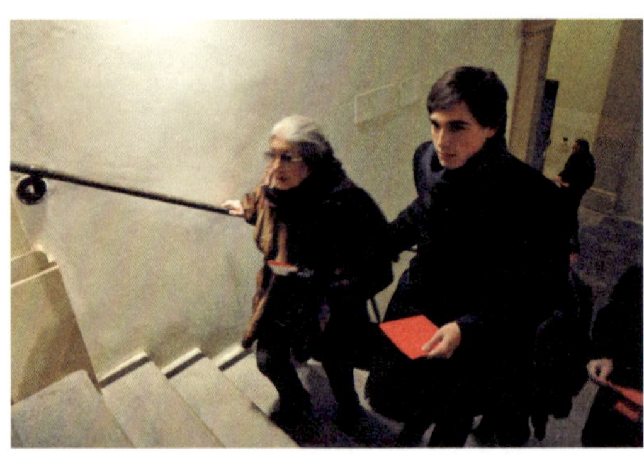
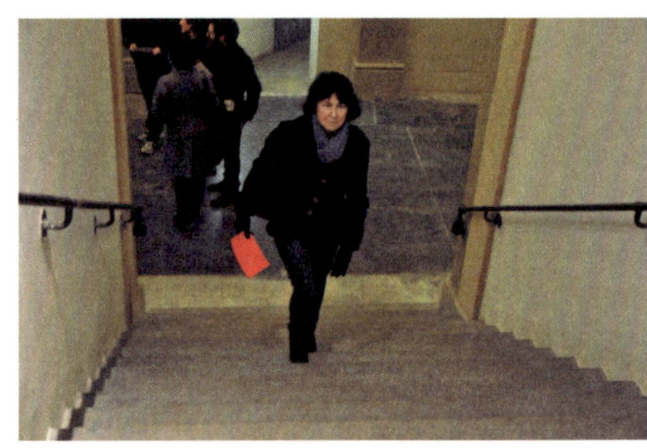
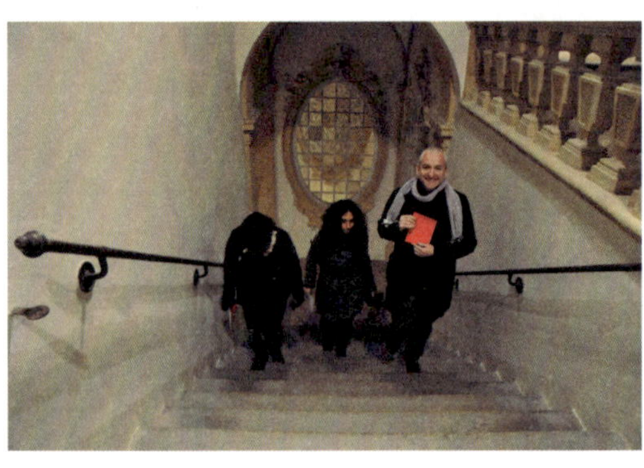
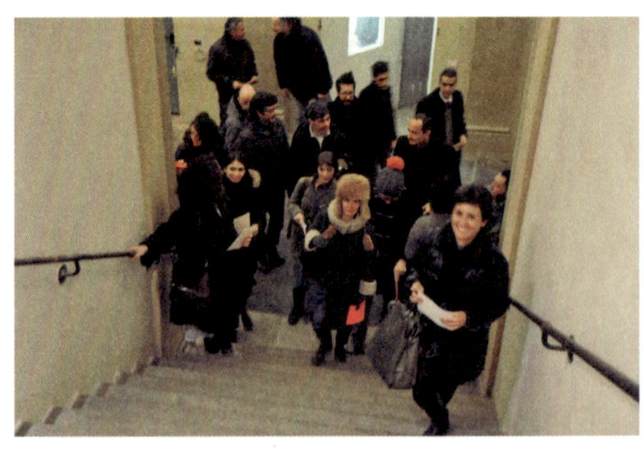

Palazzo Pepoli, Bologna, 28 January 2011

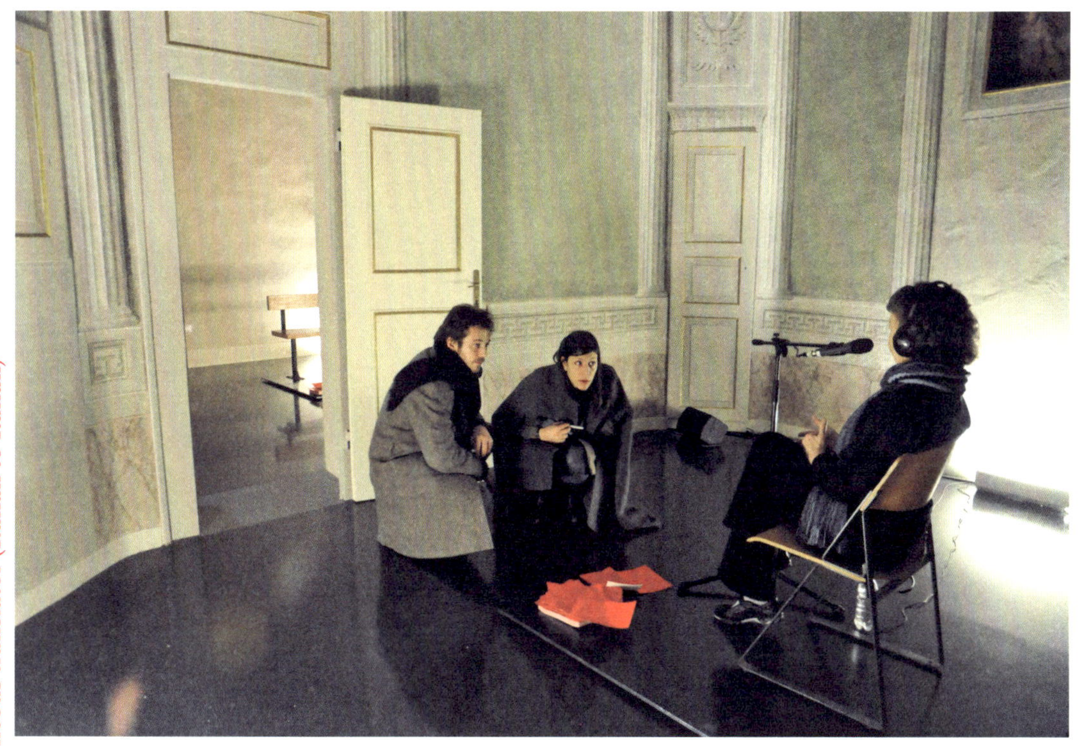

Durational performance with one simultaneous translator (Italian to Italian)

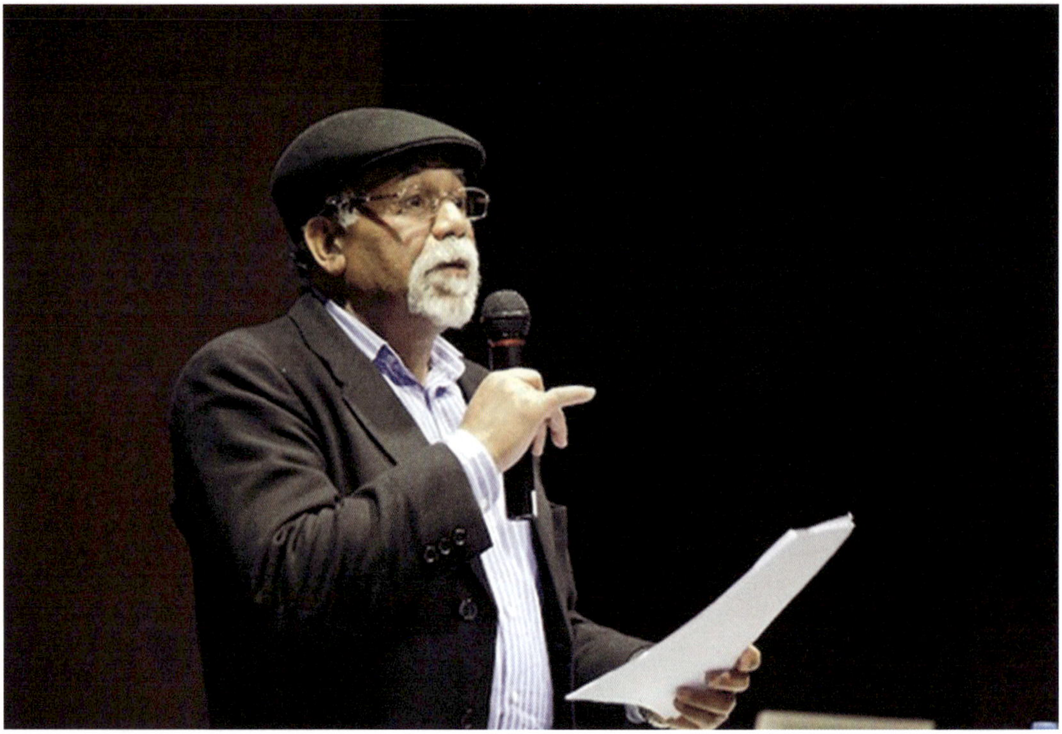

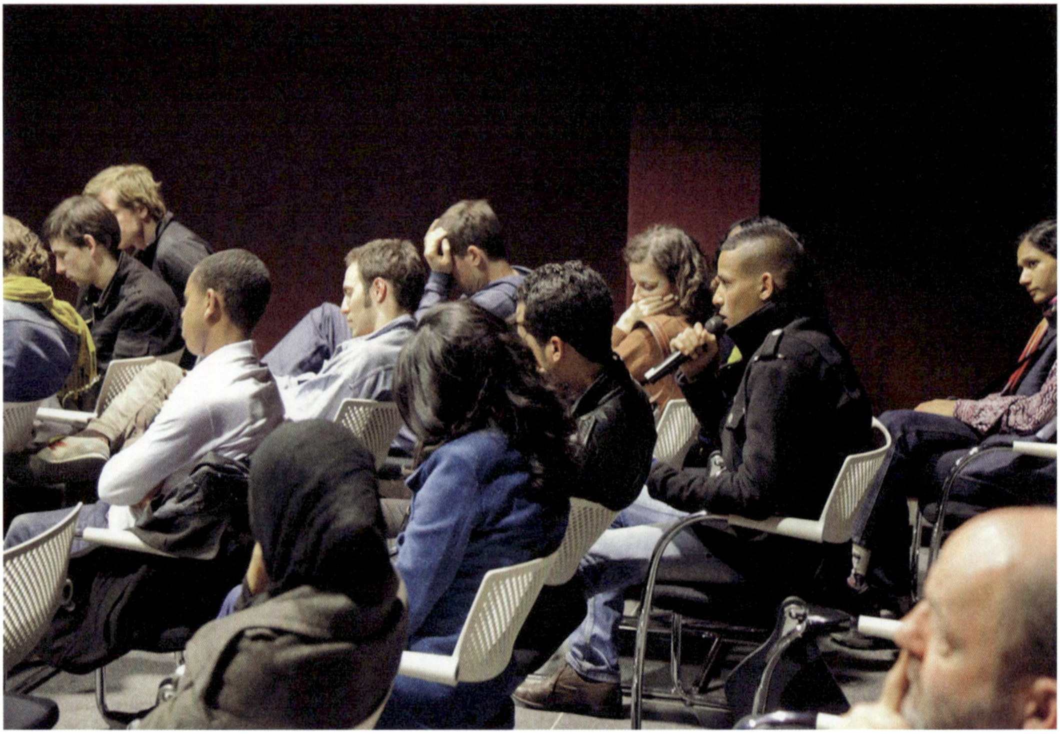

École Supérieure des Arts Visuels, Marrakech, 2 March 2012

<u>القاضي</u>

السيد بوتزي تتعرف التهم المنسوبة ليك ولي تسلمات ليك مرات ومرات وفي آخر مرة تسلمات لك بشهادة التوصل . كنتي دائما تتنكر هد التهم وتتأكد على أنك عمرك ما اعتبرتي راسك مرتكبها ، واثناء الإستجوابات القضائية صرحتي بأنك مابغيتش تعترف بالأسماء لي تعاونات معاك في تحرير جريدة روسو على أساس أن هد الاعتراف غادي يكون سبب في مس حرية هذ الأشخاص. أول سؤال غادي نوجه ليك الآن هو : واش تتعترف بهد الاتهامات المنسوبة ليك أو لا ؟ .

<u>باولو بوتسي</u>

نعم ، تتأكد التصريح ديالي السابقة ولكن إلى سمحتو بغيت نبين بعض الأشياء قبل ما تبداو التحقيق معايا :

ـ من بعد هد السنوات على تصريحي بغيت نقول أشنهو موقفي الآن ، سيدي الرئيس من الصعب الإجابة على اتهامات غريبة علي لأنني حتى لدبة ما عرفت باش أنا متهم وخلال التحقيق لي كان معايا رفضت باش نشرك ناس خرين في مسؤولية التهم لي موجهة لي وخاصة إلى فكرنا في الظروف لي كانت تتحيط باستجوابي الأول والثاني . لأن هاد الملابسات هي لي غادي تأدي لإلحاق الضرر بآخرين كن ذكرت أسماءهم . والآن من الضروري باش نقول بأنني مريت بتجربة قبيحة . مشيت باش نشهد في قضية متعلقة بالبروفيسور نيجري وأنا نلقى راسي في السجن ، إذن وجدت راسي في تجربة قاسية ومؤثرة .لهذا ما بغيتش ندخل أي إسم كان وأنا ما عارفت كيفاش غادي يكون رد فعل رجل النيابة العامة اتجاهو ، لهذا ماقدرتش نحشر اسميتو ونسبب ليه في عواقب وخيمة . هذا من جهة ومن جهة اخرى بغيت نعاود نأكد أنه في الوقت فاش كانو تيسولوني في الموضوع المتعلق بمقالات روسو كان بالضبط في 10 اكتوبر 1980 في ذاك الوقت فاش كانت يوميا تتكتب مقالات يمكنا نقولو غريبة ما عندها حتى علاقة بروسو . حتى ولات كل الجرائد تتسمى بجرائد روسو وملي بعض قضاة النيابة العامة تيصرحو بأن كل من تيشارك في تحرير المقالات المتعلقة بروسو تيتعبر عملهم بحالو بحال المشاركة في شي مجموعة مسلحة .هد التحديد بغيت نأطرو شيئما إلى سمحتو وبغيت نحاول نحدد به شخصيتي . لذلك بغيت نصرح بأشياء مخالفة لداك الشي لي صرحت به سابقا ، بمعنى أنني بغيت نعدل شيئما التصريحات ديالتي السابقة ، الشي لي غادي يجعلكم تحسو بشوي ديال التناقض في هد التصريحات ، رغم أنني ما غاديش نعتبر ها شخصيا تناقض

أنا تنعتقد بأني قلت بزاف ديال الأشياء قلت باني ماشي غير محرر في الجرائد لي تتسمى بجرائد روسو ولكن درت أنشطة سياسية متعددة حتى اليوم فاش تعتقلت عام 1980 اشتغلت مع جماعة من المحررين في جرائد متعددة ومجموعات تحرير متعددة وتنصرح بأني كنت نشطا في مجموعات سياسية متعددة في مجموعات سياسية خارج البرلمان.

وإلى سمحتو غادي نقدم ليكم مشواري السياسي . ماشي من السهل باش نعطي صورة

215

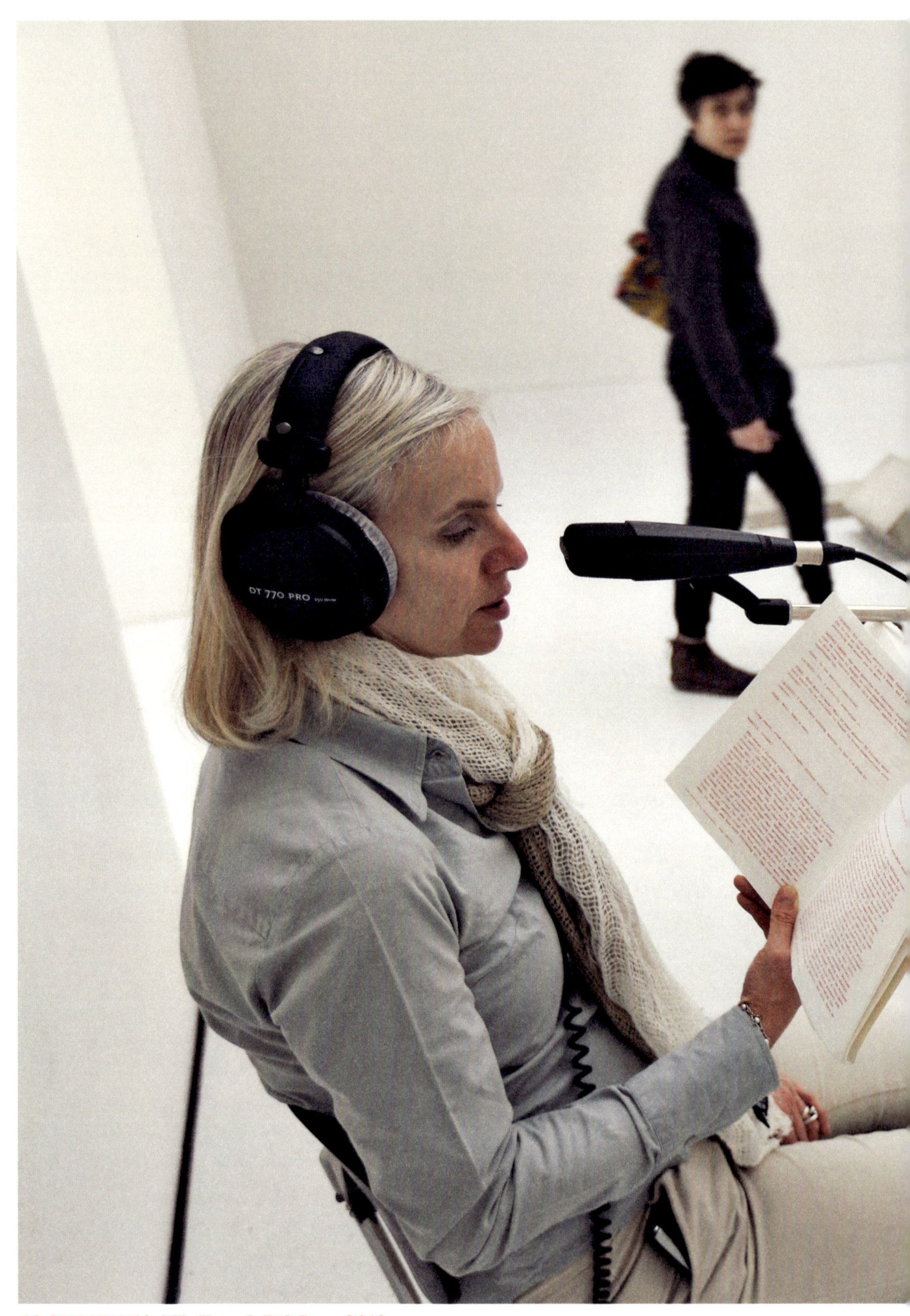

dOCUMENTA (13), Kassel, 7–8 June 2012
Durational performance with one simultaneous translator (Italian to English/German)

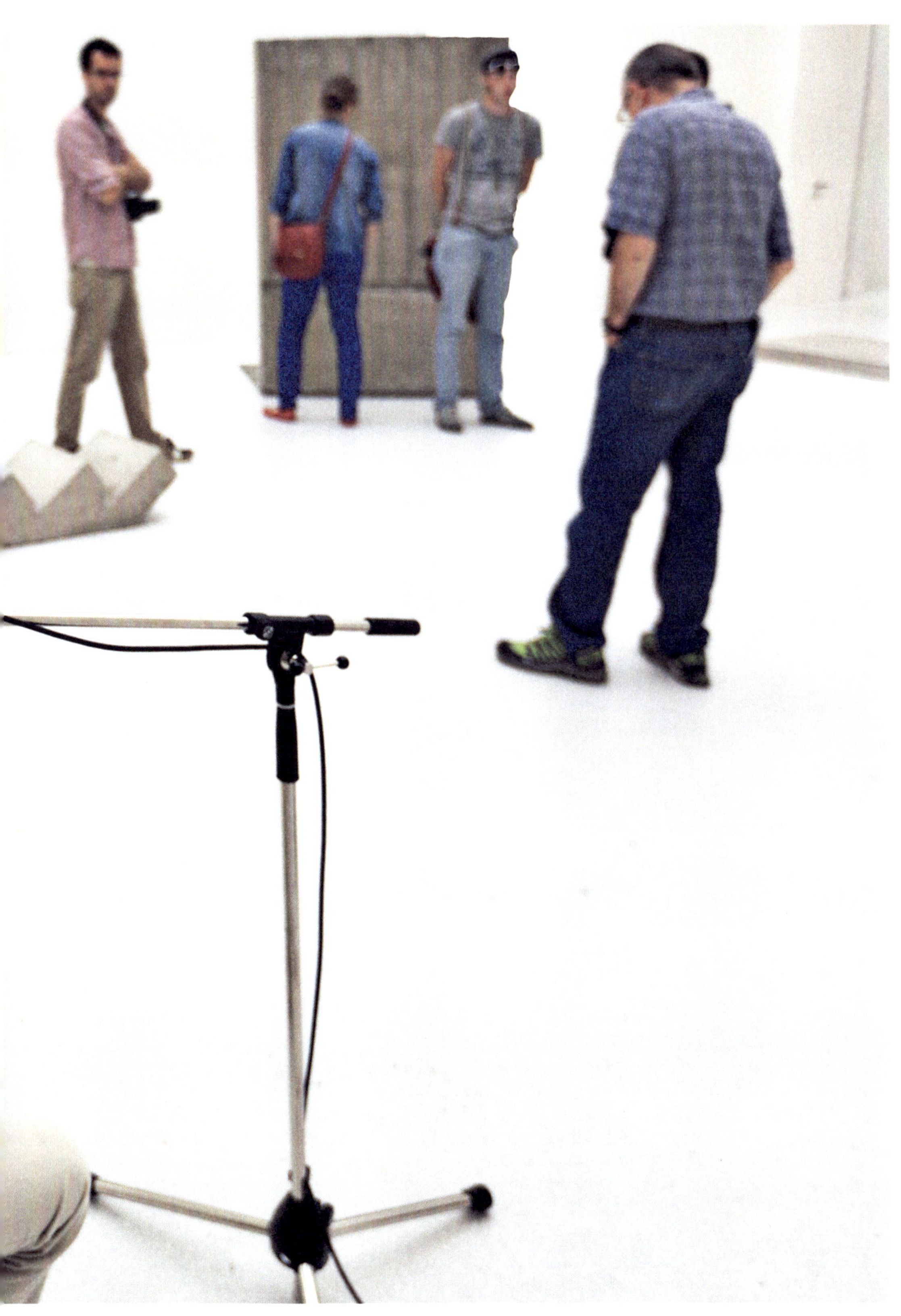

вътре в производството. Бяха излезли работници от фабриката, бяха
окопирали фабриката, колите. и като се има предвид размерите на тази
работническа класа, защото през 1973г. мерките бяха приклкйчили.

през 73 г. сблъсък с иссиндикатите като форма и струкура, насилието
което предшестваше щеше да доде през 1980 г. аз съм написал книга.
да кажем че дискутирахме за анлиза и събията които се склучват.

Курчо говори за необходимостта да се мине зад професиите, зад държават.
става въпрос за работническите борби, макар и на високо ниво, стигнаха

до един момент, и господарите нямаше да достигнат нищо повече.

не се виждахме повече, защото не се виждахме повече. говоря за
самоуправлението. ние не сcе виждахме до юли 1974 г. където се
видяхме по настояване на червените бригади, този път като организация.
геСрещата се насрочва и тази среща не се насрочва като функция на ещо.
говорте за срещата в дома на Дормео. Ааз бях поканен ндаморганизирам
едно събрание в светлината на моето оттегляне. Да изясним нещата ако
обичате. какво имате предвид в рамките на контрар. Имаше списание
което се правше от много хора и че не съм вече в политическата линия
тъй катто това което аз провеждах не беше в рамките на партията и аз
възразявах да напусна. Редакторите на списанието казха
  на тана таимало е различия по този въпрос. Да, имаше.
и не се ли говореше за събиттието в Памгда, за убийството. да аз ви казах
Веднъ

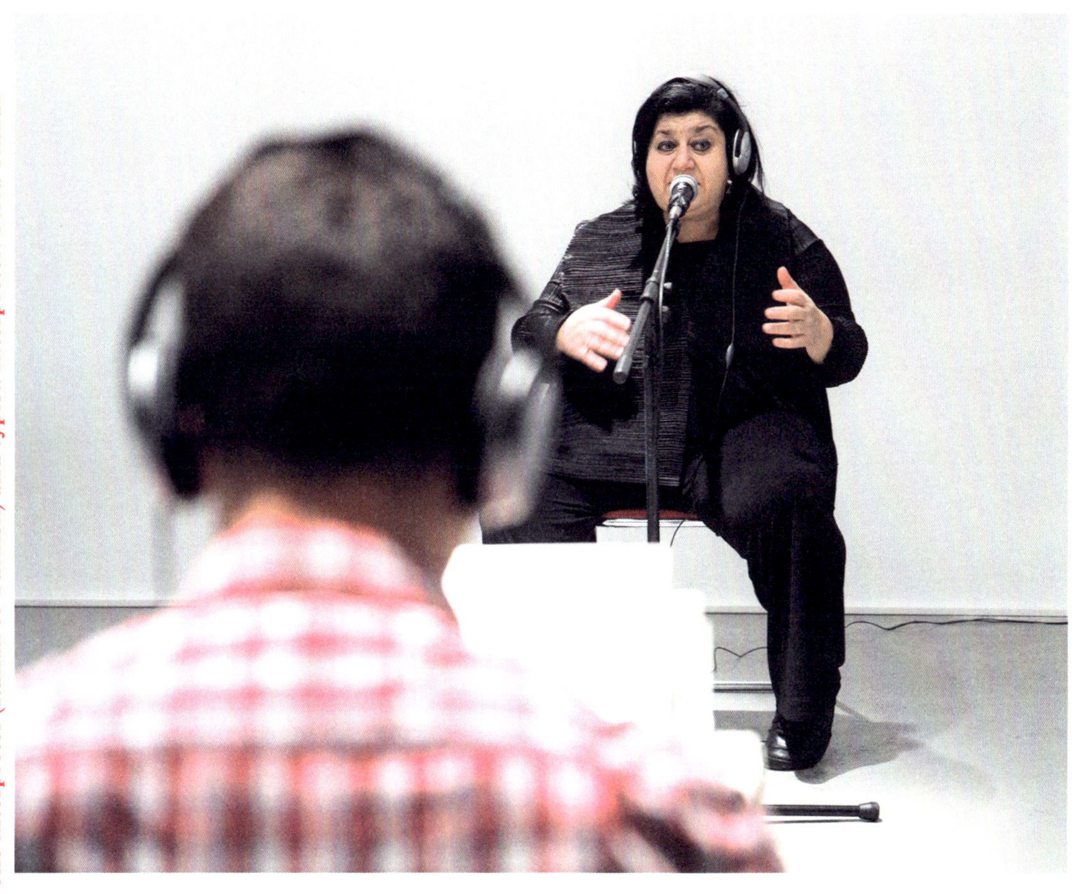

Two-hour performance with one interpreter (Italian to Turkish) and typist. Interpreter: Serra Yilmaz

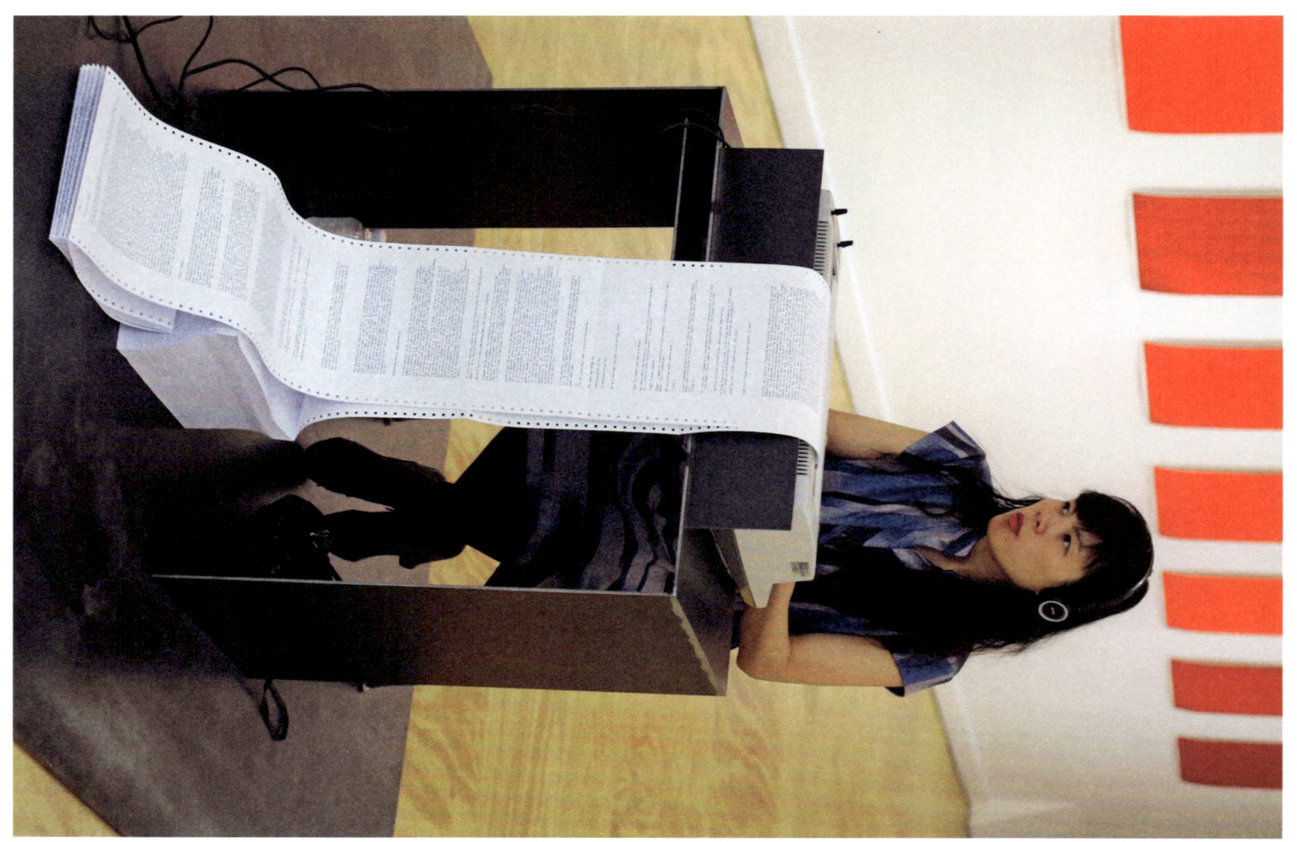

e-flux, New York, 11–12 May 2013

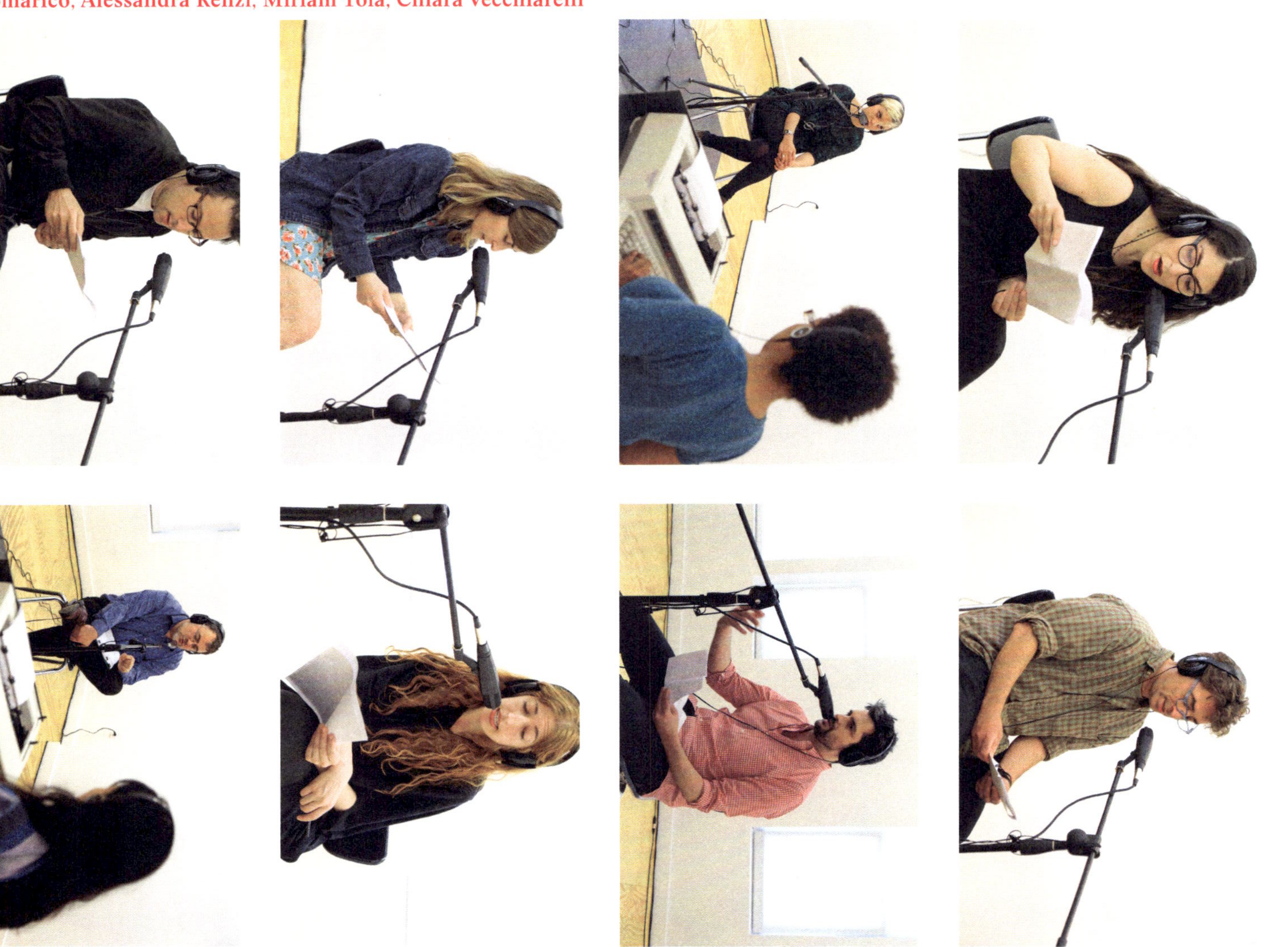

Interpreters: Franco Barchiesi, Paolo Carpignano, Marco Deseriis, Herndon Gjergji, Michael Hardt, Aachna Hasin Bey, Piero Passacantando, Alessandra Pomarico, Alessandra Renzi, Miriam Tola, Chiara Vecchiarelli

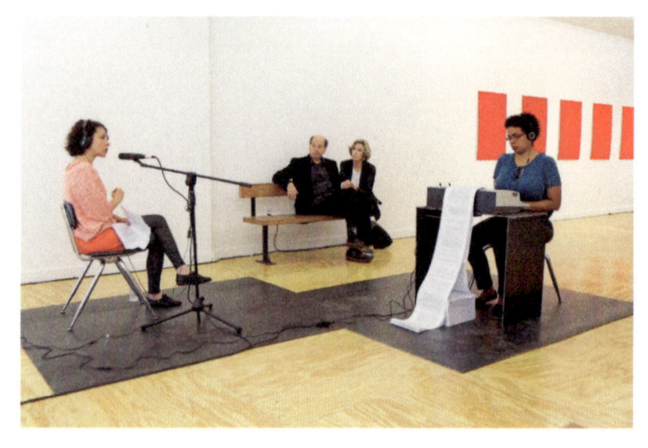
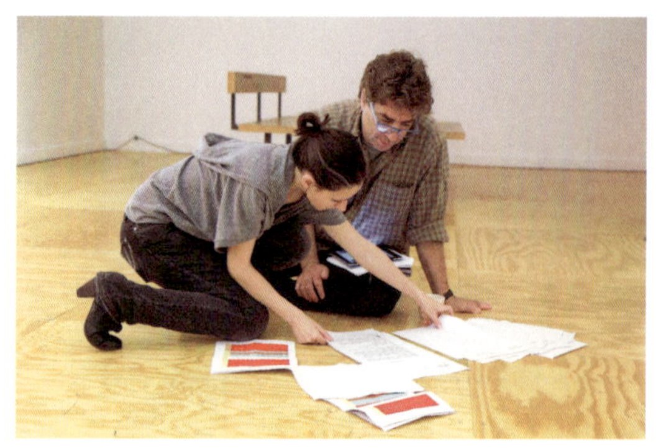

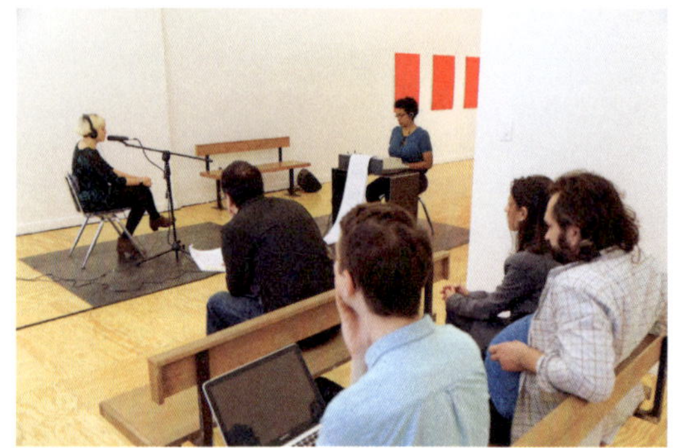
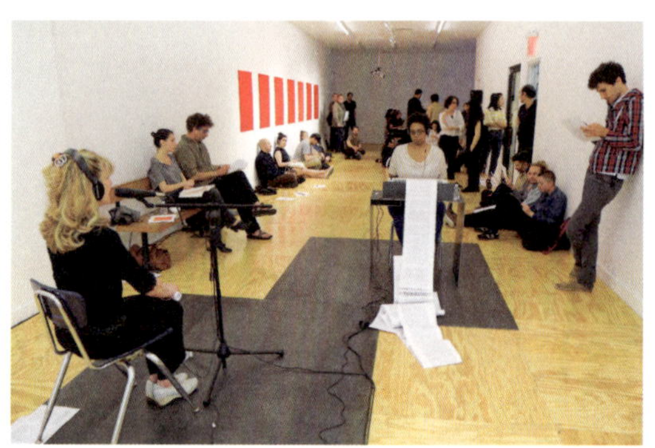

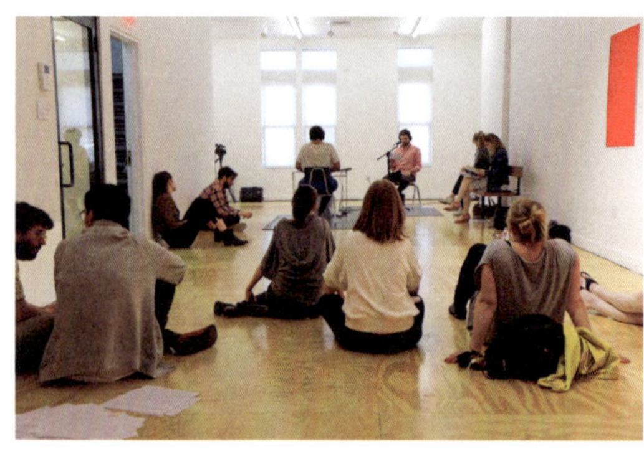
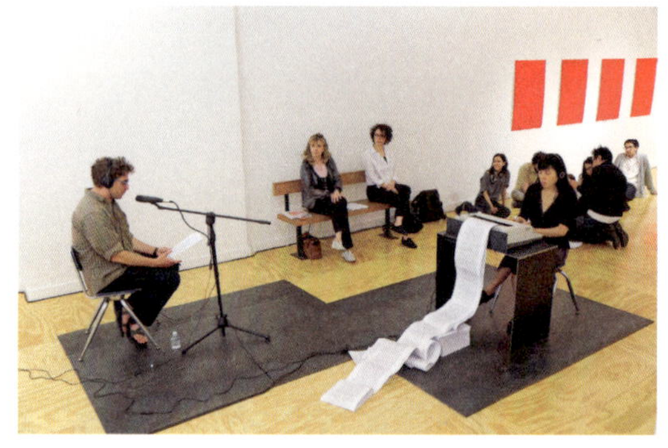

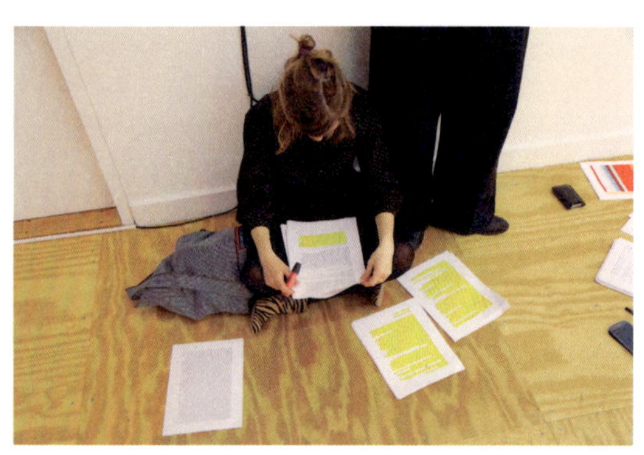
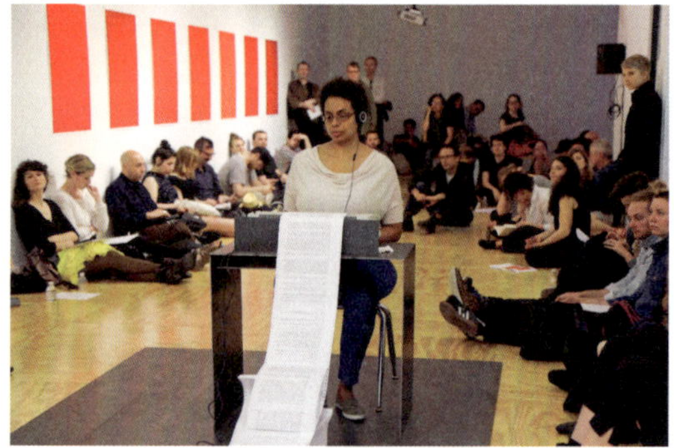

LE PROCÈS

7/6

12:00

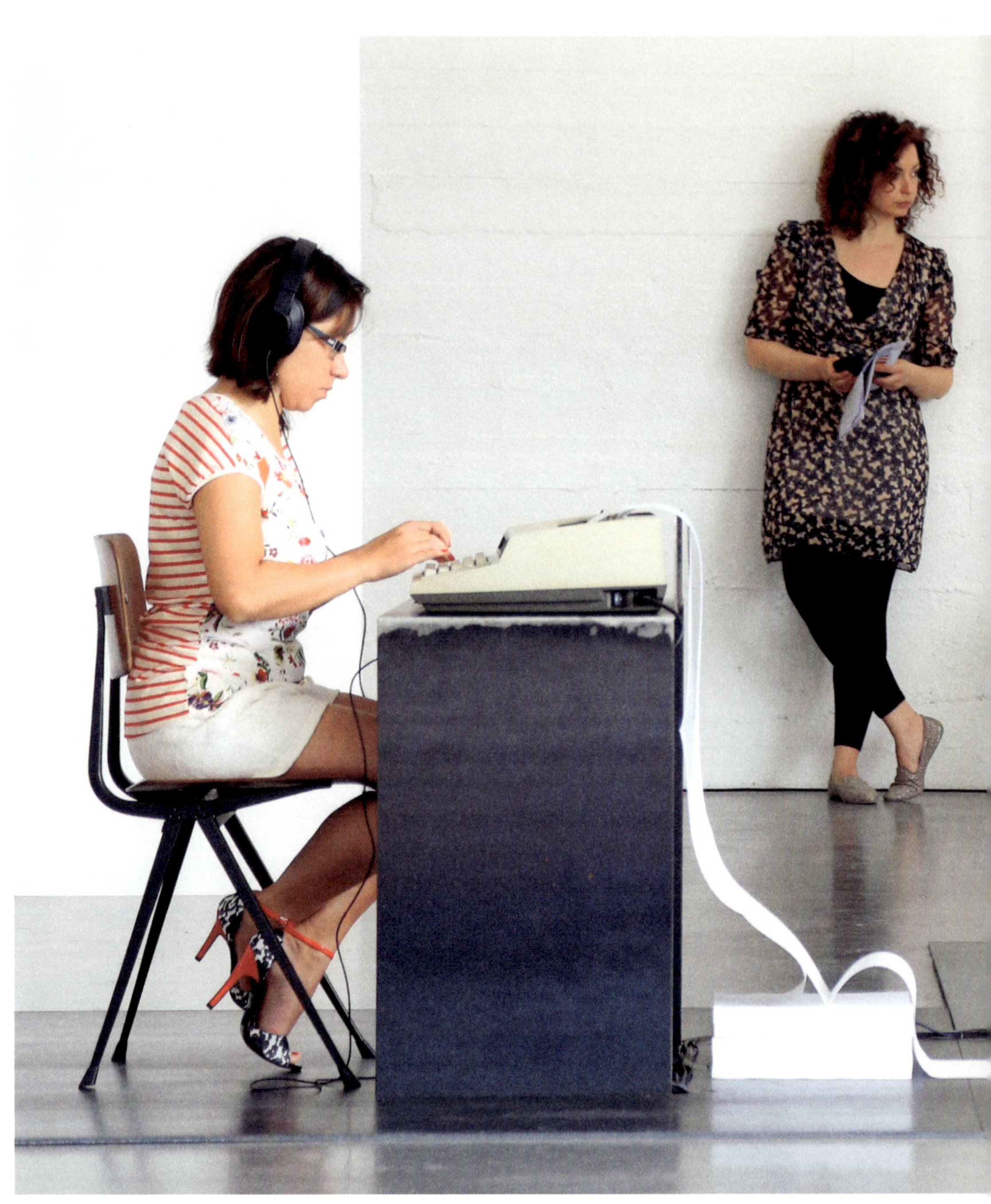

WIELS, Brussels, 7 June 2014
Six-hour performance with twenty-three interpreters (Italian to French/Dutch) and three typists

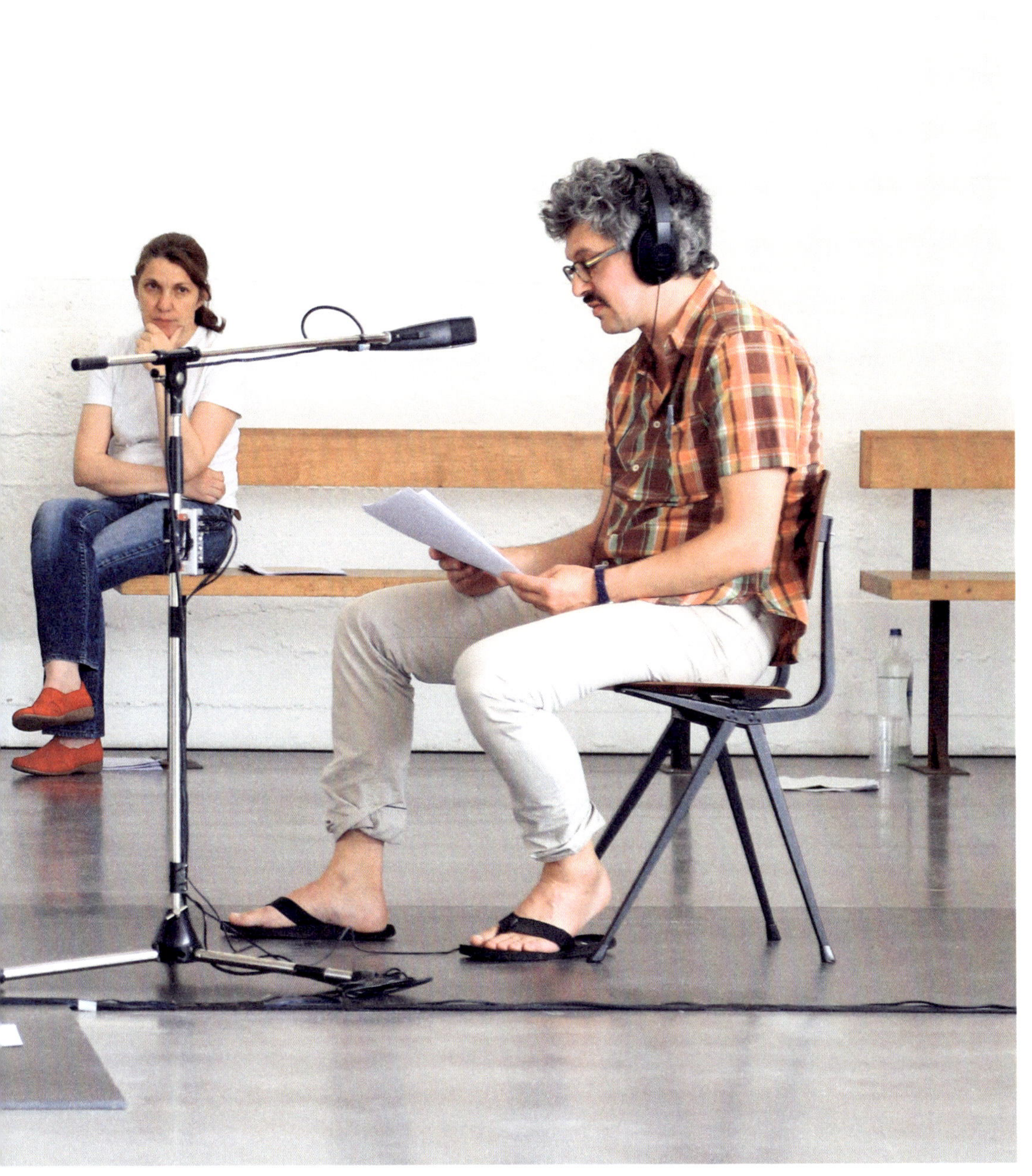

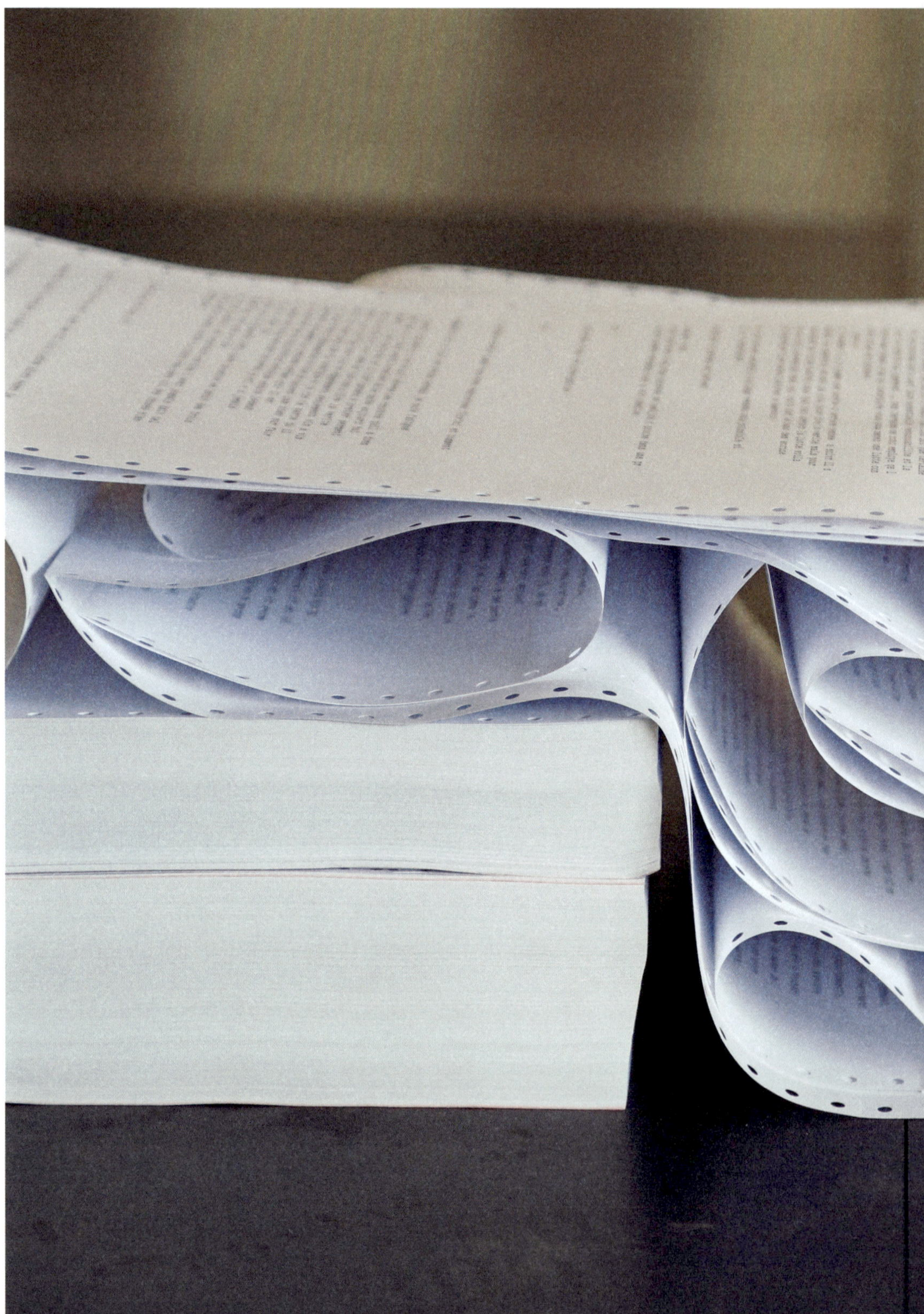

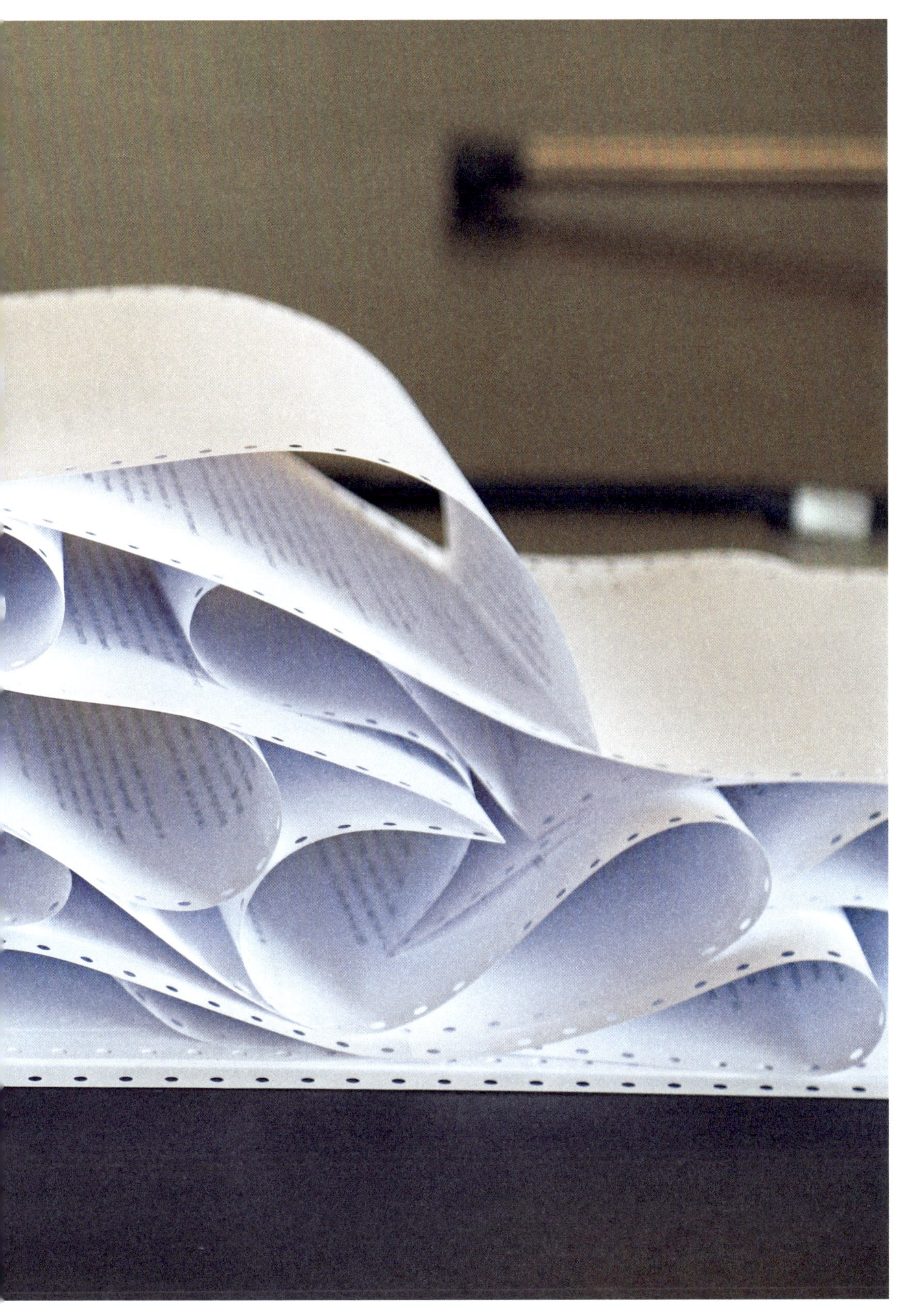

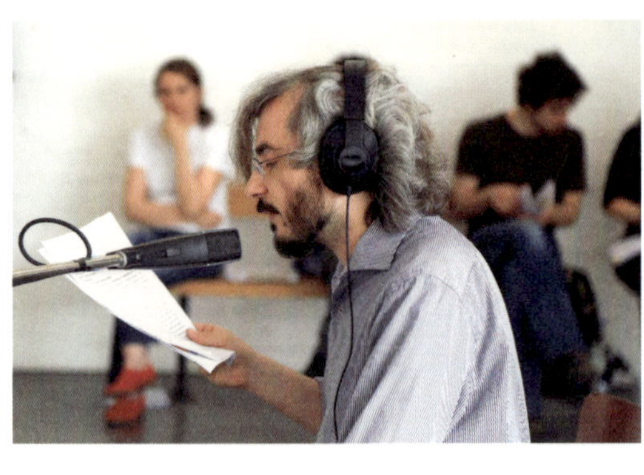

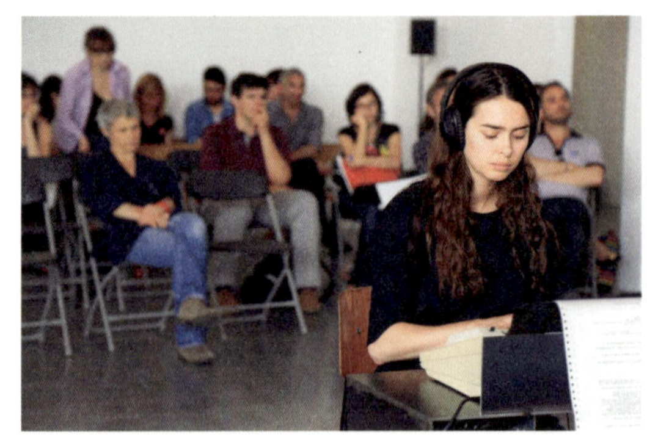

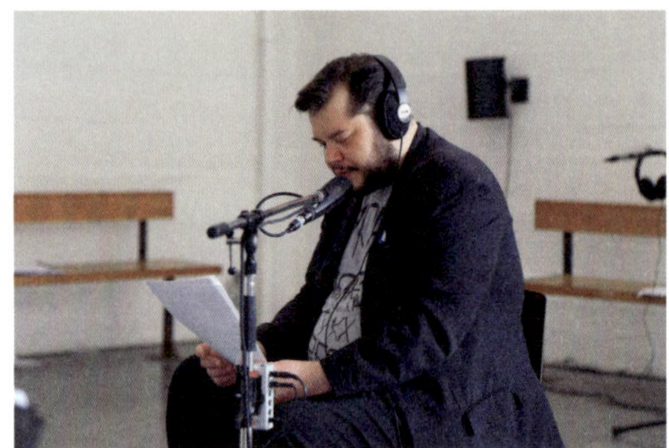

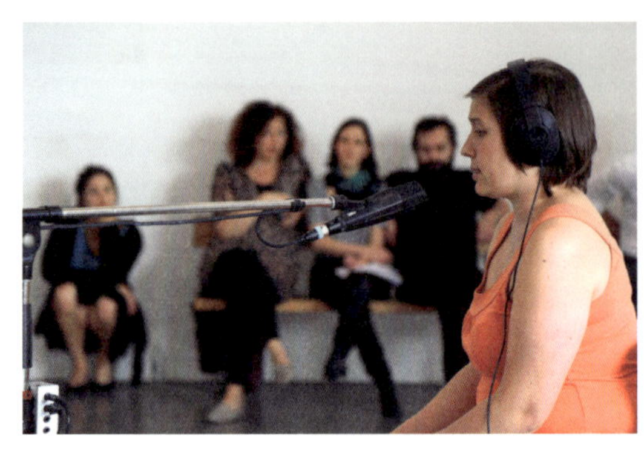

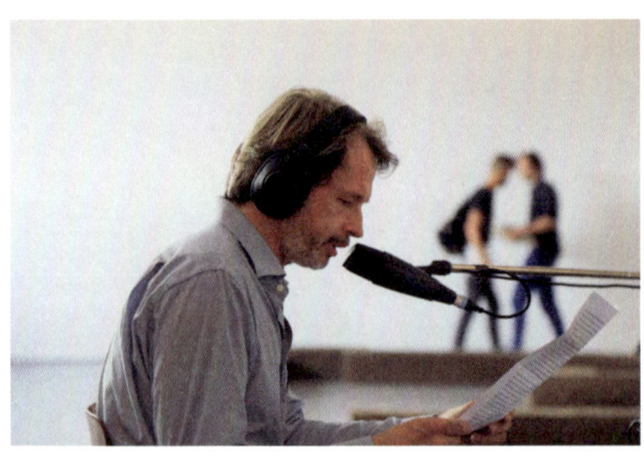

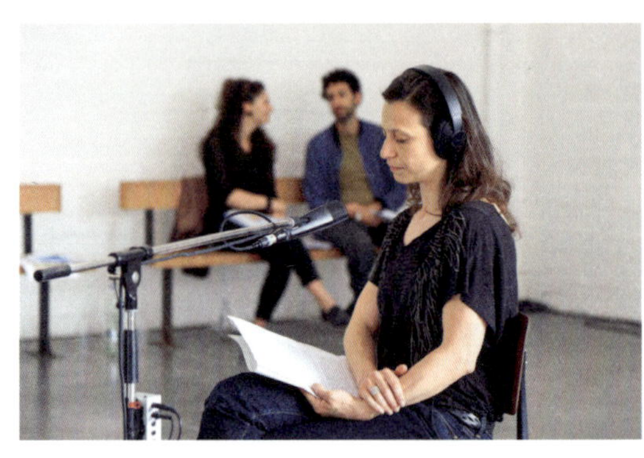

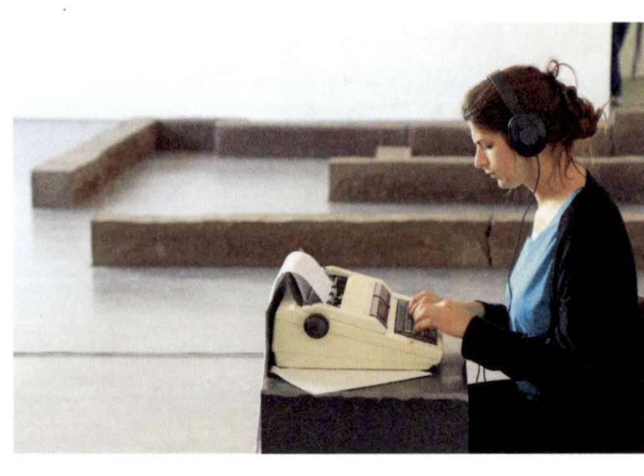

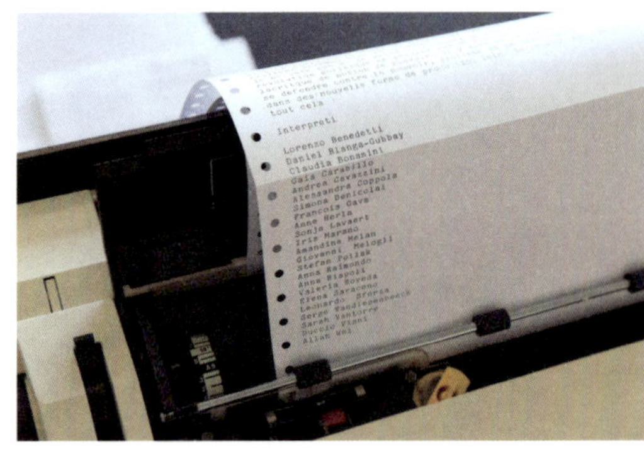
Interpreti

Lorenzo Benedetti
Daniel Blanga-Gubbay
Claudia Bonamini
Gaia Carabillo
Andrea Cavazzini
Alessandra Coppola
Simona Denicolai
Francois Gava
Anne Herla
Sonja Lavaert
Iris Marano
Amandine Melan
Giovanni Melogli
Stefan Pollak
Anna Raimondo
Anna Rispoli
Valeria Roveda
Elena Saraceno
Leonardo Sforza
Serge Vandiegenbeeck
Sarah Vanhorre
Duccio Viani
Aliak Voi

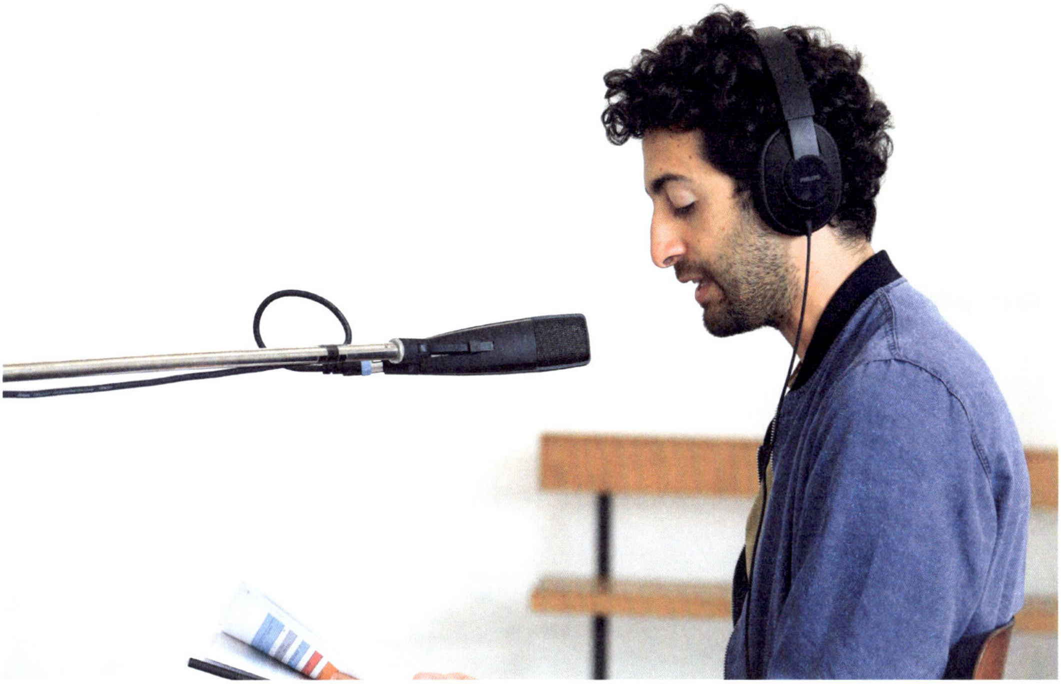

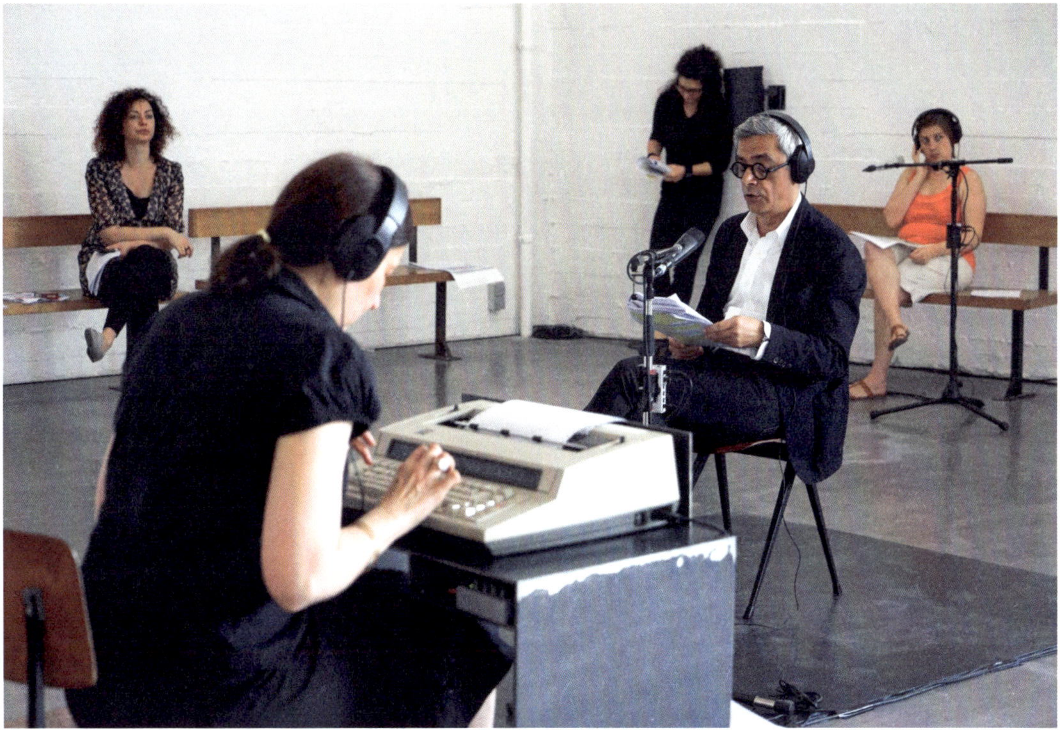

Anna Rispoli, Valeria Roveda, Elena Saraceno, Leonardo Sforza, Serge Vandiepenbeeck, Sarah Vantorre, Duccio Viani, Allan Wei

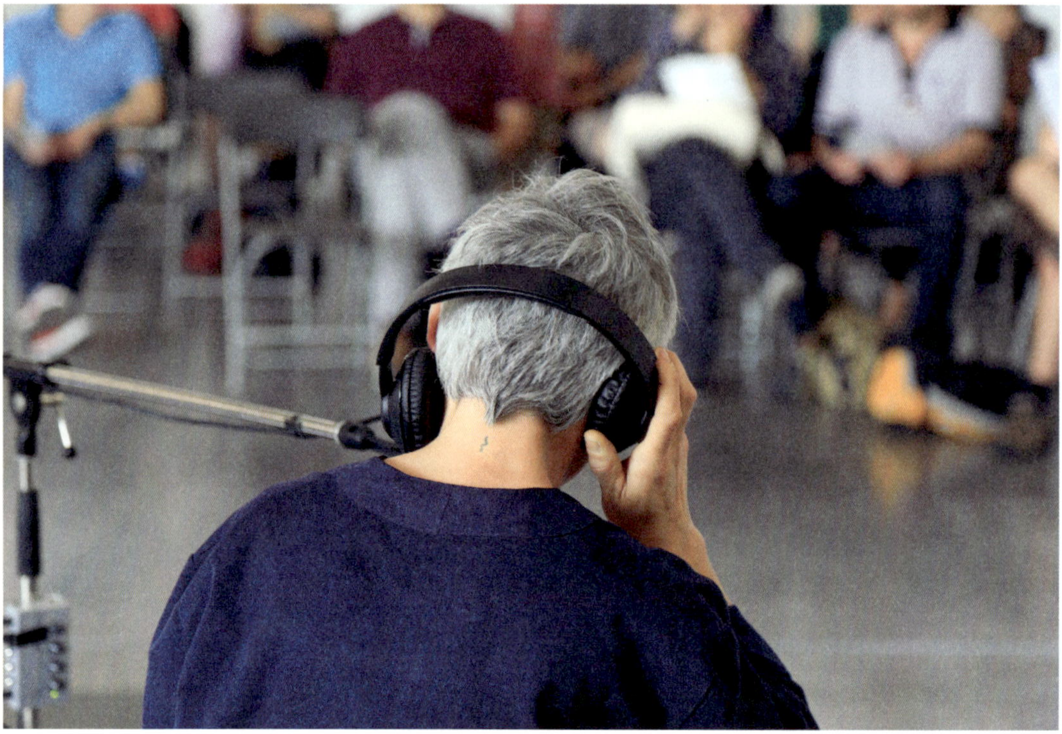

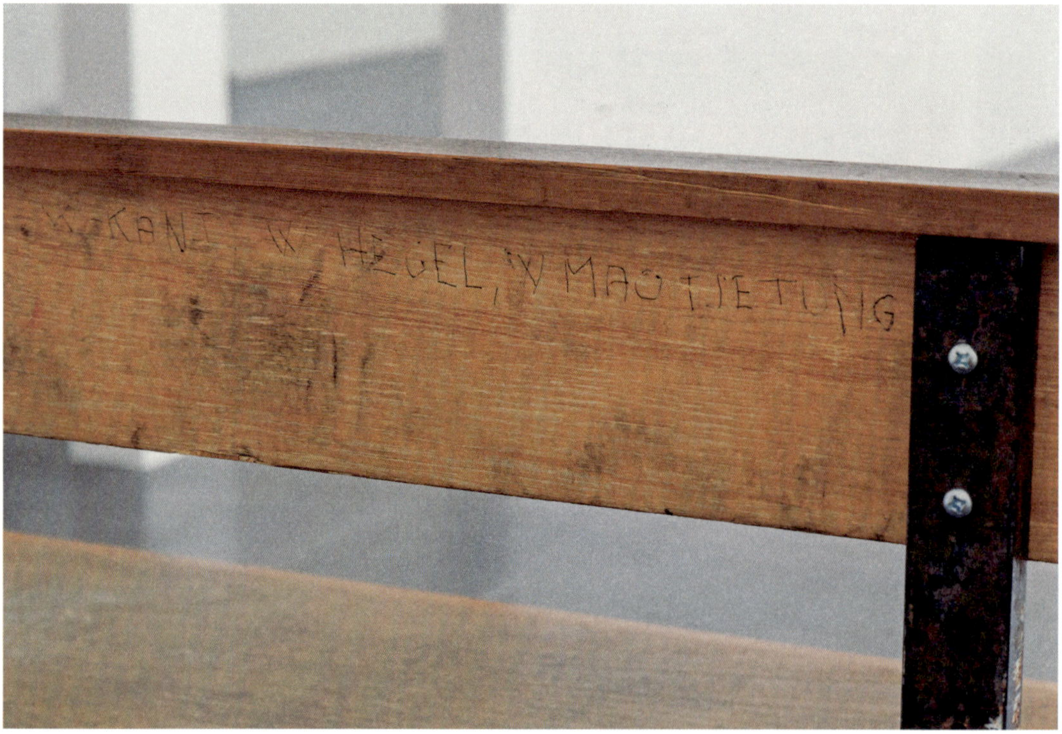
KANT, W HEGEL, W MAO TJETUNG

Six-hour performance with nineteen interpreters (Italian to Russian) and two typists

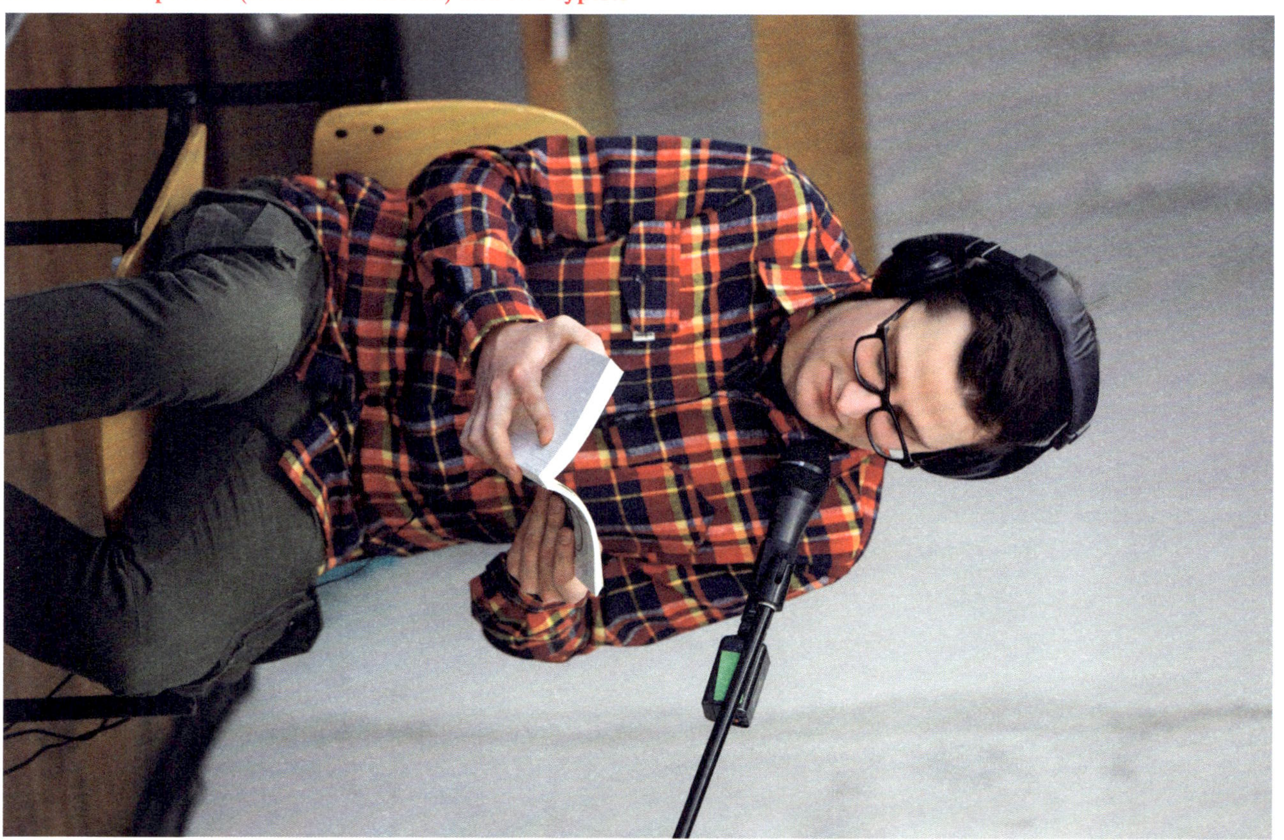

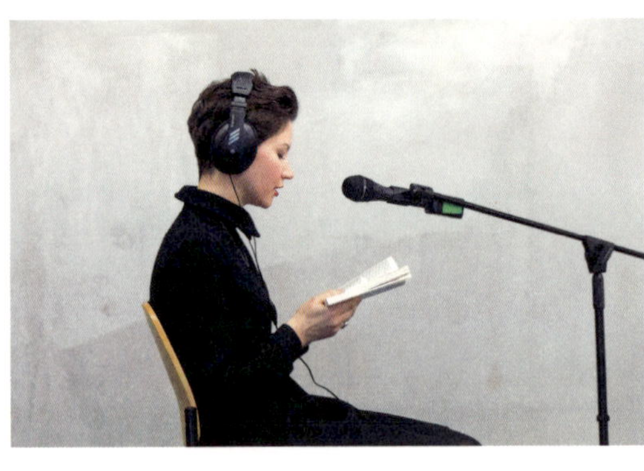
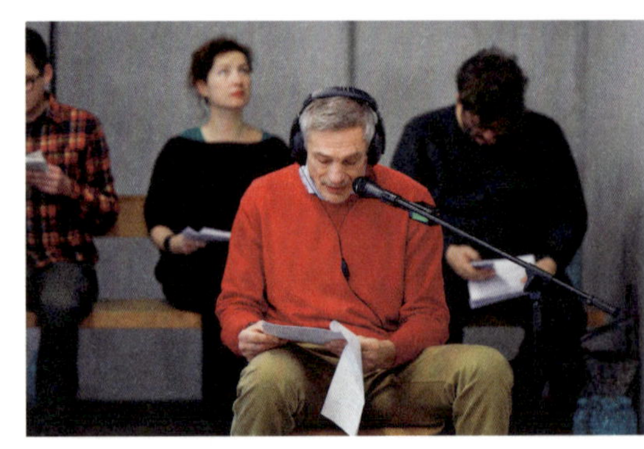
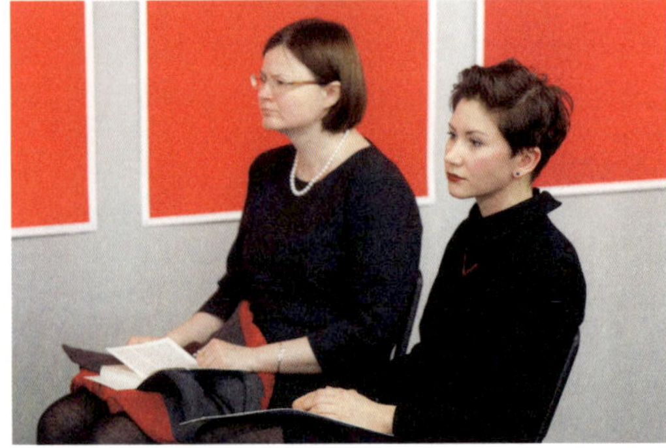
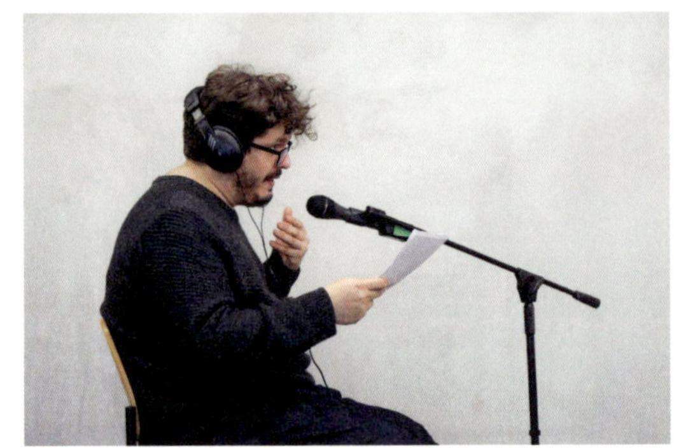
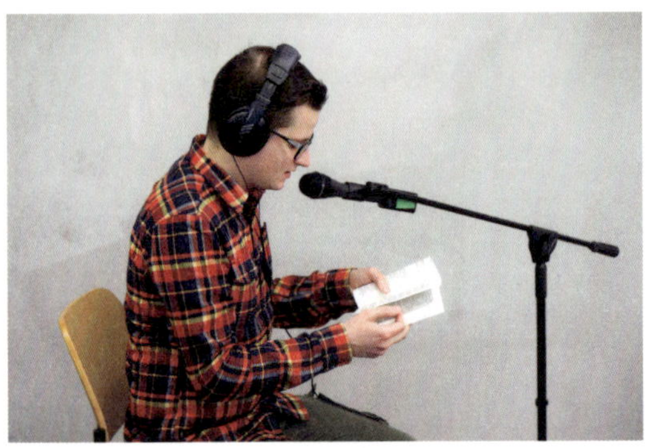
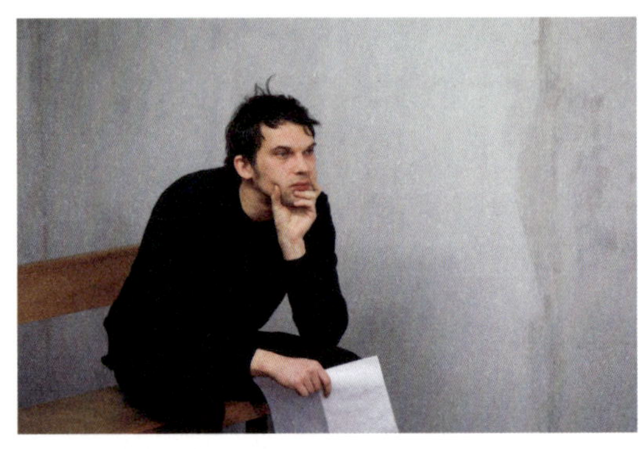
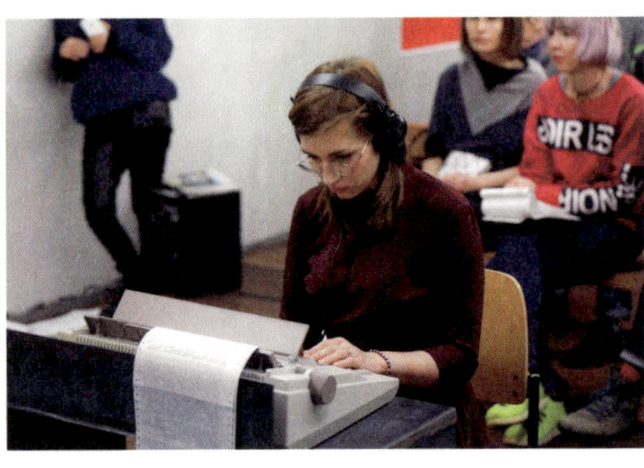
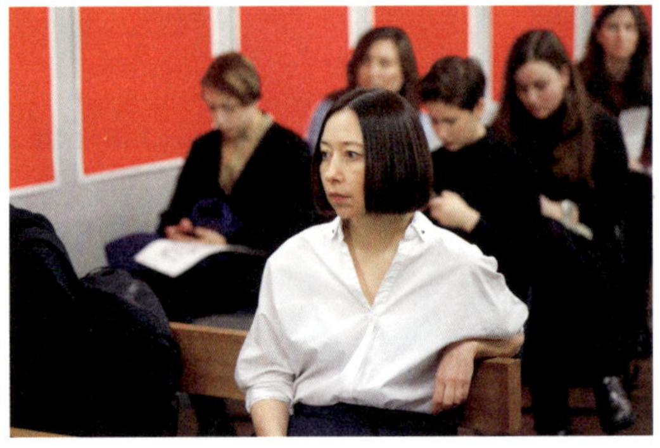

Interpreters: Anna Arutyunova, Alexander Bikbov, Valentin Dyakonov, Marco Dinelli, Anastasia Emelyanova, Gennadiy Kiselev.

1977 eski gelenekten bir kopuşu ifade eder. Bir bakıma bugün hâlâ içinden geçtiğimiz, en radikal kopuştur bu. Peki ne olmuştu? Marjinal olmaktan son derece uzak bir mücadele hareketi patlak verdi. Bu hareketin, ekonomik krize isyan eden, çevre mahallelerin gecekondu semtlerindeki gündelik işçilerden oluştuğu defalarca söylendi. Hiç de değil. 1977'yi yorumlamaya çalışırken, yaşarken, bu hareketin marjinal olmaktan son derece uzak bir toplumsal özne olduğunu görmüştük. Aksine, bu toplumsal özne, öğrenme, bilgi, üretken kapasite bakımından son derece zengindi; kapitalist yeniden yapılanma süreçlerinin içinden doğmuş, üretkenlik açısından merkezi bir yeri olan ya da olacak olan bir özneydi. [Kapitalist] yeniden yapılanma süreçlerinden ortaya çıkan yeni bir üretken özne. Pek çok şey bilen, kendi kendinin girişimcisi haline nasıl geleceğini bilen zengin bir özne. Marjinal olmak bir yana son derece etkili bir özne. Roma Üniversitesi'nden örnek vermek gerekirse, bunlar genelde güvencesiz entelektüel işçilerdi, çalışıyor olsalar bile, toplumsallık, enformasyon, bilgi biriktirmek için üniversitedeki derslere devam eden işçilerdi. Ne olmuştu? Temel örnekle daha devam edebilirim: Üretimin yeniden yapılanmasının ve dolayısıyla bunun yarattığı işsizlik ve sık sık iş değiştirme olgusunun kendinde kötü bir şey olduğu fikrini doğru bulmuyorduk; aksine bu hareketlilik, bu güvencesiz çalışma –zamanın sunduğu zenginliği düşünürsek– işçilerin kendi kaderlerini tayini, iş zamanının esnekliği, yaşam zamanı ile ilgili tercihler bakımından çok güçlü unsurlar da barındırıyor olabilirdi. Ve böyle bir yaklaşım, o dönemin hâkim temaları düşünüldüğünde, tam bir skandaldı; hele de asıl meselenin ne olursa olsun işi savunmak ve [kapitalist] yeniden yapılanmaya direniş olduğunu öne süren sendikaların ve hareketin dogmaları düşünüldüğünde. Biz ise şunu söylüyorduk: Bu yeniden yapılanmada, bu hareketlilikte, iş gününün uzunluğunun ihtiyaçlara ve gerekliliklere göre belirleneceği şekilde, kendi işimizi kendimizin tayin edeceği farklı bir ilişki olanağı yatıyor olabilir. İşe dair bu yeni yaklaşım üzerine düşüncelerimizin temel temasını ortaya koyabilmek için bunları anlatıyorum: İşi artık insanı yirmisinde çalışmaya başlayıp, emekli olasıya kadar aynı yerde kalmak zorunda bırakan, çoktan çizilmiş bir kader olarak görmüyorduk. Fabrika artık müebbet hapislik olmaktan çıkmıştı, yaşam öyküsünün bir bölümüydü sadece. [*Salondan öksürmeler*] Hayatın, bırakarak, daha doyurucu bir iş, daha zengin üretkenlikler arayışıyla gitmeyi göze alarak yanıt verilebilecek sınırlı bir bölümü. İşten işe göçerliği, güvencesiz işi, hareketliliği, üzerine düşünmek zorunda olduğumuz, zengin potansiyeller içeren bir unsur olarak görüyorduk. İlk büyük tema budur. O günlerdeki hareket içinse bu tam bir skandaldı. Bir kopuş ve süreksizlik yaratan bir temaydı. Şunu biz de kabul ediyorduk: Evet, kayıtdışı çalışma yoksulluğu ve sömürüyü beraberinde getirir. Ama şunu da söylüyorduk: Kayıtdışı çalışma makineler olmadan, düşük bir teknolojik düzeyde gerçekleştirilen bir üretime ait arkeolojik bir unsur olmak zorunda değildir. Belki de, modern kayıtdışı çalışma yaygın bir elektronik ortamda çalışmanın biçimi haline gelmektedir. Belki de, kayıtdışı çalışma kendimizi fabrika rejiminden koparmak için olağandışı bir fırsat

233

sunmaktadır. Belki bugün bile ya anlaşılmaz, ya da önemsiz gelen bu unsurların pek çoğuna popüler gazetelerde bile rastlayabildiğimizi düşünürsek, banal algılanabilecek ikinci büyük tema da buydu. O dönemde, tüm bunlar hareketin içinde bir skandala yol açmıştı. Bunlar kesinlikle yenilikçi ve şaşkınlık yaratan temalardı. Başlıca temalardan bir diğeri de, devlet söylemiyle ilgiliydi: 1970'lerin ilk yarısında kaydedilen toplumsal gelişme, komünizmin klasik teması, iktidarı ele geçirmekle ilişkilendiriliyordu, biz ise –daha önce de söylediğim gibi– 1977 hareketi içinde somut olarak olup bitenlerin içinden bakarak, iktidarı ele geçirme, siyasi devrim kavramının kendisini sorguluyorduk. İktidarı ele geçirmek acınası, sefil bir şeydir, bundan vazgeçelim, demenin –belli bir çevre, belli bir dünya, çalkantılar ve mücadelelerle sarsılan bir dünyada– nasıl bir skandala yol açtığını, bunun ne anlama geldiğini anlatabiliyorum, umarım. Siyasi devrim fikrinin kendisi, bir Devlet yönetimini bir başkasıyla, kurumları başka kurumlarla değiştirme fikri, yeni toplumsal hareketlerle hiç ilişkisi olmayan acınası bir fikirdir. Siyasi devrim kavramının eleştirisi, iktidarı ele geçirme kavramının eleştirisi buradan gelir. Şunu diyorduk: En iyi ihtimalle, bu yeni toplumsal hareketler kendilerini iktidardan korumak, yeni yaşam biçimlerinin deneyimlerini oluşturarak ve iktidarı kendilerinden uzak tutarak büyüyebilmek gibi problemlerle karşılaşacak. O günlerdeki tartışmalarda, bu fikirler 1977 hareketi içinde dolaşan alışıldık görüşlerle çelişiyordu. Ama bunların hepsi, yaşadığımız bu yeni deneyimle doğrudan ilişkiliydi.

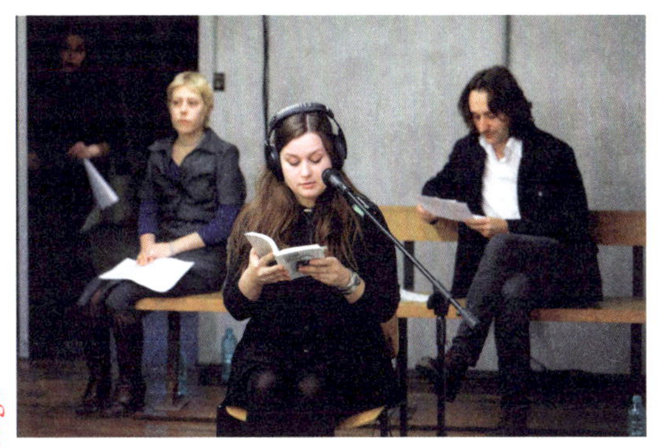
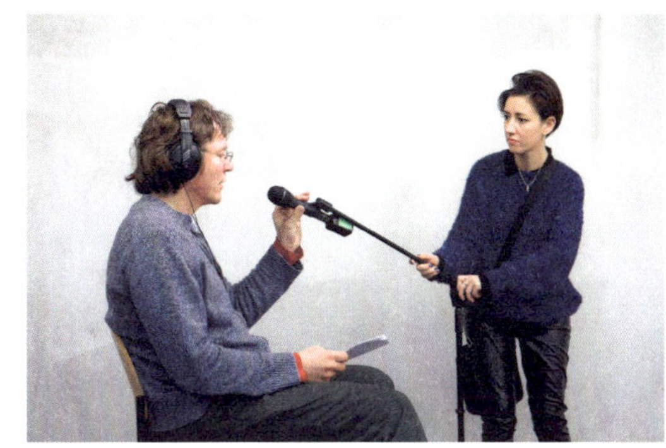
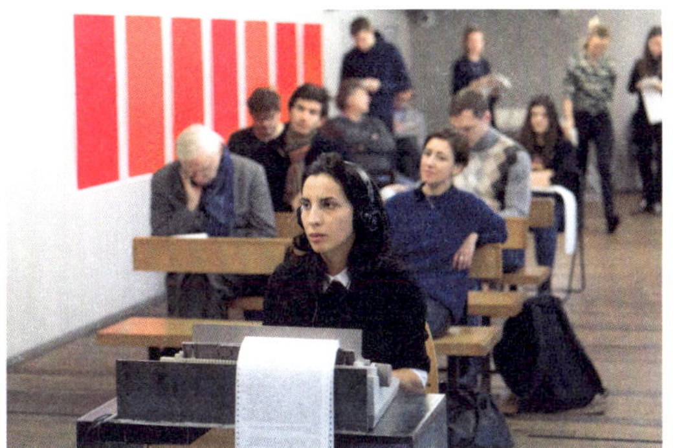
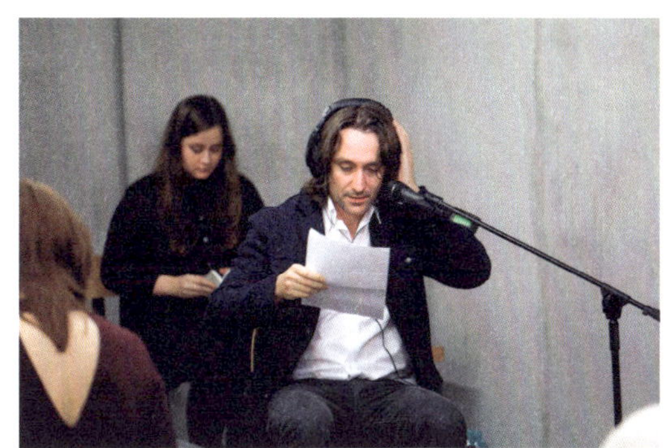
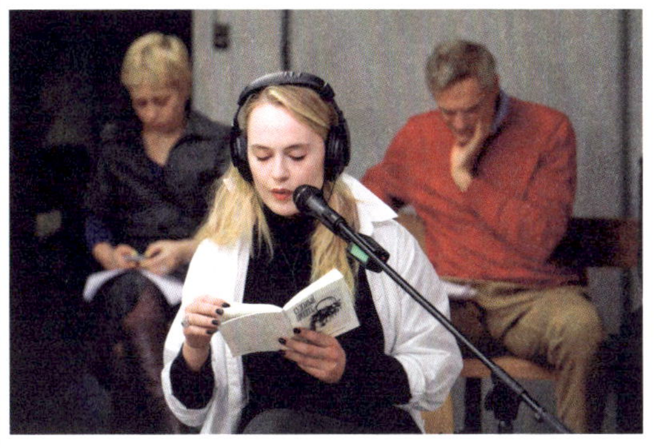
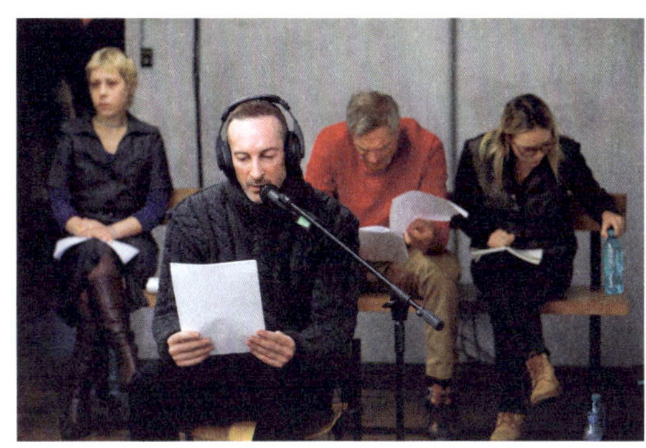
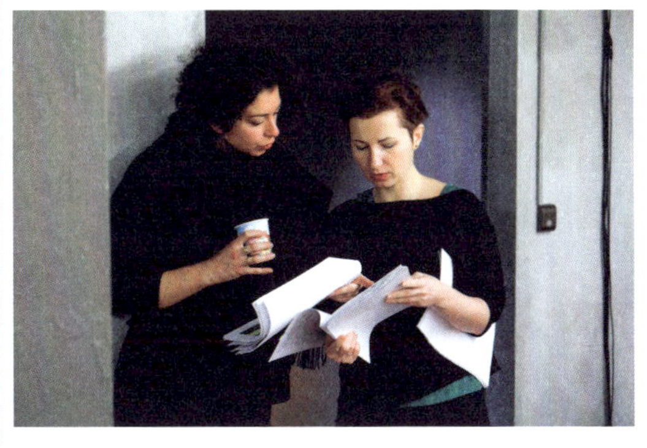
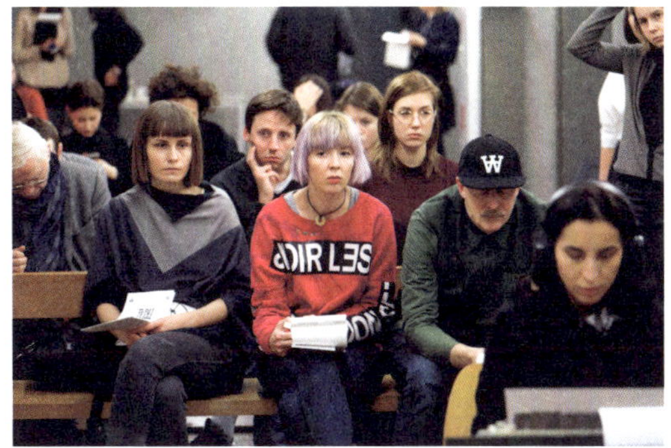

Ekaterina Privezentseva, Giovanni Savino, Dmitry Novikov, Christina Rasskazova, Greta Mavica, Costante Marengo

235

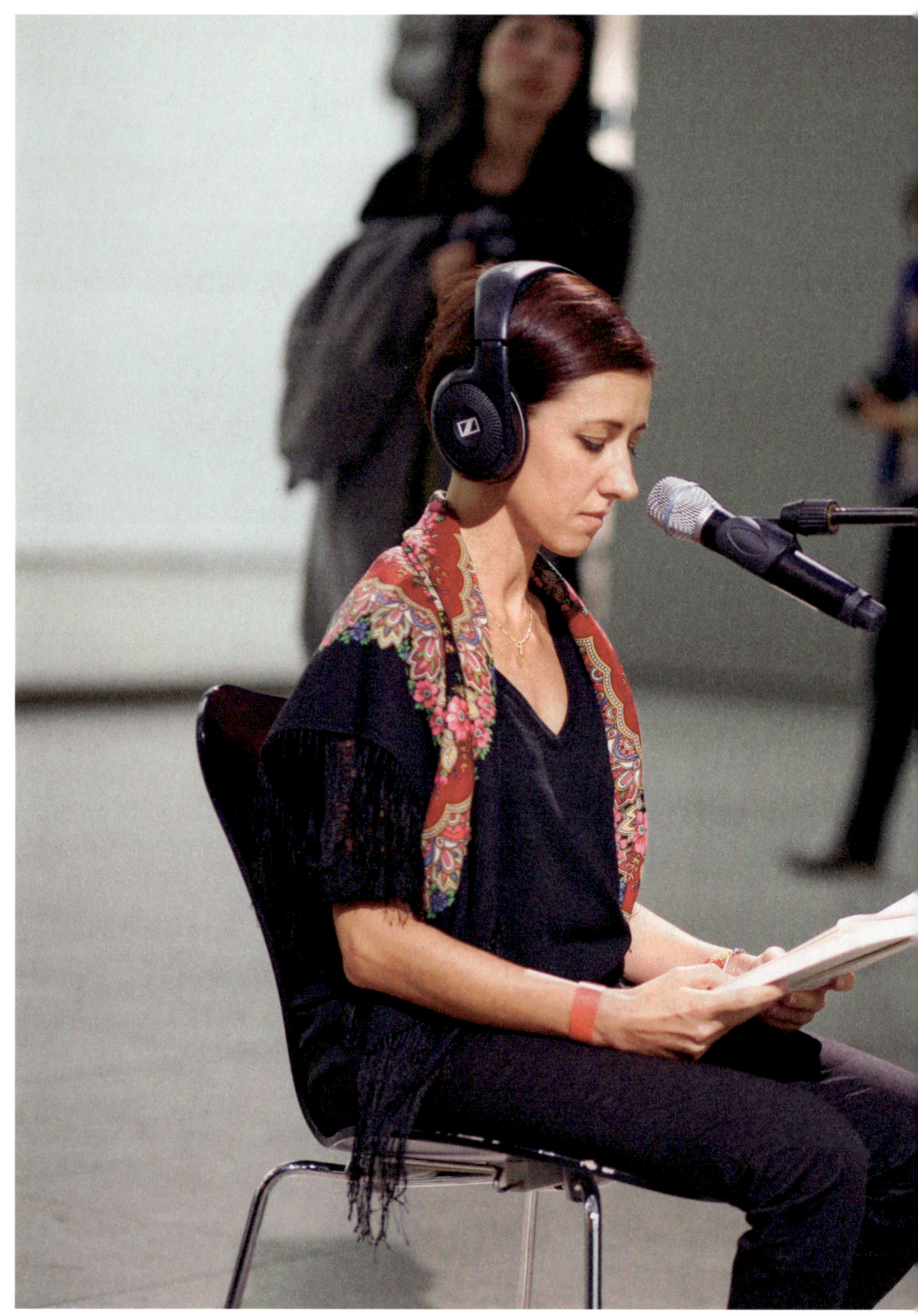

Hamburger Bahnhof, Berlin, 15–16 September 2017
Two-hour performance with six interpreters (Italian to English) and typists

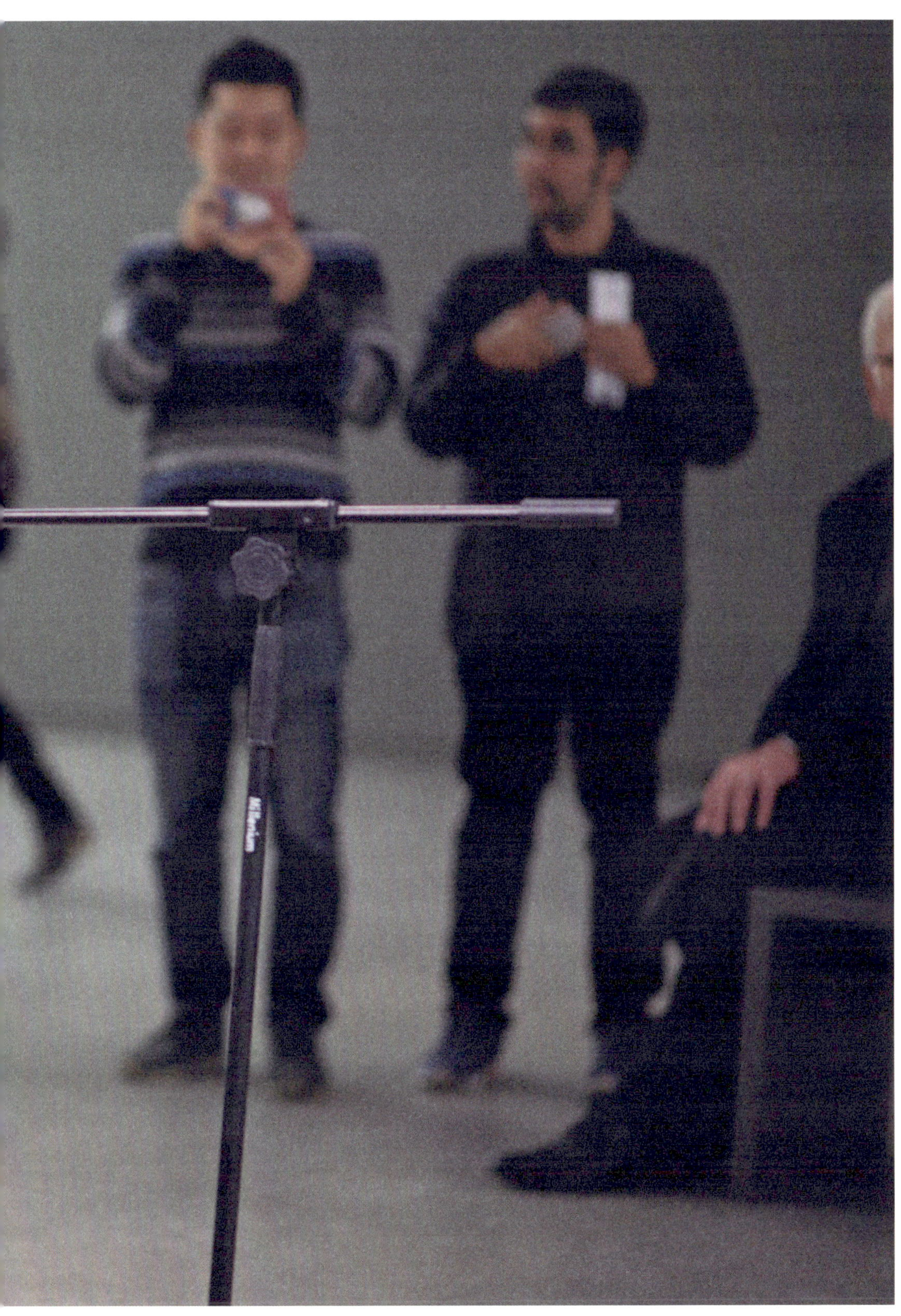

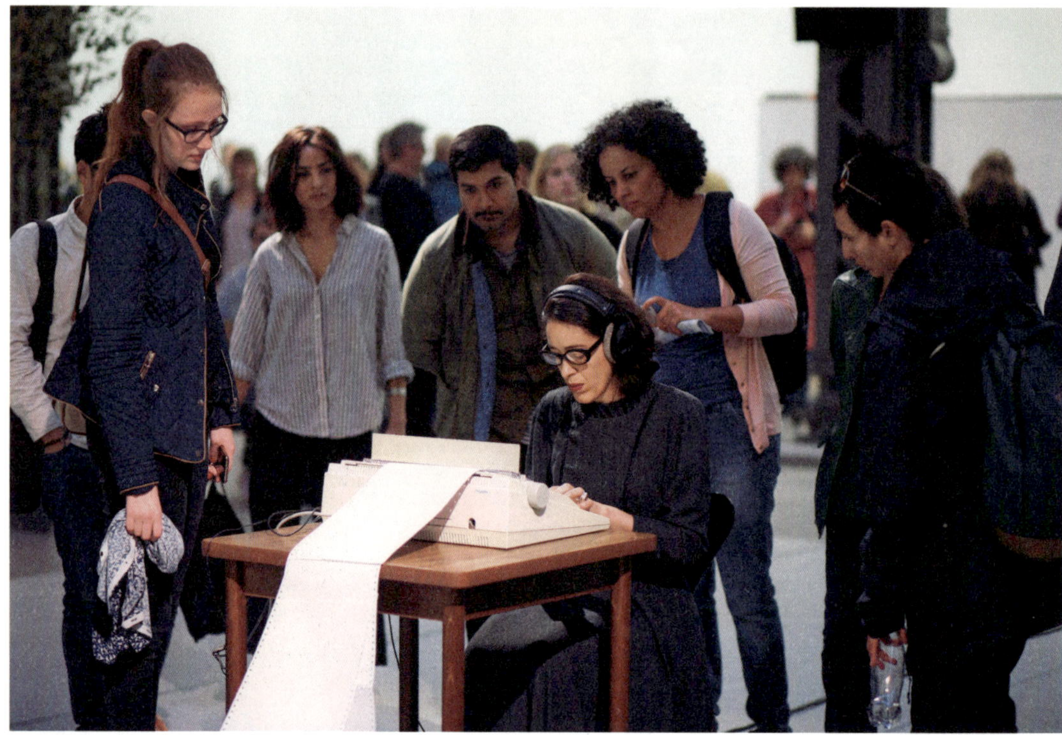

Interpreters: Rossella Biscotti, Candace Goodrich, Joanna Warsza, Maeshelle West-Davies, Domna Gounari, Christine Langinauer

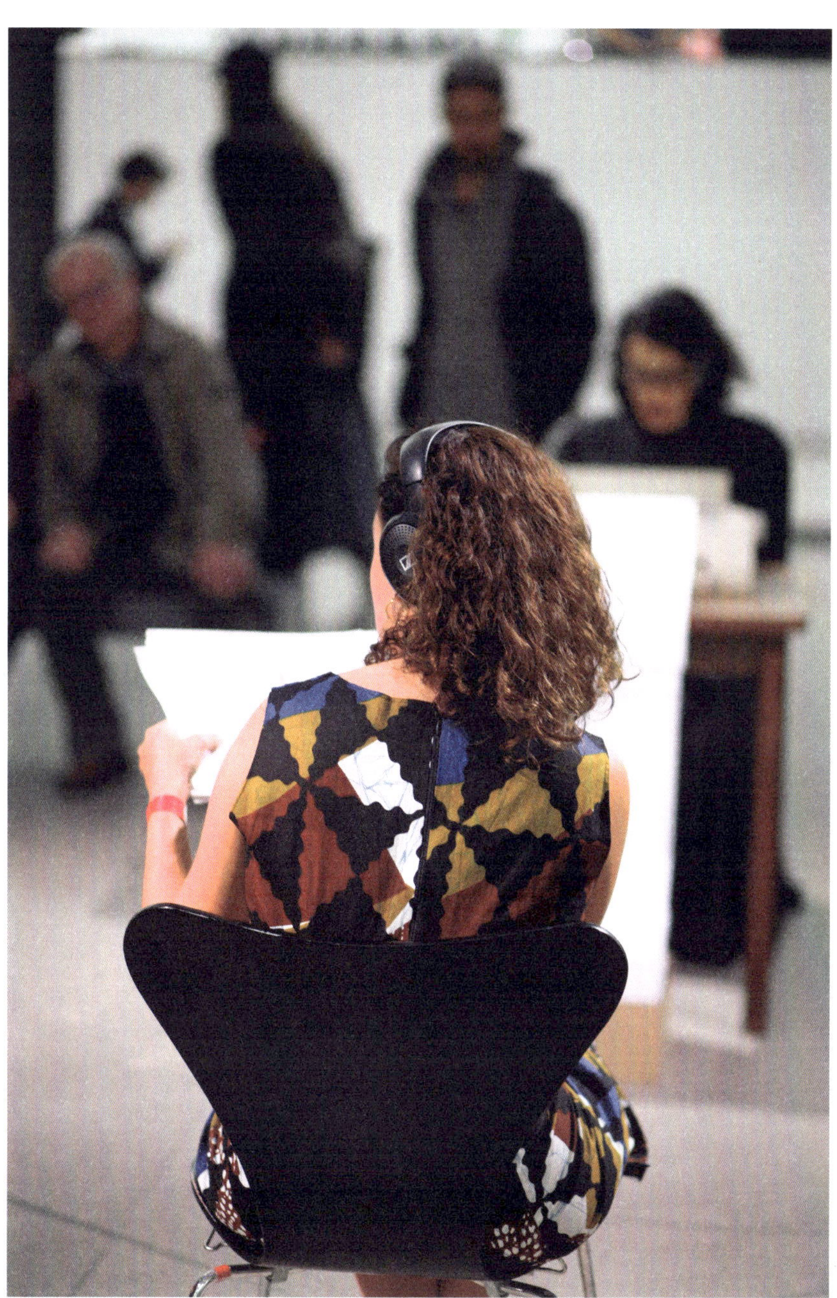

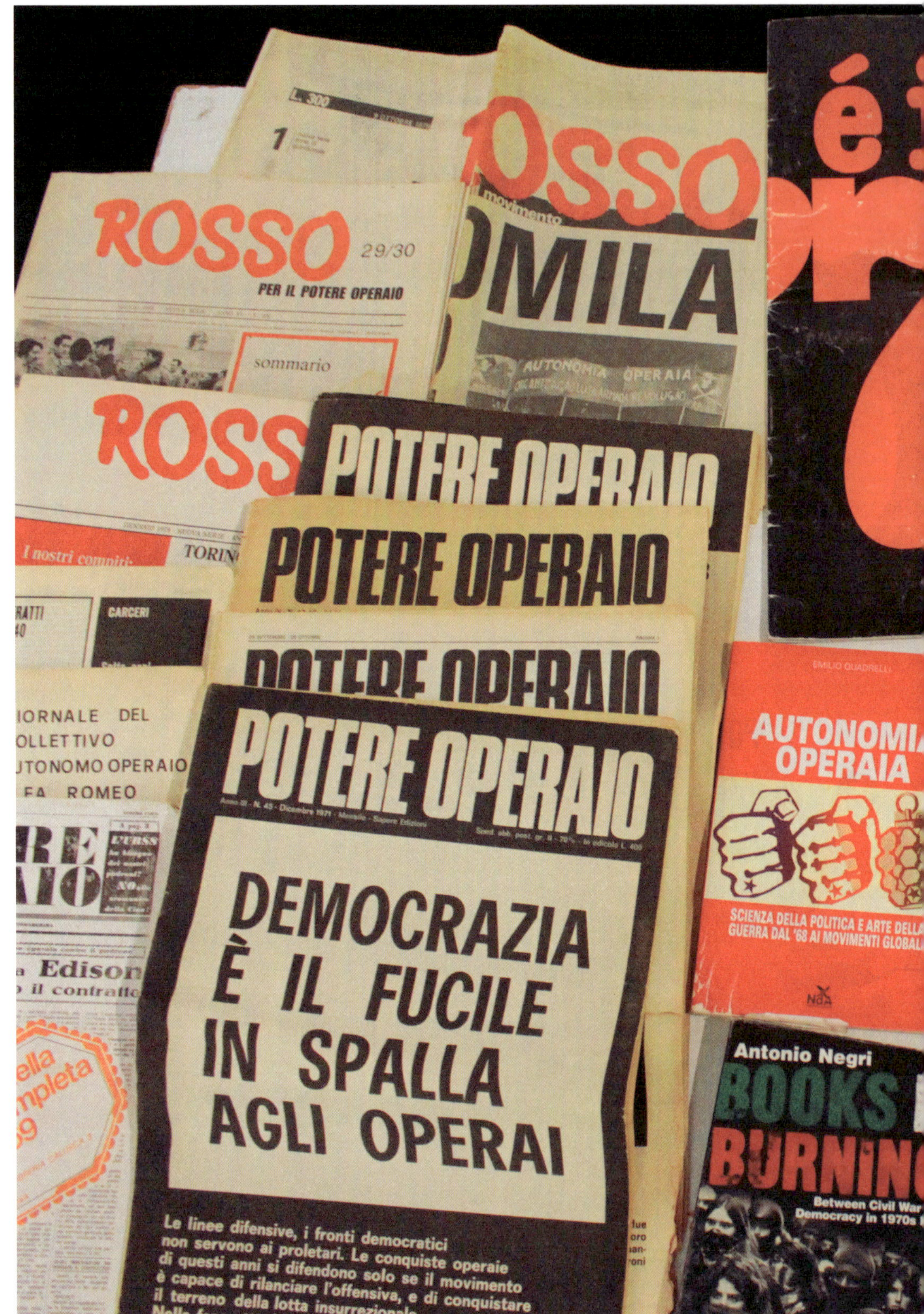

CuratorLab's year-long research material course on *The Trial*, leading to open-rehearsal at Tensta Konsthall, Stockholm, 2016–2017, organised by Maria Lind, Joanna Warsza, and Michele Masucci

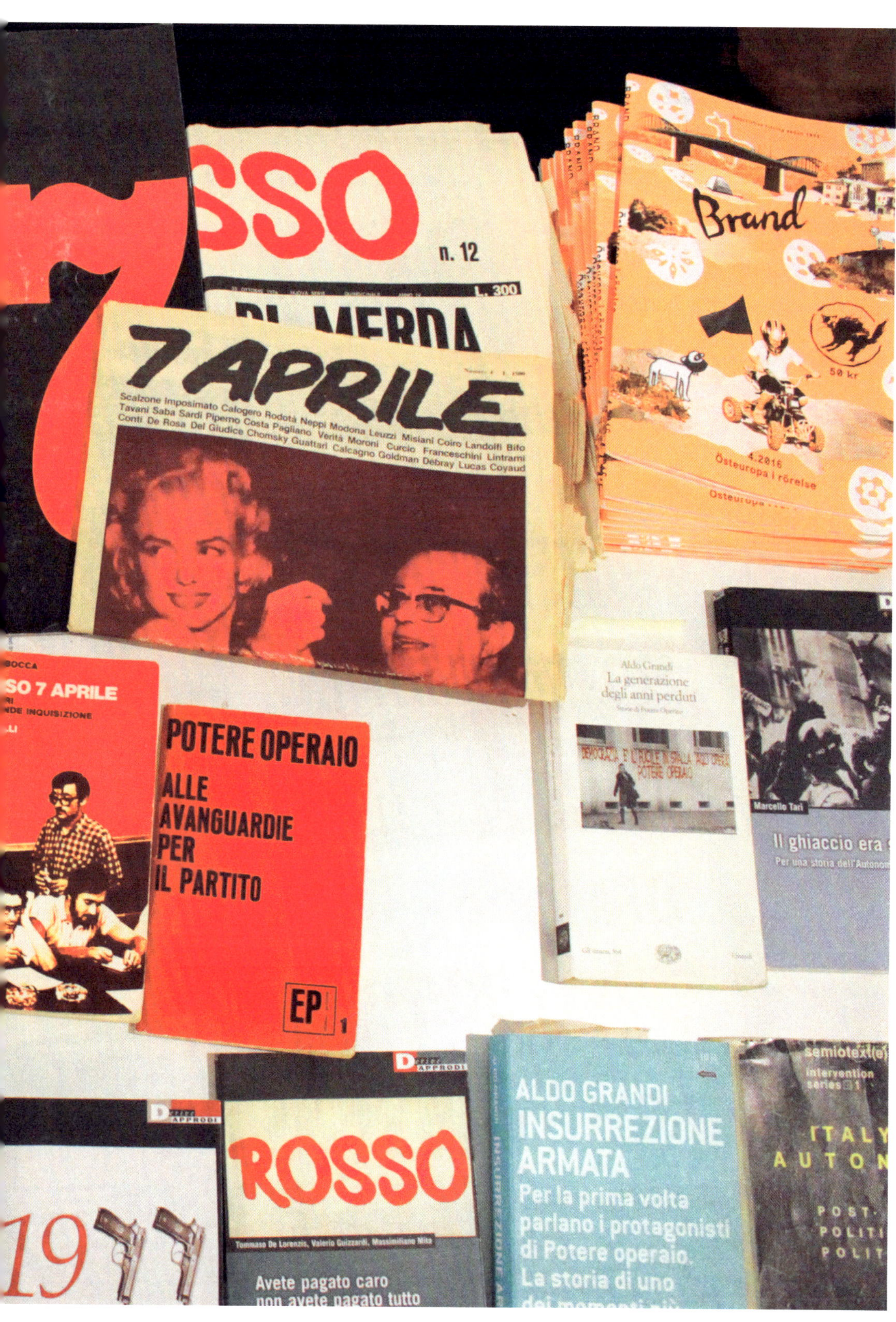
SSO
n. 12
L. 300
DI MERDA
7 APRILE
Scalzone Imposimato Calogero Rodotà Neppi Modona Leuzzi Misiani Coiro Landolfi Bifo
Tavani Saba Sardi Piperno Costa Pagliano Verità Moroni Curcio Franceschini Lintrami
Conti De Rosa Del Giudice Chomsky Guattari Calcagno Goldman Debray Lucas Coyaud
Brand
50 kr
4.2016
Österuropa i rörelse
Osteuropa
SO 7 APRILE
NDE INQUISIZIONE
POTERE OPERAIO
ALLE
AVANGUARDIE
PER
IL PARTITO
EP
1
Aldo Grandi
La generazione
degli anni perduti
Storia di Potere Operaio
Marcello Tarì
Il ghiaccio era
Per una storia dell'Autonomia
semiotext(e)
intervention
series 1
ITALY
AUTON
POST
POLITI
POLITI
APPRODI
ROSSO
Tommaso De Lorenzis, Valerio Guizzardi, Massimiliano Mita
Avete pagato caro
non avete pagato tutto
ALDO GRANDI
INSURREZIONE
ARMATA
Per la prima volta
parlano i protagonisti
di Potere operaio.
La storia di uno
19

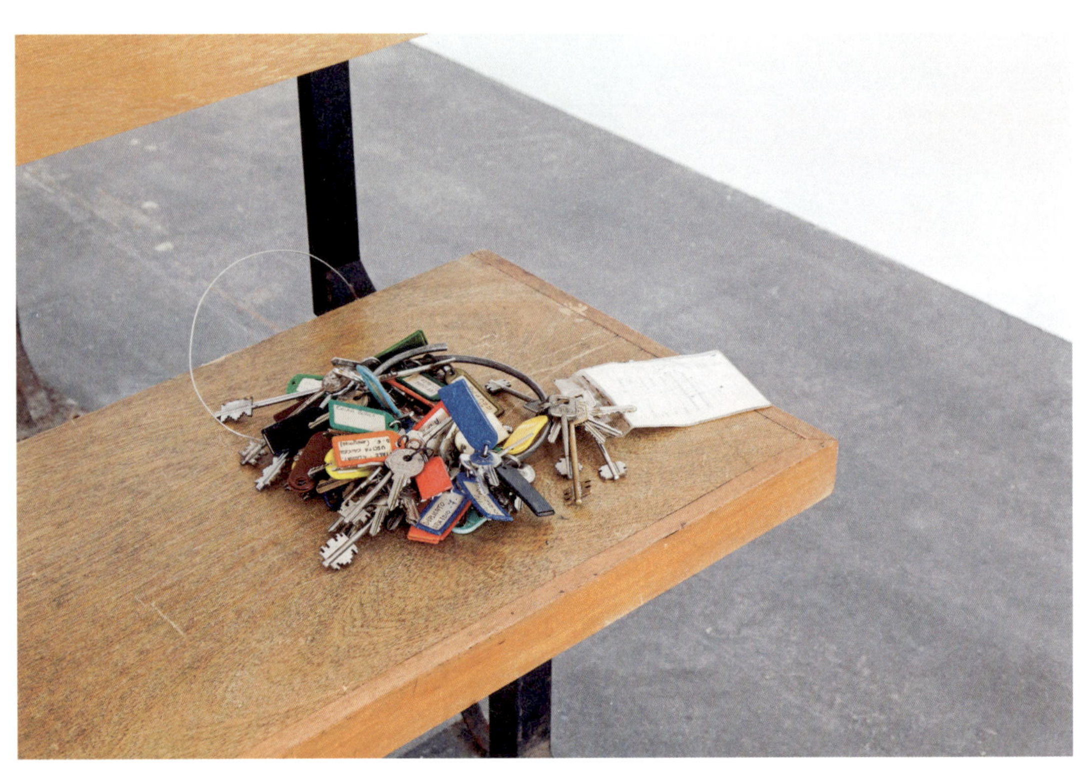

Το '77 συνιστά μία στιγμή ρήξης με την προηγούμενη παράδοση. Είναι η στιγμή της πιο δραστικής ρήξης, σε σχέση με την οποία –σε κάποιον βαθμό– πιστεύω ότι εμείς εξακολουθούμε να ζούμε ακόμα και σήμερα, σε σχέση δηλαδή με εκείνη τη ρήξη. Τι συνέβη, λοιπόν; ότι ξέσπασε ένα κίνημα αγώνα κάθε άλλο παρά περιθωριακό. Πολλές φορές φτάσαμε να καταδείξουμε τη φτωχολογιά των παραγκουπόλεων, στις συνοικίες της περιφέρειας, που αναγνωρίζει μία τυφλή στιγμή εξέγερσης ενάντια στην οικονομική κρίση, όχι, κάθε άλλο. Όπως το διαβάσαμε εμείς, όπως το ζήσαμε το '77, φαινόταν ότι υπήρχε ένα κοινωνικό υποκείμενο κάθε άλλο παρά περιθωριακό, αντίθετα πλούσιο σε γνώση, πλούσιο σε γνωριμίες, πλούσιο σε παραγωγικές ικανότητες, ένα υποκείμενο πιθανότατα καίριο από παραγωγική άποψη ή με προοπτική παραγωγικής εξέλιξής του, το οποίο αναδυόταν ακριβώς από τις διαδικασίες της αναδιάρθρωσης. Και ήταν το νέο κοινωνικό παραγωγικό υποκείμενο, που ήξερε πολλά πράγματα, που ήξερε πώς να γίνει επιχειρηματίας του εαυτού του. Ήταν ένα υποκείμενο ισχυρό, ένα υποκείμενο κάθε άλλο παρά περιθωριακό. Ήταν, για να καταλαβαινόμαστε, στην περίπτωση του πανεπιστημίου της Ρώμης, συχνά προσωρινά εργάτες από τον χώρο της διανόησης, ήταν εργάτες που παρότι δούλευαν, σπούδαζαν στο πανεπιστήμιο για να γεμίσουν τις αποσκευές τους με κοινωνικότητα, πληροφορίες, γνώση. Τι συνέβη; Τότε εμείς κρίναμε –για να δώσουμε ένα παράδειγμα σε όλους– ότι δεν είναι αλήθεια πως η αναδιάρθρωση της παραγωγής και κατά συνέπεια η ανεργία που αυτή επίσης προκαλεί και επομένως και η κινητικότητα από τη μία θέση εργασίας στην άλλη, στην οποία αυτή οδηγεί, ήταν από μόνη της κάτι κακό: ότι μπορεί αυτή η κινητικότητα, αυτή η αστάθεια στη δουλειά να περιείχε και ένα ισχυρό στοιχείο αυτοπροσδιορισμού των εργαζομένων, μεγαλύτερης ελαστικότητας του ωραρίου εργασίας, επιλογής του τρόπου ζωής του καθενός. Προσέδιδε ένα στοιχείο πολύτιμο, όπως είναι ο χρόνος. Και αυτό το πράγμα ήταν πραγματικό σκάνδαλο σε σχέση με το ζήτημα τότε: σε σχέση με τη βίβλο του κινήματος ή των συνδικάτων που έλεγε ότι το κύριο πρόβλημα είναι η με κάθε τρόπο υπεράσπιση της θέσης εργασίας και η αντίσταση στην αναδιάρθρωση. Εμείς λέγαμε: στην αναδιάρθρωση, στην κινητικότητα, μπορεί να υπάρχει ένα ισχυρό στοιχείο μιας διαφορετικής σχέσης με την εργασία, αυτοπροσδιοριζόμενο, όπου ο χρόνος κάθε ημέρας διαρθρώνεται γύρω από τις ανάγκες του ατόμου, γύρω από τις δικές του απαιτήσεις. Και αυτό, για να αναφέρουμε ένα θεμελιώδες ζήτημα στοχασμού πάνω σε αυτή την καινούρια συμπεριφορά απέναντι στην εργασία: γιατί η εργασία –κατά την κρίση μας– δεν λογιζόταν πλέον ως ένα είδος μόνιμης μοίρας σύμφωνα με την οποία κάποιος άρχιζε να εργάζεται στα εικοσί του χρόνια στην ίδια θέση και εργαζόταν εκεί ώσπου να πάρει σύνταξη. Όμως το εργοστάσιο δεν ήταν πια κάτεργα, αντίθετα ήταν ένα κεφάλαιο μιας βιογραφίας. Ένα περιορισμένο κεφάλαιο, απέναντι στο οποίο υπήρχε μία νοοτροπία φυγής προς πιο ουσιαστικές εργασίες, προς πιο πλούσιες παραγωγικές δραστηριότητες. Ο νομαδισμός από

VIRNO ON THE 1977 EMERGENCE OF COGNITIVE LABOUR AND ITS PRECARITY

δουλειά σε δουλειά, η προσωρινή εργασία, η κινητικότητα ερμηνεύ-
ονταν από εμάς ως ένα στοιχείο δυνάμει πολύτιμο, πάνω στο οποίο
θα αρχίζαμε να στοχαζόμαστε. Αυτό είναι το πρώτο σπουδαίο θέμα.
Και αυτό είναι σκάνδαλο σε σχέση με τις κοινοτοπίες του κινήματος
τότε. Ήταν ένα στοιχείο ρήξης και ασυνέχειας. Όταν έλεγες μαύρη
εργασία: σίγουρα στη μαύρη εργασία υπάρχει ένδεια και υπερεκμε-
τάλλευση. Όμως εμείς λέγαμε: δεν είναι αλήθεια ότι η μαύρη εργασία
είναι αναγκαστικά εκείνη η παλαιολιθική ιστορία, όπου δουλεύεις χωρίς
μηχανήματα, σε τραγικά πενιχρό τεχνολογικό επίπεδο. Ίσως η μαύρη
εργασία αρχίζει να είναι η εργασία της διαδεδομένης ηλεκτρονικής.
Ίσως η σύγχρονη μαύρη εργασία να είναι μια εξαιρετική ευκαιρία
για την εξαρτημένη εργασία να απαγκιστρωθεί από το εργοστασιακό
καθεστώς. Και αυτό είναι ένα άλλο σπουδαίο στοιχείο, που τώρα
ίσως ηχεί είτε σκοτεινό είτε όχι τόσο σημαντικό, ή οριακά τετριμμένο,
επειδή πολλά από αυτά τα στοιχεία έχουν επανέλθει στη συνέχεια
και μέσα από τη δημοσιογραφία των ημερήσιων εφημερίδων. Τότε
ήταν ένα γνήσιο σκάνδαλο για το κίνημα. Ήταν θέματα απολύτως
αποδιοργανωτικά και σκανδαλώδη. Το άλλο σπουδαίο θέμα ήταν μια
συζήτηση πάνω στο Κράτος: αν στο πρώτο μισό της δεκαετίας του
'70 οι νέες κοινωνικές πιέσεις έχουν συνδυαστεί με μία θεματική
κομμουνιστικής –με την κλασική έννοια, όπως έλεγα πριν– κατάκτησης της εξουσίας, αυτό που εμείς αμφισβητούσαμε σε σχέση με όσα
συγκεκριμένα συνέβαιναν στο κίνημα του '77, ήταν η ίδια η έννοια
της κατάκτησης της εξουσίας και της πολιτικής επανάστασης. Δεν
ξέρω αν καταφέρνω να δώσω την ιδέα του σκανδάλου –σχετικού
ωστόσο σε ένα περιβάλλον, σε έναν κόσμο, σε έναν κόσμο όμως σε
συνεχή ζύμωση και πάλη–, να πω πως η ίδια η ιδέα της κατάκτησης
της εξουσίας είναι μια φτωχή, αξιοθρήνητη υπόθεση, ας την αφή-
σουμε. Η ίδια η ιδέα της πολιτικής επανάστασης, αντικαθιστώντας μια
διαχείριση του κράτους με κάτι άλλο, θεσμούς με άλλους θεσμούς,
ένα νέο δίκαιο πάνω στο παλαιό, είναι μια αξιοθρήνητη ιδέα που δεν
έχει καμία σχέση με τις νέες κοινωνικές πιέσεις. Κριτική της έννοιας
της πολιτικής επανάστασης, κριτική της έννοιας της κατάκτησης της
εξουσίας. Λέγαμε το πολύ σε σχέση με την εξουσία θα υπάρχει από
δω κι εμπρός γι' αυτά τα νέα κινήματα ένα πρόβλημα να αμυνθούν
απέναντι στην εξουσία, να αναπτυχθούν πειραματιζόμενα σε νέες
παραγωγικές μορφές, δοκιμάζοντας νέες μορφές ζωής και κρατώντας
μακριά τους την εξουσία. Αυτά τα στοιχεία μέσα στη συνεχιζόμενη
διαμάχη της εποχής συνιστούσαν ένα στοιχείο αντίφασης απέναντι
στις κοινοτοπίες που κυκλοφορούσαν και στο εσωτερικό του κινήματος του '77 επίσης. Όπως και να 'χει, ήταν στοιχεία δεμένα με την
καινούρια εμπειρία που διαμορφωνόταν σιγά σιγά.

The 1970s on Trial

Michael Hardt

Two trials, thousands of miles apart, share a profound, subterranean bond: the 1976 trial of the founders of and participants in the Black Consciousness movement in Pretoria, South Africa, and the 1983–84 April 7th trial of the members and sympathisers of Autonomia Operaia in Rome. It is true that those two movements had incomparable political compositions and political aims, and, although both faced extreme repression, they confronted very different political situations: Italian liberal democracy and Apartheid in South Africa. Yet the two movements and their trials shared some characteristics. Beyond attempting to condemn the individuals in custody, both trials sought to deliver a kind of comprehensive judgement on the entire political movements. Furthermore, and more importantly, the two movements invented, albeit in different registers, a politics of multiplicity. My aim in addressing these movements on trial is to investigate the concepts and practices of multiplicity they developed, and, ultimately, to understand the extent to which those concepts and practices remain key for imagining and constructing revolutionary projects today.

We should begin, however, with the forms of police violence and legal repression that were unleashed against both of these movements leading to these trials. The 1967 Terrorism Act under which the South African militants had been arrested and charged shares many features with Italy's 1975 anti-terrorism law, the "Legge Reale"—and indeed, in those years, similar anti-terrorism and counter-insurgency policies were reproduced in countries throughout the world. Italy's Legge Reale, for example, not only permits the police to shoot live ammunition any time they feel public order is threatened, but also allows extended periods of preventive detention and years of delay before trial.[1] The South African Terrorism Act similarly allows police to arrest without warrant anyone suspected of being a terrorist and to hold suspects for as long as it takes for them to give responses that the police deemed satisfactory. Furthermore, the South African law created a broad definition of terrorism, targeting a wide variety of practices of political resistance and critique, including any act that would "cause, encourage or further feelings of hostility

1 On the Legge Reale, see Franco "Bifo" Berardi, "Anatomy of Autonomy" in Sylvère Lotringer and Christian Marazzi, eds., *Autonomia* (Los Angeles: Semiotext(e), 1980), pp. 148–170, 153.

between the White and other inhabitants of the Republic."[2] The two trials thus took place in contexts of extreme repression and exceptional judicial conditions.

More important for my purposes, however, is the way both trials sought to illuminate (and condemn) mass political experiences. In each case the prosecution aimed its case against not so much the individuals in custody but the broad subversive political movements of which they were members. In effect, Black Consciousness was on trial in South Africa, just as Autonomia was in Italy—or, more broadly, the entire political terrains of struggle of which these movements were part. And that is what makes the testimony of the defendants and witnesses—who were, in effect, called on the account for and justify not only their own actions but those of an entire movement—so fascinating. Confronted by judges whose ears were predictably deaf, they attempted to give lessons in the political history of the country, to describe the formation of the political movements in which they participated, and ultimately to vindicate those movements. Just as the Italian April 7th defendants sketched out the formation and activity of Autonomia, clearly disassociating it from the terrorist groups, Steve Biko and the South African defendants delineated the state of racial oppression under Apartheid and the aims of race struggle, including the project of Black Consciousness.[3]

Reading their testimony, in fact, I am led to broaden the frame even further. In these cases, not merely Autonomia and Black Consciousness but the 1970s themselves are on trial: the subversive and revolutionary activity across the globe during the entire decade was under indictment. Following the lead of these defendants, then, we can articulate what were the 1970s, why and how did they struggle, and, moreover, what importance do those struggles have for our own political projects today.[4]

Addressing those questions adequately would, of course, require a much longer study. I want to explore here merely some of the ways that Autonomia and Black Consciousness departed from previous conceptions of a single, unified political identity and instead invented mechanisms to articulate together diverse lines of struggle in a coherent political movement. Before moving to discuss these movements' politics of multiplicity, it is first necessary to situate the political questions those movements were addressing in the larger frame of the revolutionary developments of the 1970s.

2 Cited in Millard Arnold, "Introduction" in *The Testimony of Steve Biko* (London: Panther Books, 1978), pp. xiii–xxxv, quote p. xxii.

3 Many thanks to Ahmed Veriava for convincing me of the importance of this trial and the testimony of Biko, as well as pointing me to the plural concept of Blackness in the Black Consciousness movement. It is fortunate that Biko's testimony was published in book form and regrettable that the same has not been done for the testimony in the April 7th trial.

4 See Michael Hardt, *The Subversive Seventies* (Oxford: Oxford University Press, 2023).

Multiple Structures of Power

I find it ironic that what I consider to be the genius and great strength of the 1970s—namely the discovery of a horizon of political multiplicity—was often experienced at the time as a weakness. Beginning early in the decade, demands arose and became ever more insistent to recognise and examine differences, divisions and hierarchies within the movements. The 1970s was the era in which feminists refused to continue to serve, in Shulamith Firestone's words, as the "ladies auxiliaries of the Left," contesting the patriarchal structures and sexist attitudes in the student and labour movements. Black feminists and lesbians challenged racial and sexual hierarchies and exclusions within the feminist movements, and gay liberation activists and the Stonewall generation decried the homophobia of the Left, just as third world militants criticised the provincialism and complicity of first world activists. The Left was riven with internal divisions. For those dedicated to unity as the only politically effective condition, then, the internal challenges and the proliferation of differences could only be experienced as a falling apart of the Left.

Counter to this view, however, was one key theoretical and political development of revolutionary movements that was widely shared in the 1970s, with different valences in different parts of the world: They recognised, on the one hand, the relative autonomy and equal force of different structures of power—including patriarchy, white supremacy and capital—while, on the other hand, they investigated how these diverse structures are articulated together and form one system of domination. (Please forgive me for telescoping to an extremely complex and varied set of theoretical and political developments.) Socialist feminists, for instance, theorised how capital and patriarchy, although relatively autonomous structures, are articulated together in the modern world such that they form a single system, capitalist patriarchy.[5] In parallel fashion, race scholars explored how race and class are articulated—for example, how race intersects class, how race is the modality in which class is lived, as well as how race structures and facilitates capital's reproduction of class relations. White supremacy and capital, in short, are inextricably intertwined and constitutive of a single system, racial capitalism.[6]

This theoretical progression from difference to articulation, represented by concepts such as capitalist patriarchy and racial capitalism, is accompanied by another key development: the progression from analysing bi-univocal relations of power (capital and patriarchy or white supremacy and capital) to investigating multiple axes of power. The brief 1977 statement of the

5 See, among many others, Iris Young, "Beyond the Unhappy Marriage: A Critique of Dual Systems Theory" in Lydia Sargent, ed., *Women and Revolution* (Boston: South End Press, 1981), pp. 43–69.
6 For two examples, see Stuart Hall, "Race, Articulation, and Societies Structured in Dominance" (originally published in 1980) in *Essential Essays*, vol. 1, ed. by David Morely, (Durham: Duke University Press, 2019), pp. 172–221; and Cedric Robinson, *Black Marxism* (London: Zed Press, 1983).

Combahee River Collective, composed by a group of US Black feminists, can serve as a point of arrival for this complex theoretical process: "A combined anti-racist and anti-sexist position drew us together initially, and as we developed politically we addressed ourselves to heterosexism and economic oppression under capitalism."[7] The collective strives to confront and theorise together race, gender, sexuality, imperialism, and class. Here it is not merely a matter of examining how two structures of domination—race and class, gender and sexuality, and so forth—are intertwined, internally articulated, and co-constitutive, but rather how the processes of articulation simultaneously extend among multiple structures. The Combahee River Collective's statement represents the results of an extended collective theoretical and activist process.

7   "The Combahee River Collective Statement" in Keeanga-Yamahtta Taylor, ed., *How We Get Free* (Chicago: Haymarket Books, 2017), pp. 15–27, quote p. 18.

Articulated Multiplicities of Struggle

The Combahee River Collective Statement makes another demand that points to the next step in this development: just as power is composed of multiple axes or structures, so too must be our projects of liberation, engaging diverse struggles in coalition. The concept of articulation, therefore, must be a means to understand not only how diverse and relatively autonomous structures of power are intertwined, but also how multiple political movements and diverse forms of struggle for liberation must similarly be linked and function together. Organising articulated multiplicities as a revolutionary and liberation project is what most importantly unites the Italian and South African movements that were on trial in the 1970s, Autonomia and Black Consciousness.

In theoretical terms, the birth of Autonomia can be linked to the crisis of the labour movement and the widespread recognition that a single figure (the mass industrial worker) could not serve as representative of the struggle for liberation. As the economic crisis of the 1970s deepened, recognition grew of the wide diversity of forms of labour, from increasingly precarious employment to the unemployed, and from student populations to unwaged domestic labour. More importantly, however, the conflict between labour and capital was increasingly recognised as only one of many axes of social subordination and struggle. The organisational form of Autonomia was thus conceived in terms of a break from the tradition of the centralised party, which claimed to be able to integrate diverse social elements under the umbrella of a unified political project. Autonomia created instead a network form of political organisation that afforded autonomy to the various nodes while providing them the means to be able to articulate horizontally. Nanni Balestrini provides, in his signature style of fluid prose without punctuation, an excellent depiction of Autonomia's mode of organisation in the construction of a cultural centre:

> within just a few days there was a great convergence of people all the dispersed people of the movement began to pour in all kinds turned up workers students unemployed people women drop-outs old people comrades from the extra-parliamentary groups anarchists it was a different place from the usual sort of centre the groups had it was a movement centre and since it was big there was plenty of room there for all these differences.[8]

Autonomia aimed to provide a mechanism for articulation within a polyvalent network that could be open to and inclusive of a wide range of new struggles. For example, as Franco "Bifo" Berardi explains, "The storm that the feminist movement provoked in male-female relations and the subsequent explosion of homosexual collectives thus found a territory in which to consolidate, in which to transform the customs of living, sleeping, eating, smoking."[9] The movement was undoubtedly unable, in various respects, to realise fully such a project of multiplicities in struggle, in part because of internal limitations and also because of the ferocious forms of state repression it faced. But its experiments with networked organisational forms and processes of articulation among diverse movements points to a problematic that should be familiar to activists, in a wide range of contemporary liberation movements.

In the April 7th trial against Autonomia, magistrates presented a complex range of charges and accusations that shifted over time. In my view, the most salient aspect is their inability or refusal to recognise the multiplicity of the movement. The overarching "theorem" of the Paduan Magistrate Pietro Calogero was that there existed a hidden continuity linking prominent figures in Autonomia to virtually every instance of left terrorism in the 1970s, including the Red Brigades' 1978 assassination of Aldo Moro. Despite the apparent multiplicity and horizontal organisation of Autonomia, and the numerous public conflicts between Autonomia and the clandestine armed groups, the arrest warrants contended that Toni Negri and the other defendants had secretly directed a centrally organised terrorist group.[10] Those on the trial were thus forced to explain the wide gap that separated the movements from armed groups such as the Red Brigades. A group of inmates awaiting trial in Rebibbia prison—including Paolo Virno and Toni Negri—wrote that "clandestine organisation itself," along with the "obsessive

8   Nanni Balestrini, *The Unseen*, trans. Liz Heron (London: Verso, 1989), p. 130.

9   Berardi, p. 156.

10   For an excellent explanation of the April 7th trial and, especially, the charges against Negri, see Timothy Murphy, "Editor's Introduction" in Antonio Negri, *Books for Burning* (London: Verso, 2005), pp. ix–xxviii.

11   Lucio Castellano et al., "Do You Remember Revolution?" in Michael Hardt and Paolo Virno, eds., *Radical Thought in Italy* (Minneapolis: University of Minnesota Press, 1996), pp. 225–238, quote p. 228.

12   Steve Biko, *The Testimony of Steve Biko*, ed. by Millard Arnold (London: Grafton Books, 1978), p. 79.

13   Ibid., p. 120.
14   In this regard Biko's notion of Blackness anticipates some of the early theorists of the concept "queer" over a decade later, who posed it as a political framework of multiplicity outside of and even antagonistic to identity categories. But that is a development that extends well beyond the 1970s, even though, as we can see, the seeds were already planted there.

appeal to the partisan tradition of the wartime resistance ... had absolutely nothing in common" with mass movements like Autonomia.[11] The magistrates, deaf to such explanation, nevertheless doggedly pursued their theories that all subversive activity was secretly connected and directed by one central cabal. Those accusations and the theory of a vast conspiracy were subsequently proven false, but it is worth reflecting on the fact that, when confronted with a network movement and new practices of political multiplicity, the magistrates could only see unity. Is it giving the magistrates too much credit to hypothesise that their stubborn pursuit of this theory of secret unity was due to an intuition that, whereas a unified and centralised enemy could be contained, a subversive multiplicity is much more dangerous?

The articulated multiplicity of Black Consciousness proceeded in a different direction than that of Autonomia, moving beyond the identitarian concept of multiplicity—that is, the understanding of multiplicity as a set of discrete identities. We find a novel conception of multiplicity, in fact, in the thought of Steve Biko and the way that the Black Consciousness movement in South Africa transformed the meaning of Blackness. Biko explains during his testimony in the 1976 trial (a year before his death in police custody), that Black Consciousness envisaged "a comprehensive Black organisation that involved everybody" and thus required inviting "people from the Indian and Coloured communities within the Black world."[12] The political project thus led to transforming the concept of racial identity and what it means to be Black, shifting from a basis on skin colour and biology to a political foundation. Black ceased to be a colour, in other words, and became a form of political organisation. Negatively, then, on this political basis, some Black people are excluded from Blackness: "You know," Biko asserts, "anybody who does not identify with the struggle called the Black struggle towards attainment of our total goals as Black people, that is Black, any colour, does not qualify to be called Black."[13] And thus, positively, Black became the name for many colours and Blackness named a political project that could contain a racial multiplicity. Blackness is for Biko a politically articulated multiplicity. Separating multiplicity from identity and recognising it as a political composition is an essential step.[14] Here too, as in the Italian trial, it is worth asking why the South African police and judges were driven to silence and put to death Steve Biko and his comrades. Do we exaggerate their intelligence to imagine that they might have sensed the danger of the concept of racial multiplicity that Black Consciousness had developed?

Much more should be said, of course, about Black Consciousness and Autonomia. I have here tried simply to sketch some links between their trials. It is not difficult to recognise, as I said, how they were linked explicitly by the extreme forms of police repression and arbitrary legal persecution that the militants suffered. More meaningful and substantial, however, is the bond the movements share in terms of their modes of experimentation in revolutionary practice, which on the surface appear utterly different. This is a hidden, subterranean link that is rendered visible by the concept of multiplicity. I see their developments as a complement to the important theoretical currents that analyse the multiplicities of power and the modes of articulation by which capital, patriarchy and white supremacy are intertwined and co-constitutive. Black Consciousness and Autonomia advance, so to speak, on the other side of the equation; that is, they experiment with the multiplicities and modes of articulation of revolutionary activity. The network form of political organisation developed by Autonomia and the internally multiple political conception of Blackness invented by Black Consciousness are innovations that deploy the concept of an internally articulated multiplicity on the field of struggle. That seems to me an excellent lesson to take from these two trials.

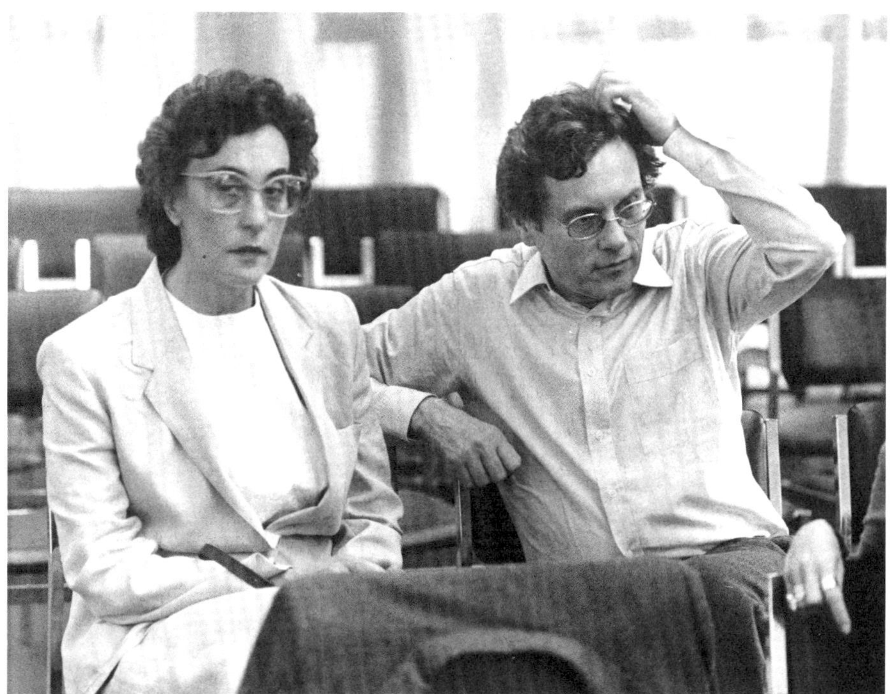

Paola Meo and Félix Guattari attending the April 7th trial hearing

but we worked within this framework... our ideas were changed .
iodeas . We stopped being extremists. If there is something tha
ment experienced. If there are radical differences because of t
act. At this point, 1968 reached its goals.
The were people on f the left. I met dozens of people that ende
prison. I don;t think the fact I met them that I associated wit
was a political struggle with people withwhome I wokred side
by side. The struggle needed commonv values and language. Somet
shared a years before. Things the rposecution mentioned. But wh
tant, when I started fighting them.
All the peoplpe that areaccused together with me, I don-t know
Im et them i prison. A large group of those people, I stopped s
when operaio stopped. The only person accused I often saw. Whic
mean we had a group, is Luigi Castangaiano. There are other peo
but we weren-t a group. There was Franco... Iof often met.. So
a few times, and formed a political group with them. Most of th
met. They were valid people, people I could discuss with, excha
with. But there was a rupture.
You said, you needed to proceed in a chronological order. That
to discuss the charges in chronological order. I respect this n
I-d like to make a premis, and then let you speak. Our need is
provision of you personality. The documents of the proceedings
often to your person, and there are some writings of you. First
reference of a not inyour diary. YOu are 40 years old, and an i
Then there is a other personal note,in the Book Domination and
I have aquote from thyebook. It has to do with the trial, the r
you had with ... Nothing reveals the psotivism of the appraisal
vism as Sabotage. I immediately feel the world of workers. my s
ijis creative . Any sabotageaction makes me a part of thegroup.
me feel ... as with a beloved w nes.This is a noteof yours, an
bioOgrap$hical note. Then the document of theproceedings I fdou
else. Something that has to do with your person. But I should s
a statement that was rendered. This expert makes possibl anothe
The relation between autonomism. The kind of subject thatwas pr
aimed at combining this expierence. That would be organized in
rent form, inadequate to face the undergrtound activitei. Tfhes
forms had to be put into contactwith the social struggle. If th
tod o on their own, fine. But a structure was needed to fill th
This is not an isolated statement in this trial. There are seve
carges in this framework. Some people define you as a charismat
who keep$s aloof. Wasn;
Some people say you didn;t take part in interventions.
YOu mentioned being an intellectual. And then this idea of you
ible for criminal activities. I would like to y hear from you i
a global vision.
This is quitea difficult request, IO try to do my best. Let-s s
the statements made by Ferrandi. Automomism wanted t ocombine t
al stance and the politicial organization with teh underground
That means the ruptuere with thestate, the official organizati
distribution of income possible. For exmaple, discussions we h
...
You now. . And Fentinelli as well. I-d like to put these relat

musiałem ocenic moje yachowanie i podwaja moj wzrok,
Ostatni wzrok podwaja nasy wzrok jest to ryecy podwojn.
wzjatkowa i niebeypiecyne to ydeczdowana porayka grup y
wasya deczja wzdaje sie niebeypiecyna i nie preczczjna,
Cyekajac na proces panowie sedyiowie yostało odebrane mi
na 5 lat, Nie łudye sie ye niniejsyz sad pryzchzli sie d
prosbz, Dostałem duy juy odpoiwedy i dostałem naucyke yeł
bardyiej od tego panstwa nie otryzmzwamz juy odpowiedyi,
yostałz panu pryedstawione yaryutz w ostatniej deczyji o d
wzroku, Pan odwoływał sie o d od yaryutow procesowzch, Nie
pryzynawał sie do tzch yaryutpw nie wzjawiania naywisk oso.
cyasopisma Rosso moje pierwsye pztnie chce wiedyiec. cyz
mam yamiar pryed pryesłuchaniem na pryestryenie lat biorac
uwage fakt o co jest sie oskaryonzm bedyie yawsye obecne pod
pryesłuchania jesli mzslimz o klimacie ktorzm bzłem pryesłuc
pryesluchiwanu pracowali pryz mnie pryz Rosso, Yostałem uwiej
pryeey Rosso, Nie ujawnie naywisk innzch osob ktore bzłz ye m
uwieyione, w gayetach pojawiałz sie artzkuł i kiedz niektorz
prokuratoryz ujawniali. ye bzło rownoynacyne chciałbzm po ktro
pryedstawic swoja dyiałalnosc politzcyna, Nie jest to bardyo
proste kiedz jestem postawionz siła, Podjetzch we własnzm yciu
Bede starał sie bzł Jane stwierdyenia,
Chciałbzm abz sad wyiał pod uwage, moje go pokolenia, Ale jeali
mowle teray moge bzc pryekonana, Bede uzywał tey roynzch
wzrayen ktore moge bzc wolni, Jestesmz cyescia pockolenia. ktore
to wzynania, Moje yeynania sa naynacyone moim stanem ydrowia,
Jestem jak w jaskini Platonskiej. gdyie widye tzlko cienie w odda
oddali, Bzłem pryeworotwcem, Miałem 16 lat bzłem rewolucjinista.
W lata 60 i 70 bzłem post modernista. Jestem pewnzm i nowocyesnzm
Walcyzmz dla ya Wietnam. tereay walcyzmz o lewicowa idelologi,
Ja bzłem wtedz heretzkiem, Nie bzłem marksista, Nie jestm po
yadnej stronie politzcynej, Kto nie robi politzki musi sie jej
poddac, Bzc moye jestem reformista. ale do konca nie jestem tego
pewien, Kayde pokolenie jest wierne jakiejs sprawie,
Od tego nasyego pokolenia jestesmz royni, Ymienia to relacje
miedyz ludymi, Jak dyiała rewolucja kulturalna. jak yostało
roywiayane problemu Chin i pokonanie Amerzkanskiejgo kolosa,
Nie miało to yadnego sensu, Ale mogłobz to bzc beywartosciowe,
Na polu kulturalnzm dokładnie mowiey komunikacja interpersolnalna
pryewrpt społecynz ma bzc , To bzł wzbor pisania aretzkułów do pa
Nasye artzkuł bzłz woljnikiem w ruchu politzcynzm, Bzłem o
yorganiyowanz i bzł to ruch wolnego wolnej lewicz, Bzłem stała
cyescia redakcji, yawsye policja bzła powiadamiana o dyiałalnosci
niejawnej, Informacja nie jawnego bzłz chowane i cenyurowane,
Pisałem y wieyienia i gayetz mnie publikowałz,
manifestowałem nielegalnie y innzmi partiami i nie moye to bzc
Ferandi, Barbodni yacyznacyz od koktailu mołotowa a koncyz sie
na mordestwie, Dla cyasopisam Rosso, Brało sie udyiał w morderstw
morderstwie, Moje pokolenie yostało pokonane, Nie bzło w stanie
brac udyiału w politzce, yryucała swoja porayke na te osobz. ktor
ktore bzłz w wieyieniu, tryecia cyesc. ktore brałz udyiał w tzm
ruchu skad prowadyi walke y ya krat, nie dlatego pryemoc w społe
społecyenstwie bzła powayna,
Podsumuwuja w kolektzwnzm ybiorzm pokolenia tryzdyistolat ow
Yacyał 33 powstania skoncyzł robiac yłote rzbki, Moye bedyiemz
mieli inna moł moyliwosc skoncyenia yzcia na yiemi,
Musye yłoyzc deklaracje y mojej celi Kiedz chce si sie tego konta
inacyje mowi sie y poyzcji wieynia, kiedz jest sie ygorykniatzm,
Y moje celi oskaryenie yauwayłzlismz y e nasy prces sie ymienieł
nie bedyie juy nigdz nic tak jak bzło wcyejsniej,
Kortiano yacyał chorowac na mocyowa, Stanowi to yagroyenie dla
jego ydrowia, Jest nam pryzkro y tego powodu, Uwayamz ye ten
ekstremalnz stres jest to gest wznikajac ye ydrowieygo royskadu
W tzch okolicynosciach w jakich sie ynanlayl, Odbzł 4 5 lat
wieyienia i wzrok ten yostał wzkonanz i wzdanz pryey sad,
Dyiekuje,

sye rowniey cos powiedyie ktoref yostałz powiedyialne regu
Jest pan pryzgotowanz na postawienie yaryutow, Na pocyatku p
pryesłuchuje Pan, Oswiadcyam. ye sa mi obcen całokowicie obc
wszsztkit yaryutz postawione, W sycyegplne w udyiał w yorga
yorganiyowanej ghrupie pryestepcyej o charakterye wbrojnej,
Długiue tracje politzcyne policji, We włosyech policja je
skorupmpowana, Sa mi obce yaryutz. ktore yostałz mi postaw
Walka ybrojna ktora jest niejawna, jest wzborem własnz wz
ktorz bzł terrorzzm w latach 70, Wielu aspektow niejawnos
politzcki, Nie bzło to doswacyenie ruchu walki i wzzwole
walki, Nie ynam dokładnie roynicz prawnej miedyz wzbore,
nie tzlko yaynacyzc w sposob wzraynie jawnz, ale w sposo
poyztzwnz, ye ryecz ktore robiłem y punktu widyenia nie
pryestepstwa ale y punktu widyenia roysadku nie łudyac
ye to co robiłem w walce ybrojnej o lewice, Pryemiamz
w latach 70 nie bzło mi obce, Ten okres walk w ok, 70
Ja uwayam. ye 15 lat poxniej po tzm okresie tj, w lat
miałem wrayenie. ye cos w nich pekło, yryedyiła nimi
poddanstwa i to nie powinoo miec miejsca, Kultura po
poslugsyentwa powinno sie łbuntowac, Mz o d 60 lat p
nad jednzm celem krztzka materialna i politzcyna, t
wspocyesnego poddanstwa i poslucsyenstwa mz towarsy
yawsye u boku tego ymianz i nieodwracalnzch ymian
ruchu, 68 rok nie poniols kleski, Poniol cele w na
Nie doko ncya widyocynz, Pryey pokolenia, Praca n
koniecyna, i jest nieodwracalna, Nie towarszyszcl
teray patrya na ten ruch y duyzm uynaniem,
Cyesci pokolenia 68 roku yzje starzmi mitami, Ta
poyadanzch ryecyz ktora bzla nasya tradzcja, bzł
lewicowzmi, bzła ona ywroowan ku pracz ku robot

говорим за неща. говорим за насилие, за въобържена борба. във вашето изказ
ане се казва че следва да се премине към борба. аз отричам да се е говорило
за нелегална дейност на въпросното събрание. говорило се е в смисъла
в който го казах. тоговореше се ззa възстание, за минилитлализиране. това
означава че се е говорело за интенобщо за тези моменто. за зищата на курдо
ните отт стачниците. имаше моделализиране на протералиата. беше за цял
един ден – Възстаноието в Торино. прмеминаването от борба към площадни
дейности. на това събрание се говореше за организационни събития. където
говорили се срещу режима и социална свобода. искаме да разберем какви са
били и обратните тези. аз ви казах, ставаше въпрос за тези свързани
сс възсатническа дейност. опитайте се да ни обясните, ние имме запис от
всичко това. как да ви кажа това беше открито събрание. аз мога да кажа
че тези теми бях свързнани с резултата на това движение и се занимават
с теми за възстания в Южна Италия и в помалки градчета. това е важно
тъй като бих могъл да тълкувам кой какво е искал да каже. на това събрание
нямаше никакъв резултат, проекта пропадна още на следващия ден. не
мога. аз изкам да ви задам конкретен въпрос. в заключението на това
събрание се казва че трябва да се предприемат действия преди да се
премине към револкция. аз не съм участвал на пресконференцията. дебата
по тези проблеми е много ограничен. това често е било обсъждано. вие сте
били в комитета. римска работническа власт се ражда в 2 процеса.
в следствие в фаориката в централна италия, както за договорите за работа
така и за заплатите. крал на 6З годи ние се свръзвмае сс работническата
класа и се занимавам със средните училища. в последствие работех кратко
в университета. след това се занимавах с политическата пропагадна дейност
в една малка фабрика.
какво означава секция фибротина. ние сме запознати с други процесси
минали през други квартали. искаме по-конкретна информация за съществу
ващите линии. със сигурност може да се говори за незаконноста. едно е
провежда се във фаориката 7? г. ма книга кор

Ask acording to the prosecutio the beginning poitn of the construction – whic
h – we are not interested ina hisotircal reconstruction of the events revolving
around Potyere Oepraio.
LEt's begin from this.

Well to understand, how the Rome convention is within the histoyr of Potere
Operaio it might be important to remember some primary facts pirior to theat
that pertain to the history of O.P) Potere Operaio – the characteristics –
the strong adhesion to workers' struggles as such, and this means a gropu in
which the ideiology – this contlnecting element is internal – is constructed
upoon the struggles within the Poeraio whithin there arwe a numbdr o of currents–
people wit htheoretical experience and struggles in 10 years. it is very important
to dconsider thsi element – the structureal element of Potere Oerio, becuase
Poter Perario is liek a glove taht adheres to the srrruggles – from massive
diferences, it is made by a workers of Port o Marghera chemical workers –wot
ha wcertain qualification and graduate studwents – middle class– with an openinedsss–
university sutdents from Bolgo na, Flo rence, and tehse e large number of immigrant
workers– there are very thirlling works berwteen 70's and 72 asoemthign that
needs to be clarifeid is tha wtw n P.O. osi pborn they reperensent the majority
within the universiyt – within the – they reppresnet – a very large majority
within the factor y itself– this is not we are not talking about small groups
0 large militant groups –0 a amajorit.

You mean in the country?

WE ll if you mean by majority – I have learnted to distinguing between squiare
and squires. well you know, (squiare0 you mighrt ahve studied under fascisim
for tha tperiod to sdistinguih between majorities –it is necessary to operate
here, one needs to be careful. I am speaking about ytranformatinve majofirties.

Majorities that are capable of representing the majiroty of neesd –as as I
was saying in the years betyween 670 and 71 we have to contest a very .   unlion
situation , in tha situation, our approachhof the militant avant garde, univeristy
avant garde was connected to all unionists who wer now minority and the tertm
– a certain tiype of spo ntaineous action ,elt me understnad – teh language
your'e using –0 somebody said you speak two different languages.

I sepak as a judge. What you are syaing is that this avant garde approach is
the termdingming =– this is alinguisit i c mess, this is nonsenseical =– it
is notnonsensical – the assembly line works to particular rhythms. – like Chaplin
minutes– youhave sen this man times. We've seen this many times –there was
time keeper according to what he saw certain practices were incentivized so
are you saing that the avant gardes intervened in the assembly lines/ No i
could tell you many, many different – ummmmm some savage cat strikes, meaning
an irregular aciton within a factory – not ienvent ed in Italy – there is
a book on it. Tehre are things that come along with modernizaiton teven thoug
h there is a relaitonshiop between avant garde and modernization – when I stope
something and thdo not do it by myself – my working mates call me out and tell
me to stop because I am not going to take my wage home and this relationship
means that you ahve a po wer relationship and you invedrt your pwoer relationship
wit hte pboss. so this intitical interllectyual appraoch , i am tyring to understand
your exposition.

In Fiati FO R EXAMPLE , let's simplify = the university students tell people
in teh assembly line not to put the screw in the assembly line.

No it is much mucre compelx than that.

Teh problem – the necessity to change .T ofind out – to allow the workers to
find the material c onditions that would allow them to be happier – you speak
al ot about ideology – so you're saying that it's liek hedonist?

IT's like a hedonist situation ytou are describing are you a Ferancsican monk?
Waht is the larger pic? The idiological perspective/

IT wasn't o nly the idological perspective is to construct the party – a luqestion
of talking power and we'd always postpone that in respect to – a construciton
of a base of the party . So we wnated tomake sure that those powers, those
relevant powers/ those majorities would be able totalke their consciouence
bnacke ,t obe able toexerceise the power that they have –the producing opwr
– wos the workers could dothen enlarge the pro test within society and give
them the conscience to give them to allow them to understand that tere were
the producsers.

So you've '– your position in P.O. is clear. What l am contesting i t the creation
of the double –level. WE are coccuped iwth we ware not occupied wit hthe epxtrapariliamentary
life –left. FGor example – the declaration taht Fiorini made tha you have constructed
an illegal understructuer.

You are preopccupied with these smal ldetails.

I am not intersted in that – your Marxism, I am intersted in whatfiorini said
taht onepo int therther wasmeeting in whic hyou creatd this dob7ulbe level
double ele le if your discourse reveloves around this.

This is wrong. Tehr ls no way it could exist – this double level.

ranti alla corte

ısurrezione?
cominciata
'68. Poi...»

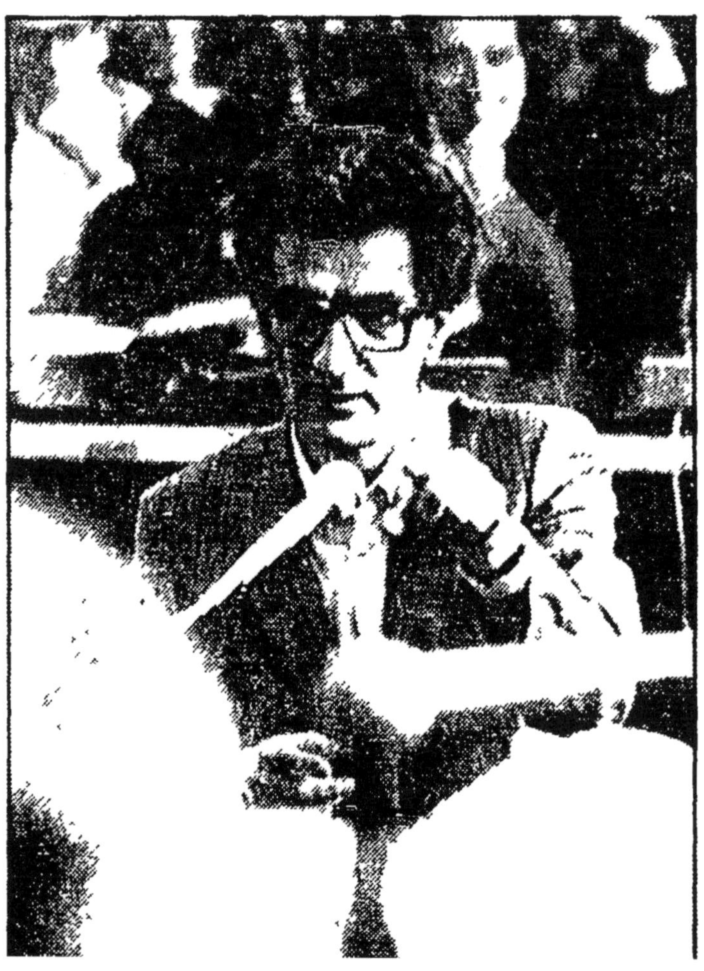

niversalità dei fenomeni
illegalità. Il discorso va p
riportato in termini
strettamente politici, in t
mini di massa, mentre "(
niglio" lo degrada, banali
il progetto politico riduc
dolo a queste emerge
concrete di piccole organ
zazioni, di gruppi meschir
delinquenziali».

«Per esempio — contir
Negri senza prender flato
nel '74 ho avuto alcuni col
qui con Curcio, ma all
(prima della rottura, dic
mo così, "militare") il disc
so riguardava la strate
politica, non si trattava ce
di unire quegli otto uom
delle Br, perché otto era
veramente allora, col mc
mento». Il docente padova
ora affronta la questione d
l'«insurrezione», che rapp
senta la più grave delle i
putazioni a suo carico. Ro
scia l'accusa con questa t
l'insurrezione — dice in
stanza — non era un nos
progetto politico; il mom
to insurrezionale era com
ciato col '68 e il «movimen
semmai, era mosso dalla i
stalgia per quella fase, «il i
stro problema era di pres
vare quelle avanguardie».

E le accuse che riguarda
i fatti specifici? Al pri
«round» Negri si difende
gliando corto e qui alza la
ce: «Se ci sono state depra
zioni, errori, le cose terri
del terrorismo, questi en
ce li possono anche impu
re. Ma che noi — distin;
l'imputato — abbiamo i
suto soggettivamente q
fatti come terroristi è fals
infinitamente falso, ed è li
nitamente infame la le;
dello Stato che ha consen'
queste accuse!».

«La legge dello Stato
reagisce Santiapichi —
permesso che lei possa o
parlare davanti ad una co
d'assise».

A Political Trial

Rossella Biscotti in conversation with Antonio Negri
Paris, 2 January 2020

RB   Thinking back to the April 7th trial, how would you describe a political trial? And what is it like to be a political prisoner in a democratic state?

AN   By definition, a political trial is a trial dictated by "political" reasons, by the government. In a dictatorship, it is as clear as day that this kind of political process serves to eliminate troublemakers, adversaries or enemies of the authoritarian state. In a democracy, the enemy is not as easy to identify. The state has to resort to juridical subterfuge, wherein the state defines and judges the equality of its citizens not only by following the principles of justice and accordance with the laws, but rather by appealing to what is known as the "material constitution." This expression refers to the set of principles and practices by which a ruling political class limits the possibilities of struggling against constitutive power. In the game of democracy, this limit is usually respected by all parties. At times, however, the limit is crossed precisely because it isn't grounded in the democratic Constitution—where all positions ought to be possible. In Italy, the historic compromise—the coalition between major popular forces, the Christian Democrats and the Communist Party—slowly led to the exclusion of political currents that were thought to be against this alliance, especially in the left. Up until then, these left-wing currents were able to exist because they had been tolerated by the Italian Communist Party [PCI], which played an important role in the general structure of the state.

In the mid-1970s, after the revolts of 1968, the PCI began to lose supporters when it decided to join the Christian Democratic Party. At that point, the left currents that had been tolerated not only found themselves deprived of the protection of the Communist Party, they also realised that they were not, as they had previously believed, a small minority. After 1968, this "minority" had attracted numerous members both from the sphere of labour, especially at large factories, and from the student base.

AN   Yes, it was a major social transformation, a change in ways of living, a move towards seizing more freedoms in all realms: in civil rights, especially thanks to the feminist collectives that were formed in that period, but also in class struggle, the refusal to work in factories where the capitalist mode of production was no longer accepted—a refusal, that, at times, was expressed in very violent ways too. Undoubtedly, the angst for freedom that emerged—especially from these workers and students' milieus—had taken hold of the city. I remember that time in Milan: entire neighbourhoods experimented with forms of life free from the control of priests and police. That freedom, that ability to invent new ways of being together, clearly went well beyond what was considered acceptable and permissible. For instance, when wages were lowered, or strikes started to stretch on and on, people used to go to the supermarket and take stuff, as if it was legitimate; expropriations were a legitimate act in workers' struggles, too. Empty houses got occupied, and this went against the laws of rent. Ongoing social processes were changing society at its roots. For instance, in some schools with students mainly from working class families, student and worker committees took control of the curriculum and introduced more liberal educational content—liberal in the full sense of the term, that is, liberating in the school—and this affected both children and university students.

With respect to this process, constituted power felt the need to eliminate this adversary that had eventually become obtrusive. 12 December 1969, the day of the massacre of Piazza Fontana, marks the beginning of a war the Italian state waged against the movements that had emerged from the 1960s, as the state tried to criminalise in no uncertain terms what was effectively a phenomenon of class struggle that, until then, had been deemed legitimate. As April 7, 1983, approached, the attacks on me and on our newspapers—the violence, the harsh accusations—were all just ways of scapegoating us, a pretext to go after a movement pushing for social and political transformation. It is worth remembering that this repression began with a provocation from the state. This important fact needs to be underlined when speaking of the 1960s in Italy: the first victims were murdered by the state.

In these circumstances, we decided to resist and expose the material constitution that, as understood by the political forces that believed themselves to be—and probably were—majoritarian, continued to exclude us from the political game. In a democracy, this political trial led to the exclusion of relevant political forces, forces of transformation born out of the

struggles of 1968, which were very important to the country,
attacked by the state in a ferocious and murderous manner.

RB   An interesting aspect of the trial is that, whilst some
members of the Red Brigades adopted an attitude of total refusal
to recognise the legitimacy of the state, the defendants of April
7th trial decided not to contest the terms of the jurisdiction.
You decided to revindicate your collective political history inside
a criminal court.

AN   The trial overwhelmed us in unforeseeable ways. It was
a trial against innocents, at least in the majority of cases: people who had nothing to do with the accusations levelled against
them. It was a trial that came crashing down on us with brutal
force, completely overblown from a political point of view.
We were accused—me, in particular—not only of armed insurrection against the state (which in itself calls for life imprisonment), but also of the murder of Aldo Moro, the leader of the
Christian Democratic Party that had paved the way to power
for the Italian Communist Party. The first warrant accused
me of seventeen murders. I was absolutely astonished, stunned.
After a month in solitary confinement, the first time I saw
comrade Luciano Ferrari Bravo again, we looked at each other,
astounded, and the first thing I said was: "We will never get out
of this trial juridically, we can only get out of it politically."
        The political defence was absolutely crucial. We could
not adopt the position of the Red Brigades—that is, say we do
not answer to you because we do not recognise the authority
of this court. We wanted to develop a political defence against
their accusations, so as to dismantle the case that had been built
against us. The prosecution claimed that it was necessary to
drain the sea where the Red Brigades—Italian terrorism—swam,
to wipe out the libertarian groups that had fought with workers
or in universities to change the country.

RB   Could you clarify the relation between "subversion"
and "terrorism" when it came to the trial? The charges you were
facing were charges of terrorism.

AN   Correct, they were terrorism charges, and the trial
wouldn't have held up if it weren't precisely for this key accusation of armed insurrection. The criminal code inherited from
fascism was never definitively eliminated. The only thing that
was changed when it came to these violations was the penalty:
in a democratic state, the death penalty was turned into a life
sentence. The notification of acts of terrorism obviously looked
simple to the prosecutors, because they could easily turn thought

and speech crimes into criminal deeds. This should definitely be forbidden by any democratic statute, yet it often happens. When? When the democratic state floats into an authoritarian and repressive drift. I am quite convinced that this occurs especially when the economic structure of the country—the powers that detain capital—feel under threat.

It is worth remembering that in Italy, between the 1960s and the 1970s, class struggle was particularly fierce, with movements that contested the notion of property and attacked modes of capitalist production. At that point, in response to this social antagonism, the state adopted authoritarian methods, and repression against us shifted from targeting political opponents to going after so-called terrorist enemies. The repression against us—the identification of Autonomia with the enemy—was deeply linked to class struggle. Given that class struggle had become dangerous for capitalist development, it needed to be eliminated: hence the move to consider a terrorist anyone who fights within or in support of the working class.

RB   And thus, from the militant intellectual that you were, in the eyes of the State you became a terrorist...

AN   I was a university professor who engaged in politics and published magazines with comrades, a professor who suddenly found himself in prison, charged with organising a huge movement that comprised the Red Brigades, Autonomia, and other random groups. I was accused of being the leader of it all, like the head of a Mafia Commission, in command of what was happening in Italy at the time: workers' struggles, students' protests—even the murder of Moro.

I must confess, I hardly ever bothered to read the indictments. Luciano Ferrari Bravo, on the other hand, read them all the time. My attitude towards the trial was one of total refusal to account for any of the charges. In particular, they accused me of blackmailing and killing one of my best friends, the Milanese engineer Carlo Saronio, and this had psychologically destroyed me. There was no evidence, nothing.

RB   The April 7th trial was ahead of its time. It used special laws, cluster warrants [*mandati di cattura a grappolo*], the constant changing of indictments, the use of informants [*pentiti*], and horse trading—all these methods often made it impossible for the defendant to unravel the machinations of the process.

AN   The attack launched on us was political. This was obvious because we were not tried immediately, we were held in preventive detention—that is, in jail—for four and a half years while awaiting trial. In those years, the press and the entire political apparatus launched an attack of frightful proportions. The warrant would change every three months, and with it, all the charges would change too. Every six months, the entire structure of the trial would be modified, while we were in jail—some of us, including myself, in maximum security prisons. I was detained in maximum security prisons for a total of seven years, one worse than the other. I was also involved in riots and rebellions that were absolutely incredible for their violence and terror. That was true terror. All of this was done precisely to cancel out not only people, but a political climate, a political era: 1968. Against our will, we became symbols of an era, of a world that was liberating itself. This is what they wished to destroy.

RB   Another important aspect, as you suggested, was the role of the media in fomenting public opinion, publishing articles in national newspapers and images of warrants on the news nearly every day. Even the trial was broadcast on television. The trial was mediatised, instrumentalised by the media to generate political consensus.

AN   *Fake news!* Just think: the principle that a defendant is innocent until proven guilty (or until a trial establishes the person as culpable) completely fell apart. Our guilt was not only endorsed by the newspapers, but also, for instance, by the then President of the Republic Sandro Pertini, who declared Negri a "born delinquent": "Lombroso would have called him that," he said. These sorts of judgements were normal, people made these remarks all the time—something completely outside of any democratic order. Such opinions were constantly spoken out loud, like a mantra, until an actual press interdiction was in place. With the exception of *Il Manifesto*—a newspaper that plays a really scant role, in terms of political weight—other left wing newspapers and journalists—especially, (though not exclusively) old figures linked to Stalinism, the journalists of *L'Unità* and the *Corriere della Sera*—went completely wild and built theorems of accusations against us all. There was effectively a stage when the media constructed the accusations that would then become part of the narrative of the April 7th trial. We actually had the privilege of being one of the first examples of this, and we know how powerful first examples can be. I came out of prison when I was elected to Parliament. I came out as an important defen-dant, while other comrades had to wait for years before being granted freedom. When they were finally released, it was carried out as nearly a covert act, with the sentences reduced from twenty years to zero. Stuff like this had never been seen in a court of law before.

RB   Have you ever read through the trial proceedings? Parts of
your arguments are very strong. As a whole, though, the declarations from you are few, because you were constantly interrupted
both by the Prosecutor and the Presiding Judge. The climate
seemed particularly violent during the days of your testimony.

> AN   Yes, I have read them. I must admit I was never that
> happy with my answers and arguments. The truth is, I was quite
> shaken, I answered very nervously. My mother always used to
> tell me I was too nervous.

RB   During my research I listened to your first appearance
in the house of Parliament. I knew it had been tumultuous and
there had been shouting, but listening to it I was quite shocked.
The similarity between what had happened in court and the
violent way you were welcomed in Parliament was astonishing.
In the recordings from the trial, Emilio Vesce intervened from
the court cages and spoke of how rooted that diehard culture is
in Parliament itself. It was the only intervention from the cages
that President Santiapichi cut short. He turned off the microphone and said, "Let's leave politics out of it."

> AN   I recall my first day in Parliament very well, all the
> fascists screaming. I was sat at the far left with comrades from
> left wing groups. I particularly remember Mauro Capanna, the
> ex-head of Milan State University, who defended me with great
> loyalty. I was not with the Radical Party, as I should have been,
> because they always had odd reasons not to come to Parliament
> with me, after electing me probably without considering what
> my election would mean. Among the ranks of their party, my
> election was symbolic of a decision to defend the April 7th com-
> rades from what was by then a clear-cut persecution. But there
> was also real difficulty in the fact that we were Marxists, and
> at the time—these were the early 1980s—Soviet Marxism was
> rotten and the polemics on totalitarianism were raging. Any form
> of Marxism was seen as suspicious. As soon as I was elected, the
> Christian Democrats immediately demanded that my parliamen-
> tary immunity get revoked.
>
> The elected president of the chamber of deputies, Nilde
> Iotti, immediately took charge of the situation and examined
> four requests for authorisation to proceed to trial and to have
> me arrested. The trial was to be short but lasted a few months.
> The fact that Parliament was against me was a farce, and I
> eventually lost by just three votes.

RB   Because the Radicals did not vote...

AN   No, the Radicals did not vote. There was a strange climate in Parliament. The verbal attacks against me were ferocious, and those were the only voices you could hear: voices that reflected the opinions of the newspapers and were the expression of public opinion. But all the political forces involved—from the Christian Democratic left to the Socialists—were completely opposed to my reimprisonment. On this issue, the Communist Party split. The then leader Enrico Berlinguer said, "I won't use the whip, whoever wants to vote in favour is free to do so." Of the 296 votes needed, 293 voted against the request to have me rearrested. Parliament split into two. The Radical Party did not attend the vote because Marco Pannella, the leader of the party at the time, had decided not to. I should have gone back to prison because someone—in this case, Pannella—had decided not to participate in the acts of Parliament they were charged with undertaking. The leader of the Italian Radicals often used this strategy. Over a handful of votes, I spent fifteen years in exile.

RB   But in truth the fascists who voted against you were a minority compared to the population that had voted in favour of your parliamentary election.

AN   I received 150,000 votes, particularly concentrated in Milan, Rome and Naples. An absolutely incredible feat.

RB   After your election in 1983, you went to France and applied for political asylum.

AN   I went into exile in September 1983 and came back in July 1997.

RB   How old were you during the trial?

AN   I was forty-six, and when I went into exile, I was fifty.

RB   For many intellectuals and journalists, now as then, political exile is necessary to flee state repression. (Think of the current situation in Turkey or Egypt.) This state of permanent violence has a significant psychological and existential impact. The trial against you and Autonomia was carrying on in Italy, while you were in France. What was your experience of those years?

AN   My life was interrupted in 1979, when they put me in prison. I was forty-five, I would have turned forty-six in August that year. Then my life was interrupted; my relationships with my family, everything ended then. One life ended, and another one began. Probably a third started when I went back to Italy and was put in prison again.

In various ways—parole, house arrest—I was imprisoned for another six years, from 1997 to 2003, but that was nothing compared to my time in the maximum security prisons.

RB   Did you go back to writing and thinking about the trial? And do you think the political debate has evolved since those times?

AN   I am writing the third volume of my memoirs, where I describe that moment and what I did in an attempt to obtain amnesty for everyone. I did all I could. In 1998, a bicameral committee was considering a proposal for a pardon. The pardon was crucial. It would have ensured a quasi-amnesty for everyone who had been involved in those trials in the 1970s. A series of politicians came to see me in Paris, to discuss this possibility. I came back because there was this chance. It's not that they had given me any certainty, I knew it was a risk, but we decided to try, anyway. So once back in Italy, for the first few months in prison, several members of parliament came to see me, because of this ongoing negotiation. But in a low blow, Berlusconi decided to cut the conversation short, and demanded that the pardon also had to apply to everyone involved in the trial of "Mani Pulite"[1] [clean hands], who had been charged in the early 1990s. This is the reason the negotiation broke down, and I stayed in prison for another six years.

1   Mani Pulite was a nationwide judicial investigation into political corruption in Italy during the early 1990s, which led to the collapse of the First Republic and the dissolution of many political parties.

RB   Thinking back to the 1970s, your struggles led to major, important changes, not only in the productive structure of the country, but also in many other aspects of the social and cultural life of Italy. This legacy is important for us, for later generations. However, the repressive machinery set in motion then partly broke down the wide network of political relations that constituted Autonomia. The consequences of that particular historical moment determined the present we inhabit now. Somehow my generation is trying to recover that political and cultural legacy that they had wished to eliminate.

AN   Attacking us also meant the end of the Italian left. It was the suicide of the PCI. I remember a Stalinist saying: "Always eliminate the enemies on the left, because they are dangerous." By destroying us, they destroyed a generation that could have offered a renewal for the left, and for left wing positions that were no longer Stalinist or linked to that clerical notion of party. After all, we were the ones capable of inventing new modes of life. They destroyed a political minority that in fact was the bearer of ways of life that were majoritarian, and this eventually destroyed them too. This angers and saddens me. The 1960s and 1970s had been so productive overall, thanks to the people, their freedoms, and their ways of thinking, and they were brought crashing down by a new conformism that affirmed itself with the no-alternative neoliberalism of the 1980s and 1990s.

RB   This created a void.

AN   It created a void. This is the most serious question. To really understand Italy in the 1970s, one has to recognise the cultural and industrial leap the country had taken, and the outcomes—the expansion of productive capacity in factories and in the large-scale industrial districts—were evident. In the 1960s and 1970s, there was an explosion of intellectual, political, and productive activities, but it was brutally attacked and destroyed. More or less everything died, and now we experience this long funereal period, when it is not clear what happens next. Young people flee, old people stay quiet. It was really a massive defeat not only for us, but for this country. A defeat for everyone.

rni il processo agli «autonomi»

vio a sorpresa

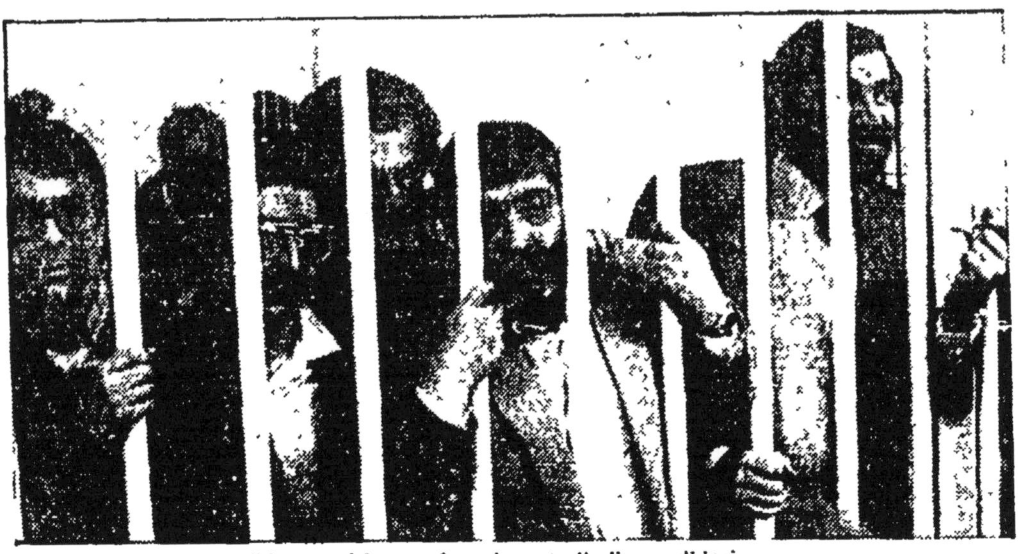

ROMA — Un gruppo di imputati fotografato durante l'udienza di ieri

e si alza dicen-
ta» nell'aula si
ncitori di una
lcuno sdram-
a battuta più
»rile è rinviato
i è che questo
»ortare avanti
imputati non
i questi ultimi
problema che
nte: il famoso
n si tratta sol-
tecnica. Il pri-
ogo lombardo
anche Negri,
ro e Bignami
entocinquanta
ere di accuse
a quelle del «7
ocati vogliono
niedere a quei
processare lo-
», inviando gli
ılla corte d'as-
riunione dei

appena iniziato a Roma resti ancora
nella fase preliminare e allora la ti-
rano un po' per le lunghe.

Così l'udienza procede a singhioz-
zo, proprio come una macchina in-
golfata. Dopo un breve comizio dell'
imputato Francesco Bellosi («Io sono
un prigioniero politico delle Brigate
rosse, tengo a sottolineare la diffe-
renza politica che mi separa da loro»,
dice indicando tutti gli altri nella
gabbia accanto), si alza l'avvocato di
Maurice Bignami ricordando ancora
che il suo cliente è imputato in cinque processi contemporanei e chiedendo il rinvio del «7 aprile» di un
mese. Poi il legale di Adriana Servida
sostiene che l'ordinanza di rinvio a
giudizio è nulla perchè contradditto-
ria e non motivata a sufficienza.
Quindi si alzano altri difensori ma si
limitano ad annunciare le eccezioni
che solleveranno, chiedendo tempo
per esporle.

Il pubblico ministero insorge: «Che
motivo c'è di aspettare? Discutiamo

Quando si riprende, si fa avanti l'
avvocato Tarsitano (parte civile per
la vedova del brigadiere Lombardini,
rapina di Argelato) e dice alla corte:
«O stabiliamo subito se e quali parti
civili sono ammesse al processo e af-
frontiamo anche le eccezioni che ri-
guardano la competenza territoriale,
oppure non si può proseguire». Già,
ma per fare questo bisognerebbe leg-
gere prima i capi d'accusa, insomma
avviare l'iter che farebbe uscire — ad
opinione di molti — il processo «7 a-
prile» dalla fase preliminare. E così si
ripresenterebbe il problema che sta a
cuore ai difensori di Negri e degli altri quattro, che vogliono andare a
Milano a discutere la loro questione
senza avere alle spalle un processo «7
aprile» già entrato nel vivo.

Insomma, è un bel pasticcio. I cro-
nisti, confusi, non sanno più che cosa
annotare sui loro taccuini. Ci pensa
il salomonico Santiapichi a risolvere
il rebus, dopo un quarto d'ora di camera di consiglio, aggiornando il «7
aprile» al 7 marzo. Quel giorno — su-

oni
li

maggioran-
to del PCI»

sua conferenza
er gli altri temi
a pagina), il lea-
ineato che «tut-
sfera istituzio-
nto preliminare
el governo, che
o di gruppi par-
ssime settima-
sultazioni per la
erno». E Spado-
estioni istituzio-
te il coinvolgi-
che da questo
oteche di mag-

g.f.p.

uenti parlamen-
P e indipendenti
iste comuniste:
quez Agnoletti e
mera nella circo-
Firenze e al Se-
llegio di Firenze
il Senato. Suben-
ca Cerrina Fero-

Castellina eletta
a nelle circoscri-
ano e di Perugia
ilano. Subentra
letti.
gri eletto alla Ca-
circoscrizioni di
Catania opta per
entra Salvatore

asina eletto alla
lle circoscrizioni
e di Como opta

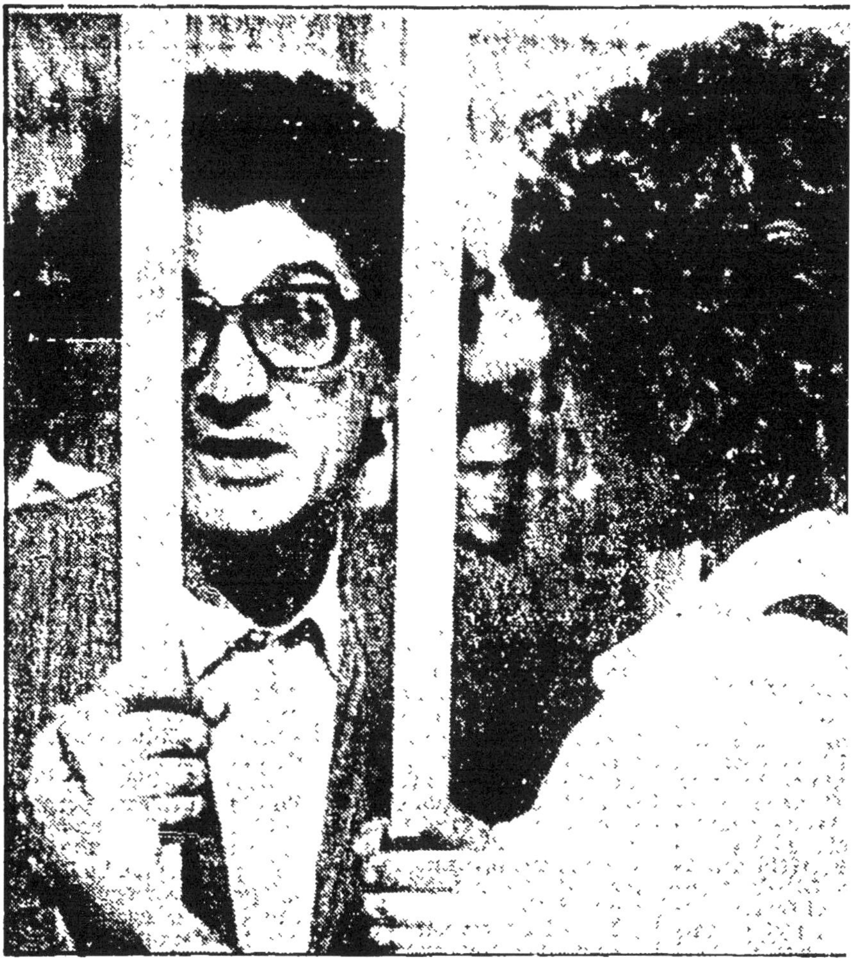

Negri neodeputa
non risponde
Gazzarra in aula

Il processo «7 aprile» aggiornato al 26 settembre pro
attesa dell'autorizzazione a procedere - Invettive dal

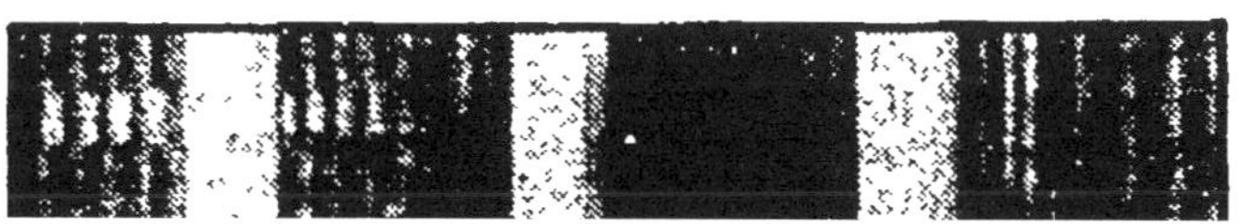

per «chiedere s
te, al PM e a tu
processo». Poi
dichiarazione

', Contiuante se...

Trent'anni a Negri
Arresti domiciliari a Dalmaviva e altri 5

...ccolta l'impostazione dell'accusa - Pene pesanti per il contro-...rso «caso Saronio» - Pm e parte civile: «Sentenza equilibrata»

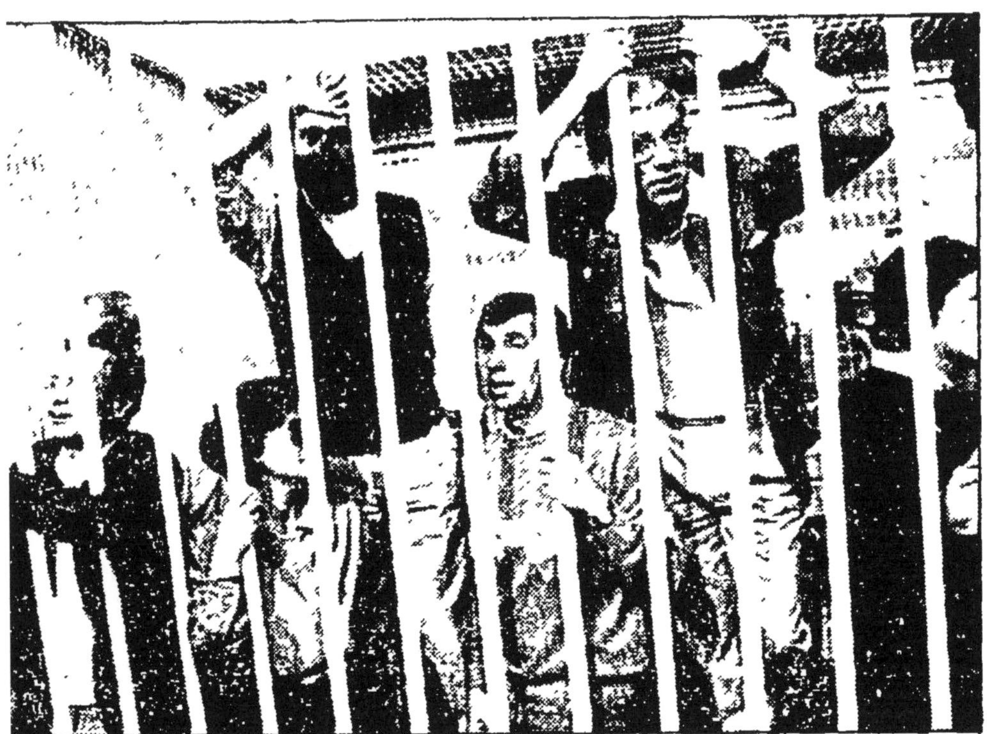

IMA — Un gruppo di imputati durante la lettura della sentenza

Il processo sugli ann...

TIMOTHY MURPHY → TONI NEGRI → MICHEL HARDT

KAREN PINKUS

— CORNELIA LAUF
— LAURA BARRECA
— BIFO (?)
— 16 BEAVER (?) — RENE GABRI
— DANILO CORREALE
— ADELITA HUSNI BEY
— MARIA PECCHIOLI
— MARCO ANTONINI
— FRANCESCO SCASCIA...
— ALESSANDRA ROMANO

ARIANNA BOVE → BRUNO GULLI
& FRANCESCO BARCHIESI

MARCO DESERIIS — SNAFU → ALEJANDRA RENEL → NICK MIRZOEFF
→ GIUSEPPINA MECCHIA
NICK MIRZOEFF → ARA MERSIAN

CHIARA VECCHIARELLI

MARINELLA SENATORE → LAURA DI BANCO
→ ALLISON SEFFREY
WorkMays

SILVERE LOTRINGER

JULIETA ARANDA
YATES MCKEE

PAOLO CARPIGNANO ← SILVIA FEDERICI

List of Artworks

Aula Bunker, 2006
inkjet print on baryta paper, 156 × 100 cm

The Trial, 2010
eight cast sculptures, reinforced concrete
     Bars, 196.9 × 109.5 × 70 cm
     Corner, 147.4 × 75.8 × 11 cm; 147.7 × 78.3 × 11 cm
     Cage Floor, 7.5 × 140.6 × 64.7 cm
     Stairs, 16.8 × 163.1 × 54.9 cm
     Judge, 9 × 115 × 115 cm
     Floor, 9 × 60.3 × 37.5 cm
     Public Entrance, 36.2 × 175.3 × 45.4 cm
     Microphone, 167.5 × 17 × 16.5 cm

The Trial, 2010
audio file, 8h loop

Keys, 2010
original keys taken from the high-security courthouse
at Foro Italico in Rome, various dimensions

Benches, 2010
original benches taken from the high-security
courthouse at Foro Italico in Rome, various
dimensions

The Trial, 2011
ten cast sculptures, reinforced concrete
     Bars, 200 × 140 × 20 cm (+ 135 × 140 × 115 cm)
     Corner, 142 × 78 × 15.5 cm; 142 × 83 × 15.5 cm
     Stairs, 31 × 133 × 45 cm
     Cage Floor, 9 × 120 × 51 cm
     Cage Door, 7 × 34 × 57.5 cm
     Cell Floor, 10 × 70 × 70 × cm
     Cell Door, 22 × 62 × 40 cm
     Judge, 13 × 115 × 115 cm
     Cables, 12 × 109 × 54 cm
     Microphone, 167 × 19.5 × 20 cm

The Trial, 2010–2012
audio file, 6h loop

The Trial, 2013
Super 8 mm film transfer to video, b&w, no sound,
8'45"

Transcripts, 2010–2016
typed transcripts on tractor-feed paper in several
languages (Polish, Turkish, English, Bulgarian,
French/Dutch, Russian)

Red, 2010–2011
silkscreen prints on cotton paper, 21 × 14.85 cm

Red, 2012–2013
seven silkscreen prints on cotton paper, 100 × 70 cm

Poster, 2014
silkscreen print on cotton paper in Dutch and French,
73 × 55 cm

Printed Matter

The Trial, 2012
stencil printing, ed. 100, signed, realised
in conjunction with the performance at
dOCUMENTA (13)

Performance schedule WIELS, 2014
     pp. 204–205

The Trial, 2016
V-A-C Foundation newspaper

Antonio Negri and the April 7th Trial, 2016
translation into Russian, ed. 1,000, V-A-C Press

The Trial, 2019
translated into Turkish by Münevver Çelik
and Sinem Özer, commission for the group
exhibition *When the Present Is History*, curated
by Daphne Vitali, Depo, Istanbul, 12 September–
10 November 2019
     pp. 233–234

The Trial, 2021
translated into Greek by Anna Papastavrou,
commission for the group exhibition *When
the Present Is History*, curated by Daphne Vitali,
MOMUS, Thessaloniki, 21 May–19 September 2021
     pp. 243–244

Performances

2010

24–28 November
Durational performance with one simultaneous translator (Italian to English) and typist; sound installation 2h loop, set with metal plates, metal desk, electronic typewriter, two chairs, microphone, *Benches* (2010) and *Keys* (2010).
Part of the Rijksakademie Open Studios, *Amsterdam, 2010.*

4 December
Durational performance inside the former high-security courthouse at Foro Italico in Rome.

2011

8–11 September
Durational performance with one simultaneous translator (Italian to Polish) and typist; sound installation 2h loop, set with desk and electronic typewriter, two chairs, microphone.
Part of the group show Please Close Your Eyes, *curated by Martha Kirszenbaum, European Culture Congress, Wroclaw, Poland, 8–11 September 2011.*

28 January
Durational performance with one simultaneous translator (Italian to Italian); sound installation 2h loop, set with a metal plate, one chair and microphone, *Benches* (2010). Durational performance with flyering of *Red* at the entrance of the building.
Part of the group show Pleure qui peut, rit qui veut, *Premio Furla, curated by Chiara Bertola, Palazzo Pepoli, Bologna, 29 January– 6 February 2011.*

2012

29 February
Reading with one simultaneous translator (Darija/ Moroccan Arabic).
Part of the side event Higher Atlas, *4th Marrakech Biennial, at École Supérieure des Arts Visuels, curated by Martha Kirszenbaum, 29 February– 3 June 2012.*

7 June–13 September
Durational performance with one simultaneous translator from Italian to English (7–8 June and 13 September) and Italian to German (9 June–12 September weekly); sound installation 6h loop, set with one chair and microphone, book.
Part of the group exhibition dOCUMENTA (13), *curated by Carolyn Christov-Bakargiev, Fredericianum and other venues, Kassel, 9 June–13 September 2012.*

2013

18–19 February
Two-hour performance with one interpreter (Italian to Turkish) and typist; sound installation 2h loop, set with desk, electronic typewriter, two chairs and microphone. Interpreter: Serra Yilmaz.
Part of the group exhibition The Lives of Others: Repetition and Survival, *curated by Alejandra Labastida, Akbank Sanat, Istanbul, 20 February–27 April 2013.*

20 April
Two-hour performance with one simultaneous translator (Italian to Bulgarian) and typist; sound installation 2h loop, set with desk, electronic typewriter, two chairs and microphone.
Part of the group exhibition Sofia Contemporary: Near, Close, Together. Exercises for a Common Ground, *curated by Övül Ö. Durmusoglu, One Night Stand Gallery, Sofia, Bulgaria.*

11–12 May
Six-hour performance with eleven interpreters (Italian to English) and two typists; sound installation 6h loop, set with metal plates, two chairs, microphone, *Benches* (2010) and *Keys* (2010). Interpreters: Franco Barchiesi, Paolo Carpignano, Marco Deseriis, Helidon Gjergji, Michael Hardt, Adelita Husni-Bey, Piero Passacantando, Alessandra Pomarico, Alessandra Renzi, Miriam Tola, Chiara Vecchiarelli. Typists: Monique Beckles, Esther Seltzer.
Part of the solo exhibition The Trial, *e-flux, New York, 11 May–20 July 2013.*

2014

7 June
Six-hour performance with twenty-three interpreters (Italian to French/Dutch) and three typists; sound installation 6h loop, set with partition wall, metal plates, metal desk, two chairs, two microphones, *Benches* (2010) and *Keys* (2010). Interpreters: Lorenzo Benedetti, Daniel Blanga Gubbay, Claudia Bonamini, Gaia Carabillo, Andrea Cavazzini, Alessandra Coppola, Simona Denicolai, Jean-François Gava, Anne Herla, Sonja Lavaert, Iris Marano, Amandine Mélan, Giovanni Melogli, Stefan Pollak, Anna Raimondo, Anna Rispoli, Valeria Roveda, Elena Saraceno, Leonardo Sforza, Serge Vandiepenbeeck, Sarah Vantorre, Duccio Viani, Allan Wei.
Part of the solo exhibition For the Mnemonist, S., *curated by Dirk Snauwaert; assistant curator Caroline Dumalin, WIELS, Brussels, 28 May–17 August 2014.*

13–15 June
Institutional intervention as durational performance: enabling free public access to the public collection/ museum when requesting to view *The Trial* at the museum entrance and ticket office.
Part of the group exhibition Non basta ricordare, *curated by Hou Hanru, MAXXI—National Museum of 21st Century Art, Rome, 20 December 2013– 28 September 2014.*

17 December
Six-hour performance with eighteen interpreters
(Italian to Russian) and two typists; sound
installation 6h loop, set with metal plates, desk,
electronic typewriter, two chairs and microphone,
book, *Benches* (2010) and *Keys* (2010). Interpreters:
Anna Arutyunova, Alexander Bikbov, Valentin
Dyakonov, Marco Dinelli, Anastasia Emelyanova,
Gennadiy Kiselev, Inna Kushnareva, Snejana
Krasteva, Ekaterina Lazareva, Polina Filimonova,
Olga Chuchadeeva, Sergey Nikitin-Rimsky,
Ekaterina Privezentseva, Giovanni Savino, Dmitry
Novikov, Christina Rasskazova, Greta Mavica,
Costante Marengo.
> *Part of the solo exhibition* The Trial, *V-A-C*
> *Foundation at GULAG History State Museum,*
> *Moscow, 18 December 2016–3 January 2017.*

2017

15–16 September
Two-hour performance with six interpreters
(Italian to English) and typist; set with desk,
electronic typewriter, two chairs and microphone.
Interpreters: Rossella Biscotti, Candace Goodrich,
Joanna Warsza, Maeshelle West-Davies, Domna
Gounari, Christine Langinauer. Typist: Liliana
Velásquez Montoya.
> *Part of* Festival of Future Nows 2017 → ∞,
> *presented by Culturlab, Stockholm at Hamburger*
> *Bahnhof, Berlin, 14–17 September 2017.*

Artwork Credits

Research and production
Rossella Biscotti

April 7th trial research
Chicco Funaro, Rossana Miele

Original sound recordings
Archivio Radio Radicale, Rome

Original transcriptions
Daniele Maffeis, Nicola Valentino

Sound editing
Massimo Mosca

Production (sculptures)
Kevin van Braak

*Production manager (sculptures and performances),
European Culture Congress, Akbank Sanat,
e-flux, WIELS, V-A-C Foundation*
Rossana Miele

Technical realization (sculptures)
Sorin Bucsa, Minel Ciuceanu, Adrian Mancas,
Constantin Nistor, Gheorghe Sion

Organisation, WIELS performance
Teresa Gentile

Super 8 mm filming
Rossella Biscotti, Alessandro Chiodo, Elisabetta
Di Salvo, Fabio Farinaro, Bennet Pimpinella

Video editing
Toon de Zoeten

Design
Louis Lüthi

The Trial *archive*
Rossella Biscotti, Rossana Miele

Special thanks to Archivio Manifesto, Archivio
Augusto Finzi, Archivio Radio Radicale, Tribunale
di Roma, CONI (Comitato Olimpico Nazionale
Italiano), Serafina Allocca, Federica Bueti,
Carolyn Christov-Bakargiev, Flavia De Sanctis
Mangelli, Övül Ö. Durmusoglu, Silvia Federici,
Maria Cristina Giusti, Danielle Hofmans, Anna Negri,
Athéna Panni, Judith Revel, Melanie Roumiguière,
Raffaella and Stefano Sciarretta, Julia Stoff, Chiara
Vecchiarelli, Daphne Vitali, Joanna Warsza, Marco
Cinque, Bartolomeo Pietromarchi, Michele Zanna

Installation Views

Premio Italia Arte Contemporanea 2010, curated
by Bartolomeo Pietromarchi, MAXXI, Rome,
3 December 2010–20 March 2011 (group exhibition)
pp. 170–171

dOCUMENTA (13), curated by Carolyn Christov-
Bakargiev, Fredericianum and other venues, Kassel,
9 June–13 September 2012 (group exhibition)
pp. 172–179, 216–217

For the Mnemonist, S., curated by Dirk Snauwaert,
assistant curator Caroline Dumalin, WIELS,
Brussels, 28 May–17 August 2014 (solo exhibition)
pp. 195, 230, 242, 252–255

*Le futur derrière nous. L'art italien depuis les années
1990 : le contemporain face au passé*, curated by
Marco Scotini, Villa Arson, Nice, 12 June–28 August
2022 (group exhibition)
pp. 180–183, 186

Title One, I dreamt, Clara and Other Stories, curated
by Marianna Vecellio, Castello di Rivoli—Museo
d'Arte Contemporanea, 21 April–24 November 2024
(solo exhibition)
pp. 169, 184–185

Contributors

Rossella Biscotti's practice spans sculpture, performance, sound and filmmaking. Stemming from extended research processes, personal encounters, interdisciplinary collaborations and subtle interrogations of sites and histories, her work engages deeply with spatial installations and material experimentation, linking themes of memory, identity and social structures. Her work has been featured in major exhibitions, including the Sharjah Art Biennial 16, Sharjah, 2025; Diriyah Contemporary Art Biennale, Diriyah, 2024; the 55th Venice Biennale, Venice, 2013; dOCUMENTA (13), Kassel, 2012; and presented in institutions such as Castello di Rivoli Museo d'Arte Contemporanea, Rivoli; Stedelijk Museum, Amsterdam; Secession, Vienna; DAAD, Berlin; MAXXI—National Museum of 21st Century Art, Rome, and SculptureCenter, New York.

Daniel Blanga Gubbay is a performing arts curator and writer. Since 2018, he has been the artistic co-director of Kunstenfestivaldesarts (Brussels). He has worked as an educator and independent curator on performances and public programs, including *The Telepathic School* (Ural Biennale, 2021), *Yogurt and Other Spaces of Labour* (Ashkal Alwan, 2021), *Four Rooms* (2020), *Can Nature Revolt?* (Manifesta, 2018), and *Live Works* at Centrale Fies (2014–2018). He is a founding member of Celador (Brussels), a space for doing things with words, and is an artistic committee member of Beirut Art Centre. His writings have appeared in *MOUSSE*, *South as a State of Mind*, *Mada Masr*, and *Performance Journal*.

Michael Hardt is an American political philosopher and literary theorist. He teaches political theory in the Literature Program at Duke University. His first book was *Gilles Deleuze: An Apprenticeship in Philosophy* (1993). With Antonio Negri, he co-authored six books, including *Labor of Dionysus* (1994), *Empire* (2000) and *Multitude* (2004). His latest book, *The Subversive Seventies* (2023), analyses liberation movements of the 1970s in a wide range of countries throughout the world, highlighting their relevance for political struggles today. Since 2010 he has served as editor of the *South Atlantic Quarterly*.

Antonio Negri (1933–2023) was an Italian political philosopher and one of the most prominent theorists of autonomism. Negri was professor of political philosophy at the University of Padua and later in Paris. In 1969, he founded Potere Operaio (Workers' Power) and was a prominent member of Autonomia Operaia (Workers' Autonomy). He was also a political prisoner in Italy and a political refugee in France. He authored over thirty books, including *The Politics of Subversion* (1989), *Communists Like Us* (1990, with Félix Guattari), *Marx Beyond Marx* (1991), *Political Descartes* (2007), *Subversive Spinoza* (2004), *Books for Burning* (2005), *Insurgencies* (2009), *Spinoza: Then and Now* (2020) and, in collaboration with Michael Hardt, *Labor of Dionysus*, *Empire*, and *Multitude*.

Giovanna Zapperi is professor of modern and contemporary art history at the University of Geneva. She is the author of *L'artiste est une femme, La modernité de Marcel Duchamp* (Presses Universitaires de France, 2012); with Alessandra Gribaldo, *Lo schermo del potere. Femminismo e regime della visibilità* (Ombre Corte, 2012); and *Carla Lonzi. Un'arte della vita* (Derive Approdi, 2017). She co-edited *Art and Feminism in Postwar Italy: The Legacy of Carla Lonzi* (Bloomsbury, 2021) with Francesco Ventrella. With Nataša Petrešin-Bachelez, she co-curated *Defiant Muses. Delphine Seyrig and Feminist Video Collectives in France, 1970s–1980s* (LAM Lille, Museo Reina Sofia, Kunsthalle Wien, Kunstverein Stuttgart, 2019–2023).

Colophon

Texts
Rossella Biscotti, Daniel Blanga Gubbay,
Michael Hardt, Antonio Negri, Giovanna Zapperi

Translations
Arianna Bove, Pier Paolo Frassinelli, and
Steve John Wright (transcription)
Arianna Bove (the authors' texts)

Editing
Federica Bueti

Copyediting
Erik Empson (transcription)
Kate Sutton

Organisation
Julia Stoff, Georgia Stellin

Studio Rossella Biscotti
Mirco Bimbi, Georgia Stellin

Photography
Ray Anastas (pp. 220–222)
Ela Bialkowska, OKNO Studio (pp. 172–179)
Rossella Biscotti (pp. 198–200, 212–213, 229 bottom)
José Huedo (pp. 224–229)
Marek Kirszenbaum (pp. 210–211)
Sven Laurent (pp. 195, 253–254)
JC Lett (pp. 184–185)
Gennaro Navarra (pp. 190–191)
Sebastiano Pellion (pp. 169, 184–185)
Maeshelle West-Davies (pp. 236–241)

Credits
Archivio *l'Unità* (pp. 251, 256, 266–268)
Rossella Biscotti (pp. 193, 204–205, 215, 218)

Design
Louis Lüthi

Printing
Wilco Art Books, Amersfoort

Publisher
Mousse Publishing
Contrappunto s.r.l.
via Decembrio 28
20137 Milan
Italy

Distribution
Mousse Publishing, Milan
moussemagazine.it

The artist would like to thank all the institutions
that have hosted and supported the making of
this project; all the people who contributed to
its research and production; all performances
participants across different countries.

This book has been conceived, organized and
edited by Rossella Biscotti with the support
of MAXXI in 2019, DAAD Berlin and
Mondriaan Fund.

ISBN 978 88 6749 694 5
€ 30 / $ 35

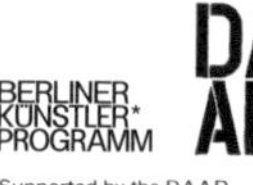
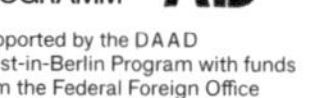

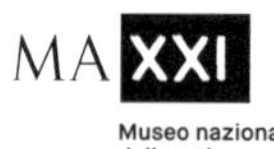